The Gospel

EXPLAINED

BY THE

SPIRITIST

DOCTRINE

Allan Kardec

First edition, 2000
Second edition, revised, 2003
Copyright © 2003

Published by:
Allan Kardec Educational Society
P.O. Box 26336
PhiladelphiaPA 19141
Phone (215) 329 4010

Manufactured in the United States of America

Library of Congress Control Number: 2003096337

Main entry under title:
The Gospel – Explained by the Spiritist Doctrine
1. Religious Philosophy 2. Spiritist Doctrine 3. Christianity. I. Kardec, Allan,
1804
ISBN 0-9649907-6-8
(translated from Le Evangile Selon Le Spiritisme, 3rd edition, 1866)

The Translation Of The Gospel — Explained By The Spiritist Doctrine: Our Guiding Principles

Sensus non verba (Meaning not words)

Cicero

The Translation and Editorial Team has seen the challenge of translating *L'Evangile Selon Le Spiritisme* from its original French in two ways. We might best describe them metaphorically.

Imagine that two individuals have been invited to give the same talk to different audiences. The first speaker takes the theme to heart, delves into its ideas, convinces himself of its facts and, once on stage, speaks with a profound conviction. He allows his audience to share in his emotions to the point that it enthusiastically affirms every major point and endorses his conclusions. This audience is captivated by the ideas, applauds warmly, and avidly seeks to learn more from the speaker during the break.

The second speaker delivers basically the same speech—as far as content goes—but takes a methodical approach, lacks humor and feeling, and speaks in a monotone. The audience stays to the end, applauds respectfully, and quietly heads for the exits.

Always our challenge has been to make sure that the audience for *The Gospel - Explained by the Spiritist Doctrine*, which has come hoping for the first kind of experience, won't find itself surprised—and disappointed—by the second kind. Both presentations may be correct in their details. Only one is memorable.

Thus, from the outset we sought to deliver an experience like our first example, one wherein the book's emotions, its intimacy with the Christ, and the soulful poetry of its many spirit contributors would have the same meaning and music in English as it has in French. Allan Kardec, himself a classic translator from German, provided us with the theory and guide in his reflective commentary in Chapter 23, section 3. In undertaking this work, we assembled a team of translators and reviewers who upheld Dolet's five rules of translation: (a) that the would-be interpreter must have a perfect grasp of "the sense and spirit" of his author; (b) that the interpreter must possess in-depth knowledge of the original language as well as that of his own tongue; (c) that the interpreter ought to be faithful to the meaning of sentences, not to their word order; (d) that the interpreter must aim for a version in plain speech; and (e) that the translator must achieve harmonious cadences, composing in a sweet and even style so as to ravish the reader's ear and intellect.[1]

The difficulties of such an enterprise are the same that have confronted literary translators since Cicero and Quintilian, and have concerned those who have written about the art and theory of translation for over two thousand years. The approach we chose decidedly avoided a literal, strictly word-for-word matching, or the other extreme, that of adaptation or free interpretation. Instead, we embraced what John Dryden, great English poet and translator of Ovid and Chaucer, established as the high road of the process, which he called *"paraphrase"* or translation with latitude, where the author is kept in view by the translator, so as never to be lost, but his words are not so strictly followed as his sense, and that, too, is admitted to be amplified, but not altered.'[2] Paraphrasing assured us that the rational spirituality of Kardec's personality was alive and continuously engaged in our interpretive frame.

Thus, we have tried in these pages to eliminate anything that by its cultural and linguistic particularity would create a barrier between our American readers and the book's message. The content is completely faithful to the ideas of Allan Kardec and the teachings of the ennobled spirits who graced its pages. We wanted to offer you a book as Allan Kardec might have written it had he been writing in English—a book that would evoke in the American reader the same feelings of reverence, faith, and spiritual comfort experienced by the readers of the original. This, we believe, is that book.

This is *not*, then, the work of translators in the strictest sense of the word, but the work of interpreters of a powerful experience expressed in a new garment by inspired writers and poetic souls. We hope you enjoy the experience.

The Editorial Team

[1] *Chassaigne M. Étienne Dolet, Paris, 1930, pp. 230-233, 272.*

[2] *Cited in George Steiner, After Babel: Aspects of Language and Translation (Oxford University Press, 1998), p. 269. For a full discussion of Dryden's position, the author makes reference to W. Frost, Dryden and the Art of Translation (Yale University Press, 1955).*

Preface

As science and technology redefine the human experience on earth and place their stamp on the new century, the quest for "purpose and meaning" will continue to seduce our imaginations. Back at the dawn of the Christian era, humanity fell enraptured by Christ's announcement, "I am the way and the truth and the life."[1] At every major stage of our evolution we have been asked to rethink our understanding of His words, and redraw the map of our resolutions. This book is an invitation for you to experience again His voice, and to rework the blueprint of your own life. This New English Edition of *The Gospel — Explained by the Spiritist Doctrine* holds the hope, in our evolving world community, for a new path of love, understanding, and justice. As the English language assumes the role of international language, the importance of this accomplishment must not be missed.

Originally published with the title *L'Imitation de l' Evangile* in 1865, this book was completely revised and reformulated by Allan Kardec and gained its current title, *L'Evangile Selon Le Spiritisme*, in 1866. The present translation is based on the third edition, considered by Allan Kardec as the definitive one.

The Gospel - Explained by the Spiritist Doctrine is the third book in a series of five, all compiled by Allan Kardec, based on the teachings of a team of evolved spirits. Together with *The Spirits' Book, The Mediums' Book, Heaven and Hell,* and *Genesis*, it comprises the foundation principles of the Spiritist Doctrine.

The core message it presents transcends time and religious form, as Allan Kardec carefully chose passages from the Gospel that deal exclusively with moral matters and timeless truths. In doing so, he deliberately avoided what might be interpreted as circumstantial to the Jewish nation and customs. These scripture excerpts became the basis for the explanations provided by the spirits, and the explications by Allan Kardec himself. This is therefore a book that invites the reader to ponder her or his life through the vivid accounts from those who have already mastered their lessons, and the reflections of those who were willing to reevaluate their own past experiences on earth. This is what makes the Gospel a true guide for our own inner transformation, and for engaging the self in the discovery of each person's true purpose in life.

---

[1] John 14:6

This is not a book written for scholars or destined to serve the intellectual pleasure of philosophers. Its pages offer a treasure of lessons that can have an immediate and positive impact in your life. Its principles will influence everything you do, from simple activities like choosing a television program to watch or a magazine to read, up to the more complex endeavours of human relationships. It will soothe your suffering through the most painful trials and help you focus on the real meaning of this existence. This book illuminates our perspectives, throwing the light on the reality of continuous life and our continuous evolution toward perfection.

The task of translating a work of such significance was not taken lightly. The backbone of the translation project was a team of people with solid skills in both French and English, but who foremost had a profound knowledge of the Spiritist Doctrine in its triple aspects: philosophical, scientific, and religious. In this we agreed with Stephen Mackenna, a renowned practitioner and scholar of literary translation, who said, "Nothing could serve the classics more than superbly free translations—backed of course by the thoroughest knowledge—accompanied by the strict text."[2] Since 1994 the translation and editorial team has worked following a very detailed and disciplined approach. The methodology comprised the following stages: (a) first draft in English; (b) blind editorial revision by three parallel teams; (c) comparative revision against the French by three independent reviewers; (d) discussion and consolidation of individual interpretations; (e) consolidated draft; and (f) final editorial revision. The intellectual breadth of the team combined well with a methodology designed to create sufficient redundancy and assure the faithful interpretation of ideas.

This is, for all purposes, a comprehensive version. It has been enriched by detailed scientific support of its ideas and a review of facts current in Kardec's era but affected by the passage of time. It also provides extensive research aimed at reconstructing the sources for Allan Kardec's references. This was particularly the case in the discussion of Socrates's ideas in the Introduction.

Like Allan Kardec in his time, the team wrestled with some serious problems created by the evolution of meaning of some critical words and concepts. The most important regarded the translation of the title *L'Evangile Selon Le Spiritisme*. The issues concerned the accurate English meaning for selon and the appropriateness of a direct translation of the word *Spiritisme*, given the connotations it already

[2] E.R. Dodds (ed.), Journal and Letters of Stephen Mackenna, *London, 1936, cited in George Steiner, After Babel, London, 1998, p. 282.*

carries in modern English vernacular. Kardec faced similar dilemma when he named the first edition *L'Imitation de l'Evangile*. A man of superior intellect and culture, he took the word *Imitation* in its highest literary meaning, which poet Ben Jonson, a respected translator of Horace's poetry, defined as "to draw forth out of the best and choicest flowers, with the bee, and turn all into honey; work it into one relish and savour; make our imitation sweet."[3] The ideal of choosing the choicest flowers from the Gospel and turning them into the honey of practical spiritual inspiration was Allan Kardec's intent. However, the French reader saw the word "Imitation" quite differently, and considered it as a cheap rework of a sacred book. The translation team was faced by a no less daunting challenge.

The word selon has in French an elastic range of meaning and could be equally interpreted as "in light of," "in accordance with," "as understood by," and so on, depending on the context. Portuguese and Spanish translations have chosen "according to" but this equivalence in English proved to be perilous. A small scale survey of American readers showed what we feared the most, that it would be understood either as (a) a new version of the Gospel parallel to the Bible's own (e.g., a complete exegesis of the Gospel According to Matthew) or (b) the gospel of Spiritism (unrelated to Jesus'). Neither of these came close to the original meaning. As for the word *Spiritism*, the common usage catalogued in the Oxford English Dictionary considers it to be a synonym of the word spiritualism, i.e., the religion of modern spiritualism. Though the two share many common principles, there are sufficient differences to justify the distinction. Foremost among these differences stands church organization, the role of religious ministers, and the remuneration of mediums—features not present in the Spiritist movement. Further, modern spiritualism opposes the idea of reincarnation, which is a central pillar of Spiritist thought. In addition, whereas in French Spiritisme was a new coinage (Allan Kardec was the first to claim the word and to associate it directly with a new body of doctrine), in English the word was already in use before the Spiritist Doctrine was launched in 1857. Thus, to prevent the development of misconceptions, and at the same time affirm the unique characteristics of the Doctrine, the team realized the importance of new thinking on the matter. It eventually opted for a solution that clearly and accurately conveyed the true essence of the book, and what it should represent to the average reader—a work of practical Christian spirituality. We believe that the title *The Gospel - Explained by the Spiritist Doctrine* does just that without producing any further difficulties of comprehension.

---

[3] *Cited in George Steiner*, After Babel, *London, 1998, p. 269.*

The title also positions the book as a work of explication and explanation of Jesus' teachings in light of the perspectives that constitute the
Spiritist Doctrine.

As with any such large scale translation project, many people have
been involved and have contributed to this process, which started in
October 1994. We are indebted to all for their support of this work
and we thank everyone who so kindly volunteered their time and
resources to make it possible. We have to acknowledge the devotion
and dedication to this work of Dr. John Zerio, the originator and
director of a project meant to bring to the English-speaking world the
works of Allan Kardec; he has worked continuously and relentlessly
to see this dream come true. Similar thanks go to Dr. Antulio Bomfim,
who tirelessly contributed his superb command of the French language, and Dr. Robert Champ, who was annointed our "chief editor"
and on whose poetry and art we relied for the design of a truly
superb literary experience. The whole Vision2000[4] team is deserving
of our recognition, but we especially acknowledge the excellent contributions of Brenda Haney, Mike Highsmith, Zaida Knight, Lucia
Machado, Barbara Paulin, Maria Payas, and Anna Sinclair. Many special thanks go to the spouses who supported this effort and endured
it all with patience and friendship. However, our most heartfelt
thanks go to our Maker and the team of "angels" assigned to inspire
and sustain this venture.

We, of the Allan Kardec Educational Society, invite you to take a
journey with us, to slowly navigate through the pages of this classic
in the field of human spirituality. We are convinced that when you
turn the last page, you will feel enlightened and closer to the Creator.

If this work brings you a new vision of your reality, we'll feel that
this effort was not in vain; if you want to share your thoughts with us,
learn more about our activities, start a study group, or begin a Gospel
At Home practice, please write to us at AKES or visit our Web site:
http://www.allan-kardec.org.

Miguel Bertolucci, eng., M.Sc.A.
Project Director
Allan Kardec Educational Society

---

[4] *Vision2000 is a project started in 1992 by individuals interested in the dissemina-
tion of the Doctrine in the English language. The launching of* The Gospel—
Explained by the Spiritist Doctrine, *together with* The Spirits' Book, *constitute
two of the team's most important achievements. The team is made up of volunteers
representing diverse regions of North America.*

Table of Contents

Introduction

1. THE PURPOSE OF THIS WORK

The Gospel[1] can be divided into five parts: the events in the life of Christ; the miracles; the prophecies; the passages chosen by the Church as the basis of its theology; and the moral teachings. The first four have always been subject to controversy. The last has remained pure and uncontested through the ages. This Divine Code of morals transcends even disbelief in religious ideas. It is the common ground where people of all religions can come together, the banner under which we can unite. Religious disputes are often based on specific articles of faith—not on the moral teachings of the Gospel, since a focus on these teachings would end up exposing our own frailties. It is little wonder then that many organized religions are quicker to embrace the mystical aspects of the Gospel than to heed their call for moral improvement.

The moral teachings of the Gospel constitute a system of principles concerning our behavior in every key circumstance of our private and public lives. These principles, centered on the most exacting justice, illumine every aspect of human relations. They are, finally and above all, our one unfailing route to lasting inner peace and the means by which we can lift a corner of the veil that hides the future life. The purpose of this book is to reflect on these principles.

Everyone, you will find, admires the moral content of the Gospel. Everyone will tell you what an elevated concept its content divulges and how much need we have for it. Yet many of these words of praise rely primarily on what others have said about it or on biblical precepts that have been turned into simple proverbs. Few people actually have an in-depth knowledge of the moral teachings of the Gospel; fewer still can understand them or reason about their implications. In many cases, the cause of this difficulty lies in a misunderstanding of the Gospel itself; often it appears incomprehensible to readers. Its allegorical form and intentionally mystical language make it something we read because we feel we should, or because our conscience tells us

---

[1] *Translator's Note: Refers to the first four books of the New Testament, namely Matthew, Mark, Luke, and John. The ethical principles of the Spiritist Doctrine are essentially based on Christ's message as presented in the four Gospels.*

to—as someone would recite prayers, without understanding them and without benefiting by them. In this way, the Gospel's moral principles usually go unnoticed, scattered as they are in bits and pieces throughout long stretches of narrative material. This, in turn, makes it nearly impossible to get a general idea of the whole or to take these principles as specific subjects for reading and meditation.

Many works on the moral doctrine of the Gospel have, of course, already been written. But once translated into modern prose, the precepts in which this doctrine is embodied lose much of its original simplicity, which accounts for both their appeal and their authenticity. Many other works deal with the best-known precepts but reduce them to the form of truisms. The precepts become then no more than adages, deprived of a large part of their value and interest because, presented in isolation, they lose the meaning lent to them by the original context.

To avoid these unfortunate results, we have brought together in this work the Gospel passages that make up a moral code of universal application, regardless of denominational emphasis. In these citations, we have kept everything that is necessary to the development of the ideas. We have also kept painstakingly to the translation by Sacy[2] and to the division of the verses. The reproduction of the verses in the exact order in which they appear in the Gospel would little benefit our comprehension and perhaps even undermine it. Thus, we have methodically grouped and classified different passages according to subject matter in such a way that the ideas develop one from the other as much as possible. Indication of specific chapters and verses allows reference to the original textual placement whenever desired.

The procedure described above is, taken by itself, only of secondary importance. Our main purpose has been to put these teachings within the easy reach of everyone by using clear explanations, especially of passages that have until now been obscure. By doing so, we hope to unfold the full implications of the teachings and the way they can be applied to all our life circumstances. This is what we have tried to do, helped always by the spiritual inspiration of higher friends.

---

[2]*Translator's Note: Allan Kardec used the French version by Le Maistre de Sacy. For this translation we have chosen the* New International Version, *1995. The* NIV *was chosen for its wide acceptance in the United States, and its reputation among religious scholars.*

Many points in the Gospel, the Bible, and sacred writings in general, are practically unintelligible (indeed, some appear to be nonsense) because the key to their true meaning has been lost. This key can be found in its complete form in the propositions contained in the Spiritist Doctrine. Those persons who have already seriously studied the Spiritist Doctrine can verify this fact. Many more will do so in the future as they come to recognize its soundness. The principles behind the Spiritist Doctrine can be found throughout human history, some dating back to ancient times. We find traces of them everywhere—in the form of writings, in particular beliefs, and in engravings on monuments. This is the reason that the Spiritist Doctrine, at the same time that it is opening new horizons to the future, is also casting a no less brilliant light on the mysteries of the past.

The examination of the precepts selected from the Gospel relies on a series of commentaries taken from among many dictated— in various countries and through different mediums—by spirits. Now if these instructions had come entirely from one source, they would unquestionably have been affected either by the influence of the particular medium or by his or her environment. The great diversity of sources we have used, however, proves that the spirits give teachings freely and that no one person is especially privileged.[3]

This work is for everyone's use. From it, all of us can discover the ways to best apply Christ's moral teachings to our daily lives. It applies most especially, though, to those who embrace the Spiritist Doctrine. Thanks to the relationship between living human beings and the invisible world, now established through

---

[3]*We could easily have presented many more spirit communications on each subject, all given in cities and centers different from the ones we cite in this work. This, however, would have involved a good deal of useless and tedious repetition. Consequently, we have limited our choice to those communications that, from their base and form, most nearly harmonize with the plan of this work. We reserve for future publication the communications we have been unable to use here.*

Regarding the individuals through which the instructions were transmitted, we made a conscious decision not to identify them by name. In most cases, they themselves asked not be be mentioned and we have made anonymity the general rule. In any case, mentioning their names would add no real value to the spirits' work and would accomplish little more, perhaps, than inflating their egos, a temptation no serious person should succumb to anyway. These mediums (or channels) understand fully that, since their part in the work is merely passive, the value of the communications they impart in no way contributes to their personal merit. They know, too, that it would be foolish to become conceited about an intellectual work to which they had only lent mechanical assistance.

the present communications on a permanent basis, the moral doctrine of the Gospel which the spirits have taught throughout the world will no longer be a matter of dead words. Each person will be able to understand those words and to strive always to put them into practice. These instructions are really voices from higher realms that have come to enlighten humanity and invite us to fulfill the Gospel in our lives.

2. UNIVERSAL CONTROL: THE ULTIMATE AUTHORITY

If the Spiritist Doctrine was entirely a human idea, it would only be as good as the person who conceived it. Yet no one on earth can credibly claim to be in exclusive possession of absolute truth. By the same token, if the spirits who brought us the Doctrine had chosen to speak through one individual alone, we would have had no guarantee of its real source, other than that medium's claim that he or she had received it. And even if we believed that this medium was perfectly sincere, he or she would never be able to do more than convince the small circle of acquaintances who would personally be touched by that sincerity. The Doctrine, in that case, might well attract a few followers, but it would never capture the attention of the world.

Thus, according to the Divine Plan, the new revelation came to us by a quicker, more authentic route. That's why the enlightened intelligences of the spirit world were entrusted to spread it from pole to pole, making their presence felt everywhere so that no one individual could claim the exclusive privilege of hearing their words. One person might be deceived, might even be self-deceived. But when millions of people see and hear the same thing, the chances of such deception grow very slim. This provides a guarantee for each of us personally and for all of us generally. Moreover, while we can ignore one person, we can't ignore the masses. You can burn books; you can't burn spirits. And even if all the books were burned, the basis of the Doctrine would still not be exhausted. Why? Because the origin of the Spiritist Doctrine isn't found on earth. Thus, it would soon reappear worldwide and everyone could share in it once again. Additionally, should there be a shortage of men and women to spread it, there will always be spirits whose actions reach all of us, and who cannot be silenced by human beings.

We should all understand that it is the spirits themselves who, with the help of many mediums, are engaged in spreading this doctrine throughout the world. If there had been a single interpreter, favored though that individual might have been, the Spiritist Doctrine would be virtually unknown. Regardless of social class, he or she would have been treated with suspicion by many people and would certainly not have been accepted in so many countries. But the spirits communicate to the four corners of the earth, to all peoples, all denominations, all parties, and everyone accepts them. The Spiritist Doctrine has no nationality. It doesn't stem from any known religious movement. It isn't imposed by any social class. Anyone can receive instructions from parents, relatives, and friends from the beyond. This was how the doctrine had to spread if it was to lead all humanity toward brotherhood. Without this neutrality, it would promote disagreements rather than ease them.

The strength of the Spiritist Doctrine, and the cause of its rapid spread, comes from the universality of its teaching. Where the word of a solitary person, even with the press's help, would take centuries to become known worldwide,[4] millions of voices are now making themselves heard simultaneously in every corner of the planet. All assert the same principles, transmitting them at every level—from the scholarly down to the most uneducated—so that no one will be disinherited. So far, this is an advantage that no other doctrine can offer. In addition, because the Doctrine is in accordance with truth, it doesn't need to fear the ill will of some people, cultural or moral revolutions, or even physical cataclysms, because none of these can touch the spirits.

But this isn't the only advantage to come from this exceptional situation. The Spiritist Doctrine also offers an unassailable guarantee against any internal contention that might arise, whether caused by someone's personal agenda or the occasional contradictions found in the statements of particular spirits. We don't deny that these contradictions present obstacles; but they bring with them the seeds of their own solution.

We know that spirits, because they have different individual aptitudes, are far from possessing all the truth. Not all spirits have equal access to some mysteries, since their knowledge depends on the extent of their evolution. Ordinary spirits, in fact, don't know any more than the average human being, and sometimes even less. There are even spirits, just as there are men and women, who presume to know much more than they actually do.

---

[4] *Translator's Note: This statement was made in the 1850s. The advent of the Internet and satellite-based telecommunication has made possible the almost instantaneous diffusion of information worldwide.*

There are also those who concoct elaborate theories to support their own ideas, which they construe to be the truth. Finally, there are the highly evolved spirits, completely free from matter and immune to earthly conceptions and prejudices. We must be aware, however, that less honest spirits won't hesitate to deceive others by taking names that don't belong to them, all in an attempt to impose their utopian ideas. As a result, every new piece of information received from the spirits, especially in topics that go beyond moral teachings, should be taken as an individual expression, subject to verification of authenticity. Such revelations should be considered (until otherwise proven) the personal opinion of this or that spirit, making it unwise for us to accept them and spread them thoughtlessly as absolute truths.

There are, fortunately, tests by which we can validate spirit assertions. The first of these is the test of reason, to which everything that comes from a spirit should be submitted, without exception. Any theory that obviously contradicts good sense, rigorous logic, or positive facts, should be rejected, no matter how highly regarded the name that the spirit uses. Still, this test will probably never be more than partial, since it is limited by the extent of human knowledge and the tendency on the part of some people to confuse their own opinions with the truth. When this is the case, what should people who do not possess the required expertise do? Their best course is to try to find what seems to be the majority view and take this as a guide. This is the method you should follow when judging what is said by serious spirits, who are the first to support your effort to verify their assertions.

The best proof of authenticity, then, is the agreement of a spirit assertion with the assertions of other spirits. It is important, however, that this test be applied only under specific conditions. For instance, the weakest type of agreement comes about when a sensitive person, on his or her own, questions many different spirits about a doubtful point. It is obvious that if the medium has fallen under a controlling influence or is dealing with a devious spirit intelligence, the latter may simply repeat the same thing under different names. For the same reason, it is not a real guarantee of agreement when communications are received by different sensitives at the same center: They may be acting under the same influences.

There is, in fact, only one sure guarantee in judging spirit teachings—the agreement that exists among revelations that have been received spontaneously by a large number of mediums who don't know each other and are located in different places.

Here, it should be understood, we aren't referring to communications that deal with secondary matters, but those that concern the basic principles of the Doctrine. Experience has taught us that when a new principle is to be presented, its announcement always happens spontaneously in different places, at the same time, and in the same way (if not in actual form, then at least in general content). Thus, if a spirit happens to come out with a peculiar doctrine, one based entirely on its own ideas and devoid of truth, you can be sure that—as has happened numerous times in the past—this doctrine will collapse the moment it is examined against knowledge received in other places. This principle of universality of the teachings has debunked many theories that, during the early times of the Doctrine, tried to explain certain phenomena on the basis of personal experience and a deficient knowledge of the laws that govern the relationship between the physical and spiritual realms.

This guideline is one we have relied on ourselves when formulating a principle. We don't accept a principle as being true just because it happens to agree with our own ideas. And we have no desire to present ourselves as being the sole possessors of the whole truth. We have never said to anyone, "Believe in this because I am the one who is telling it to you." We consider our own opinion to be nothing more than personal, one that might be true or false, since we aren't any more infallible than anyone else. It isn't because we've been taught a principle that we believe it is true; it is true because it is validated by facts and observations collected in different parts of the world.

Currently we find ourselves in the position of receiving communications from almost a thousand serious spiritual centers scattered over many different areas of the globe. This has given us the opportunity to identify areas of strict agreement. This method has been central to this work and will continue to be so. While studying communications obtained both in France and elsewhere, we have noticed, from the very special nature of the information, that a new path is being sought and that the moment has arrived to take a step forward. Often composed in an allegorical style, these communications were only partially understood by their recipients, and in other cases, judged of value to those recipients solely. Indeed, taken in isolation, we would have considered them unimportant ourselves. It is, however, in the pattern of coincidences that their value comes to the fore. Later, when these new teachings reach the public, there will be many individuals who will remember having received the same instruction. The general threads we are able to observe and study, often with the assistance of our spiritual guides, are what help us decide what position, if any, to take on a particular principle.

The method of universal verification guarantees the integrity of the Spiritist Doctrine and will cancel out all contradictory theories. In this method, we will find the criteria for the truth in our future endeavours. The success of the Doctrine, as described in *The Spirits' Book* and *The Mediums' Book*, was due to the fact that everyone could obtain empirical confirmation (i.e., speak to spirits) on his or her own. If, on the other hand, the majority of other spirits had offered an incompatible perspective, these books would have met the same end as others that have offered misconceived ideas. Not even the support of the press would have saved them from shipwreck. Yet, even without press support, they have made rapid advances. This is because the Doctrine has the support of the enlightened intelligences of the spirit world, whose good will has more than offset the ill will of some men and women. This is the normal path of new ideas, whether they come from human minds or spirits. From this process of validation they derive their undeniable power.

But suppose that a group of spirits decides to dictate a book that offers an opposite perspective with the purpose of challenging the Spiritist Doctrine. Worse yet, imagine that they misrepresent themselves by assuming highly respected names. Still, what influence could their material have if it were refuted by the teachings of a majority of spirit intelligences? Indeed, before attributing truth to any new revelations from one or a few spirits, we must first be sure that these new principles are actually consistent with the position of the spirit majority. The distinction between a principle proposed by only one spirit and an opposing principle embraced by all is as wide as the distance that separates the number 1 from infinity in real numbers. What can the attacks of a few detractors do when they are countered by millions of friendly spiritual voices who come from across the globe and go everywhere, speaking with astounding consistency? Doesn't such concordance of views and positions already provide some support for the claims of the majority? Furthermore, what has happened to the many publications that have attempted to put an end to the ideas proposed by the Spiritist Doctrine? Not one has caused as much as a hesitation in its march. One fact must be highlighted in no unclear terms: Those responsible for such publications often relied solely on their personal opinions, disregarding the accounts of the enlightened intelligences of the spirit world.

The principle of universal agreement also assures that no group can tamper with the foundations of the Spiritist Doctrine to satisfy its own particular agenda. Anyone who tries to steer it away from the design of Providence will fail, for the simple reason that the spirits will cause mistaken ideas to collapse.

Nevertheless, the fact remains that those who position themselves against established and well-founded ideas may for a while cause a limited disruption. But they will never be able to rule the Spiritist movement; not now or, even less likely, in the future. We should also like to point out that spirit teachings on points incompletely developed in the body of the Doctrine should not be considered tenets as long as these teachings remain confined to a few groups. They should be taken with reservations and for information only. From this we conclude that greater care needs to be taken before making spirit teachings public. And even if we decide to bring these teachings to the public, they should be presented as individual opinions, which may or may not be right because they haven't yet been fully confirmed. We wait for this confirmation before announcing any communication to be factually true—otherwise, we run the risk of being accused of gullibility or a lack of seriousness.

The enlightened spirits make their revelations to us very wisely. They address important questions only gradually, waiting until our intelligence is ready to accept more advanced illations and until circumstances are favorable to a new idea. This is why they didn't reveal everything to us from the beginning—and haven't told us everything yet. Moreover, they never heed the call of impatient individuals who want to eat the fruit before it is ripe. Consequently, it's simply wasting time to hurry things forward, before their natural time. When the circumstances are not proper, the enlightened guides will refrain. Frivolous spirits, on the other hand, are not the least interested in the truth and will give answers to anything and everything. They are the reason that, whenever a question is premature, contradictory answers invariably result.

The principles mentioned above do not originate from some personal theory. They are a result of the very conditions surrounding spirit communication. We maintain that if one spirit says one thing while thousands of others say the opposite, the presumption of truth doesn't lie with the single communicant. To imagine that one possesses the truth against all the rest is to be illogical. The truly wise spirits, when they don't feel sufficiently sure about a subject, never give a definite answer; instead, they state that they are merely giving their own point of view and suggest that we await the necessary confirmation.

Moreover, no matter how all-encompassing, how beautiful, or how just an idea appears, consensus about its truth, at the first moment that it appears, is impossible. The debating that ensues is unavoidable, but healthy. Indeed, open discussions help to focus on the key issues, and the sooner they occur the better, for they help weed out false ideas. Nobody should feel worried about this situation; groundless ideas will wilt away before the enormous force that comes from universal concurrence.

It is not behind the opinion of any single individual that we rally, but behind the unanimous voices of the spirits. The Spiritist Doctrine is not centered on any one person, least of all myself, or on the communication of any individual spirit. The Doctrine is based on principles universally taught by enlightened spirits whose presence has been felt the world over, and according to the designs of Providence. This is the essential character of the Spiritist Doctrine; this is its source of vitality and power. It was part of the Divine Design that the Spiritist Doctrine should be set on the soundest of foundations. Thus, its basic principles were not trusted to one fragile being only.

Before this magnificent forum of discerning entities—where rivalries, sectarianism, and divisions are unknown—all base ambitions and personal agendas are powerless. We will ourselves fall if we try to substitute our own ideas for their divinely inspired vision. The universality of their teachings is the final arbiter of all legitimate questions and will resolve all disagreements. In the face of this imposing consensus what impact can the opinion of one person or one spirit have? No more than a drop of water in the ocean or the voice of a child in a great storm.

This broad and universal agreement, like the ruling of a supreme court, is the definitive opinion; it is the sum and synthesis of all the individual opinions. If an individual opinion is sound, it is given its appropriate weight, and if it is false, it will die away. In this all-encompassing consensus, names and personalities disappear, leaving no room for inflated egos and personal arrogance. This harmonious picture is already in the making. And it will shine ever more brightly before the century comes to an end, shedding much-needed light on many unresolved questions. High-minded beings have been instructed with one mission: to prepare the field, to make themselves felt in every heart, and to unite humankind under one banner. But until this actually happens, we can develop a position in relation to two opposing matters by relying on our observation of the non-prejudiced majority. In this, we often find the best indicators of the views the spiritual world propounds, and an even more accurate sign as to which positions will prevail in the long run.

3. HISTORIC FACTS

Deepening our understanding of the Gospel requires that we know the true meaning of many of the words pertaining to Jewish customs and society at the time the Gospel was written. The meanings of some of these words have changed over time and, not surprisingly, have frequently been misinterpreted, generating some confusion. Yet once the full meanings have been explained, the real sense behind certain seemingly odd precepts becomes very clear.

Samaritans: After the division of the Ten Tribes, Samaria became the capital of the dissident kingdom of Israel. Destroyed and rebuilt several times, under Roman rule it became the administrative center of one of the four divisions of Palestine. Herod the Great beautified the city, built magnificent monuments within its precincts, and to flatter Augustus Caesar, gave it the name of Augusta, in Greek, *Sébaste.*

The Samaritans were almost constantly at war with the kings of Judah. The profound hatred between the two tribes, dating from the time of the division,[5] assured the impossibility of any reciprocal relations between them. In order to widen the schism, and to avoid going to Jerusalem for religious festivities, the Samaritans built their own temple and instituted some religious reforms. For instance, they only admitted the Pentateuch (the first five books of the Old Testament), which contained the laws of Moses, and rejected all other books that had since been added. In addition, all their sacred books were written in the ancient Hebrew characters. Orthodox Jews regarded them as heretics and consequently despised, anathematized, and persecuted them. The antagonism between the Samaritans and the Judeans

---

[5] *Translator's Note: After Solomon's death, about 922 B.C., the kingdom of Israel was divided into 12 tribes, organized like this: ten in the north became the kingdom of Israel, and two to the south became the kingdom of Judah.*

was, then, based entirely on religious differences, despite the fact that their beliefs had a common origin. The Samaritans were the Protestants of their time.

Samaritans can still be found in certain regions of the Levant, especially near Nablus and in Jaffa. They observe the laws of Moses more strictly than other Jews and only marry among themselves.

Nazarites: In biblical times, the name referred to Jews who took a vow of perfect purity. The vow could be either temporary or for a lifetime. The Nazarites promised to remain chaste, refrain from alcohol, and wear their hair uncut. Samson, Samuel, and John the Baptist were Nazarites.

Later, the Jews gave this name to the first Christians, using it to allude to Jesus, who came from Nazareth. It was also the name given to a heretical sect dating from the first phase of the Christian era. Like the Ebonites, from whom they adopted certain principles, the Nazarites mixed the practice of the Mosaic law and the teachings of early Christianity. The Nazarite sect disappeared during the Fourth Century A.D.

Publicans: In ancient Rome this was the name given to individuals who had obtained the right to collect public taxes and other state incomes, both in Rome and throughout the Empire. They were much like the tax collectors of the old regime in France, or of other countries today. These were risky but profitable arrangements. Publicans were usually very rich. Later on, the name Publican came to refer to anyone who oversaw public monies. Today,[6] the term is used, in some corners, in a disparaging sense to mean dishonest financiers and their agents. We sometimes hear phrases such as "greedy as a Publican" or "as rich as a Publican" in reference to a financier's ill-gotten gains.

During the Roman occupation, the Jews found the imposition of taxes difficult to accept. Taxation was, in fact, a cause of considerable agitation among them and resulted in a number of revolts. Invariably, the problem turned into a religious question, with the Jews considering the taxes contrary to the law. Indeed, a powerful party was formed—led by a man called "the Gaulite, from Judah"—which had, as its main objective, the abolition of all taxes. The Jews hated Rome's taxes and anyone connected with their collection. From this feeling arose a hatred for Publicans of all kinds, as well as for their friends and associates. Many Publicans were, of course, worthwhile persons, but their function guaranteed that

---

[6] *Translator's Note: This refers to the usage in France of the mid-1850s.*

they would be despised. Prominent Jews considered it morally compromising to have any personal relationships with them.

Toll Collectors: These were the lowest-level public collectors, entrusted primarily with collecting tolls on travelers entering a city. Their functions somewhat resembled those of our customs and passport officials. They shared in the general distaste accorded all Publicans. For this reason, we frequently find, in the Gospel, the word "Publican" along side the expression "sinful people." This term, however, didn't imply immorality or abusiveness; it was, rather, a term of scorn, another term for people who kept bad company, who weren't worthy to mix with decent people.

Pharisees (from the Hebrew, meaning division or separation): Tradition played an important role in ancient Jewish theology. It was according to tradition that the Scriptures were interpreted and reinterpreted numerous times and that ancient dogmas came into being. The interpretations became, among scholars, the subject of endless discussions, many devoted to simple questions concerning the meanings of words and their forms. In many ways, these discussions were similar to the theological disputes and subtle reasonings of the Schoolmen in the Middle Ages.[7] All this resulted in the formation of different sects, each of which wanted to establish a monopoly on the Truth. As often happens, the end result was a great deal of animosity amongst them.

The Pharisees, the origin of whose sect dates to approximately 200 years before Christ, were the most influential sect. Its most prominent leader was Hillel, a doctor born in Babylon and a staunch defender of the view that religious truth resided only in the Scriptures. The Pharisees were persecuted at different times, especially under Hyrcanus (religious leader and ruler of the Jews), Aristobulus, and Alexander, a king of Syria.[8] However, Alexander later restored their confiscated properties, making it possible for them to maintain their social structure and political status. This situation continued until the fall of Jerusalem in 70 A.D. With the ensuing Jewish diaspora, the name disappeared altogether.

---

[7] *Translator's Note: Schoolmen or Scholastics, persons engaged in the Scholasticism movement predominant in the Middle Ages which was based on the authority of the church fathers and of Aristotle and his commentators. They attempted to use natural human reason to understand the supernatural content of the Christian revelation.*

[8] *Translator's Note: John Hyrcanus (died 104 B.C.), ruler from 134 to 104 B.C., freed Judea from all Syrian influence. Aristobulus I (140?-103 B.C.), king of Judea, son of the High Priest John Hyrcanus and the first of the Hasmonean (Maccabean) family to assume the royal title. Alexander Jannaeus (died 76 B.C.) brother and successor of Aristobulus.*

The Pharisees took an active part in religious controversies. They were strict observers of religious rituals and exterior practices, avidly sought converts, opposed all new ideas, and strictly observed the Jewish law. All too often, this meticulous religiosity was a cover for corrupt practices, enormous arrogance, and above all, an excessive desire to wield power. Religion was for them a means to an end, not an object of sincere faith. Apart from outward show, it had little value. Still, they exercised great influence over the Jews, who considered them holy men—a view that gave them power in Jerusalem. They believed, or at least claimed to believe, in Divine Providence, the immortality of the soul, eternal punishment, and the resurrection of the dead (see Chapter 4, item 4). They viewed Jesus with great disfavor. He, Who preached against hypocrisy, valued simplicity and the qualities of the heart above all else, and preferred the "spirit that gives life to the letter that kills,"[9] was viewed as a threat. Along with the high priests, the Pharisees were instrumental in stirring up the people to get rid of Him.

The Scribes (or teachers of the law): Initially this was the name given to the secretaries of the kings of Judah and to certain posts in the Jewish army. Later, it was applied to scholars who taught and interpreted the law of Moses. By the time of Jesus, these scholars had thrown in their lot with the Pharisees, sharing with them the dislike of new ideas. This is why Jesus included them in his references to the Pharisees.

Synagogue (from the Greek synagoge meaning assembly, congregation): The only temple in Judah was that of Solomon in Jerusalem. Here all the major ceremonies of worship took place. Each year the Jews would go to this temple as pilgrims to take part in such important festivals as the Passover, the Dedication, and the Feast of Tabernacles.[10] This is why Jesus is seen in Jerusalem on so many occasions. Other Judean cities had synagogues. In these buildings, the Jews would gather for their Sabbath meetings and to pray under the leadership of their Elders, the scribes or scholars versed in the law. It was also in the

---

[9] *Translator's Note: 2 Corinthians 3:6.*

[10] *Translator's Note: Passover commemorates the Exodus from Egypt, begins on the eve of the 14th day of Nisan, and is celebrated for either seven or eight days. Dedication (Hanukkah or Festival of Lights) commemorates the rededication of the Temple of Jerusalem and is characterized by the lighting of the menorah on each night of the festival. Feast of Tabernacles marks the close of the harvest in Palestine; it begins on the 15th day of Tishri (in the fall) lasting seven or eight days.*

synagogues that the Jews read and studied the Torah. The fact that all who attended these readings could take part in the ensuing commentary explains why Jesus was able to freely teach in the synagogues on the Sabbath. After the destruction of Jerusalem, the synagogues became, in the cities where the Jews went to live, the main gathering places for religious worship.

Sadducees: Another Jewish sect, founded about 248 B.C., took its name from its founder, Sadoc. The Sadducees did not believe in immortality or resurrection, or in good and bad angels. They did believe in God. But with nothing to hope for after death, they served God only with worldly rewards in mind; for them God's purpose was limited to the dispensation of such rewards. Under the influence of these ideas, their main purpose in life was the satisfaction of their physical senses. Where the Scriptures were concerned, they adhered to the literal form of the ancient laws and refused to accept any interpretation or tradition not explicit in these laws. They put good works and the observance of the law before outward practices of worship. In many ways, they were the materialists, deists, and hedonists of their time.[11] The sect had few followers, but counted among these a number of important people. The Sadducees became a political faction, constantly opposing the Pharisees.

Essenes: These were members of a Jewish sect founded about the year 150 B.C.—in the time of the Maccabees. The sect's members lived in monasteries, forming a kind of ethical and religious order. They were notable for their peaceful ways, and their plain and simple virtues. They taught the love of God and neighbor, the immortality of the soul, and the reality of the resurrection. They were celibate, condemned war and slavery, held all their worldly goods in common, and devoted themselves to agriculture. Distancing themselves from the Sadducees, who were highly sensual and denied immortality, and from the Pharisees, who were concerned with rigid external practices and the outward show of goodness, the Essenes refused to take part in the disputes that caused hostility between the two sects. In their way of life, they resembled the first Christians to the extent that the moral princi-

---

[11] *Translator's Note: Materialism: the doctrine that nothing exists except matter and its movements, and that the phenomenon of consciousness is purely a physical event arising from processes of the brain. Deism: the belief that God created the world, as proven by reason and the order of nature, with rejection of revelation and any supernatural doctrines. Hedonism: the theory of ethics in which pleasure is regarded as the chief good, or the proper end of action.*

ples they professed have led many scholars to assert that Jesus belonged to their community before He began His mission. However, while it seems certain that He knew of them, there is nothing to prove that He had any association with them, and works written to show otherwise are simply hypothetical.

Therapeuts (from the Greek *therapeutay,* formed from *therapeueyn,* to serve, meaning "servants of God or healers"): These were Jewish sectarians and contemporaries of Christ who were established mostly in Alexandria in Egypt. Like the Essenes, whose principles they adopted, they practiced all the virtues. They were frugal in diet, celibate, dedicated themselves to meditation, and lived solitary lives. In short, they made up a truly religious order. The Platonist philosopher Filon, an Alexandrian Jew, was the first to speak of the Therapeuts, which he considered a Jewish sect. Eusebius, Saint Jerome, and other Church Fathers believed them to be Christians. Whether they practiced Judaism or Christianity, however, the fact remains that, like the Essenes, they represent a link between the two faiths.

4. SOCRATES AND PLATO, FORERUNNERS OF THE CHRISTIAN IDEA AND SPIRITIST PRINCIPLES

We can't conclude from the simple fact that Jesus knew the Essenes that His teachings arose from theirs; or that, if He had lived in another environment, He would have adopted other principles. Great ideas—those founded on truth—do not appear suddenly; they always have their precursors, which partially prepare the path for them. Later, at the appointed time, Providence sends an individual whose mission is to unite and compile scattered principles into a doctrine. As a result of this process, new ideas are not introduced suddenly but evolve gradually, germinating fully when humanity is ready for them. This happened to the Christian idea, which had been predicted many centuries previously; the principle forerunners of Christianity were Socrates and Plato.

Socrates, like Christ, wrote nothing himself; at least he left no written work of which anyone is aware. Like Christ, he also was the victim of fanaticism and a criminal's death because he dared to challenge accepted notions and inveighed against the hypocrisy of the times. In short, he died because he fought against religious bigotry. Just as with Jesus, Whom the Pharisees accused of corrupting the people through His teaching, Socrates was also accused by the "Pharisees" of his time of corrupting the people by proclaiming the One God, the immortality of the soul, and the existence of a future life. Moreover, just as Jesus' teachings became known only through the writings of His disciples, so the teachings of Socrates became known through the work of his disciple Plato.

For these reasons we find it fitting to offer here a brief summary of the basic points in Socrates' teachings in order to show their agreement with Christian principles.

Some readers may well consider this parallel between Jesus' and Socrates' teachings blasphemous and claim that there can be no similarity between a pagan doctrine and Christ's. We reply by saying that the teachings of Socrates were not pagan because he objectively fought against Paganism. As to the teachings of Jesus, which are the more complete and purer of the two, they have nothing to lose by the comparison because nothing can affect the greatness of Christ's mission. In the case of any remaining objections, we reply that we are dealing here with historical facts. Humanity has now reached a point where the light is, on its own, emerging from beneath the bushel. We are now mature enough to meet truth face to face, and it would be sad to miss this opportunity. The time has arrived to consider matters in a fuller manner, not from the perspective of the narrow and backward concerns held by various sects and denominations. The following excerpts show that, in addition to being forerunners of Christian ideas, Socrates and Plato also advanced some of the fundamental principles of the Spiritist Doctrine.

A SUMMARY OF THE TEACHINGS OF SOCRATES AND PLATO[12]

1. As human beings, we are incarnate souls.[13] Before incarnating, we existed in union with the primordial forms, i.e., the ideas of truth, goodness, and beauty. Separating from them at birth, we forgot them momentarily but, on remembering our past, we become consumed by the desire to return to the original reality.[14]

    Comment: The independence of, and the distinction between, the intelligent principle and the vital principle couldn't be expressed more clearly.[15] It is also an affirmation of the notion of pre-existence of the soul, the vague intuition of another reality to which the soul aspires, the concept of survival, the idea

---

[12] *Translator's Note: This collection of Socratic ideas about the soul, compiled by Allan Kardec, was based on French sources at the time of the writing, approximately 1857 to 1859. However, no bibliographical citation is offered in the original L' Evangile Selon Le Spiritisme. The references in the remainder of this section represent the translation team's attempt at reconstructing the bibliographical work. Except for a few cases,*

Footnote continues on page 20

of leaving the spirit world in order to incarnate, and a return to this same world after death. Finally, it offers the seeds of the doctrine of fallen angels.

2. When the soul makes use of the body to consider any material object, it becomes dizzy, as if intoxicated, because it is dragged by the body to things which never remain the same. By contrast, when it inquires about its very essence, it finds itself in the realm of the pure, the everlasting, the immortal, and being akin to these, it dwells always with them whenever it is by itself and is not hindered, and it has rest from its wanderings and remains always the same and unchanging with the changeless, since it is in communion therewith. And this state of the soul is called wisdom.[16]

    Comment: The person who considers things from an earthly, matter-bound viewpoint is under an illusion. To see things in their true perspective, he or she must look at them from on high—that is to say, from the spiritual point of view. The discerning person must be able to distinguish the soul from the body, and see with the eyes of the spirit. This is what the Spiritist Doctrine also teaches.[17]

3. As long as we possess bodies, and our soul is contaminated by such an evil, we'll surely never adequately gain what we desire— and that, we say, is truth. Because the body affords countless distractions, owing to the nurture it must have; and again, if any ill-

---

Footnote continued from previous page

the references were located and transcribed from English translations. In those few cases, where apparently Allan Kardec paraphrased his references or combined different sections of text, the direct matching was not possible. When it occurred, the book and section in which the topic is discussed has been referenced. In some instances, the differences in linguistic usage and style between the French of the mid-1850s and modern English represented a barrier, which was overcome by following a principle of "closest approximation" of ideas. In such particular cases (item 7, part of item 10, item 14 and 15) the original text was directly translated from the French. The interested reader will benefit from reading Plato's Phaedo and Phaedrus, which contain the essence of the Socratic thought about the soul, and its origin and destiny. For online research visit the Tufts University's Perseus Project at http://www.perseus.tufts.edu.

[13] Translator's Note: Plato's Phaedrus, 246c; Discussion in Phaedo 71c-72d

[14] Translator's Note: Plato's Phaedrus, 250a.

[15] Translator's Note: See Allan Kardec, The Spirits' Book, Chapter 2 and 5, for a more extensive discussion.

[16] Translator's Note: Plato's Phaedo, 79c-d. Perseus Project, http://www.perseus.tufts.edu November, 1999.

[17] See also Chapter 2, item 5, for a more extensive discussion.

nesses befall it, they hamper our pursuit of reality. Besides, it fills us up with lusts and desires, with fears and fantasies of every kind, and with any amount of trash, so that really and truly we are, as the saying goes, never able to think of anything at all because of it. Because if we can know nothing purely in the body's company, then one of the two things must be true: Either knowledge is nowhere to be gained, or else it is for the dead. And being thus pure through separation from the body's folly, we shall probably be in like company, and shall know through our own selves all that is unsullied. Truly then, those who practice philosophy aright are cultivating dying, and for them, least of all humans, being dead holds no terror.[18]

> *Comment:* Here we find the notion that the faculties of the soul are dimmed by the physical body, and that the soul returns to its normal state after death. However, this is the case of advanced souls only, those already purified; it does not apply to impure souls.[19]

4. And such a soul is weighed down by this and is dragged back into the visible world, through fear of the invisible and of the other world, and so, as they say, it flits about the monuments and the tombs, where shadowy shapes of souls have been seen, figures of those souls which were not set free in purity but retain something of the visible; and this is why they are seen.... And it is likely that those are not the souls of the good, but those of the base, which are compelled to flit about such places as a punishment for their former evil mode of life. And they flit about until, through the desire of the corporeal which clings to them, they are again imprisoned in a body. And they are likely to be imprisoned in natures which correspond to the practices of their former life.[20]

> *Comment:* Here we clearly see demonstrated not only the principle of reincarnation but also the state of souls who remain in bondage to matter, just as spirit communications describe it to us. Additionally, reincarnation is said to be the result of a soul's imperfection, while the perfect soul finds itself released from having to undergo rebirth. This is exactly what the Spiritist Doctrine teaches. The doctrine adds only that the soul that has made good resolutions in the spirit world

---

[18] *Translator's Note: Plato's* Phaedo, *transl. David Gallop (Oxford University Press, 1993), 66b-c, 66e, 67b, 67e.*

[19] *See also Allan Kardec's* Heaven and Hell, *Part 1, Chapter 2; Part 2, Chapter 1.*

[20] *Translator's Note: Plato's* Phaedo, *Perseus Project, 81d-e.*

has acquired knowledge and brings fewer defects and more virtues and intuitive ideas into its new life than it had in its preceding existence. In this way each lifetime represents a step toward greater intellectual and moral progress.[21]

5. And so it is said that after death, the tutelary genius of each person, to whom he had been allotted in life, leads him to a place where the dead are gathered together; then they are judged and depart to the other with the guide whose task it is to conduct those who come from this world; and when they have there their due and remained through the time appointed, another guide brings them back after many long periods of time.[22]

> *Comment:* This is the doctrine of guardian angels or spirit guides, and of consecutive reincarnations after varying time intervals in the spirit world.

6. Daemons occupy the space that separates heaven from earth. This occupied space forms the link that unites the different parts of the Universe into one. Divinity enters into contact with human beings only through the mediation of the daemons, with whom the Deity deals solely. The daemons occupy themselves with humanity both during waking and sleeping.[23]

> *Comment:* In ancient Greek, the word daemon, from which we get our synonym for devil, didn't refer to something bad, as it does today. Nor was it used exclusively for evil beings, but for spirits in general, including superior beings called gods and less elevated spirits (the actual demons) who communicated directly with human beings. The Spiritist Doctrine also says that spirits inhabit space, and that God only communicates with humanity through the intermediary of pure spirits. Spirits also communicate with us during sleep and wakefulness. Put the word spirit in place of daemon and we have the Spiritist Doctrine. Substitute the word angel and we have the Christian doctrine.

7. The occupation of the philosopher is to care for the soul less in

---

[21] *See also Allan Kardec's* Heaven and Hell, *Part 2, Examples.*

[22] *Translator's Note: Plato's* Phaedo, *Perseus Project, 107e.*

[23] *Translator's Note: Plato's* Epinomis, *984e, "The daemons or divine spirits had their existence and activity 'between mortal and immortal' and they served as interpreters and conveyors of men's prayers and offerings to the gods, and of the god's behests and requitals to men." See also Plato's* Symposium 202e-203a.

regard to the present than to life in eternity.[24] Since the soul is immortal, it would be wise to live our lives with this fact in mind.

> *Comment:* Both the Spiritist Doctrine and the Christian faith teach the same thing.

8. The soul, the invisible, which departs into another place which is, like itself, noble, pure, and invisible (while) the body is liable to be dissolved and fall apart and to disintegrate.[25] It is important to distinguish between the pure soul and the soul that is stained by material imperfections which prevent it from rising to everything divine and that, in fact, cause the soul to stay attached to the earthly environment.

> *Comment:* As we can see, both Socrates and Plato understood perfectly the different levels of dematerialization of the soul. They also asserted the differences in the situation faced by the soul according to its greater or lesser purification. What they concluded by pure intuition, the Spiritist Doctrine confirms through the many examples it places before us. [26]

9. For if death were an escape from everything, it would be a boon to the wicked, for when they die they would be freed from the body and from their wickedness together with their souls. This, then, is why a man should be of good cheer about his soul, who in his life has rejected the pleasures and ornaments of the body, thinking they are alien to him and more likely to do him harm than good, and has sought eagerly for those of learning; and after adorning his soul with no alien ornaments, but with its own proper adornment of self-restraint and justice and courage and freedom and truth, awaits his departure to the other world, ready to go when fate calls him.[27]

> *Comment:* The notion of annihilation is tantamount to saying that materialism, when it asserts that there is nothing after death, cancels out all moral responsibilities—a situation that only encourages evildoing, and allows the evildoer not to worry about consequences. On the other hand, the above statement teaches that persons who have stripped away all their vices and clothed themselves with the best of qualities can look calmly forward to their wakening into the other life. By

---

[24] *Translator's Note: Discussed in Plato's* Phaedo, *transl. David Gallop, 67d and 107b.*

[25] *Translator's Note: Plato's* Phaedo, *transl. David Gallop, 80d, 80c.*

[26] *See also Allan Kardec's* Heaven and Hell.

[27] *Translator's Note: Plato's* Phaedo, *107c and 114d-115a. Perseus Project.*

means of objective examples, the Spiritist Doctrine demonstrates how painful passing on and adjusting to the future life
are for wrongdoers.[28]

10. "The body retains impressions of both the good care it has
received and all the accidents it has suffered. The same holds true
for the soul. When it disposes of the body, it retains its character
and emotions, as well as the influence of all the events that have
happened during life....[29] For no man fears the mere act of dying,
except he be utterly irrational and unmanly; doing wrong is what
one fears for to arrive in the nether world having one's soul full
fraught with a heap of misdeeds is the uttermost of all evils....[30]
But as it is, you observe that you three, who are the wisest of the
Greeks in our day—you and Polus and Gorgias—are unable to
prove that we ought to live any other life than this, which is evidently advantageous also in the other world. But among the
many statements we have made, while all the rest are refuted this
one alone is unshaken—that doing wrong is to be more carefully
shunned than suffering it; that above all things a man should
study not to seem but to be good both in private and in public."[31]

> *Comment:* Here we meet with still another point of capital
> importance, and one that observation has confirmed—i.e., the
> unpurified soul retains the ideas, tendencies, character, and
> emotions that it had while on earth. Isn't the precept "doing
> wrong is to be more carefully shunned than suffering it" in
> agreement with Jesus' teachings? Jesus expressed the same
> thought when He said, "If someone strikes you on the right
> cheek, turn to him the other also."[32]

11. "Either death is a state of nothingness and utter unconsciousness,
or, as men say, there is a change and migration of the soul from
this world to another. Now if you suppose that there is no consciousness, but a sleep like the sleep of him who is undisturbed
even by dreams, death will be an unspeakable gain. But if death
is the journey to another place, and there, as men say, all the dead
abide, what good, O my friends and judges, can be greater than
this? Above all, I shall then be able to continue my search into
true and false knowledge; as in this world, so also in the next;

---

[28] *See also Allan Kardec's* Heaven and Hell, *2nd part, Chapter 1.*

[29] *Translator's Note: Generic discussion of this theme in Plato's* Georgias, *Perseus Project, 524c-d.*

[30] *Translator's Note:* Georgias, *Perseus Project, 522e.*

[31] *Translator's Note:* Georgias, *Perseus Project, 527b.*

[32] *Translator's Note: Matthew 5:39. See also Chapter 12, items 7 and 8.*

and I shall find out who is wise, and who pretends to be wise, and is not…. The hour of departure has arrived, and we go our ways —I to die, and you to live" [Socrates to his judges].[33]

Comment: According to Socrates, those who live on earth meet again after death and recognize each other. The Spiritist Doctrine shows that relationships continue and that death is not an interruption of, or an end to, life but an inevitable transformation.

If Socrates and Plato had known what Christ was to teach five hundred years later, and what the Spiritist Doctrine teaches now, they would have been in perfect agreement with both. There is nothing surprising in this fact, however: All fundamental truths are eternal and all advanced spirits must have known them before they come to earth. We might further consider that Socrates and Plato, together with other great philosophers of antiquity, were among those chosen to prepare the way for Christ—chosen because of their intimate understanding of His convictions. It would not be farfetched to assume that they are today among the host of spirits charged with reminding humanity of these same truths.

12. If, then, anyone affirms that it is just to render to each his due and he means by this, that injury and harm is what is due to his enemies from the just man and benefits to his friends, he was no truly wise man who said it. For what he meant was not true. For it has been made clear to us that in no case is it just to harm anyone…."It [Justice] belongs in the fairest class, that which a man who is to be happy must love both for its own sake and for the results." "Yet the multitude," he said, "do not think so…." If it is the business of injustice to engender hatred wherever it is found, will it not, when it springs up either among freemen or slaves, cause them to hate and be at strife with one another, and make them incapable of effective action in common?" The business of injustice will make them incapable of effective action in common.[34]

Comment: Isn't this the principle of love, which requires that we refuse to return evil for evil and that we forgive our enemies?

13. "So we may fairly describe each of these workings as follows: as you call either of them evil because of the evil it produces, so you must call it good because of the good it produces."[35]

---

[33] *Translator's Note: Plato's* Apology, *Perseus Project, 40c-41b, 42a.*

[34] *Translator's Note: Plato's* Republic, *Perseus Project, 335e, 358d, 351d-e.*

[35] *Translator's Note: Plato's* Alcibiades, *Perseus Project, 115e-116a.*

Comment: The precept "It is by the fruits that we know the tree" is repeated many times in the Gospels.

14. "Wealth is a great danger. People who love wealth, love neither themselves, their family members, nor their associates."[36]

15. The most beautiful prayers and sacrifices mean less to Divinity than the effort of a virtuous soul who struggles to take on godly qualities. It is a great mistake to think that the gods pay more attention to offerings than to our souls. If this were true, some of the greatest culprits would be among the most favored. But it is not so. The truly just and honorable are those individuals who, by their words and deeds, fulfill their duties to the gods and humanity. [37]

16. By "wicked" we mean that popular lover, who craves the body rather than the soul. "(Love is everywhere and it springs) in such love-connections as are studied in relation to the motions of the stars and the yearly seasons....Love was originally of surpassing beauty and goodness, and is latterly the cause of similar excellences in others. And now I am moved to summon the aid of verse, and tell how it is he who makes—Peace among men, and a windless waveless main; repose for winds, and slumber in our pain."[38]

   Comment: Love—the force which will eventually unite humanity—is according to Plato, a Law of Nature. Socrates said, "Love is a great spirit: for the whole of the spiritual is between divine and mortal."[39] This statement was held against him by his Athenian opponents as if it expressed a criminal idea.

17. At the moment, if, through all this discussion, our queries and statements have been correct, virtue is found to be neither natural nor taught, but is imparted to us by a divine dispensation without understanding in those who receive it.[40]

   Comment: This is very nearly the Christian doctrine of grace. But if virtue is a gift from God, then it is a favor, and one may feel like asking why it isn't given to everyone. Further, if it is a gift, its possessors can't claim any real merit for receiving it. The

---

[36] *Translator's Note: Generic discussion of this theme in Plato's* Republic, *550a-e, 553d, 555a-e, 556a-c, and Laws 831c-e, 919b.*

[37] *Translator's Note: Generic discussion of this theme in Plato's* Republic, *Perseus Project, 364b-c. See also chapter 10, items 7 and 8.*

[38] *Translator's Note: Plato's* Symposium, *Perseus Project, 183d, 188b, 196b.*

[39] *Translator's Note: Plato's* Symposium, *Perseus Project, 202e.*

[40] *Translator's Note: Plato's* Meno, *Perseus Project, 99e.*

Spiritist Doctrine is more objective when it says that individuals who demonstrate a good quality have earned it through their own efforts during successive lives—lives in which they have rid themselves, little by little, of their imperfections. In this way, grace can be understood as the force that God gives to all well-meaning men and women so that they can cleanse themselves of all that is bad and so embrace good in their lives.

18. "You really strike me, indeed, as following the average man's practice of keeping an eye on others rather than on oneself."[41]

    Comment: The Gospel says: "Why do you look at the speck of saw-dust in your brother's eye and pay no attention to the plank in your own eye?"[42]

19. "Let nobody persuade you to treat his head with this remedy, unless he has first submitted his soul for you to treat with the charm. For at present," he said, "the cure of mankind is beset with the error of certain doctors who attempt to practice the one method without the other."[43]

    Comment: The Spiritist Doctrine offers the key to understanding the relationship between the soul and body, and proves that each constantly interacts with the other (an idea that opens up a new field for science). With the possibility of uncovering the real causes of certain illnesses, the cure becomes easier to find. When medical science takes into account the importance of the spiritual element in the human organism, failures will be much less frequent.

20. Men do many more bad things than good, from childhood up, and commit many errors involuntarily.[44]

    Comment: In this sentence, Socrates touches on the serious question of the predominance of wrong-doing on earth, a question that cannot be resolved without a knowledge of the existence of many worlds and the destiny of our planet earth, where only a fraction of humanity lives. Only the Spiritist Doctrine offers a logical explanation for this problem.[45]

[41] *Translator's Note: Plato's* Laches, *Perseus Project, 200b.*

[42] *Translator's Note: Matthew 7:3. See also Chapter 10, items 9 and 10.*

[43] *Translator's Note: Plato's* Charmides, *Perseus Project, 157b.*

[44] *Translator's Note: Plato's* Greater Hippias, *Perseus Project, 296c.*

[45] *See also Chapters 3, 4, and 5.*

21. For you will have the wisdom not to think you know that which you do not know. [46]

> *Comment:* This statement is directed against people who offer criticism concerning matters about which they don't know even the basic terms. Plato completes this thought of Socrates by saying, "In the first place, if it is possible, we must make them more honest in their words; if they are not, we cannot bother with them and must seek nothing but the truth. We will do our best to instruct them, but we will not insult them."
>
> This is how the Spiritist Doctrine should be presented to those individuals who, whether from good or bad motives, oppose it. If Plato were living today, he would find things almost as they were in his own time and would be able to use the same words. Socrates would also meet persons who would jeer at his belief in spirits and would consider him and his disciple Plato disturbed. Indeed, it was for professing these principles that Socrates saw himself ridiculed, accused of impiety, and condemned to drink hemlock, the poison that caused his death. Likewise, we must not expect that new truths, which stir up controversy among many interests and strike against many prejudices, will be accepted without a fight, or without making martyrs.

---

[46] *Translator's Note: Plato's* Theaetetus, *Perseus Project, 210c.*

Chapter 1

I Have Not Come to Abolish the Law

SCRIPTURES AND COMMENTARY[1]

1.   *"Do not think that I have come to abolish the Law or the Prophets; I have not come to abolish them but to fulfill them. I tell you the truth, until heaven and earth disappear, not the smallest letter, not the least stroke of a pen, will by any means disappear from the Law until everything is accomplished."*

(Matthew, 5: 17-18)

MOSES

2.   There are two parts to the laws enacted by Moses: the Law of God, which Moses received on Mount Sinai, and the civil (or secular) law, which he devised and mandated himself. The first Law is unalterable; the second, which was designed to suit the customs and character of the people of Moses' era, changes over time.

The Divine Law is based on the following ten commandments:

I.   I am the Lord your God, who brought you out of Egypt, out of the land of slavery. You shall have no other gods before me. You shall not make for yourself an idol in the form of anything in heaven above or on the earth beneath or in the waters below. You shall not bow down to them or worship them.

II.   You shall not misuse the name of the Lord your God.

III.   Remember the Sabbath Day by keeping it holy.

IV.   Honor your father and your mother, so that you may live long in the land the Lord your God is giving you.

V.   You shall not murder.

VI.   You shall not commit adultery.

VII.   You shall not steal.

VIII. You shall not give false testimony against your neighbor.

IX.   You shall not covet your neighbor's wife.

---

[1] *Translator's Note: Scripture excerpts taken from the* Holy Bible, New International Version (NIV), *International Bible Society, 1984.*

X.   **You shall not covet your neighbor's house. You shall not covet your neighbor's wife, or his manservant or maidservant, his ox or donkey, or anything that belongs to your neighbor.**[2]

The Law presented in the Ten Commandments is for all times and all nations, a universality that gives the commandments a divine character. The other laws decreed by Moses were devised to instill, at times through fear, a sense of order in a people very much agitated and unorganized, whose behavior and prejudices were still freshly colored by many years of bondage in Egypt. To sanction his authority, Moses did claim a divine origin for his secular laws. In doing so, he followed a practice common among the leaders and lawgivers of many early peoples. In those days authority over people was often exercised under the guise of a divine power. Only the notion of a harsh God could impress a relatively unaware people, whose sense of justice and moral values were still very limited. Today, we realize that a God Who would include among the Divine commandments "you shall not murder, and do no harm to your neighbors" wouldn't contradict that law by sanctioning any type of bloodshed.[3] This only highlights the transient nature of Moses' secular laws.

THE CHRIST

3.   Jesus didn't come to abolish the Law defined in the Ten Commandments. He came to fulfill and amplify it, to clarify its real meaning, and to interpret it at humanity's level of progress at the time. Those elements of the Mosaic code that emphasize love of God and fellow human beings constitute the very basis of Jesus' teachings. As for the secular laws, Jesus advocated fundamental reforms both in form and substance. He fought constant-

---

[2] *Translator's Note: Exodus 20: 1-17.*

[3] *Translator's Note: The following are some among the instances in the Bible where Moses is apparently commanded by God to kill: Exodus 32: 27-28 (Then he said to them, "This is what the Lord, the God of Israel, says: 'Each man strap a sword to his side. Go back and forth through the camp from one end to the other, each killing his brother and friend and neighbor.' The Levites did as Moses commanded, and that day about three thousand of the people died."); Numbers 21:34-35 (The Lord said to Moses, "Do not be afraid of him, for I have handed him over to you, with his whole army and his land. Do to him what you did to Sihon, king of the Amorites, who reigned in Heshbon." So they struck him down, together with his sons and his whole army, leaving them no survivors. And they took possession of his land.); Numbers 31:7 (They fought against Midian, as the Lord commanded Moses, and [the soldiers] killed every man.)*

ly to correct the abuses of ritualistic worship and to right misconceived interpretations. His call for reform could not have been
any more revolutionary than when He reduced the Law to this
one principle: "Love the Lord your God with all your heart and
with all your soul and with all your mind; and Love your neighbor as yourself." He said Himself, "All the Law and the Prophets
hang on these two commandments."[4]

Furthermore, by the words "until heaven and earth disappear,
not the smallest letter, not the least stroke of a pen, will by any
means disappear from the Law until everything is accomplished" Jesus wanted us to realize that the Law must be respected and lived in all its purity over the whole earth, and with all its
amplifications and consequences. What, otherwise, would have
been the purpose of proclaiming the Law if it was only going to
benefit one nation or a few people? All human beings are sons
and daughters of God; they are without distinction in God's eyes
and subject to the same care and attention.

4.   But Jesus wasn't simply a lawgiver who was offering His word
as the one and final authority. He also came to fulfill the prophecies that had foretold His coming. He derived His moral authority from the exceptional nature of His spirit and from the divine
mission with which He was entrusted. Jesus came to teach
humanity that true life is not the one lived here on earth but in
the kingdom of heaven. He came to show us the pathway to this
kingdom. Jesus taught us that the way to reconcile ourselves
with God is by experiencing the events of our lives with an
awareness of our higher purpose as human beings. But He did
not reveal everything. On many subjects He limited Himself to
offering only the initial part of the truth, explaining His silence
about the rest by saying that human beings weren't capable yet
of understanding the whole truth.[5] He did talk about all things,
but often in a veiled manner. He knew that, in order for people to
be able to assimilate the integral meaning of His words, new
ideas and knowledge would first have to come into being that
would provide the key to unlock the full extent of His doctrine.
These ideas would only come once the human spirit had reached
a certain level of advancement. Science, especially, still had an
important part to play in the emergence and development of
human knowledge, and it needed time to mature.

---

[4] *Translator's Note: Matthew 22:37-39.*

[5] *Translator's Note: John 16:12.*

THE SPIRITIST DOCTRINE

5. The Spiritist Doctrine is the new body of principles that reveals, through indisputable evidence, the existence and nature of the spirit world and its relationship to the material one. The spirit world is presented not as a supernatural element but as one of the living and active forces of Nature, the source of a vast number of phenomena that even today we don't understand and so relegate to the realm of fantasy or miracles. Christ hinted at such a development on several occasions, and it is because He only hinted that many of the things He said have remained beyond our grasp or been wrongly interpreted. The Spiritist Doctrine offers a key that will help explain all these matters.

6. The Law of the Old Testament was personified in Moses; that of the New Testament in Christ. The third revelation can't be personified, however, because it isn't given by a human being but by spirits. Having transcended the bondage of matter, spirits now constitute the heavenly voices which communicate to all parts of the world and through countless intermediaries. The Spiritist Doctrine is, in this sense, the collective work of the illuminated intelligences of the spirit world. This work brings us enlightenment and offers the means of understanding the destiny that awaits each of us on our return to the spirit realm.

7. Just as Christ said, "I have not come to abolish the Law or the Prophets but to fulfill them,"[6] so it is with the Spiritist Doctrine, which has not come to defy Christian principles but to help carry them out. The Spiritist Doctrine teaches nothing contrary to Christ's message. Rather, it develops that message, explains it in a way that everyone can understand, and makes plain that part of it which has been known, until now, only in an allegorical form. The Doctrine has come at the predicted time to confirm Christ's foresight and to prepare the way for the realization of future things. The Spiritist Doctrine is, then, part of the design of Christ. As He said Himself, Christ presides over the spiritual renewal of humankind, laying the foundation of a more divine order on earth.

THE ALLIANCE BETWEEN SCIENCE AND RELIGION

8. Science and religion are the two levers of human intelligence. One reveals the laws of the material world, the other the laws of the spiritual one. Now, since these laws stem from the same first

---

[6] *Translator's Note: Matthew 5:17.*

cause, which is God, they can't contradict each other. If they did, it stands to reason that one would have to be right and the other wrong, which would be inconsistent with the Divine design. Consequently, the apparent incompatibility that exists between science and religion is simply the result of incomplete views of the world and one-sided positions taken by both parties. This conflict of ideas has often given rise both to unbelief and intolerance.

The time has come, however, when the teachings of Christ can be interpreted in their fullest significance. The veil of allegory that He purposely used on many occasions must be lifted. Science must see beyond matter and acknowledge a spiritual perspective; religion must stop ignoring the fundamental laws of matter. Only in this way will both sides come together and learn to lean on each other. As a result religion will no longer be discredited by science. Its accordance with reason and with the compelling logic of the events of nature will give religion a new, unshakable power.

Until our own day, science and religion struggled with their differences. Each had a tendency to see matters only according to its own particular point of view, and each rejected the other. Clearly, something more was needed—something that would allow these two realms of knowledge to close the gap between them. The missing link is contained in the knowledge of the laws that govern the nonphysical (spiritual) realm and its interactions with the world of matter—laws, it should be pointed out, as constant as the ones that govern the movement of the stars and the existence of living beings. Once these interactions are empirically demonstrated, we will see things in a new light. Faith will speak to reason; reason will find nothing illogical in faith; materialism will be overcome.

Nevertheless, in this case as in many others, there will always be those who initially choose to stay behind. They might, for a while, resist the new views, but they too will eventually be overtaken by this new wave of progress. A new moral revolution is taking place whose foundation has been maturing for over eighteen centuries. Directed by the higher intelligences of the spirit world, this silent revolution, which will bring about a new era for the human race, now nears its completion. Its consequences are easy to predict: The new order will produce inevitable changes in all aspects of social relations. We say inevitable because no one will be able to circumvent these changes; they are part of the designs of Providence, a natural by-product of the Divine Law of Progress.[7]

----

[7] *Translator's Note: See Allan Kardec's* The Spirits' Book, *Chapter 28.*

SPIRIT TEACHINGS

THE NEW ERA

9. ■ God is One and unique. Moses was the spirit entrusted by God with the mission of making the Divine Presence known, not only to the Jewish people but also to the entire pagan world. Through Moses and the prophets, the Jewish people were the means through which Divinity was to be revealed. The many misfortunes along the way served to call attention to God, lifting the veil that obscured humankind's comprehension of the Divine.

God's commandments, as revealed through Moses, contain the seeds of the moral teachings brought by Christ. The biblical text, however, restricts their meaning, and for a good reason: If the full extent of Christ's message had been advanced by Moses, his contemporaries would not have been able to understand it. Still the Ten Commandments were a shiny doorway to a new journey, a beacon lighting up a new path for the human race. Moses' moral teachings were very appropriate to the state of progress of the people he wanted to renew and uplift. But with respect to their spiritual development, these people were in a relatively primitive stage. It is true that in scientific and artistic matters they had achieved some impressive things. But they wouldn't have understood that they could worship God by any other means than by animal sacrifices or that they had to learn to forgive their enemies. The spiritual awareness of Moses' contemporaries was very limited. A wholly spiritual religion would not have reached their hearts. They needed a more materialized form of worship. In that environment, animal sacrifices spoke to the believers' senses at the same time that the idea of a Supreme Power touched their spirits.

Jesus unveiled a more elevated moral doctrine. Pure and sublime, His is the doctrine which will one day renew the world by bringing together all humanity. This doctrine will cause compassion and the love of one's neighbor to spring forth in every heart, and establish unity and fellowship among all peoples. Finally, His moral doctrine will transform earth into a planet that will become the home of a far greater number of high-minded beings. This is the Law of Progress, to which all nature must submit. The Spiritist Doctrine is a lever the Almighty makes use of to spring humanity toward a new era.

The time has come when moral values must be developed in order to bring about the advancement intended by Providence.

These ideas will follow the same route as the one taken by the idea of liberty, which was a precursor of moral progress. And no less than liberty, these developments will not come about without a fight. Attacks and opposition are, however, good for that development, and for keeping it in the public eye. Once this passes, the beauty and sanctity of this new vision will touch all spirits, who will then embrace a system of knowledge (and way of thinking) that will give them the key to the future life and open doors to happier living.

Moses showed humanity the way, Jesus continued his work, and the Spiritist Doctrine will help bring the work to completion. ■ —An Israelite Spirit (Mulhouse, 1861).

10. ■ Once, out of undying compassion, God let humanity see the light of truth pierce through the darkness. This was the coming of Christ. After the departure of that living Light, the darkness returned; and humankind, which had been given the opportunity to choose between truth and ignorance, once again lost itself. Then, just like the prophets of the Old Testament, the spirits began to speak and finally to give warning that the world is trembling on its very foundation, that thunder is ready to resound. But, dear friends, remain steady.

Rest assured that because the Spiritist Doctrine has its very basis in the Laws of Nature, it has a divine essence. As such, its principles serve a great and useful purpose. Whenever your scientific advances lack a sound moral orientation, they often misguide you. The result can be a relentless and exclusive pursuit of one's own material well-being—a reality that better serves the interest of darkness than of light. But those whose lives are in keeping with the teachings of Christ know that love and kindness of heart must go hand in hand with science.

Think of it: Nineteen centuries of bloodshed and martyrdom, and yet Christ's reign hasn't come! Christians, go back to the teacher who wants to redeem you! Everything is easier when you have faith and love in your heart: Love fills you with a joy that can't be measured. Yes, the world is being shaken to its foundation, as spirits of light have repeatedly told you. Bend, then, with the wind that announces the storm, and it won't knock you down. Prepare yourselves so you won't be like the foolish virgins who were taken by surprise at the arrival of their bridegroom.[8]

---

[8] *Translator's Note: Matthew 25:7-10.*

The revolution that nears will be primarily of a moral, not physical, nature. High-minded spirits were entrusted by God to inspire faith among you. Enlightened and committed workers, make your voices heard! You might think you're just a grain of sand, but that's the stuff mountains are made of. The words "We are unimportant" have no real meaning. Each person has a mission, a particular task. Don't the ants build vast colonies? Don't tiny micro-organisms, which you can hardly detect, raise up continents? A new crusade has begun. Apostles, not of war but of universal peace—modern Saint Bernards—look ahead and march forward. The law of the universe is the Law of Progress. ■
—Fénelon (Poitiers, 1861)

11.   ■ From the spirit realm, Saint Augustine is among the greatest advocates of the principles behind the Spiritist Doctrine, and his intellectual influence is felt throughout this work. The reason for Augustine's association with the Doctrine can be found in the life story of this great Christian philosopher. Augustine belonged to a dynamic vanguard of men known as the Fathers of the Church, to whom Christianity owes its most solid bases. Like many others he was converted from paganism, or rather from a life of deep disregard for religious and moral concerns. Once, in the midst of a pleasure binge, he felt deep in his soul an unusual sensation. This experience called him to himself and made him realize that he couldn't find real happiness in the debilitating and fleeting entertainments he pursued. He had an experience similar to Paul's, who heard a saintly voice saying to him on the road to Damascus: "Saul, Saul, why do you persecute me?"[9] When Augustine heard his voices he cried out, "My God! My God! Forgive me! I believe; I am a Christian!" From this moment, he became one of the greatest supporters of the Gospel. You can read, in his famous Confessions, the characteristic and prophetic words he spoke after the death of his mother, Monica: "I am convinced that my mother will visit me and give me advice, letting me know what waits for us in the future life."[10] What great teaching there is in these words, which are a remarkable anticipation of the doctrine that was to come. This is why today, when the time has come to spread the truth as he had foreseen, he has become one of its ardent supporters and has, in a sense, multiplied himself so that he can attend to the needs of everyone who seeks his assistance. ■ — Erastus, a disciple of the Apostle Paul (Paris, 1863)

---

[9] *Translator's Note: Acts 9:4*

[10] *Translator's Note: Inferential conclusion based on Confessions, 9.13.37, and 9.12.29-33.*

Comment: Would it be possible for Saint Augustine to tear down what he himself built? Certainly not. But, like many others before him, he now sees with the eye of the spirit what he couldn't see while he was in a physical body. Free from matter, his soul sees new brightness and understands what he had found incomprehensible before. New ideas have revealed the true meaning of certain words to him. On earth he judged things according to the knowledge he possessed at the time. Since seeing the new light, he can appreciate those words in a fairer and more rational way. For example, he has reconsidered his beliefs regarding incubus and succubus spirits, as well as his condemnation of the theory of the antipodes.[11] Now that he understands Christ's doctrine in its purest dimension, he finds it natural to think differently on some points from the way he did on earth, though this in no way affects his standing as a Christian apostle. Indeed, he can even establish himself as an advocate of this new order of ideas without repudiating his original allegiance, because he has seen what was predicted so long ago come to pass. By proclaiming this doctrine today, he assists us toward a more correct and logical interpretation of the scripture. The same is true of all illuminated spirits that find themselves in a similar position.

---

[11] *Translator's Note: In medieval Europe, incubus was a male demon believed to have sexual intercourse with women in their sleep. A succubus was its female counterpart. Union with an incubus was thought to produce demons, witches, and deformed children. The word incubus is Latin for nightmare.*

Chapter 2

My Kingdom Is Not of This World

SCRIPTURES AND COMMENTARY

1. *Pilate then went back inside the palace, summoned Jesus and asked him, "Are you the king of the Jews?"*

    Jesus said, "My kingdom is not of this world. If it were, my servants would fight to prevent my arrest by the Jews. But now my kingdom is from another place."

    "You are a king, then!" said Pilate.

    Jesus answered, "You are right in saying I am a king. In fact, for this reason I was born, and for this I came into the world, to testify to the truth. Everyone on the side of truth listens to me."

    (John, 18: 33, 36-37)

THE FUTURE LIFE

2. Here Jesus' words clearly refer to a future life. At every opportunity He presents the future life as the destiny of every person and a reality that we should, while on earth, make our chief preoccupation. All of his precepts refer to this great principle; indeed, without it, there wouldn't be a real reason for most of His moral teachings. This is why people who don't believe in a future life can't understand His teachings or consider the whole business foolish—they think of Jesus' precepts in the context of the present life only.

    The idea of a future life is the cornerstone of Christ's teachings and important enough to be featured at the very beginning of this book. It is a notion to be pondered seriously. Without it, finding meaning in the many oddities of life or reconciling them with God's Justice is difficult.

3. Early Jewish notions about the future life were vague. The Jews believed in angels, for instance, whom they regarded as privi-

leged beings in creation; but they didn't fathom that human beings could themselves aspire to become angels and take part in the same happiness. They believed that the primary rewards for observing God's Law were worldly gain, the supremacy of their nation, and victory over their enemies. On the other hand, they viewed crises and natural disasters as punishments for disobeying the Law. Moses could not have said anything different to a people then made up mostly of unenlightened shepherds. Moses' contemporaries were still primarily impressed by the events of the physical life. Much later, as we know, Jesus revealed that there is another world where God's justice follows its course. This is the world He promises to everyone who observes the Divine commandments, the world where the good find rewards in the things of the spirit. This is His kingdom, the realm to which He returned when He left earth.

Nevertheless, Jesus also had to conform His teachings to the understanding of the men and women of His time. He knew that too much light dazzles and that his message would be incomprehensible otherwise. So He limited Himself to the presentation of the future life as a principle, a natural law whose action no one could escape. Nowadays, though all Christians necessarily believe in a future life, in some respects this belief is either too vague, incomplete, or misguided. For many, the future life is no more than an article of faith, accepted without much conviction. It's not surprising then that skepticism and even outright rejection still surround this issue.

As it has done with other ideas offered by Jesus, the Spiritist Doctrine brings to completion His teachings on the future life. Humanity has now matured enough to appreciate the true significance of these teachings. Under the Spiritist perspective, the future life is no longer a simple article of faith, a mere theory; it's an undeniable reality, demonstrated by facts. Those who've described it to us have seen different aspects and stages of this life with their own eyes, so that doubt is no longer possible. The accounts of the future life, moreover, are accessible to anyone, regardless of the level of understanding, just as anyone can pick up a book and read a detailed description of a country. These accounts are supported by so many details, and the conditions of existence for those who live there (whether they are happy or not) are so rational, that we have to agree that it couldn't be any other way and that life in the spirit realm is perfectly consistent with God's Justice.[1]

JESUS AS KING

4. All of us realize that the kingdom of Jesus is not of this world. But isn't He of the highest royal lineage for us? The title "King" doesn't always refer to temporal authority. We give it—by popular consent—to individuals who, by the use of their talents, rise to the highest level in their professions, dominate their time, and influence human progress. We frequently use the expression "king" or "prince" in this sense when we speak about philosophers, artists, poets, writers, etc. This kind of royalty, which comes from personal merit and represents a legacy for all posterity, often indicates a superiority far greater than the one we associate with a royal crown. This royalty is everlasting; it is admired and respected by future generations. By contrast, the royal titles of earth are of shifting value, and sometimes even hated by future generations. Earthly royalty ends with death. But the supremacy of a truly moral person is only strengthened in the future life. From this vantage point, isn't Jesus a mightier and more powerful King than all the earthly monarchs? It was with good reason that He said to Pilate, "I am a King, but my kingdom is not of this world."

THE (SPIRITUAL) VANTAGE POINT

5. The clear and precise idea that we can form of a future life gives us unshakable confidence in what is to come. Moreover, this confidence has enormous consequences for our moral development because it completely changes the vantage point from which we look at life on earth. For those who can contemplate the eternity of life in the spiritual realm, life in the body is but a temporary stay in an unpleasant country. The sufferings and trials of our lives become nothing more than incidents, which we can patiently endure since we know they'll last only a short time and be followed by a far happier state. Death, too, loses its terror for us; it stops being a door that opens onto nothingness and becomes

---

[1] *Translator's Note: Vast literature on the subject of life after death is offered also by studies of individuals who experience clinical death. This field of research was pioneered by Dr. Raymond Moody with* Life After Life *(1977).The primary vehicle for scientific studies on clinical death is the* Journal of Near-Death Studies, *published by the International Association for Near Death Studies, Inc. (http://www.iands.org).*

instead the door to freedom, through which the exiled spirit enters into a blessed sphere of blissfulness. The realization that the sojourn on earth is temporary makes us pay less attention to the busyness of life and, as a result, we attain a measure of calmness that soothes the wounds of daily living.

To the contrary, simply by doubting the existence of a future life, we direct our minds solely to the here and now. Where we are unsure of what lies before us, we give everything to the present. We come to the mistaken conclusion that nothing is more precious than earthly things, and so we behave like children who can see only their toys. We'll go to any lengths to acquire all forms of material goods. The loss of even the smallest possession causes us considerable anguish, disappointment, and feelings of self-pity. It's then that our own exaggerated sense of self-worth is hurt and we turn the minor mishaps of life into a series of excruciating torments. Everything around us is magnified. The harm we experience, and the good that touches others, takes on great importance in our eyes. We become like the person who, while in the center of a large city, sees every building on a monumental scale without realizing that from the top of a mountain it all looks pretty minute.

So it is with a person who looks at life from the vantage of a future existence. For him or her, life is but a moment in the infinity of time, much as the stars are tiny points of light in the immensity of the night sky. We begin to see that the wellborn and the common folk are parts of the same whole, like ants on top of an ant hill, and that the worker and the industrial tycoon really have little to distinguish them. We can't avoid a tinge of sorrow for the toil that some people put themselves through to conquer things that will do them so little good, and that they will enjoy for so little time. From this we can conclude that the value we give earthly things is inversely related to the strength of our belief in a future life.

6. But—someone might argue—if everybody thought this way, everything on earth would soon be in ruins because no one would bother to do anything. Not exactly. Human beings instinctively look after their own well-being and will do their best to improve their lot even when they know that their stay on the planet is short. There is no one who finds a thorn in their hand who doesn't pull it out, just to stop the pain. Likewise, our desire for comfort drives us to improve things, because this same desire is part of the drive toward progress and self-preservation which are part of the Laws

of Nature.[2] Driven partly by this desire to meet our needs and partly by our sense of personal fulfillment and duty, we work and so honor the designs of Providence that placed us on earth for this very purpose. In this regard, the only difference between those who consider the future life and those who don't is that the former attach only a relative importance to the current life. From this perspective, it's easier for them to face the misfortunes of earthly life because they know what awaits them afterwards.

God doesn't condemn the enjoyment of earthly pleasures but their abuse at the expense of spiritual matters. It was against these abuses that Jesus warned us when he said, "My kingdom is not of this world."

If you will, think of those people who identify themselves with a future life as being like the rich who are not troubled when they lose a small amount of money. By contrast, the person whose interests are centered on earthly things is comparable to a pauper who falls into total despair after having lost all possessions.

7. The Spiritist Doctrine opens up and broadens our perspective; it offers new horizons. In place of a narrow vision that focuses only on the present and makes our brief time on earth the one central lever to an eternal future, the Spiritist Doctrine shows us that this life is nothing more than a link in the magnificent, harmonious progression that is God's work. It also reveals the unity that connects all the lives of one being, all the beings of the same planet, and all the beings of the universe. It offers the basis and the reason for universal brotherhood. In this sense it differs greatly from the doctrine of the creation of the soul at birth, which makes each individual a stranger to everyone else. This unity among the parts of the whole explains what couldn't otherwise be explained when we consider life from a purely physical view. Yet such an integrated view would have been impossible to understand in Christ's time, and for this reason He waited until now to make this knowledge known.

---

[2] *Translator's Note: see Allan Kardec's* The Spirits' Book, *chapter 23, "The Law of Progress."*

SPIRIT TEACHINGS

EARTHLY ROYALTY

8. ■ No one understands better than I the truth of these words of Jesus: "My kingdom is not of this world." During my life on earth, I lost myself because of an all-consuming conceit. Who if not I, then, can really understand the worthlessness of a royal title? Was I able to bring any of my titles with me here? No, I brought absolutely nothing. To make my lesson more poignant, my royal condition didn't go with me even as far as the grave. Among men and women, I was a queen, and I thought I would enter heaven as a queen. A great disappointment was in store for me. Imagine my shame when, instead of being received as a sovereign, I saw above me—a long way above—spirits I had judged unimportant on earth, whom I had despised because they weren't of noble blood.

Now I understand the insignificance of the honors and glittering prizes people run after so eagerly on earth.

In order to win a place in this kingdom, you must show selflessness, humbleness, benevolence, and charity in their most celestial form. Here, you are not asked who you are or what position you held but what good you have done and how many tears you have dried.

Oh Jesus! You said that Your kingdom was not of this world because it is necessary to know human suffering in order to get to it. An earthly throne brings no one closer to it. The path to Your kingdom is often found among briars and thorns, not flowers.

On earth, men and women are always in such a huge rush, running back and forth, hoping to make a fortune—as if they could keep it forever. Here, these illusions disappear. Once free from matter, spirits soon realize that they were chasing shadows and neglecting the pursuit of the only lasting and valuable possessions. These are the only goods that count in the spirit realm, the only ones that grant us access to a true spiritual heaven.

Take pity on those who squandered their opportunities. Help them with your prayers, because prayer helps humanity approach the Most High. It is what links heaven and earth. Don't forget! ■ —A Queen of France (Havre, 1863)

Chapter 3

In My Father's House Are Many Mansions

SCRIPTURES AND COMMENTARY

1.   *"Do not let your hearts be troubled. Trust in God; trust also in me. In my Father's house are many rooms; if it were not so, I would have told you. I am going there to prepare a place for you. And if I go and prepare a place for you, I will come back and take you to be with me that you also may be where I am."*

(John, 14: 1-3)

THE DIFFERENT STATES OF THE SOUL IN THE SPIRIT WORLD

2.   The "Father's house" Jesus speaks of is the Universe. The many places are the planets orbiting in space. They offer the spirits dwelling places corresponding to their level of development.

But Jesus wasn't only talking about the diversity of planets; He was also referring to the condition of the soul in the spirit world, where it can be happy or unhappy. In that world, depending on how purified and detached from material ties spirits have become, the manner in which they experience their environments can vary enormously. For example, there can be distinct differences in the way things appear to them, in the sensations they feel, and in the perceptions they have.

Whereas some spirits can't distance themselves from the physical world they've just left, others are high enough on the spiritual ladder that they can journey through space and to different spheres. Some spirits feel blemished by guilt and wander aimlessly, as if trapped in darkness; others rejoice in a state of radiance that opens to them the grand spectacle of Infinity. Finally, those who did evil often find themselves full of regret and remorse. Often feeling lonely, comfortless, and separated from the ones they love, these spirits suffer intense moral anguish. By contrast, those who did good find themselves in the company of their loved ones and enjoy an indescribable happiness. In this

sense, too, there are "many places," though they have no boundaries or specific locations.[1]

THE CATEGORIES OF INHABITED WORLDS

3.   The characteristics of the many inhabited worlds vary greatly
      depending on the spiritual evolution of the individuals living on
      them. In some, the inhabitants are less evolved, physically and
      spiritually, than we on earth. Others fall into the same category
      as earth; and still others are superior to us in every respect. On
      less developed worlds, we learn, life is completely material, pas-
      sion rules everything, moral concerns are almost non-existent. As
      they develop, however, the influence of matter wanes so that in
      more advanced worlds life is, so to speak, all spiritual.

4.   There are also worlds in an intermediate state where good and
      bad are intermixed, with one or the other being the controlling
      influence, as the inhabitants' ethical progress dictates. Thus,
      although an absolute classification of the many orbs in the cos-
      mos is impossible, we can at least group them in a general way
      by their condition and purpose. According to their dominant
      characteristics the following groups can be identified: primitive
      (or unevolved) worlds, where the earliest incarnations of the
      human spirit take place; worlds of trials and purifications, where
      wrongdoing predominates; worlds of regeneration, where spirits
      who are still in assignments of purification can replenish their
      energies; blissful worlds, where good far outweighs bad; and
      celestial (or divine) orbs, inhabited by purified spirits, where
      goodness prevails uncontested. Earth belongs to the category of
      worlds of trials and purifications, which explains why we are
      often exposed to so much suffering.

5.   Spirits who live their physical lives in a particular world are not
      attached to it indefinitely. Nor do they have to go through all the
      different phases of their journey towards perfection on that one
      planet. When their own spiritual advancement surpasses that of
      the world they live in, they pass on to a more evolved one. In
      consecutive stages, they reach the state of complete purification.
      The different orbs are, in effect, stations where the spirits find all
      the elements they need for their progress—elements, in other
      words, that correspond to their particular stage of evolution. It is
      naturally a reward to ascend to a more evolved planet, just as the

---

[1] *Translator's Note: An extended discussion is found in Allan Kardec's* The
Spirits' Book, *Chapter 5, "Spirits."*

lengthening of one's stay on a world of lesser condition is an opportunity for the spirit to correct its own faults. Those who choose to persist in their unruliness risk reincarnation in a world even inferior to the one where they currently live.

EARTH'S DESTINY; CAUSES OF HUMAN SUFFERING

6. Some people find it surprising that earth is filled with so much wrongdoing, so many raw passions, and all sorts of disease. From this, they may conclude that the human species is very unfortunate. This assessment is often the result of failing to consider things in their entirety, which occurs whenever we limit our vantage point to the here and now. The human beings who live on earth are only a small fraction of our kind if we define humankind as the set of all the reasoning beings who inhabit the countless orbs of the universe. How large is earth's population relative to the total population of the universe? Much smaller than a village's population when compared to a great empire's. Thus, the material and moral situation of earth isn't particularly surprising, especially when one considers earth's purpose and the nature of its inhabitants.

7. It would be a great mistake to judge the entire population of a city by the people who live in its worst sections. Likewise, in a hospital we only see the sick and injured; in a prison we find all kinds of corruption and vice gathered in one place; in unhealthy climates we discover that the inhabitants are, for the most part, pale, puny, and sickly. Picture earth as a combination of these: a slum, a hospital, and an unhealthy place. It is all of them together. You will understand then why hardships outweigh pleasures here: after all, we don't send healthy people to hospitals or put innocent ones in houses of correction. These institutions can't, by definition, be places of pure enjoyment.

But just as the total population of a city isn't found in its hospitals and prisons, we don't find the total population of spirits here on earth. And just as sick people leave the hospital when they're cured and inmates who have served their sentences leave prison, the spirits of men and women on earth will also leave earth's environment and go on to happier realms once they've rid themselves of their moral frailties.

SPIRIT TEACHINGS

PRIMITIVE AND ADVANCED WORLDS

8.   ▓ When we say that a world is advanced or primitive we speak in relative terms, not in an absolute sense. Such and such a world is more or less advanced only when compared to another one at a different stage of evolution. If you take earth as your point of reference, you can conceive what a less advanced world would be like. In particular, its inhabitants are likely at a stage of evolution that is akin to that of earth's primitive peoples. In fact, the very existence of these peoples on earth is a reminder that earth too was once a less advanced world.

On more backward spheres the inhabitants are, to some extent, at a rudimentary stage: They have human form but no physical beauty. More important, their instincts are not tempered by notions of social grace, goodwill, or even fairness. Brute force is the only law they know. In the absence of industry and technology, they live their lives gathering food. However, these beings, like all others, are not forgotten by God. Deep within, they have the vague intuition of a Supreme Being. This intuition is enough to make some of these primitives more advanced than others; and it is through these more evolved individuals that all the rest are prepared for the ascent to a more complete life. These people aren't degraded beings but children who are growing.

Between the higher and primitive orders of spirits are countless degrees. Consequently, seeing the pure spirits, diaphanous and brilliant with glory, you would find it impossible to recognize in them the primitive beings they once were. To do so would be as difficult as to recognize the adult in the embryo. ▓

9.   ▓ In worlds that have reached a highly evolved level, the ethical and material aspects of life are very different from those on earth. Their inhabitants have, as elsewhere in the universe, material bodies, but they have a more refined beauty. Their physical forms are more perfected, their looks, especially, are more serene. The bodily form has nothing of earth's materiality about it, and so isn't subject to the same needs, sicknesses, or wearing out that the strong influence of matter causes here. And this isn't all. Because of their higher refinement, the senses of the people who live on these worlds are far more developed than earthly senses. The lightness of their bodies allows for easy and rapid movement. They don't drag laboriously over the ground; instead, their

bodies float, as it were, above the surface and glide through the air—the only effort being the spirit's intent—much like the popular conception of angels or the ancient Greek's notion of the inhabitants of the Elysian fields. Further, by their own will, the inhabitants of such places can keep the appearance they had during a prior life and show themselves to their friends as they once knew them—except that they now project a radiant light and exhibit the outward marks of the finer inward impulses that are characteristic of evolved natures. Instead of downtrodden faces stricken by anguish and earthly passions, life and insightfulness sparkle in them with the same kind of splendor that is symbolized in works of art by the halos of saints.

As we know, physical matter offers only slight resistance to enlightened spirits. Thus, in advanced worlds the physical body develops more rapidly and the period of infancy is very short, almost non-existent. Without worry and anguish, their lives are proportionately longer than on earth. (In principle, the life span corresponds to the degree of advancement on each planet.) Nor does death bring with it the horrors of decay. Far from being feared, death is seen as a happy transformation since there is no doubt as to the future. As for the soul during its incarnate life there, it is not constrained by matter and enjoys a clarity of consciousness that places it in an almost constant state of freedom, giving it the ability to communicate by means of thought. ■

10. ■ In addition, on these highly evolved spheres, relationships among different peoples are always friendly. Because no nation ever tries to dominate another, there are no wars. There are no masters, no slaves, and birth doesn't confer special privileges. Only moral and intellectual superiority determines social rank. Authority is respected, as it is only conferred on people who earn it and strive to exercise it with justice. In these higher realms, individuals don't try to elevate themselves above one another; they strive instead to rise above the self, to reach perfection. Their objective is to attain illumination, although this desire isn't a torment but a noble goal spurring them to work hard to join the ranks of pure spirits. In these realms, all the higher feelings of human nature are exalted and refined. Hate is unknown; so are jealousy and envy. Love is the common bond; it unites all, and the strong are always ready and willing to help the weak. As a result of their different abilities, some individuals might have more than others, but nobody suffers from want because the need for such trials doesn't exist in these realms. ■

11. ■ Conversely, note that on your planet, wrongdoing is still needed so that you can come to know true goodness, just as you need night before you can admire light, and sickness before you can appreciate health. On more evolved planets, there is no need for these contrasts. There, spirits revel in an everlasting light, an undying beauty, and a permanent state of inner calmness. They enjoy uninterrupted joy. Their feelings are not, in any measure, tainted by the anguish and fears of material life, or by the contact with less evolved beings. These are the things that the human spirit on earth has the most trouble understanding. Humans are more clever at painting the torments of hell than at imagining the glories of heaven. Why? Because, being in a less advanced state, they've known only pain and suffering and haven't yet experienced celestial enjoyments. They can't speak of things they don't know. Now however, as humanity progresses and achieves greater purification, horizons are expanding; at last human beings have begun to appreciate the good that is before them, and comprehend the extent of the bad they're leaving behind. ■

12. ■ Yet these happy worlds of which we have been speaking aren't especially privileged ones. God doesn't play favorites in that way. God gives the same rights and the same opportunities to all. Everyone starts at the same point; no one receives more from God than any other. The highest ranks are accessible to everyone. Getting there depends on the individual, who can choose to put forth the necessary effort and so reach the goal more quickly, or remain inactive for centuries and centuries in the quagmire of human matter. (This is a summary of teachings from enlightened spirits.) ■

WORLDS OF TRIALS AND PURIFICATIONS

13. ■ What more is left to say about worlds of purification that you don't already know? You only have to look at the one on which you're living to know one. Yet the great number of superior intelligences among you indicates that earth is not a primitive world, destined to accept newly created beings. The innate qualities that different souls bring with them prove that they've lived before and achieved a certain degree of progress. But the number of vices you're subject to also shows that you have great moral imperfections. This is why Providence has placed you in your unfriendly world, where you can purify yourselves through hard work and by undergoing the hardships of life. By doing so, you'll earn the right to ascend to happier realms. ■

14. ■ Nevertheless, not every spirit incarnated on earth came here for the purpose of expiation. Those peoples that you include among the so-called "savage" or uncivilized societies of early times were formed of spirits who had barely left their infancy and who were here enrolled, so to speak, in an educational experience in which learning was accomplished through interaction with spirits farther along in the evolutionary scale. Later on, these same spirits progressed enough to become the semi-civilized populations of earth. In general, these are earth's indigenous peoples. They have been advancing gradually over the centuries, and some have attained a level of intellectual development common to more cultivated societies.

    Indeed, the spirits who are in expiation—if we may use the term—are the rare ones of the earth. They've already lived on other planets, from which they were banned for persisting in wrongdoing or causing great distress to the social order there. They were, therefore, sent away to live for a time in an environment with less evolved spirits. They received the assignment to help, through the use of their more developed intelligence and by sharing their knowledge, the less evolved spirits to advance. This is how spirits under correction are found among the more developed peoples of earth. It's also why the misfortunes of earthly life seem so very bitter to them: They have a higher degree of sensitivity, and reverses and trials test them more severely than less evolved beings whose sense of right and wrong is not yet fully developed. ■

15. ■ Earth, is then, a planet of expiation. The variety of such planets is infinite, but all of them have one thing in common: They serve as places of exile for spirits struggling to adjust themselves to the Divine Law. This means that these spirits have to endure, at one and the same time, the meanness of human beings and the harshness of the physical environment. Their work here is doubly hard, but it develops the superior qualities of heart and intelligence simultaneously. Thus, out of undying goodness, God turns a journey of redemption into an opportunity to reach greater heights. ■—Saint Augustine (Paris, 1862)

REALMS OF RENEWAL

16. ■ Among the many dazzling stars you see in the sky, there are many planets like yours that are designed for the purpose of correction and trial. But there exist also many other categories of worlds, some worse off than yours, some happier. Among the lat-

ter are the transitional places, which we call worlds of renewal. In the Universe, each swirl of planets that gravitates around a common center, contains a broad range of these worlds, from primitive places to places of exile, trial, renewal, and bliss. It has been explained to you about planets to which spirits in early development are assigned. Notwithstanding their unawareness of both good and evil, these spirits are endowed with the faculty of growing toward God through use of their own free-will. It has also been revealed that every soul is endowed with amazing gifts to do good. Unfortunately, there are those who fail miserably in this endeavor. But God, Who doesn't desire their annihilation, consigns them to planets where, in the course of successive incarnations, they gradually rid themselves of their imperfections. From these worlds they eventually return worthy of the glory that is their destiny. ■

17. ■ Realms of renewal are intermediate places between worlds of expiation and bliss. There the wounded soul finds a calm space to finish its purification. It is true that the soul still finds itself subject to the laws of matter, and still experiences earth-like sensations and desires. But it is free from the unbridled passions that enslave, from the excessive pride that numbs the heart, from the envy that torments it, and the hate that suffocates it. On such planets every soul displays the seal of love; fairness presides over social relations; everyone recognizes the Supreme Being and strives to live in a godly manner.

Although their inhabitants are still distant from perfect bliss, they experience the dawning of happiness. They still have physical bodies so they are subject to physical needs and tribulations from which only completely dematerialized spirits are free. The spirit still has to undergo trials, although these don't bring with them the poignant anguish typical of expiatory circumstances. Compared to earth, these planets are pleasant dwellings and most of you would be happy to live there forever. For you, they represent the calm after the storm, the recuperation period that follows a serious illness. However, being less absorbed by material concerns, their inhabitants have a more penetrating comprehension of the future than you do and grasp clearly that there are even higher joys reserved in the true life (after death) for spirits who show themselves worthy. Once free, the soul hovers on high. It no longer experiences the sensations of gross matter; instead, it comes to revel, through the sensitivity of an untainted perispirit (spiritual body), in the fragrances of love and compassion that emanate from God. ■

18. ■ But even on these worlds, individuals remain fallible. The spirit of wrongdoing hasn't completely lost its empire in the heart. The soul still has to make progress, for not to advance is to fall behind, and if a spirit isn't firmly placed on the pathway to goodness, it may stumble and risk having to return to a planet of expiation where it may have to face new and more trying challenges.

So at night, at the time of prayer and rest, raise your eyes to the sky and think on the countless worlds of light that shine over your head. Ask yourself which of these may lift you closer to God, and pray that one of these realms of renewal will open up to you after your time of trials here on earth is over. ■ —Saint Augustine (Paris, 1862)

THE PROGRESS OF THE PLANETS

19. ■ Progress is a Law of Nature. All created beings are submitted to this Law. God's generosity sees that everything improves and everyone prospers continuously. Even bodily destruction, which appears to you to be the end of everything, is only a means of reaching a more perfect state. Everything dies only to be reborn, and nothingness is an impossible state.

At the same time that living beings progress morally and ethically, the planets on which they live progress materially. If you were to follow a planet through its different phases—from the first moment its atoms came together—you would see a continuous line of progress. Though this underlying progress often goes unnoticed by each generation, it is such that the conditions of physical life become succeedingly more agreeable, keeping stride with the evolutionary pace of the inhabitants of the planet. This is true because nothing in nature stays static, everything evolves in tandem: human beings, animals, plants, the environment. This glorious idea is entirely worthy of God's grandeur—and contrasts sharply with the notion that the Supreme Being is solely concerned with the earth, this tiny grain of sand in the Universe. The view that God is exclusively devoted to our planet, as if we were the only form of life in the cosmos, is limited and incompatible with God's magnificence.

Earth, consistent with the Law of Progress, was in the past at a more backward moral stage than today, and it is bound to improve continuously in both dimensions. In truth, the earth is approaching a time of transformations, the result of which will be its accession to an abode of regeneration (no longer a place of

trial and expiation) where there will be greater happiness as
more and more people will live by God's precepts.[2] ■ —Saint
Augustine (Paris, 1862)

---

[2] *Translator's Note: The earth is gradually leaving the stage of a world of expiation
and beginning a transition to a world of regeneration. Evidence of this is found in
the scientific accomplishments since the last world war, the economic progress that
benefits a growing number of countries, and the advances in medical science that
have improved the quality and duration of human life. The same holds true for
social life, where the spread of democratic principles, the adoption of more enlightened legal codes, the repudiation of discrimination and so on, have made the task of
living less difficult. Clearly the characteristics of an expiation stage—e.g., occasional spurts of crime, violence, and wars, as well as the existence of personal
hatreds, abuse, promiscuity, etc.—will stay with us for quite some time yet, but the
transformation is already visible and significant. In a world of regeneration, the
primary purpose of life (for the incarnate spirit) will center on the cultivation of
new values and virtues, the manifestation of creative gifts, the acquisition of new
intellectual skills, and the development of one's own divine talents.*

Chapter 4

No One Can See the Kingdom of God Unless He Is Born Again

SCRIPTURE AND COMMENTARY

1.   *When Jesus came to the region of Caesarea Philippi, he asked his disciples, "Who do people say the Son of Man is?"*

They replied, "Some say John the Baptist; others say Elijah; and still others, Jeremiah or one of the prophets."

He asked, "But what about you? Who do you say I am?"

Simon Peter answered, "You are the Christ, the Son of the living God."

Jesus replied, "Blessed are you, Simon son of Jonah, for this was not revealed to you by man, but by my Father in heaven."

(Matthew, 16: 13-17; Mark, 8: 27-30)

2.   *Now Herod the tetrarch heard about all that was going on. And he was perplexed, because some were saying that John had been raised from the dead, others that Elijah had appeared, and still others that one of the prophets of long ago had come back to life. But Herod said, "I beheaded John. Who, then, is this I hear such things about?" And he tried to see him.*

(Luke, 9: 7-9; Mark, 6: 14-15)

3.   *[After the transfiguration] The disciples asked him, "Why then do the teachers of the law say that Elijah must come first?"*

Jesus replied, "To be sure, Elijah comes and will restore all things. But I tell you, Elijah has already come, and they did not recognize him, but have done to him everything they wished. In the same way the Son of Man is going to suffer at their hands." Then the disciples understood that he was talking to them about John the Baptist.

(Matthew, 17: 10-13; Mark, 9: 11-13)

RESURRECTION AND REINCARNATION

4.   Reincarnation was always part of Jewish belief, but it was taught using the term resurrection. Among the Jews, only the Sadducees, believing that everything ended with death, rejected the idea. But about this subject, and many others, Jewish ideas were never clearly defined; the Jews had only vague and incomplete notions about the soul and its connection to the body. They believed that people could live again; they didn't understand the mechanism by which this could occur. Accordingly, they used the word "resurrection" to designate what the Spiritist Doctrine calls, more appropriately, reincarnation. What is the difference? Resurrection assumes that life returns to a dead body, a concept science has demonstrated is impossible, especially after the body has decomposed and its elements have been reabsorbed by nature. The term reincarnation refers to the return of a soul, or spirit, to physical life in another body that has been newly formed for it. This new body has nothing to do with the previous one. Strictly speaking, in the Bible only Lazarus was resurrected; the word doesn't apply to Elijah or the other prophets. After all, if the Jews believed that John the Baptist was Elijah, the body of John couldn't have been the body of Elijah because John was seen as a child and his parents were known. John couldn't have been Elijah resurrected; he could have been Elijah reincarnated.

5.   *Now there was a man of the Pharisees named Nicodemus, a member of the Jewish ruling council. He came to Jesus at night and said, "Rabbi, we know you are a teacher who has come from God. For no one could perform the miraculous signs you are doing if God were not with him."*

   In reply Jesus declared, "I tell you the truth, no one can see the kingdom of God unless he is born again."

   Nicodemus asked, "How can a man be born when he is old?"

   "Surely he cannot enter a second time into his mother's womb to be born!" Jesus answered, "I tell you the truth, no one can enter the kingdom of God unless he is born of water and the Spirit. Flesh gives birth to flesh, but the Spirit gives birth to spirit. You should not be surprised at my saying, 'You must be born again.' The wind blows wherever it pleases. You hear its sound, but you cannot tell where it comes from or where it is going. So it is with everyone born of the Spirit."

   "How can this be?" Nicodemus asked. "You are Israel's teacher," said Jesus, "and do you not understand these things? I tell you the truth, we speak of what we know, and we testify to what we have seen, but still you

people do not accept our testimony. I have spoken to you of earthly things and you do not believe; how then will you believe if I speak of heavenly things?"

(John, 3: 1-12)

6.   The idea that John the Baptist had been Elijah and that the prophets would live again on earth can be found in many New Testament passages, but it is most notably mentioned in this extract. If the belief had been wrong, Jesus would have attacked it, as He did many others. But far from taking this course, He gave it His complete sanction and authority. In fact, He made it a basic principle and a necessary condition when He said, "No one can see the kingdom of God unless he is born again." He insisted on the point further by adding, "You should not be surprised at my saying, 'You must be born again.'"

7.   The words "unless he is born of water and the Spirit" have been interpreted to mean spiritual renewal through the water of the Baptism. Here, where the original text simply says "born of water and the Spirit," some translations have replaced the word "spirit" with "Holy Spirit," so that the translated meaning doesn't correspond to the original one. This important point emerged in early commentaries on the Gospel and will one day be proved beyond all possible doubt. [1]

8.   In order to understand Jesus' real meaning, we must also pay attention to the significance of the word "water," which is not used here in its usual sense.

       Ancient peoples had a very imperfect knowledge of the natural sciences. They believed that earth had risen out of water and that water was the basic and sole life-generating substance. This is why we read in the book of Genesis: ". . . the Spirit of God was hovering over the waters; ...Let there be an expanse between the waters; ... Let the water under the sky be gathered to one place and let dry ground appear.... Let the water teem with living creatures, and let birds fly above the earth across the expanse of the sky."[2]

       According to this belief, water represents the essence of matter, just as Spirit represents the essence of intelligence. The words

---

[1] *Translator's Note:* The New International Version Bible *employs the correct translation, confirming the correctness of Allan Kardec's position.*

The translation by Osterwald follows the early texts. It says "not born of water and Spirit." The translation by Saci says "of the Holy Spirit," and the version by Lammenais equally says "from the Holy Spirit."

[2] *Translator's Note: Genesis 1:2, 1:6, 1:9, 1:20.*

"without being born through water and the Spirit" (or in water and in Spirit) mean then "without being born in body and soul." This is how the Jews understood these words originally.

Jesus justifies this interpretation completely when He says to Nicodemus, "Flesh gives birth to flesh, but the spirit gives birth to spirit." Here Jesus establishes a clear distinction between body and the spirit. "Flesh gives birth to flesh" clearly indicates that only the body is produced out of the body and that the spirit is independent.

9. Continuing with Jesus' remarks, the words "The wind blows where it pleases, you hear its sound, but cannot tell where it comes from or where it is going" may apply either to the Supreme Being or the soul. The words "you cannot tell where it comes from or where it is going" indicate that we don't know who the spirit was or who it will be in the future. On the other hand, if the spirit or soul was created at the same time as the body (the usual interpretation), we would know where it came from because we would know its beginning. No matter how you look at the passage, it confirms the principle of the preexistence of the soul and the fact that we have all led many lives.

10.   *"From the days of John the Baptist until now, the kingdom of heaven has been forcefully advancing, and forceful man lay hold of it. For all the Prophets and the Law prophesied until John. And if you are willing to accept it, he is the Elijah who was to come. He who has ears, let him hear."*

(Matthew, 11: 12-15)

11. Even if the doctrine of reincarnation, as John expressed it, is interpreted in a purely mystical sense, this passage from Matthew allows no room for ambiguity: "He is the Elijah, who was to come."[3] Here there is nothing figurative, nothing allegorical, only a complete affirmation.

"From the days of John the Baptist until now, the kingdom of heaven has been forcefully advancing, and forceful man lay hold of it." What can these words mean when John the Baptist was still

----

[3] *Translators' Note: Some biblical scholars counter this argument with John the Baptist's words in John 1:21 "They asked him, 'Then who are you? Are you Elijah?' He said, 'I am not. "However, to accept this position is to affirm that Jesus is wrong. Since Jesus repeatedly affirms that John is Elijah, we have to accept that Jesus has the final authority on the matter. Indeed, this authority is confirmed by John the Baptist, when he claims that "He (Jesus) is the one who comes after me, the thongs of whose sandals I am not worthy to untie." See John 1:27.*

alive at the time they were spoken?[4] Jesus explains them to us when He says,"he is the Elijah who was to come." Given that John was Elijah, Jesus could only be speaking of the time when John was living under the name of Elijah. "Until now, the kingdom of heaven has been forcefully advancing, and forceful man lay hold of it" is another allusion to the violence of the Mosaic laws, which ordered that unbelievers be put to death[5] so that the Promised Land, the Paradise of the Jews, could be reached. This is in contrast with the new law of Jesus, under which heaven is to be won through love and kindness.

Jesus then added, "Anyone who has ears should listen!" These are words He frequently uses, reminding us that not everyone was in a condition to understand certain truths.

12.   *"But your dead will live; their bodies will rise. You who dwell in the dust, wake up and shout for joy. Your dew is like the dew of the morning; the earth will give birth to her dead."*

(Isaiah, 26: 19)

13. This passage from Isaiah is also very explicit: "Your dead will live." If the prophet had been speaking of the spiritual life, if he had meant to say that those whom we consider dead have not really died, spiritually speaking, he would have said, "They are still alive" and not "They will live." In fact, taken in the strictly spiritual sense, these words are a contradiction, since they imply an interruption in the life of the soul. Alternatively, if Isaiah had been referring to a moral rebirth only, his words would be at odds with the ancient belief in eternal punishment because they would establish, in principle, that all those who are (morally) dead will live again. [6]

---

[4] *Translator's Note: the* NIV *Bible lends a softer tone to Jesus' words. Other English translations are closer to the earlier texts and to the French text employed by Allan Kardec. The French Bible reads "Or, depuis le temps the Jean-Baptiste jusqu'à présent, le royaume des Cieux se prend par violence, et ce son le violents qui l'emportent." The* Jerusalem Bible *(1968) reads "Since John the Baptist came, up to this present time, the kingdom of heaven has been subjected to violence and the violent are taking it by storm." The* New American Bible *(1990) reads "From the days of John the Baptist until now, the kingdom of heaven suffers violence, and the violent are taking it by force."*

[5] *Translator's Note: See Chapter 1, footnote 3.*

[6] *Translators Note: The French quote is more akin to "your dead will live again" ("Ceux de votre peuple qu'on avait fait mourir vivront de nouveau…") while modern English translations prefer the meaning "your dead will come back to life," i.e., resuscitate. (The* Jerusalem Bible: *"Your dead will come to life, their corpses will rise," and* The New American Bible, *"But your dead shall live, their corpses shall rise.")*

14.   *"But when a man hath died once, when his body, separated from his spirit, has been consumed, what happens to him? Having died once can a man live again? In the war in which I find myself, each day of my life, I await my mutation."*

(Job, 14: 10, 14)

[Catholic translation by Le Maistre de Sacy]

"When a man dies, he loses all his strength, expires. Afterwards, where is he? If a man dies, will he live again? Will I wait all the days of my combat, until there comes some mutation?"

[Protestant translation by Osterwald]

"When a man is dead, he lives forever; when my days of existence on earth have finished, I will wait, seeing that I shall return again."

[Greek translation][7]

15. Each of these translations clearly expresses the principle of many lives. Nobody can imagine that Job is referring here to renewal through baptismal water, because he had never heard of such a thing. "Man having died once," he asks, "can he live again?" This idea of dying once and living again implies dying and living many times. The Greek version is even more explicit, if that is possible; "When my days of existence on earth are finished, I will wait, for I will return again" that is to say, will return to earth. This is perfectly clear, as if someone were saying, "I am leaving my house, but I will return."

   "In the war in which I find myself each day of my life, I await my mutation." Evidently, Job is referring here to his struggles against the hardships of life, to which he adds an expression of resignation, "I await my mutation." In the Greek version "I will wait" seems more likely to apply to a new lifetime: "When my

---

[7] *Translator's Note: The above is a free translation of the French versions of the Scripture. For the benefit of the interested reader, the passages in their original form are transcribed here: "Mais quand l'homme est mort une fois, que son corps, séparé de son esprit, est consumé, que devient-il? —L'homme étant mort une fois, pourrait-il bien revivre de nouveau? Dans cette guerre où je me trouve tous les jours de ma vie, j'attends que mon changement arrive." (Le Maistre de Sacy) "Quand l'homme meurt, il perd toute sa force, il expire; puis où est-il? —Si l'homme meurt, revivra-t-il? Attendrai-je tous les jours de mon combat, jusqu'à ce qu'il m'arrive quelque changement?" (Osterwald) "Quand l'homme est mort, il vit toujours; en finissant les jours de mon existence terrestre, j'attendrai, car j'y reviendrai de nouveau." (Greek Church). Consider for comparison purposes the NIV text: "But man dies and is laid low; he breathes his last and is no more. If a man dies, will he live again? All the days of my hard service I will wait for my renewal to come."*

existence has ended, I will wait, seeing that I shall return again." It is as if Job is placing himself, after death, in the interval that separates one life from another and telling us that he will wait there until the moment of his return arrives.

16. There is no doubt then that, though it went under the name "resurrection," reincarnation was a fundamental belief among the Jews. Jesus and the prophets confirm this, so that a denial of reincarnation is also a denial of the words of Christ. One day, when we have meditated on them in the proper frame of mind, without preconceived ideas, His words will be recognized as the ultimate authority on this point and on many others.

17. The Bible's sanction of the notion of reincarnation is confirmed by the deductions offered by rigorous observation of the facts. When, from the observations of certain effects, we try to deduce their causes, reincarnation becomes a logical necessity, an inherent part of human existence—in short, a Law of Nature. The notion of reincarnation reveals itself in a way that impresses it on our senses—in the same way, for instance, that a hidden motor reveals itself in the movement of a machine. Reincarnation is the one doctrine through which we can find out where we came from, where we are going, and why we are here on earth. It's the only way we can understand the many (apparent) oddities and injustices of human life.

    Without the principle of the soul's preexistence and of many lives, the wise precepts of the Gospel would, for the most part, be unintelligible, which is why they have given rise to so many contradictory interpretations. This principle offers the key that will help restore them to their true and original meaning.

REINCARNATION STRENGTHENS FAMILY TIES—A SINGLE LIFE WOULD DESTROY THEM

18. Some people believe that family ties are destroyed by reincarnation: They aren't. Indeed, they become stronger and closer. It's the opposing principle—of a single life—that would certainly destroy them.

    In the spirit world, spirits form groups or families that are bound together by affection, feelings of empathy, and similar interests and ideas. These spirits seek each other out because being together brings them joy. Incarnate life separates them only for a while; on returning to the spirit world they reunite, like friends who have just come back from a journey. Frequently, they will even follow each other into the incarnate life, unite on earth in the same family or circle of friends and acquaintances and, through these relationships, help each other progress. When some members of the same spiritual family incarnate and others do not, they continue their contact by means of thought.

Those who are free watch over those who are in the flesh. Those more advanced do everything they can to help the less advanced progress. Each physical lifetime is a step forward along the path toward perfection. Eventually, as these spirits become less bound by matter, the strength of their affections grows and their sentiments become more sublimated. They are no longer tainted by selfishness or passions. Consequently, the fact that we live many lives strikes no blow at our mutual affections.

It is to be understood that we refer here to real affection, soul to soul—which is the only love that survives after the destruction of the body. Individuals who come together solely through physical attraction will have no motive to look for each other in the spirit world. The only lasting relationships are the ones established through spiritual affection: All sensual affections die out along with the cause that brought them into being, i.e., the physical body. But the soul exists eternally. By the same token, relationships between people who join together exclusively out of self-interest have no lasting significance. Death ends these relationships both on earth and in heaven.

19. The sense of unity and affection that exists between relatives indicates prior feelings of empathy. This is why, when we see a family member whose character, tastes, and inclinations differ markedly from other members of the same family, we often say that the person doesn't belong to that family. The remark expresses a deeper truth than we realize. In certain families, God lets spirits who are uncongenial, or strangers to each other, reincarnate together with the dual purpose of serving as a test for some members of the family, and as a means of progress for others. In this way, less enlightened spirits have a chance to improve themselves by living among higher-minded ones, and benefiting from the affectionate care they receive. Their characters grow milder, their dispositions become more refined, and their hostility disappears. In the end, this is how solidarity among the different orders of spirits comes about. In the same manner solidarity develops among the peoples and nations of earth.

20. The fear some people have about ever-expanding circles of relationships as the result of having lived many lives is basically selfish: It shows that their ability to love is too limited for them to

embrace a large number of people. Look at it this way: Would parents who have many children love them any less than they would love only one child? But selfish people can rest easy on this score: Their fear is groundless. The fact that a person may have had ten incarnations doesn't mean that in the spirit world that person will find ten fathers, ten mothers, ten wives, and a corresponding number of children and relatives. In all likelihood, we will meet there the loved ones we knew on earth. In some instances they may assume the same roles they played here; in others they will not.

21. Let's turn now to the consequences of the anti-reincarnationist doctrine. Automatically it rejects any previous existence of the soul, since in this belief, the soul is created together with the body. Thus, no previous link can exist and people are complete strangers to each other. In other words, parents are strangers to their children, so that family relationships are reduced to mere physical relations without any spiritual links whatever. This means, if the anti-reincarnationists are correct, that there wouldn't be any motive for anyone to claim the honor of having had such and such a person as an ancestor. By contrast, with reincarnation, ancestors and descendants may have known each other, lived together, and loved one another in other lives; and they may also reunite later in order to strengthen the bonds between them.

22. But all this refers to the past. We come now to the future. According to one of the fundamental tenets of the anti-reincarnationists, the destiny of every soul is permanently determined after only one lifetime. This fixed and definite idea of fate implies an end to individual progress, for if there were progress in the after-life there would be no fixed and irrevocable fate. In this view, depending on whether we've lived a good or bad life, we should go immediately either to the home of the blessed or to an eternal hell. The souls are then immediately and forever separated, without hope of ever being reunited. For this reason, fathers, mothers and children, husbands and wives, brothers and sisters, and even friends would never be sure of seeing each other again. This belief means, in short, the absolute rupture of all family ties.

However, once we accept reincarnation, and the continued progress that it implies, we recognize that all of us who love each other will meet again on earth and also in the spirit world, and that we are all moving together in the direction of God. Some may weaken along the path and delay their own progress and happiness; but there will never be a total loss of hope. Helped, encouraged, and sustained by our loved ones, those who falter will one day be able to pull themselves out of the quicksand of wrong they have fallen into. Here is the comfort of reincarnation. With it, there is an everlasting solidarity among souls in the physical and spiritual realms, which only strengthens their ties of mutual love.

23. In conclusion, four alternatives present themselves to us as far as our future beyond physical death is concerned: first, nothingness, according to the materialist doctrine; second, absorption into the universal Whole, according to the pantheistic idea;[8] third, individual existence with a fixed and settled destiny, according to the traditional churches; fourth, individual existence with constant progress, according to the Spiritist Doctrine.

In the first two alternatives, family ties are cut forever at the time of death, without any hope that souls will ever meet again. With the third alternative, there is a possibility of meeting again, but only if each soul goes to the same region, which may be heaven or hell. But with the alternative of many lives, which is inseparable from the idea of continuous progress, the continuation of relationships among loved ones is certain. It is this that makes up the true family.

SPIRIT TEACHINGS

LIMITS OF INCARNATION

24. ■ What are the limits of incarnation?

No clearly defined limits to incarnation exist, if by "limits" we mean the spirit's experience in the physical realm, enveloped by the material covering that constitutes its body. Nevertheless, the type of matter that constitutes this covering becomes more subtle and refined as the spirit attains greater purity. On domains more advanced than earth, this covering is less coarse, less heavy, and so less subject to the natural limitations and needs of a material body. On still more elevated realms, it is diaphanous. Almost in its entirety, it is energy. This is because, on advanced worlds, the material covering is so subtle that it practically merges with the

[8] *Translator's Note: The pantheistic doctrine claims that God is the transcendent reality of which the material universe and human beings are only manisfestations, and that taken together they make up the essence of God. See Allan Kardec's* The Spirits' Book, *question 15, for a more detailed discussion.*

perispirit (spiritual body).[9] Accordingly, depending on where the spirit is called to live, it "reclothes" itself with a covering appropriate to its present environment.

The perispirit itself undergoes successive transformations. It becomes more and more etherealized as the spirit becomes more purified, until it achieves the ultimate subtleness that is characteristic of pure spirits. In the worlds designated for these spirits, they do not find themselves bound to the physical environment, as spirits do in less advanced spheres. Their special condition allows them to travel to any place which their assigned missions require.

From a physical perspective, the process of incarnation, as we know it on earth, is characteristic of less evolved planets. Spirits free themselves from this process as they work toward purification. We should also consider that in the spirit world, in the intervals between physical lives, each spirit's condition reflects the level of the moral progress of the world with which the spirit is associated. In the spirit world, then, our happiness and inner illumination will be determined by how attuned we still are to material concerns. ■ —Saint Louis (Paris, 1859)

THE NEED FOR INCARNATION

25. ■ Is incarnation a punishment? Is it the case that only guilty spirits are subject to incarnation?

Life in a physical body allows the spirit to function in the physical world and fulfill its part in the designs of Providence. Spirits need it in order to develop their intelligence. Being just, God offers everyone the same conditions; every spirit started from the same point, with the same aptitudes, the same obligations to fulfill, and the same freedom of action. Any type of privilege would denote favoritism, which would be an injustice. Incarnation is, in reality, a transitional state for all spirits. It is an opportunity granted to them so that they can exercise their free will. Those

---

[9] *Translator's Note: Human beings can be thought of as consisting of three elements: (1) a body, or physical being, similar to that belonging to animals and animated by the same vital principle; (2) a soul, an immaterial spirit incarnated in the body; (3) an intermediate link which unites the soul and body—the spiritual body or perispirit. The spiritual body is a semimaterial envelope, akin to a subtle energy field, to use modern scientific terminology. At death, the spirit sheds the physical body, the grosser of the two, but preserves the spiritual body. In modern popular culture this is well represented by the diaphanous image of angels. The concept of spiritual body is also insightfully captured in video and movie depictions of the clinical death phenomena.*

who excel in early experiences progress faster and more easily, and can quickly reap the fruits of their work. By contrast, those spirits who make bad use of their freedom delay their progress and, depending on how stubborn they are, may prolong the need for reincarnation indefinitely, in which case, reincarnation does indeed become a punishment. ■ —Saint Louis (Paris, 1859).

Comment: A simple analogy may help make this distinction clearer. A student can't take up higher-level studies in science until she has passed through the series of classes that lead to that level. These classes, no matter what kind of work they require, are the means for the student to reach her objective and aren't a punishment for her. If she works hard, she will shorten her path and consequently encounter fewer obstacles. However, this isn't what happens to the student who neglects her work and is lazy: These attitudes will only cause her to have to repeat some of her lessons. It isn't the work of the class that is the punishment but the necessity to begin the same work over again.

This is what happens to human beings on earth. For the unevolved spirit, who is at the beginning of its spiritual life, incarnation is the means of developing its intelligence. Nevertheless, it is a form of correction for an individual who has attained a higher level of awareness to have to experience again the hardship associated with physical life. Because such individuals have not yet completed their learning programs, they are faced with the need to prolong their stay in less advanced worlds. Conversely, if the spirit actively works toward moral progress, it not only shortens the incarnation period but may also jump over steps that separate it from more evolved realms.

Isn't it possible for spirits to incarnate only once on a given planet and then continue their learning on different ones? This view would make sense only if every being, on a given planet, were at exactly the same state of intellectual and moral development. But the differences among you— from the savage to the highly educated—show the range of degrees each of you on earth have yet to attain. Besides, an incarnation on a given planet must have a useful purpose. Yet what, one may ask, is the purpose of the short life of a child who dies at a tender age? Has that soul's experience on earth been without benefit to itself, or anyone else? The Supreme Lawgiver doesn't do useless things. Accordingly, spirits—by reincarnating on the same planet—

have multiple opportunities to interact with one another and work out their differences. Through these new opportunities, family ties are accorded a solid spiritual foundation and spirits have a chance to reaffirm in themselves the principles of the natural law of solidarity, brotherhood, and equality.

Chapter 5

Blessed Are the Afflicted

SCRIPTURES AND COMMENTARY

1.　*"Blessed are those who mourn, for they will be comforted. Blessed are those who hunger and thirst for righteousness, for they will be filled. Blessed are those who are persecuted because of righteousness, for theirs is the kingdom of heaven."*

(Matthew, 5: 4, 6, 10)

2.　*Looking at his disciples, he said: "Blessed are you who are poor, for yours is the kingdom of God. Blessed are you who hunger now, for you will be satisfied. Blessed are you who weep now, for you will laugh."*

(Luke, 6: 20-21)

　　"But woe to you who are rich, for you have already received your comfort. Woe to you who are well fed now, for you will go hungry. Woe to you who laugh now, for you will mourn and weep."

(Luke, 6: 24-25)

THE JUSTICE OF SUFFERING

3.　The reward Jesus promises earth's sufferers only becomes a reality in the future life. Without the certainty of this future, His words here would be contradictory; even worse, they would be deceptive. Yet, even given certainty, it is hard to understand why suffering is necessary before we can claim our happiness. Some suggest that it's a way for us to earn greater merit. But then we ask, Why do some people suffer more than others? Why is one person born into poverty and another into wealth without either having done anything to justify the situation? Why do some people never manage to achieve anything, while everything seems to fall into place for others? Even less understandable is why benefits and misfortunes are divided up so unequally between the good and bad. Why do we find good people suffering side by side with bad ones who flourish? It is true that faith in a future life can be a source of consolation and instill patience in us. But it can't explain these apparent oddities, which seem to negate God's Justice.

Once God's existence has been admitted, we can't imagine God being less than infinitely perfect. Without being all power-ful, all just, and all loving, God wouldn't really be God.[1] And if God is supremely good, and just, then no divine act can ever be clouded with caprice or favoritism. We must conclude, then, that the hardships of life stem from a cause, and since God is just, that cause must also be just: This is the reality of which we must final-ly convince ourselves. Through the teachings of Jesus, God start-ed us on the path toward understanding that cause. Now humanity has advanced to the point where it can appreciate this more encompassing and objective revelation, which has been brought forth through the words of illuminated spirits.

PRESENT CAUSES OF SUFFERING

4.   There are two kinds of suffering on earth; or, if you prefer, our tri-als have their origin in two different sources. The first kind has its cause in present-day life; the second arises from causes out-side the present life.

In considering the troubles of earthly life, it is evident that a great number of them are the consequence of a person's own atti-tudes and actions. Many of us flounder because of our faults— victimized by our thoughtlessness, arrogance, and ambition. Many of us destroy ourselves through lack of discipline and per-severance, and through bad conduct and an inability to control our own desires. Likewise, many marriages turn sour simply because they are built not by the heart, but by the partners' calcu-lating self-interest and vanity. So many disagreements and disas-trous hostilities could be avoided with the help of a little restraint and more tolerance. In the same way, how many illnesses and dis-eases result from overindulgence and abuses of all sorts?

Families, particularly, pay a price for these failures. Parents find they are disappointed in their children because they didn't inter-vene early enough to overcome their children's harmful impulses. In spoiling or neglecting their children, these parents let the seeds of pride, selfishness, and foolish conceit take root in them, so that their hearts became dry and shriveled. Later on, when the parents

---

[1] *Translator's Note: see Allan Kardec's* The Spirits' Book, *chapter 1, questions 1-3.*

start reaping what they have sown, they're surprised and hurt at the indifference and lack of gratitude their children show them.

We ask each of you who has experienced heartaches because of disappointments and losses to study your own consciences closely, going back, step by step, to the origins of each problem that is causing you pain. More likely than not, most will be able to say: If I had done, or not done, such and such a thing, I wouldn't be where I am today.

Who is, in such cases, responsible for the sufferings if not the person who suffers? In most cases, men and women are the architects of their own troubles. Yet rather than admit this fact, they usually find it easier and less humiliating to their egos to blame their troubles on fate, God, bad luck, or even on an unlucky star. However, this "unlucky star" is actually no more than their own carelessness.

When we consider life's problems, we find that this kind of suffering makes up the greatest part of our problems. Only when we make the commitment to work at self-transformation, raising ourselves both morally and intellectually, will we be able to avoid suffering of this kind.

5. Human laws deal with various offenses and prescribe punishments for them. In such cases, persons convicted of a crime are said to bear the consequences of their own wrongdoing. But the law doesn't—and can't—deal with every wrong. The law is concerned mostly with actions that cause injury to society, not with those that hurt the doer only. However, God, Who desires the progress of every soul, doesn't allow detours from the upright path to go unnoticed. There is no wrong, no infraction of the Divine Law, however small, that doesn't carry its own consequences. In small things, as in great, people are always corrected according to their wrongs. The suffering that follows is always a warning. Through it, we humans gain valuable knowledge that allows us to distinguish between right and wrong. Thus we realize the necessity of bettering ourselves so that in the future we can avoid the behavior whose negative consequences we now feel. Without such consequences, progress would be slower and human beings would be even farther from our blissful destination.

Unfortunately for some people, understanding this principle arrives rather late, when the life has already been wasted and filled with trouble. In many cases, the physical life is nearing its end and remedying the wrong is no longer possible. Then the person will frequently say, "If I had only known then what I know now, how many errors I could have avoided! If only I could begin again, I would act differently! But my time is up." Like a lazy worker who says, "I've wasted my day," this type of person says, "I've wasted my life!" But just as the sun rises on a new day and gives the worker the chance to make up for lost time, the dawning of a new physical life provides the spirit a renewed opportunity to take advantage of its past experiences and newly acquired understanding, and put its good resolutions for the future into practice.

PAST CAUSES OF SUFFERING

6.   Although many of life's hardships seem to be the result of our own doing, others are apparently completely outside our control, as if they were entirely the force of destiny. As examples, we can list: the loss of a loved one or a family breadwinner; accidents that no planning could have prepared us for; reversals of fortune that neither precaution nor good advice could have turned around; natural disasters; birth defects, especially ones that make working and supporting ourselves impossible, such as certain physical handicaps, mental disease, retardation, etc.

When people are born with restricting conditions like these, they can't have done anything in this life to deserve them. They couldn't have avoided them, have no power to change them, and often find that their only recourse is to depend on society for assistance. Why should someone experience such misfortune, when right next to them, under the same roof, are family members who've been blessed in every way? Why should some children die at a very young age and know only suffering during their short lives?

These are problems that modern philosophy hasn't been able to answer and that religion cannot satisfactorily explain. If the soul were created at the moment of birth and its fate irrevocably sealed after a short stay on earth, the unfortunate fate of many young children would be the very negation of God's kindness, fairness, and foresight. After all, if these souls had just left the hands of God, why should they have to come into the world facing any suffering? And how, if they die at a tender age, could they receive any reward or deserve any correction since they haven't been able to practice either good or evil?

In contrast, if we admit the principle that says every effect has a cause, these hardships are effects and so must have a cause for being. And if we admit that God is just, that cause must also be just. Now, given that a cause always comes before an effect, if the cause can't be found in the present life, it must come from before this life, that is to say, from a previous life. God, in this instance, allows us to suffer not for the good we've done or the wrong we didn't do, but for the wrong we did. If we can't find the wrong-doing in this life, it must have taken place in a previous one. This is a logical deduction we cannot avoid; its implications are in perfect agreement with God's Justice.

Naturally, people don't always experience the consequences of their wrongs in the present life. But they can't escape these consequences indefinitely. Ill-meaning people prosper only for a while; if they don't make up for their wrongs today they will do so tomorrow. Likewise, those who suffer today are undergoing a process of purification for wrongs committed in the past. Accordingly, even a misfortune that may at first seem undeserved must have its reason for being, and those who experience it can always say, "Lord, forgive me, for I have sinned."

7.   Whether the cause is in the present or a previous life, our misfortunes can be traced back to a wrong done in the past. Through the action of an evenly and exactly dispensed justice, we come to experience what we have made others suffer. If we have been hard and inhumane, we may be treated with harshness and inhumanity; if we were too proud, we may be born in humble circumstances; if we've been stingy, selfish, or have made bad use of our money, we may find ourselves lacking the necessary means of survival. If we've been bad sons or daughters, our own children's behavior may cause us grief.

The uneven distribution of happiness and misery on earth—between well-meaning and ill-meaning people—can be explained only in the context of many lifetimes, and only if we accept earth's current state as a place of expiation. Inequities exist in appearance alone. Our trouble is that, for the most part, we see them entirely from the point of view of the present. Once we broaden our perspective—to the point where we can see the succession of lives—we realize that every person is given just what he or she needs to experience (that is, after taking into account progress made in the spirit world). Then it becomes clear that God's Justice is unvarying.

We must never lose sight of the fact that we live on a lesser planet, to which we have been assigned because of our imperfections. We should remind ourselves that the hardship we endure on earth is nonexistent in more advanced worlds and that it depends on us alone—through working at our own betterment—to see that we have no need to return to this planet.

8. Earthly trials may be imposed upon rebellious spirits and upon those whose discernment is not yet sufficiently developed to allow them to choose for themselves. However, spirits that have come to realize the extent of their misdeeds may freely choose their trials. They do so as they try to right their wrongs and do better, much like the worker who asks for an opportunity to correct a job badly done so as not to waste the effort already put into it. Trials are, at the same time, a means of correcting past wrongs, and also a test of our resolve to stay the course as we face the future. For this reason we should praise God, Who grants us the means for reparation, and doesn't condemn us to eternal suffering for our faults.

9. Still, no one should think that every instance of suffering indicates the existence of a previous misdeed. Often these are experiences requested by the spirit itself to help in its purification and accelerate its own progress. In other words, every hardship is a trial, though not every trial implies a prior fault. Nevertheless, the need for trials and purification indicates imperfection, since nothing that is already perfect needs testing. Even spirits who already have a certain degree of elevation, but who want to progress further, request a task to perform. The more challenging the task, the more rewarding it will be for those who complete it. This is the case of persons who are naturally kind-hearted, who are high-minded, and have an inborn refinement of feeling and attitude. They seemingly bring no taint with them from their past lives and suffer with true Christian resignation, despite undergoing great ordeals, asking only that God help them bear their trials calmly. It is when a trial is met with moaning and contempt toward God that it's likely tied to some prior wrong-doing. That said, many hardships that are endured without moaning do correspond to an opportunity for redressing the past. In these cases, the soul has willingly accepted the experience. Typically, such life ordeals are borne with resignation and fortitude, denoting real progress on the part of those undergoing them.

10. Spirits can't hope to ascend to the realms of bliss until they've become completely pure. Any blemish prevents access. On earth

their situation is similar to that of passengers on a plague ship who can't enter a port until they have been cleansed. Likewise, the imperfections of spirits are gradually overcome by means of various lives in the physical realm. The trials of life, when borne well, help them to progress. In instances where these trials are also an opportunity for correction, they enable spirits to erase faults and improve themselves. As such, they are the remedy that clears up the soul's sores and heals the sickness. The more serious the illness, the stronger the remedy must be. Therefore, those who are faced with a great deal of anguish can view their circumstances as opportunities to correct wrongs of the past and to heal their spirit. In contrast, if, in the face of adversity, all we can do is despair and complain, we squander valuable learning opportunities and risk having to start over in similar circumstances at a future date.

FORGETFULNESS OF THE PAST

11. It doesn't make much sense to object that forgetfulness prevents us from using the experience we've gained in past lives. If God saw fit to throw a veil over our past, we must conclude that it was for our benefit. In fact, the memory of the past would be a considerable inconvenience. It could, in certain cases, embarrass us or perhaps tinge us with conceit, which would interfere with the exercise of our free will today. In any case, it would push social relations into a state of greater turmoil.

Why should this be so? A spirit is frequently reborn into the same environment in which it has already lived, and establishes relationships with many of the same people. In this way, the spirit is nudged into situations where it might redress a wrong done. Consider now what would happen if we could recognize in our current relatives and associates the very same people we hated in a previous life. Perhaps the old animosities would be rekindled. Or perhaps we would feel terribly humiliated upon realizing the harm we inflicted on these persons in the past. Thus, in our new life, God provides us only with what is essential and sufficient, i.e., the voice of conscience and our inner tendencies—and takes away what would hurt us.

We do, of course, have hints of our past. On being reborn, we bring with us the progress we've attained before. In this sense, we are born exactly the way we have made ourselves. Yet, in another way, each life begins for us from a new starting point. Regardless of what we were in the past, we live today with the consequences of previous actions. In our frailties and bad dispositions, we have a glimpse of what we need to be working on. We should work hard at ridding ourselves of these problems until no trace of them is left. Here is where conscience serves us. The good resolutions we make are the voice of conscience, which both calls attention to what is right and wrong and gives us the strength to resist temptation.

Moreover, our forgetfulness of the past only occurs during the incarnate life. On returning to the spirit world, we regain our memory of the past. Our forgetfulness is temporary, a slight interruption that on earth is analogous to a night of deep sleep from which we wake with an integral recollection of what we did the day before.

And it isn't only after so-called physical death that the spirit can recover its memory of the past. Past memory is never lost, even during the incarnate life. This is demonstrated by the fact that during sleep—a period when we enjoy a certain amount of freedom—the spirit is aware of its past acts. It knows then why it suffers and sees that its suffering is just. Our forgetfulness of the past, then, only occurs when the spirit is reimmersed in the flesh for everyday life. But even though the spirit has no precise memory of its past lives—a remembrance that could prove painful and disrupting to personal relations—the spirit can draw strength from the fuller awareness it enjoys while the body sleeps.

REASONS FOR FORTITUDE

12. By saying that those who suffer are blessed because they will be comforted, Jesus points to the reward that awaits those of us who toil under adversity and whose fortitude allows us to look at life's afflictions as the beginning of our inner healing.

    Jesus' words can also be interpreted in another way, i.e., that we should be accepting of adversity, since the distress we have to endure in this world serves to settle debts we've incurred in the past. If we bear them with patience on earth, these pains will save us centuries of future suffering. We should be happy, then, that God allows us to clear our debt logs now, guaranteeing us a more peaceful future.

    The suffering person is really like a debtor who owes a large amount of money. Suppose one day the creditor said to this debtor, "If you pay me even a hundredth part of what you owe me today, I'll forgive the entire debt and you'll be free of it forever; if you don't, I'll hound you until you pay every last penny." Wouldn't the debtor in this situation feel happy to undergo all kinds of hardships if it meant freedom from his or her burden and paying only a hundredth part of the money owed? Instead of complaining to the creditor, wouldn't this person feel grateful?

This is the meaning of the words "Blessed are those who mourn, for they will be comforted." They have been blessed with an opportunity to pay their debts and to set themselves free afterwards. It is crucial to remember, however, that if someone, while paying a debt, does new wrongs and thus creates new liabilities, he or she will greatly postpone freedom. Each new fault only increases the person's liabilities, and there is no fault that doesn't carry with it the need for reparation. Of this you can be certain: If the reparation doesn't happen today, it will happen tomorrow; if not in this life, then in a future one.

Which, in the list of our failings, should we put first? The lack of reverence for God's Will. If all we do is complain about our sufferings and refuse to accept them with fortitude, as an experience we need to go through, or if we accuse God of being unjust, we incur new debts without benefiting from lessons we could have learned from those difficult circumstances. This is why we often have to start over. In many respects, it is like borrowing money to pay an outstanding loan: One is always in debt.

In returning to the spirit realm, the soul is like the day laborer who goes to collect his wages. To some, the boss will say, "Here is your salary for the days you've worked." Others who lived all too easily on earth, wasting their lives in frivolous pursuits and overindulging themselves, will hear something very different: "There's nothing more to come: You've already received your reward on earth. Go and begin your tasks again."

13. The attitude with which we approach earthly life may lighten or heighten the harshness of our trials. The longer we think our sufferings will last, the worse they will feel to us. But if we consider things from the vantage point of spiritual life, we realize that a single life is only a point in Eternity, that our lifespan is very short, and that the painful moment will soon pass. Where we are certain of a better future, we're also sustained and energized. Far from complaining, we should offer thanks to God for the adversity that fosters our growth. On the other hand, for anyone who sees a lifetime in the body as the only reality, the pain of our adversity bears down with all its weight.

The result of accepting the reality of an independent spirit life is that worldly things become far less important to us. If we hold this view, we feel compelled to rein in our desires and content ourselves with our position in the world without being jealous of others. This in turn lessens the anguish of the misfortunes and disappointments life may offer, and engenders an inner peace and healthy resignation that benefits both body and soul. By contrast, envy and unchecked ambition cause us suffering that only compounds the difficulties of a short existence.

SUICIDE AND INSANITY

14. The inner peace and fortitude that a spirit-centered view of earthly life brings—as well as the confidence it offers in a happier future, gives the spirit a serenity that works powerfully to counteract insanity and suicidal ideas. Most cases of insanity are caused by the inability to cope with the many tribulations of life. But the moment the things of this world are seen from the perspective of the Spiritist Doctrine, all the reverses and disappointments that would otherwise plunge us into despair can be accepted with calmness, even ease. This outlook communicates an inner strength that puts individuals above such events and protects them from shocks to the mind that, in the absence of a spiritual orientation, would likely cause serious damage.

15. The same applies to suicide. Omit the suicides that result from alcoholism or mental illness (and can be classified as unconscious for this reason), and we find that in every case the underlying cause is inner discontentment, regardless of the suicide's announced motives. Consider the following analogy: If we knew that a particular hardship would last no more than a day and be followed by much happier times, wouldn't we bear it patiently? Why would we despair if we could clearly see the end of our difficulties? Now consider this. What is our lifetime vis-à-vis eternity? Much less than a day in our conception of time. However, for the person who doesn't believe in the continuity of life, death represents an end to the grief and sorrows of a troubled life. For this person, suicide becomes an appealing, almost logical solution to his or her anguish.

16. Unbelief, skepticism about the future life, and all sentiments born of materialistic beliefs contribute to suicide since they add justification to a person's faintheartedness. When scientists of recognized stature dedicate so much effort to argue that nothing exists after death, aren't they leading us to conclude that killing our-

selves is the best alternative to our misfortunes? What arguments can they put forward that would prevent someone from ending his or her life? What rewards can they hint at to inspire us? What hope can they offer? None at all. They think up only nothingness. From this view we can only infer that if nothingness is the ultimate relief—the sole course before us—then it would be better to seek it immediately and not later, so as to suffer less.

The spread of materialistic doctrine is the toxin that poisons the minds of a large number of people who entertain suicidal ideas. Accordingly, advocates of such doctrines assume tremendous responsibility. With the Spiritist Doctrine, however, skepticism has no raison d'être and our outlook on life changes completely. We know that existence continues well beyond the grave, although in modified conditions; and from this belief comes patience and acceptance, i.e., moral strength.

17. Along these same lines, the Spiritist Doctrine brings about another and equally positive result—one perhaps even more decisive. It brings us into contact with the spirits of suicides. These spirits tell us about the unhappy situation into which their act has plunged them in the spirit world, proving that no one violates God's laws without consequence (and the Divine Law forbids us, certainly, to take our own lives). Among these spirits, we meet those whose suffering, while not eternal, is still terrible and of a kind that should make anyone who is considering this act think carefully about leaving the world sooner than ordained by Providence.

These same communications lead Spiritists to still other reasons for rejecting suicide. First, there is the certainty of a future life where, we know, our happiness will be in proportion to the fortitude we showed when facing our earthly trials. Second, there is the certainty that if we terminate our lives, we will ensure the exact opposite of the result we desire. Indeed, freeing ourselves from trouble in this way guarantees that a longer and far worse trial will take its place.

Spiritists know, too, that people who imagine that they will reach heaven more quickly by killing themselves are seriously mistaken; we know that suicide becomes an obstacle that will prevent these individuals from joining loved ones, whom they hope to meet on the other side.

From this, we conclude that suicide, with its disappointing implications, is contrary to our own interest. For these reasons alone, the number of suicides prevented by the Spiritist Doctrine is already considerable—which is why we conclude that conscious attempts on one's own life will dwindle fast as acceptance of this spiritual reality becomes widespread.

When we compare the results of materialist philosophies and those of the Spiritist Doctrine, as far as suicide is concerned, we are forced to recognize that the logic of the first supports it and that of the second prevents it—a fact proven on many occasions.

SPIRIT TEACHINGS

TO SUFFER WELL OR BADLY

18. ■ When Christ said that those who suffer will have the kingdom of heaven, you should not think that He was referring to everyone in general. Everyone on earth experiences some pain, regardless of whether sitting on a throne or sleeping on the floor. What really counts is how well you take suffering. A mere handful understand that only trials that have been endured well lead to the kingdom of God. Despair is a weakness, and the Supreme Being will not shower comfort on those who lack courage and give in to despair. Naturally, you have prayer to sustain your soul, but for prayer to be a source of solace it must be rooted in total confidence in the absolute compassion of God. You have heard it said many times that God doesn't put a heavy burden on weak shoulders. The burden always depends on the degree of your strength, just as the reward for bearing it always depends on the degree of your fortitude and courage. In fact, the reward is often of much greater import than the hardship. You would be wise, then, to make yourselves worthy, since it is for this purpose that life presents you with so many faith-testing challenges.

The soldier who isn't sent to the front is a discontented person. Sitting in camp, he is aware, will never provide a chance for promotion. Try to be like that soldier: Don't seek refuge far from the battlelines, for inaction rusts the body and freezes the soul. Be pleased when you are sent into battle—not the battle of the firing line but of life. Paradoxically, many who can stand firm before an enemy attack, flinch when faced with soul-wrenching afflictions. There is no reward for this kind of courage on earth. But God will keep laurels of victory for you, and a place of glory, if you hold fast. If, in confronting difficulties and suffering, you can place yourself above the situation and manage to temper your impulse to blow up, get angry, or depressed, you can rightly say to your-self with satisfaction, "I was the stronger."

You may, then, translate "Blessed are those who mourn" in the following manner: Blessed are those of you who have an oppor-tunity to prove your faith, fortitude, perseverance, and respect for the Will of God. You will have earned a hundred times the happiness you lacked on earth, for it is only after work that you deserve rest. ■ —Lacordaire [2] (Havre, 1863).

A MEDICINE FOR ALL SORROWS

19. ■ Is earth a place of enjoyment, a garden of delights? If you think so, you must no longer hear the prophet's voice echoing in your ears. Didn't He proclaim that there would be weeping and gnashing of teeth for everyone born into this valley of pain? Every person who lives on earth experiences tears and suffering. But no matter how wrenching the pain, lift up your eyes and offer thanks to the Lord for the test. Oh humanity! Will you rec-ognize the power of God only if the ills of your bodies are cured and your days are showered with beauty and good fortune? Will you recognize God's love for you only when the stars shine in your path and success follows you? You should follow the exam-ple of the faithful man who, finding himself in misery and total destitution and even as he lay in the arms of indigence, said to God, "Lord, I have known all the delights of wealth and You have reduced me to the most absolute misery; thank you, thank you, for wishing to test your servant!" For how long will you have your eyes fixed on a horizon limited by death? When will you finally see beyond the boundaries of the grave? Even if your whole life is fraught with suffering and tears, consider how little this is, compared to the bliss reserved for you if you bear up under your trials with faith, love, and fortitude. For the troubles you cannot change, seek consolation in the future God has pre-pared for you, and search for the causes of those troubles in the past. As for you who have suffered the most—consider your-selves the blessed of this earth.

Remember that before taking a new life on earth, and while enjoying complete freedom in the spirit realm, you made choices about the trials to undergo and chose those you felt strong enough to endure. Why, then, complain of them now? You asked for riches and glory because you wanted to overcome the temp-

---

[2] *Translator's Note: See Biographical Sketches at the end.*

tations they bring. You wanted to master your base desires both physical and moral, and you knew full well that the harder the trial was, the greater and more satisfying the victory would be. You recognized, too, that, as long as you overcame and despite the fact that you may be in the most abject misery at death, your triumph would release a soul of radiant brightness, purified in the fire of hardship and suffering.

As for those of you plagued by spiritual afflictions or suffering catastrophic illnesses, what cure is there? There is only one infallible way to come through: faith—the humble appeal to the Supreme Power. If, at the moment when your suffering is greatest, you sing praises to the Lord, the guardian spirit at your bedside will direct your eyes to the signposts of wholeness and show glimpses of the future that awaits you.

Faith is the one medicine for all suffering. It illuminates your perspective of Eternity and makes the cloudy days of life feel unimportant. Don't ask us, the spirits, then, what the remedy is for an ulcer or sore, a torment or a trial. Remind yourselves that those who have strong faith already possess a powerful medication, and those who waver, harbor in themselves an extra burden of distress and suffering. Those of you who believe in God have His seal engraved upon your soul. Christ told you that it was possible to move mountains by faith alone, and I would add that those who suffer, but are upheld by faith, will remain under His protection and will suffer no more. The moments of greatest pain will become the first happy notes of Eternity. The soul will detach itself from the body in such a way that, while the body is still writhing in agony, the soul will be gliding into the celestial regions, chanting odes of gratitude and love. Blessed are those who, strong in faith, endure the misfortunes and tears of earth because God will heap blessings on them. ■ —Saint Augustine (Paris, 1863).

HAPPINESS IS NOT OF THIS WORLD

20. ■ So often we hear people of all classes complain: "My life is a mess, I hate it" or "I'll never be happy." This, dear friends, demonstrates better than any philosophical argument the truth of that verse in the book of Ecclesiastes: "Pleasures are meaningless."[3] Riches, power, youth are not the essential conditions for

---

[3] *Translator's Note: Ecclesiastes 2:1-16*

happiness. Even when these three elements—which so many desire—are united, there's no guarantee that happiness will be the result. In fact, we constantly hear people of all ages, and even the well-to-do, bitterly complain about their plight.

In view of this, it makes little sense for working people to envy those whom fortune has appeared to favor. In this world, despite what anyone can do, human beings face their own share of toil and hardship, their own individual share of suffering and deceptions. This is why we can say with such assurance that earth is a planet of trials and expiation.

Consider also those who advocate that earth is humanity's only home and that humans have only one existence to attain the highest level of fulfillment. They delude both their followers and themselves. As history shows, it is only in exceptional cases that earth can offer the necessary conditions for complete realization for any one person. In general terms, we can assert that true happiness on earth is a utopian ideal that generations have tried to find—invariably without success. If the reasonable man or woman is a rarity in the world, the absolutely happy one is even harder to find.

What some people consider happiness on earth is something so fleeting that for every year, month, or week of complete satisfaction, many may spend the rest of their lives trapped on a wheel of sorrows and illusions. And notice, dear children, that these words refer to individuals who, apparently, now have it all and are considered the luckiest ones on earth and the envy of everyone.

If, then, your earthly journey is punctuated by trials and purifications, there must be elsewhere more favorable dwellings where the spirit, though still robed with a physical envelope, can enjoy the delights of life to a fuller extent. This is the reason that God has created those beautiful planets in the universe. You will gravitate toward them one day when, through your own effort and desire, you have become sufficiently pure and discerning.

Don't assume from my words, however, that earth is forever destined to remain a reformatory for unevolved souls. Far from it. From the progress that has already taken place, you can anticipate the social advancements to come, and, yes, the enormous improvements to human life on earth. The progress of earth is the mission of this new doctrine, which the spirits have revealed.

Dear children, I hope that a saintly fervor will fill your hearts so that you can work at remaking the old self with unbridled enthu-

siasm. All of you should dedicate yourselves to spreading the principles of the Spiritist Doctrine, through which your own spiritual renewal has already begun. It is a duty of solidarity to allow your fellow human beings to share in this sacred light. So set to work! Let us all cherish in our hearts this sublime aspiration, which is to help build a world for future generations where people will experience and understand happiness in its true colors. ■
—Francois Nicolas Madeleine, Cardinal Morlot (Paris, 1863).

LOSS OF LOVED ONES—PREMATURE DEATHS

21. ■ When death pays a visit to someone in your family—especially when it takes the young and spares the old—you often say that God isn't fair. You say that God has sacrificed someone full of life and with an entire future ahead of him, and prolonged the lives of those who have already lived too many years ridden by all sorts of disappointments. You complain that God has taken those with much to contribute to society instead of those with little left to do. Or you say that God has broken the heart of a mother by depriving her of her innocent infant, her only joy.

Friends, it is at this juncture that you should raise yourselves above commonplace notions about life and realize that goodness frequently hides where you see only tragedy, that the wisdom of Providence often operates where you only perceive the blind force of destiny. Why do you equate the working of Divine Justice with your own standards? Do you think that the Almighty is a capricious dispenser of cruel punishments? The fact is that everything that happens has a purpose and a reason. Indeed, if you examine the pains and sorrows of your life closely, you will always find in them a divine purpose as they present valuable opportunities for renewal of self. You'll conclude, then, that many of your immediate concerns are only of secondary importance. Believe me, sometimes a twenty-year life on earth is preferable to a longer life ruined by abuses of all sorts that shame an entire family, torture a mother's heart, and cause parents' hair to turn gray before its time. In reality, an early death may be, in a spiritual sense, a great blessing, for it saves the person from many sorrows of life and from temptations that might set him or her back. The person who dies in the flower of youth isn't a victim of fate. Rather, it is Providence that has ascertained that the continuation of life was no longer beneficial, spiritually speaking, for that person.

But what a terrible tragedy, you say, when the thread of life is cut short and someone who was so full of hope dies. What hope are you talking about—an earthly one? The hope, for instance, that this young person might have become famous or rich? Your restricted vision here prevents you from rising above the material reality. Who can say what would have actually happened to that life? How do you know it wouldn't have been filled with sorrow and anguish? Besides, do you value the joys offered by the future life so little, even to the point of preferring the fleeting pleasures of earthly life? Do you suppose that a high position in society is worth more than a good place among illuminated souls?

Instead of wailing in desperation, you should accept and honor God's decision to call back a child from this valley of tears. Wouldn't it be selfish to want him or her to go on suffering at your side? We can imagine this attitude among those who lack faith and who see death as an eternal separation. But the spirit-minded among you should know better. You know that the soul lives better and more fully when it is separated from its material form. We can say, then: Mothers, know that your beloved children are near you—yes, very near. As spirits, they embrace you, their thoughts inspire you, and the memories you have of them are fond ones to them. In the same vein, your agonizing troubles them because it reveals your lack of faith and represents a breach of trust in the Supreme Will. To those of you who are spirit minded, I suggest listening to your hearts when you think of these loved ones. As you lift up your thoughts in prayer to God, you will feel great comfort—the kind that will dry your tears—and see your aspirations for the future, which the Master has promised you, nourished. ■ —Samson, former member of the Spiritist Society of Paris, (1863).

IF SHE HAD BEEN A GOOD PERSON SHE WOULD HAVE DIED

22. ■ Sometimes you find yourself saying about a bad person who has escaped some danger: "If she had been a good woman she would have died." Though these words are usually said out of contempt toward God, they may be closer to the truth than you think. It often does happen that a spirit in the early stages of development is assigned a longer trial than a more advanced one that has earned the grace of a final release when its task is finished, i.e., a shortening of the time of purification.

Likewise, if a good woman dies while her mean-spirited neighbor flourishes, people are quick to remark that it would have been better had the neighbor died instead. This saying shows a great deal of poor judgment. The departed person has presumably completed her tasks; the one who is left may not even have started. Why would you deny the bad person the necessary time to finish her work and condemn the good one to linger unnecessarily in the physical realm? What would you say if, after you had served a prison sentence, you were kept in prison, while some other convict, who had no right to it, was set free? True freedom for the spirit, you must understand, lies in the breaking of ties that bind it to the physical body. For as long as it remains on earth, a spirit is never truly free.

Make it a habit not to make rash judgments about things that you don't fully understand, and be certain that God is just in all things. What in many cases appears to be a curse may really be a blessing. Often, your limited faculties prevent you from seeing things in their larger context—in many ways, your senses are still too dull to encompass the whole picture. Nevertheless, if you try hard to expand your mental horizon beyond the material reality, you'll find that worldly things become less important. In this manner, you will correct your perspective and realize that the present lifetime is a mere speck in the infinite course of your spiritual life, which is the only true life. ■ —Fénelon (Sens, 1861).

SELF-IMPOSED SUFFERING

23. ■ Human beings are engaged in an endless search for happiness; yet, because true and uninterrupted happiness does not exist on earth, this search is always tinged with some frustration. Still, despite the challenges of ordinary life, people may at least enjoy a relative measure of happiness. The key to finding happiness on earth is not to search for it among material playthings—that is, in those pleasures that are subject to the same decay and transitoriness as the physical body. earthly happiness can only be found in the delights of the soul, to experience it is to catch a glimpse of the true joy that characterizes life in the higher realms. Sadly, rather than striving for this heartfelt peace, human beings look for happiness by eagerly pursuing anything that stirs up and creates commotion in their lives. It is thus that, paradoxically, you often bring upon yourselves troubles that only you can prevent.

And look at the results. Are there any worse ordeals than the ones created by envy and jealousy? The envious and jealous never rest; they suffer in a state of constant emotional fever. The thought of other people's belongings causes them sleepless nights; the success of their rivals makes their heads spin. Striving to succeed, in their eyes, simply means beating out the people around them. All their happiness consists in fueling jealousy in people as ill advised as themselves. They are indeed poor, foolish folk who have no idea that tomorrow they may be forced to leave behind their trifles, the avid pursuit of which has poisoned their lives. The words "Blessed are those who mourn, for they will be comforted" certainly don't apply to them, since their ordeals aren't worth a reward in heaven.

On the other hand, if you are content with what you have, if you can see things you don't own without feeling envy, and if you don't try to appear better than you are, you will avoid many heartaches. In fact, you will constantly see yourselves as rich since it's always possible, by looking below your economic station in life, to quickly realize that you have quite a lot. If you are a person of this kind, you can remain calm because you don't fill your mind with imaginary needs. Amid all the chaos and confusion of ordinary life, wouldn't this calmness afford you a real measure of happiness on earth? ■ —Fénelon (Lyon, 1860).

TRUE MISFORTUNE

24. ■ Everyone talks about misfortune, everyone has experienced it, and everyone believes that he or she understands it in all its forms. However, I want to tell you that almost everyone is wrong. Real misfortune isn't what humans—that is to say, unfortunate humans—believe it to be. They see it in poverty, in an unheated stove, a threatening creditor, an empty cradle; in tears, a funeral procession, the anguish of betrayal; in the reversals of fortune that lay bare the exaggerated pride ensconced in lavish clothes. All this, and a great deal more, they call "misfortune." And for those who are only aware of the present, these are misfortunes indeed. But it's not in these events that true misfortune is found, but in their consequences. Tell me, isn't an event that is thought to be positive at first, but later turns out to have terrible consequences, really more unfortunate than an event that looked awful at the beginning, but finally proved beneficial? Isn't a storm that uproots trees but purifies the air of health-threatening substances more of a blessing than a curse?

To evaluate an event well, it is necessary to understand its consequences. In similar fashion, to evaluate that which is a cause of happiness or unhappiness, you have to see beyond the limitations of this life and into the future life, where consequences also are felt. Moreover, situations you consider wretched according to your limited vision may have quite joyful consequences in the future life.

We will tell you more about a different kind of misfortune, the one that hides beneath the fragrances and hues of glamour that your deluded souls long for. It lies in pleasures, in noisiness, in pointless agitation, in overindulgence—all of which cause you to ignore your conscience, confuse your mind, and numb you to your spiritual future. They are the real misfortunes, the opium of oblivion you so eagerly seek.

Oh, you who cry today, have hope! But you who have lived your days to satiate your desires, be worried. It isn't possible to deceive God, or evade the destiny you chose for yourself. Life trials are like a pack of hungry wolves: They have a way of coming around, of constantly lurking behind the illusion you have of peace. For the soul that has grown heartless and selfish, they mean gloomy times.

May the Spiritist Doctrine be a source of illumination, an instrument to shed light on often-distorted views of what is right and wrong. With it you can act like brave soldiers who choose to engage the enemy rather than seek a safe and quiet position that leaves you without glory or recognition. What does it matter to a soldier who loses his weapons, his gear, his uniform, if he comes out of the battle a winner, covered with glory? What does it matter to those who have faith in the future if they leave their riches and their fine clothes on the battlefield of life, if their souls enter the celestial realm full of radiance? ■ —Delphine de Girardin (Paris, 1861).

DEPRESSIVE MOODS

25. ■ Why is it that you are sometimes overcome by a vague sadness that makes life seem so difficult to bear? Your spirit, which nurtures a yearning for freedom and joy, finds itself tied to and unable to cut the bonds with the physical body—where it feels confined, as if in a cell. Eventually the spirit realizes the futility of its efforts and occasionally becomes discouraged. This state of mind is then reflected in your physical body. You feel listless, tired, apathetic. It is at this moment that you fall into a depressive mood.

Believe me when I tell you to resist these moods with all your strength. They only sap your will. While the desire for a better life is inborn in everyone, you should not pursue it solely in this world. As God is now sending enlightened spirits to instruct you about the blissful future in store for you, learn to wait patiently for your day of deliverance when the angels finally will lead you to true freedom. During your time here on earth, remember that you have a job to do, whether it is dedicating yourself to your family or fulfilling the various obligations God has given you. If, as you tend to your life responsibilities, you are stricken by worries, misgivings, and sorrows, face them with strength and courage. They bring you closer to those you long for, who, overjoyed at seeing you among them once more, will hold out their hands toward you and guide you to regions where earthly troubles can never intrude. ■ —François de Genève (Bordeaux).

SELF-IMPOSED TRIALS AND THE TRUE MEANING OF SELF-SACRIFICE

26. ■ You ask us if one is allowed to lighten his or her life trials. I will restate your question as follows: Is it right, if you are drowning, to try to save yourself? Should you remove a thorn from your hand? Should you call a doctor when you are sick?

The reason for trials is to help you use your intelligence, patience, and fortitude. Sometimes a person is born into a difficult and painful situation precisely to make him or her look for means of overcoming these problems. The merit is in bearing the unavoidable without complaining, in fighting the good fight and never giving in when success isn't quick. To passively face the trials of life is more a sign of laziness than virtue.

This leads to another question: When Jesus said "Blessed are those who mourn," did He mean that there is merit in self-inflicted suffering—that is, in seeking out situations that increase one's burden in life? To this we can reply very decisively: Yes, there is considerable merit in it—but only if the suffering and self-privation are beneficial to others. This is compassion through selflessness. You gain nothing, however, if your suffering and privations are meant only to benefit yourself; this is simply a form of selfish fanaticism.

Let's make a clear distinction in this matter. Concerning yourself personally, be satisfied with the trials Providence has assigned you. Don't look to increase them, since they may already be almost too heavy to bear. Take them with a steady attitude and with faith; that is all that is asked of you. Nor should you weaken your body with useless deprivations that have no purpose: You're going to need all the strength you have just to perform your work on earth. To willingly torture and martyr the body is to go against God's Law. God has given you the means to sustain life so that weakening the body needlessly is more like a slow suicide. Use your body wisely, don't abuse it: This is the law. Remember, abuses to the treasure you were granted are not free from consequences.

But the very opposite happens when you undergo suffering as the result of easing someone else's pain. If you endure cold and hunger in order to provide heat and food for another person, and your body ails you in the process, you are making a sacrifice that God will bless. When you leave your clean homes and go to an infected shanty to comfort its inhabitants, or dirty your hands to treat someone's wounds, or lose sleep so that you can keep watch at the bedside of the sick (who are your brothers and sisters in Christ), or endanger your health in the practice of good, then it is here that you find a worthwhile sacrifice. You haven't let the delights of this world dry up your heart; you haven't fallen asleep on the seductive breast of your good fortune. Rather, you have become a consoling angel to people who've seemingly been forgotten.

Some people choose to retire from the world and live secluded lives as a way of avoiding earth's enticements. What purpose do they serve on earth? Where is their will to face up to life's trials? Aren't they similar to deserters fleeing the fight? If you want to mortify yourself, then mortify your soul, not your body. Chastise your spirit, not your flesh—whip your pride, handle offenses without anger, purge yourself of ostentation, harden yourself against moral aggressions, usually sharper than physical pains. It is in these things that you find your true sacrifice. And your wounds will be taken into account because they will testify to your courage and respect for God's Will. ■ —A Guardian Spirit (Paris, 1863).

27. ■ Should anyone help end another person's trial when the possibility arises? Or should God's purpose be respected and things be left to take their own course?

We have said repeatedly that you are on this planet of purification in order to carry out your trials, and that everything that happens is the consequence of prior actions. You are settling here a small portion of your debt. However, in some people this realization prompts attitudes that must be corrected since they may have disastrous effects.

Some people think that being on earth for the purpose of expiation means that every trial must follow its course. There are even some who believe not only that nothing should be done to ease suffering, but that they can best help others progress by making their sufferings, more acute! This is a very big mistake. Yes, it is quite true that trials must take their course as intended by Providence, but—and this is the difference—how do we know God's plan for someone else? Can anyone know how far a trial must go? What if Providence determines that it has gone far enough? Perhaps, not by accident, you are now in a position to soothe, to console, to help heal wounds. Never say, then, "It is God's Justice and has to follow its course." Rather say, "Let me see what means God has given me to lessen the suffering of my brother or sister. Let me see if moral support, material assistance, or advice can help the person endure this predicament with greater strength, patience, and courage. Perhaps this possibility has been given to me as a test or even a correction, allowing me to ease grief and substitute it with peace."

Always help each other and never allow yourself to serve as a punishing agent for someone else's presumed good. Every person with a minimum sense of compassion should rebel against such an idea, especially you Spiritists because, more than anyone else, you should understand the infinite extent of God's mercy. Spiritists should be convinced that their whole lives must be acts of love and devotion and that, regardless of what they do, Divine Justice always follows its course. Hence Spiritists should apply themselves wholeheartedly, without any reservations whatsoever, to alleviating the plight of their fellow men and women, conscious, however, that only God (Who sees the appropriateness in all things) has the right to shorten or prolong a trial.

It is, really, arrogant on the part of people to think that it could be right to turn the knife in someone else's wound, so to speak, or give an extra dose of poison to someone who is suffering, and then try to excuse the act on the pretext that the additional pain meets that person's need for readjustment. No. Always consider yourselves as agents for the easing of pain. In the end, everyone is on earth for the purpose of purification; but everyone, without exception, must also strive to ease others' plights, and thus observe in themselves the law of love and compassion. ■ — Bernadin, a Guardian Spirit (Bordeaux, 1863).

28. ■ A dying person is experiencing cruel suffering. Her state inspires no hope. Would it be right to save her an instant of pain by hastening her death?

And who gave you the right to prejudge God's purpose? Couldn't it be that Providence brings the person to the brink of death as a wake up call for her to change her ideas? Even when a dying person has reached what appears to be the last crisis, no one can be absolutely sure that his or her final moment has arrived. Hasn't medicine ever been wrong in its predictions? Of course, there are cases that can be considered desperate with good reason. But even if there's no hope of a return to life and health, there always exists the possibility, witnessed on many occasions, of a sick person recovering his or her faculties at the last instant. Indeed, this moment of grace may be of utmost importance for the soul. Unfortunately, you can't penetrate the reflections of the spirit during unconsciousness, or imagine the inner torments a moment of contrition can ward off.

The materialist, who only sees the body and doesn't consider the soul, isn't likely to understand these things. But the spirit-minded person who knows what happens in the afterlife, realizes the value of last thoughts. You should, then, ease a person's terminal moments as much as you can. But guard against the temptation to shorten a life, even if only for a minute. This might be the healing minute that avoids many future tears. ■ —Saint Louis (Paris, 1860).

29. ■ Would someone who is disenchanted with life, but doesn't want to commit suicide, be wrong to risk his life on the battlefield in the hope of making his death serve a useful purpose?

Whether he killed himself or caused someone else to kill him, the intention is always to cut the thread of life short. Consequently, the intent to commit suicide exists even in the absence of the act. The idea that this person's death would serve some purpose is an illusion—just an excuse to cover up the intention and allow him to justify himself in his own eyes. If he seriously wanted to serve his country, he would do his best to stay alive so that he could continue to defend it. He wouldn't seek death, since he wouldn't be helpful any more. Real devotion consists in serving with honor, facing danger with courage, and risking your own life in the line of duty, if called for. But to seek death by intentionally exposing yourself to risk, even if it's in service, cancels any merit the action may have had otherwise. ■ — Saint Louis (Paris, 1860).

30. ■ If someone exposes him or herself to impending danger in order to save another person's life, and knows that death is certain, will this act be considered suicide?

If you aren't actively seeking to die through such an act, then there is no suicide; there is only devotion and self-sacrifice. But who can be positively sure? Providence may have reserved an unexpected means of salvation at the last moment. Isn't it possible to save someone even when he's standing before the cannon's mouth? It may happen that Providence wants to test your fortitude in an extreme situation and then offers you an unexpected circumstance that wards off the fatal blow. ■ —Saint Louis (Paris, 1860).

31. ■ But aren't people who accept their plight with fortitude, because they accept God's wishes and are mindful of their future well-being, working only for their own benefit? Isn't it possible for them to make their experience useful to others?

Materially and morally, your sufferings may be useful to others: in the material sense, when your privations and sacrifices contribute to the well-being of your fellow human beings; in the moral sense, when your example of faith inspires the unfortunate to live with greater acceptance, therefore steering them away from desperation and its disastrous consequences for the future. ■ — Saint Louis (Paris, 1860).

Chapter 6

Christ the Counselor

SCRIPTURES AND COMMENTARY

THE GENTLE YOKE

1.   *"Come to me, all you who are weary and burdened, and I will give you rest. Take my yoke upon you and learn from me, for I am gentle and humble in heart, and you will find rest for your souls. For my yoke is easy and my burden is light."*

(Matthew, 11: 28-30)

2.   For all our sufferings—the sorrows, disappointments, physical pains, and loss of loved ones that everyone sooner or later experiences—we can find solace in the certainty of the future and confidence in God's Justice, both of which Christ came to teach us. By contrast, people who expect nothing after death, or who are simply skeptical, feel the full brunt of their troubles because their souls are barren of the hope that lightens our burdens. This is what prompted Jesus to say, "Come to me, all you who are weary and burdened, and I will give you rest."

The comfort and bliss promised to those of us who are overburdened depends on our fulfilling the principles He revealed. Obedience to these principles is the "yoke" He alludes to. However, the yoke is light and gentle because it prescribes only love and compassion.

THE PROMISED COUNSELOR[1]

3.   *"If you love me, you will obey what I command. And I will ask the Father, and he will give you another Counselor to be with you forever—the Spirit of truth. The world cannot accept him, because it neither sees him nor knows him. But you know him, for he lives with you and will be in you."*

---

[1] *Translator's Note: Greek parakletos: advocate, counselor, or protector.*

"But the Counselor, the Holy Spirit, whom the Father will send in my name, will teach you all things and will remind you of everything I have said to you."

(John, 14: 15-17, 26)

4.   In this passage from John, Jesus promises another Counselor, the Spirit of truth, about which the world of His time had no awareness, since it wasn't mature enough to understand such an idea. The Spirit of truth would be sent by God to teach us all things and to remind us of Christ's words. But if the Spirit of truth was to come at a later time to teach additional matters, we can only assume it was because Christ hadn't told us everything. And if it was to come to remind us of what Christ had said, we must also assume it is either because we've forgotten His words or, more likely, not properly understood them.

In our era, the Spiritist Doctrine has come to fulfill Christ's promise.[2] With the Spirit of truth at the helm, the Spiritist Doctrine calls on all of us to obey the law and reveals everything Jesus meant when He spoke to the people of his time in parables. Christ Himself warned against taking His examples in the literal sense: "He who has ears, let him hear."[3] Now the Doctrine has come to open our eyes and ears. It speaks without the use of symbols and allegories that purposely hid certain mysteries. It has come to bring ultimate solace to the earth's disinherited, show those who suffer the cause of their distress, and reveal the healing purpose of pain.

Christ said: "Blessed are those who mourn, for they will be comforted."[4] But how can we feel blessed if we are unaware of

---

[2] *Translator's Note: The Spiritist Doctrine has been given to humanity by the ennobled intelligences who have preceded us in the earthly quest, as a revelation of our true spiritual nature, purpose, and destiny. Objectively, the Spiritist Doctrine endorses the notion that revelation is a continuous process, and that the progress of humanity is accomplished by the incarnation of exceptional individuals with responsibilities in every major field of human endeavor to reveal or expand continuously the frontiers of our knowledge* (The Spirits' Book, Q. 622). *The Doctrine in no way claims to have access to the absolute truth. This enlightened stance is cemented in the motto: "The only unshakeable faith is that which can withstand reason, face to face, in every stage of humankind's development." Besides, Allan Kardec made it a cornerstone of the Spiritist thought that the Doctrine is dynamic and that its evolution should occur always in agreement with the development of scientific knowledge.*

[3] *Translator's Note: Matthew 11:15.*

[4] *Translator's Note: Matthew 5:4.*

why we suffer? The Spiritist Doctrine shows that the major sufferings of our lives often have their causes in past lives and that the form they take is in accordance with the state of earth. Reincarnating, we have the opportunity to make up for past mistakes. The Doctrine explains that suffering is part of the healing that assures the soul's future well-being, much like the ache that follows a surgical procedure. From this we come to understand that our misfortunes have a valid reason for being. We also learn that they help us progress; this, in turn, allows us to face life's many challenges without moaning, just as a laborer accepts the hard work that guarantees his or her salary. The Spiritist Doctrine gives us an unshakable faith in the future and helps us cleanse skepticism from our souls. In addition, it lets us see things from a higher perspective, opening up such a broad and splendid horizon that our earthly problems become trivial. The bliss we come to expect becomes, then, the source of that patience, strength, and courage we need to continue to the end of the path.

In this way the Spiritist Doctrine gives actual form to what Jesus said about the promised Counselor: It enlightens us as to where we came from, where we are going, and why we are on earth. Further, it reminds all to observe God's Law and to find comfort in the faith and hope of a better future.

SPIRIT TEACHINGS

THE COMING OF THE SPIRIT OF TRUTH[5]

5.   ▇ I have come, as I came to the lost children of Israel, to reveal

---

[5] *Translator's Note: The authorship of the messages signed by "the Spirit of truth" may be seen as the contribution of a collective of enlightened spirits who represent the purest aspect of the Christian thought and ideal. The authorship is divine, in a logical sense, if one considers that the ideas originate from those who live in oneness with Jesus, and are inspired purely by their love of God. The sacred source of the voice that sings the sublime purpose of life as "the Spirit of truth" finds echo in the Gospel in the union between Jesus and his disciples. Jesus was the light that illuminated the souls of his disciples as God was the light of His own life. [He who receives you receives me, and he who receives me receives the one who sent me. (Matthew 10:40); He who listens to you listens to me; he who rejects you rejects me; but he who rejects me rejects him who sent me. (Luke, 10:16)] Through the Spiritist Doctrine, "the Spirit of truth" reaffirms the morality of the Gospel as the highest creation of human conscience, and encourages the quest for knowledge through science and reason.*

the truth and to sweep away the darkness. Listen closely then to what the words tell you. As these words have done in the past, the Spiritist Doctrine must now remind unbelievers that there is above them one immutable truth: the loving God, the Supreme Force that causes the plants to blossom and the waves to rise. I come as a harvester who, after gathering into sheaves the sparse stalks of goodness from human hearts, compassionately says, "Come to me, all you who suffer."

Yet humankind, in its ungrateful way, has abandoned the straight and narrow path that leads to the kingdom of God, and prefers instead the rough pathways of ungodliness. God, however, desires the redemption of humankind, and for the living and the dead—that is to say, the dead according to the flesh, for death doesn't exist—to help each other. Thus, not only the teachings of the prophets and apostles of biblical times, but also guidance from the elevated spirits that no longer live on earth, will tell you, "Pray and trust! Death is a rebirth, and life is the rich soil in which your virtues will grow and develop, straight and firm as the cedar tree."

You are still immature souls who have started to discern the shadows in your own minds. Be careful not to lose sight of the torchlight that illuminates your path and guides you back to the bosom of God.

I am too overcome with compassion for your sufferings and your immense struggle. I extend a guiding hand to make sure that even as you catch glimpses of heaven, you do not fall into the same traps again. Trust, love, and meditate on the knowledge now being revealed to you. Don't mix the chaff with the good seed, or confuse chimeras with the truth.

Spiritists, love one another. This is the first precept. Educate yourselves. That is the second. In true Christianity you will find the truth. You will find mistakes in today's Christianity, but these are purely of human origin. Here, from beyond the grave, where you thought there was nothing, our voices call to you: "Brothers and sisters, nothing dies! Jesus Christ is the victor over all wrong. You, too, can be victors over your own frailties." ■ —The Spirit of truth (Paris, 1860).

6.   ■ I have come to teach and give comfort to the rejected and the disowned. I have come to nurture their courage until it rises to the level of their trials. I want to tell them to cry if they feel like it, for pain was made whole in Gethsemane. I want to tell them, too, to have trust, for the consoling angels will come to dry their tears.

Workers, plan your paths well. Begin every day where you left off the day before. The work of your hands provides your bodies with food. But your souls are not forgotten. Like a gardener, I nurture your souls in the silence of your thoughts. When the time comes for you to rest, when the thread of life slips through your fingers and your eyes are closed to earthly light, you will feel a surging inside and then a precious seed will flower within you. Nothing is lost in the kingdom of our God. Your toil and tears form treasures that will make you rich in the higher spheres, where light replaces darkness and the neediest among you may well become the most dazzling.

In reality, those of you who bear your burdens well, and help your brothers and sisters, already know the essence of my love. Occupy yourselves, then, with this marvelous doctrine that both tempers human rebelliousness and shows the purpose of human trials. Just as the wind scatters the dust, the gentle breeze of spirituality will carry off from your hearts any traces of resentment against the triumphant ones of the world. (Remember that sometimes their inner miseries are great and fraught with more pitfalls than yours.) I am with you and my disciples instruct you. Quench your thirst in the living spring of love and prepare yourself, while in the flesh, to one day rise, free and happy, toward God, Who created you to reach perfection, and Who wants you to sculpt your own self, becoming artisans of your own immortality. ■ —The Spirit of truth (Paris, 1861).

7. ■ I am the great healer of souls, and I have come to bring you a treatment that truly cures. The weak, the suffering, the sick are most dear to me and I have come to save them. Come to me, then—you who suffer and find yourselves overburdened. You will be relieved and comforted. Don't search for strength and consolation elsewhere; The world is incapable of offering them. In the principles of the Spiritist Doctrine, God delivers a powerful message to your heart. Listen to the call. Clear your aching souls from ungodly ideas, fallacies, lies, and skepticism. They are like creatures that suck out your life's blood and leave you wounded. Be humble and surrender yourself to the Supreme Love, and soon your life will be in harmony with the Law. Love, pray, be responsive to the help of good spirits. Pray with all your faith, and God will send the beloved Son to guide you and to lift you with these goodly words: "You called me, here I am!"■ — The Spirit of truth (Bordeaux, 1861).

8. ■ God comforts the humble and gives strength to the suffering when they ask for it. God's love covers the earth, and in every place, God provides a consoling remedy for each tear shed. Those who practice dedication and selflessness are in a continuous state of prayer. These two qualities carry a very powerful message; in them you will find the key to human wisdom. If only all suffering people could understand this truth instead of crying out against their pain, which in fact they rightly experience! Take as your motto these words: Devotion and Self-Sacrifice. Practice them and you will be strong, since they cover all the obligations that love and humbleness impose on you. Afterwards, the feeling you have of fulfilled duty will bring your spirit rest and fortitude. Then your heart will beat more steadily, your soul become calmer, and your body more relaxed, for the body reflects the state of the soul. ■ — The Spirit of truth (Havre, 1863).

Chapter 7

Blessed Are the Poor in Spirit

SCRIPTURES AND COMMENTARY

THE MEANING OF THE WORDS "POOR IN SPIRIT"

1. *"Blessed are the poor in spirit, for theirs is the kingdom of heaven."*

   (Matthew, 5: 3)

2. Skeptics have mocked this saying, as they often mock things they don't understand. But by "the poor in spirit" Jesus didn't mean people lacking in intellect; He was talking about the humble of heart.[1] The kingdom of heaven, He said, would be reserved for them, not the proud.

   Men and women of learning—at least those the public view in this light—generally hold such a high opinion of themselves and their intellect that they think the things of the spirit are beneath their notice. They focus all their attention on themselves, and, not surprisingly, are unable to lift up their eyes to God. Arrogance of character frequently leads them to deny that anything might be above them, even Divinity itself. For them, to admit the existence of a Higher Being would be tantamount to acknowledging their own inferiority. Moreover, even when they do admit a Superior Being, they invariably attack one of its most beautiful qualities— the rule of Providence over the things of this world. Why this scorn? Because they believe they're capable of living and ordering their lives and the lives of others entirely on their own terms. Taking their own intelligence as a measure of Supreme Intelligence, and believing that they can understand everything, they refuse to believe in the possibility of something they cannot explain. They consider their opinion to be law.

---

[1] *Translator's Note: Throughout the book, the words humility and humbleness are used for the French "humilité." They should be primarily considered in the Biblical sense as the negation of arrogance, pride, haughtiness. In the Christian Spiritist literature, the attributes of a humble person are associated with that special tolerance, compassion, and reverence for all that is born from self-knowledge.*

But if they won't admit the existence of an invisible world and of a Higher Power, it isn't because this is beyond their comprehension. It's because their pride causes them to rebel against the idea of something that they can't surpass and that would bring them down off their self-erected pedestals. Consequently, they have nothing but contempt for what doesn't belong to the visible, tangible world. According to them, the things of the spirit are only good for simple people. To their way of thinking, "poor in spirit" merely refers to anyone ignorant enough to take such matters seriously.

Scoff as they like, however, they (like everybody else) will inevitably be drawn into this invisible world that they despise. There, their eyes will be opened and they will realize the extent of their errors. Yet, being just, God can't dispense similar treatment to the scornful as to the ones who've kept the laws with love. Nor can God let them share equally in spiritual riches.

When Jesus says that the kingdom of heaven belongs to the poor in spirit, He teaches that no one will enter this kingdom without humbleness of heart and meekness of spirit. He also tells us that the uneducated person who has these qualities will be favored over the learned person who trusts more in him- or herself than God. In every circumstance, Jesus put humility in the category of virtues that brings us near to God, and pride in the category of failings that keeps us removed from God. The reason for this is clear: To be humble toward God is an act of reverence; pride, on the other hand, is a slight against God. Thus, being poor in spirit (and rich in moral qualities) has much greater value as far as our future happiness is concerned.

EVERYONE WHO EXALTS HIMSELF WILL BE HUMBLED[2]

3.   *At that time the disciples came to Jesus and asked, "Who is the greatest in the kingdom of heaven?"*

He called a little child and had him stand among them. And he said: "I tell you the truth, unless you change and become like little children, you will never enter the kingdom of heaven. Therefore, whoever humbles himself like this child is the greatest in the kingdom of heaven.

"And whoever welcomes a little child like this in my name welcomes me."

(Matthew, 18: 1-5)

---

[2] *Translator's Note: Luke 14:11.*

4.   *Then the mother of Zebedee's sons came to Jesus with her sons and, kneeling down, asked a favor of him.*

He said, "What is it you want?"

She said, "Grant that one of these two sons of mine may sit at your right and the other at your left in your kingdom."

"You don't know what you are asking," Jesus said to them. "Can you drink the cup I am going to drink?"

"We can," they answered.

Jesus said to them, "You will indeed drink from my cup, but to sit at my right or left is not for me to grant. These places belong to those for whom they have been prepared by my Father."

When the ten heard about this, they were indignant with the two brothers. Jesus called them together and said, "You know that the rulers of the Gentiles lord it over them, and their high officials exercise authority over them. Not so with you. Instead, whoever wants to become great among you must be your servant, and whoever wants to be first must be your slave— just as the Son of Man did not come to be served, but to serve, and to give his life as a ransom for many."

(Matthew, 20: 20-28)

5.   *One Sabbath, when Jesus went to eat in the house of a prominent Pharisee, he was being carefully watched.*

When he noticed how the guests picked the places of honor at the table, he told them this parable: "When someone invites you to a wedding feast, do not take the place of honor, for a person more distinguished than you may have been invited. If so, the host who invited both of you will come and say to you. 'Give this man your seat.' Then, humiliated, you will have to take the least important place. But when you are invited, take the lowest place, so that when your host comes, he will say to you, 'Friend, move up to a better place.' Then you will be honored in the presence of all your fellow guests. For everyone who exalts himself will be humbled, and he who humbles himself will be exalted."

(Luke, 14: 1, 7-1 1)

6.   These precepts of Jesus stem from the principle of humbleness of heart which He constantly presented as an essential condition for the happiness promised to the chosen. He was referring to this principle when He said, "Blessed are the poor in spirit, for theirs is the kingdom of heaven." Jesus also took the child as a symbol of humbleness of heart when He said, "…whoever humbles him- self like this child is the greatest in the kingdom of heaven"—that

is to say, the person who doesn't pretend to be greater or more perfect than others.

We find the same fundamental idea in the following saying: "Whoever wants to become great among you must be your servant," and in this: "Whoever wants to be first must be your slave"; and also in this: "Everyone who exalts himself will be humbled, and he who humbles himself will be exalted."

The Spiritist Doctrine supports this interpretation with real case studies. It shows us that the great in the spirit world are often those who were small on earth, and that the great and powerful on earth frequently find themselves extremely small on the other side. This is because the former take with them, when they die, those qualities that make for greatness in heaven—the virtues that are never lost. On the other hand, the latter, forced to leave behind the things responsible for their status on earth—wealth, titles, fame, birth into the upper reaches of society, etc.—become have-nots in the spirit world. They arrive there very like people who are shipwrecked and have lost all their belongings, down to their clothes. In such cases, only their pride remains, making their position all the more humiliating when they discover that the people they stepped on, while on earth, have been raised to places of glory far above them.

In the process of successive reincarnations, the Spiritist Doctrine also shows another side of the principle of humbleness of heart. In reincarnation, people who have, in one life, raised themselves up are often born into very modest circumstances in the next—if they've let themselves be ruled by pride and greed. It is wiser, then, not to become fixated on high earthly status or fascinated by positions of dominance since you may have to descend dramatically later on. Instead, seek simplicity, and God will, according to your merit, assure your right place in the next realm.

MYSTERIES HIDDEN FROM THE LEARNED AND THE CLEVER

7.   *At that time Jesus said, "I praise you, Father, Lord of heaven and earth, because you have hidden these things from the wise and learned, and revealed them to little children."*

(Matthew, 11: 25)

8.   It may appear odd that Jesus would give thanks to God for having revealed things to the little and humble, i.e., the poor in spirit, while hiding them from the learned and clever (who, one would think, are more capable of understanding them).

However, we should understand "little" here to mean the ones who don't think excessively of themselves and are full of respect for God. "Wise and learned" we should interpret as a reference to the arrogant, proud of their worldly knowledge, and those who admire their own perceptiveness so much that they deny God. They forget that, in ancient times, "wise" was a synonym for "savant." This is why God has left them to discover the secrets of nature, and has revealed the secrets of heaven to the humble in heart who honor the presence of the divine.

9.   The same thing happens today regarding the truths revealed by the Spiritist Doctrine. Many skeptics are surprised that the spirits take so little trouble to convince them. They don't realize that, from the spirits' point of view, looking after seekers who bring good faith and humbleness with them is preferable to trying to offer enlightenment to people who think they already have it— people who imagine, perhaps, that God ought to be grateful for the minutes of attention they spare to consider proofs of God's own existence.

The power of God reveals itself in everything, from the infinitely small to the vastness of the cosmos. Rather than hide it, God shines forth the divine light into every corner of the Universe, so that only those blinded by their own misconceptions fail to see it. God will not open people's eyes by force, however, if they are happy keeping them shut. Their time will come. It is necessary, though, that they first feel the pangs of grief so that they can recognize that it is Divinity, and not mere chance, that wounds their pride. In overcoming their unbelief, God uses the means most suitable to each individual. But it isn't their unbelief that determines what is to be done, just as it isn't their option to say, "If you want to convince me, you have to do this or that, but on this more convenient occasion and not on that one." Unbelievers shouldn't be unduly surprised, then, if neither God nor the spirits, who carry out the Divine Plan, submit to these demands. For a clear appreciation of those circumstances, they should ask themselves how they would react if one of their lowest employees tried to tell them what to do. The Creator is not subject to the circumstances surrounding our lives. God is the force behind these circumstances. By contrast, those who approach the Maker with a humble heart are able to feel divine love; those who believe themselves greater than God, can't.

10. One might ask if God couldn't touch each unbelieving person by offering some unmistakable sign, a proof so convincing that it

would bend even the most hardened skeptic. Beyond all doubt, God could. Yet what merit would they gain if God did so, and more importantly, what use would it be? Every day we see people who refuse to bow down, even in the face of such evidence; they say, "Even if I saw it, I wouldn't believe because I know it's impossible." Denying truth in this manner only proves that their spirits haven't become mature enough to understand it, or their hearts to feel it. Pride is a speck in the eye that mars their vision. And what good does it do to show a light to one who's blind? The cause of the blindness must be cured first. This is why, as a skillful doctor, God first of all corrects their pride. God will never abandon any of these lost children because sooner or later their eyes will be opened. But God wishes this to happen of their own free will. Then, crushed by the torments of unbelief, they will open themselves up to God of their own accord, asking, like the Prodigal Son, to be forgiven.

SPIRIT TEACHINGS

PRIDE AND HUMBLENESS OF HEART

11. ■ Our dear friends, may the peace of the Lord be with you. We have come in order to encourage you to follow the straight path. The spirits who once lived on earth have been assigned to aid in your quest. Blessed be the Lord for this opportunity to be part of your growth. May the Holy Spirit illuminate us and make our words so clear in meaning that they will be within the reach of everyone who hears them. You who are incarnate, who undergo trials and are searching for the light, we pray God's Will comes to our aid and that we can make God's teachings shine before your eyes.

Humbleness of heart is a virtue you too often neglect. While many examples have been placed before you, few have ever been followed. Yet can you love your neighbor when you neglect this virtue? Not really. With humbleness of heart, you see everyone as equals. It makes you realize that you are all brothers and sisters who should help each other; and in this way, it prepares you to live more compassionately. Without humbleness of heart, you might present a good outward show of virtue, but, in fact, you are simply assuming qualities you don't have—as if you were dressing up in fancy clothes to hide a bad bruise. For inspiration, remember the sublime Teacher; remember His meekness of heart which was so genuine that it made Him the greatest among all prophets.

Pride is the terrible enemy of humble-heartedness. If Christ promised the kingdom of heaven to the poor, it was because the powerful ones of the earth considered their titles and wealth to be rewards of merit, implying that they were of stock superior to that of the common person. They thought titles and wealth were their due, so that when they lost these things, they accused God of injustice. What a mockery of that justice, and what blindness on their part! God doesn't pass judgment by looking at physical appearances. The physical covering of a poor person is just the same as that of a rich one. Nor has God made two kinds of human beings. Everything God makes is wise and great. Don't attribute to God, then, ideas your own proud minds have created.

As for the rich—sleeping beneath your gilded ceilings and safe from the cold— don't you know that thousands of your brothers and sisters, who are as worthy in God's eyes as you, have nothing but a pile of hay to sleep on? Those who go hungry are your equals. We know that your pride rebels at these words. You say you give alms to the poor. Yet when have you ever shaken a poor person's hand? But "There is nothing in this," you will say. "I am descended from the finest families on both sides, and carry a prominent name. Now you tell me that one of these paupers dressed in rags is my equal! This is utopian thinking, the product of crackpot philosophers. If we are equals, why would God have placed me so high and them so low?"

Well, it's quite true that your clothes differ; but undressed, what difference is there between the two of you? Though some in the past have claimed to have a purer blood, it's a fact that there is no difference between the blood of a noble and a common person. The blood that runs in the veins of the upper and lower classes is the same. Besides, who can guarantee that you haven't been as destitute in the past as they are now? Perhaps you too begged on the street. And one day in the future, you may find yourself begging for pennies from someone you only look down on today. Wealth and status aren't eternal. They disappear with the death of the body, which is nothing more than the perishable covering of the spirit. To you we say: Seek humbleness of heart. Look honestly at the reality of this world, and upon what makes for distinction or degradation in the next realm. Remember, too, that you won't be spared from death—no one is. Your titles can't save you from it; it may strike today, tomorrow, at any time. And if you are buried already—buried in your pride—you'll have a great deal to be sorry for and will stand in need of compassion yourself.

To the proud ones, we say: What were you before you became so high and powerful? Perhaps in another life your position was beneath even the lowest of your employees. Drop your haughty brows then, for Providence may trip you in your haughtiness when you think you're flying very high. In the Divine Scale of Justice, everyone is equal, and only virtue gives distinction in God's eyes. All spirits share the same essence; all bodies are formed from the same matter. Your titles and names mean nothing. They stay with your body in the grave and in no way assure you the bliss of the angelic souls, whose nobility is based solely on love and simplicity.

Consider this poor woman, a mother whose children are cold and malnourished. She goes out, bent under the burden of her cross, struggling but courageous, to get food for her family. We bow down before her! In our eyes she is saintly, noble, great. So we tell her: Pray and have hope, because true happiness isn't of this world. For the poor and oppressed who place their trust in God, the next realm will be a place of joy.

And you, young woman—a child, in reality— toiling so hard and carrying such a burden. Don't give in. Don't allow sadness into your heart. Instead, let your eyes glide gently on high. God, Who minds the well-being of even the smallest birds, will do no less for you. Trust. Have hope: You are not forgotten. Perhaps the loud music of lavish parties and the pleasures of this world make your heart beat faster. You might want to dress in fancy clothes and join all the lucky ones you see from a distance. You dream about the women you see passing by (women who seem so carefree and full of laughter), and you want to be like them. But don't say such things. If you only knew how many tears, what unmentionable pain, are hidden beneath those expensive dresses, how many sobs are drowned out by the sound of that noisy orchestra, you would prefer your simple home job and your modest means. Keep yourself clean in God's eyes. Don't shame your guardian angel away from you or remorse will be your company. Without a loving guide and without spiritual support, your life will be devoid of true meaning, with only reparations in the next world to look forward to.

We say to you who suffer injustice at the hands of your fellow human beings: Be indulgent toward their faults, for you aren't without faults either. This is love and also humbleness. If people say bad things about you, accept it as another trial. What they say doesn't matter if your conduct is clean. For that act, God will reward you.

Withstand as courageously as you can the offenses you suffer from others. Be humble and realize that in God there is strength.

Dear God, does Christ have to return to earth a second time in order to teach humanity Your divine laws once again? Has humanity forgotten them? Will He have to throw the money-changers out of the temple again for defiling Your house, which should be kept exclusively for prayer? Humanity, if God granted this grace again, would you reject Christ a second time? Would you accuse Him of blasphemy because He humbled the pride of the modern Pharisees? Perhaps you would make Him, once again, walk the road to Golgotha.[3]

When Moses climbed Mount Sinai to receive the Ten Commandments, he left the people of Israel to themselves, and they soon abandoned the true God. Men and women gave what-ever gold they had in order to make an idol, which they then worshipped. Modern people still imitate them. Christ left you His doctrine and gave examples of all the virtues. And yet you disregard His examples and precepts. Each one of you has made a god according to your own desires. For some this god is bloody and vengeful; for others it is indifferent to the world. Nevertheless, the god you have fabricated is still the golden calf, adapted to your own tastes and ideas.

Friends, brothers and sisters, wake up. Let the voices of the good spirits echo in your hearts. Be generous, but not simply to show others how good you are; be loving—that is to say, do good quietly. Little by little, begin to tear down the altars you have erected in your hearts to pride. Live by the teachings of Christ; it will earn you a place in His kingdom. Stop questioning the good-ness of God. You already have plenty of proofs of that goodness. We have come to prepare the way so that the prophecies can be fulfilled. At some future time, when God gives you a more resounding demonstration of divine mercy, let us pray that God's celestial messenger finds you gathered together as a great family. By then, we hope, your hearts will be gentle and mild, and you will be worthy to hear the divine words the messenger has to offer. May the Chosen One find the path filled with laurels, placed there to celebrate your return to the road of goodness,

---

[3] *Translator's Note: Golgotha: from the Hebrew 'skull', is the site at which Jesus was crucified. Calvaria in Latin. The site may have been near the Church of the Holy Sepulcher, within the present walls of Jerusalem, but most religious scholars hold that it is outside the Damascus gate, north of the city.*

compassion, and love. Then your planet will be a Paradise. But if you refuse to listen to the voices from on high who have been sent to awaken and guide your society—which is rich in science but poor in compassion and love—there will be nothing left for you but tears and grief. This need not happen! Accept God into your life, and all of us who serve the Divine Plan will join together to sing a hymn of thanksgiving for God's unbounded goodness, glorifying God throughout all the coming ages. So be it. ■
—Lacordaire (Constantine, 1863).

12. ■ Why, humanity, are you always complaining about the afflictions you've heaped on your own heads? You've ignored the saintly and divine ethic of Christ—so don't be surprised when the cup of wrongdoing overflows on all sides.

The ills of society are festering. Yet you can only blame yourselves since you try constantly to push each other off. Without good will toward others, peacefulness of heart is impossible. But how can good will coexist with haughtiness? Pride is the root of all your problems. Devote yourselves to overcoming it; otherwise, you will perpetuate its harmful effects. There is only one way to accomplish this end, but it is infallible: Take Christ's Law as your one rule of conduct—the same Law you have so often mocked and defiled in its interpretation.

Why do you put greater value on the things that please your eyes than on those that touch the soul? You follow with great interest the loose morality of the rich, and yet you ignore the virtues of the ordinary person. Whenever a celebrity shows up, even one with a twisted life, people rush to open their doors and shower him or her with attention. But to the godly person who lives by work and good deeds, you hardly bother to say good-day. When the deference you bestow on someone is occasioned by her fortune or status, what motivation does she have to correct her faults?

It would be very different if public opinion condemned the moral vices of the rich with the same harshness that it does the ordinary person's. Unfortunately, people often inflate their egos to the point that they find it easier to identify themselves with the excesses of the wealthy than with the plight of the common person. You say that this is an age of money and greed. No doubt, it is. But this is no excuse to let material things overshadow your good sense and reason, or to always scramble to get ahead of your brother. Today, society is suffering from the consequences of all these attitudes.

Never forget that this state of affairs is a sign of moral decay and decline. When pride reaches an extreme, it indicates an imminent transformation, for Divine Justice never fails to correct the proud. If sometimes they are allowed to rise, it is only so they will have time to reflect on their condition. Occasionally, however, they reel under the blows life sends their way; these are warnings calling on them to mend their ways. Unfortunately, they usually rebel instead of becoming less full of themselves. Thus, when their cup is full, the higher they have risen, the worse their fall will be.

We ask you, suffering humanity (whose selfishness has ruined everything it has touched), to renew your courage despite everything. Infinite in mercy, God has sent you a powerful and unexpected cure for your sorrows. Open your eyes to its light! Free souls, no longer living on earth, have come to remind you of your true duties. With the wisdom of their accumulated experience, they tell you that, compared to Eternity, what you think of as the great events and crises of your passing life are mere trifles. The greatest among you is the humblest of the humble; and the most loved in heaven is the person who has most loved his or her fellow human beings. By contrast, the powerful of earth who abuse their authority will find themselves reduced to a position of obedience to their own servants. Finally, humbleness of heart and love, like two siblings going hand in hand, are the best means of attaining grace from God the Eternal. ■ — Adolf, Bishop of Argel (Marmande, 1862).

MISSION OF THE INTELLIGENT PERSON ON EARTH

13. ■ Never be too proud of what you know because the limits of your knowledge on earth are very narrow. Even if you are a prominent intellectual on earth, you have no right or reason to be boastful about it. If God causes you to be born into an environment in which you can develop your intelligence, it was because God wanted you to use it for the benefit of everyone. The fact that you have this instrument, through which you can help the progress of others and hence bring them close to the Creator, indicates that you have been given a mission. Doesn't the nature of an instrument indicate its purpose? Doesn't the hoe the gardener gives his assistant show what use it should be put to? What would you say if, instead of working with the hoe, the assistant raised it against the gardener with the aim of hurting him? You would say it was outrageous, that the assistant should be fired.

The same situation applies to the person who uses his or her intelligence to destroy the idea of God and Providence. This is like raising the hoe, which was made for weeding, against the gardener. Does the assistant then have the right to receive the promised salary? On the contrary, he or she deserves to be driven out of the garden. And don't doubt that this will happen. The individual who works contrary to God's purpose will endure many unhappy lives full of frustrations until, learning meekness of heart at last, he or she accepts the One to whom everything in life is owing.

Where it is used for its proper end, intelligence is rich in its effects. Indeed, if every man and woman of intelligence used it as God wished, the spirits would find performing their task of helping humanity advance much easier. Unhappily, for many people, their sharp intelligence leads to an inflated sense of themselves, and to wasting a life opportunity. Humanity abuses intelligence as it does all its other faculties. Nevertheless, there is no lack of teachings that warn of a powerful Hand that may withdraw what it has given. ■ —Ferdinand, a Guardian Spirit (Bordeaux, 1862).

Chapter 8

Blessed Are the Pure in Heart

SCRIPTURES AND COMMENTARY

LET THE CHILDREN COME TO ME

1.   *"Blessed are the pure in heart, for they will see God."*

(Matthew, 5: 8)

2.   *People were bringing little children to Jesus to have him touch them, but the disciples rebuked them. When Jesus saw this, he was indignant. He said to them, "Let the little children come to me, and do not hinder them, for the kingdom of God belongs to such as these. I tell you the truth, anyone who will not receive the kingdom of God like a little child will never enter it." And he took the children in his arms, put his hands on them and blessed them.*

(Mark, 10: 13-16)

3.   Purity of heart can't be separated from simplicity and humility, and excludes all ideas of selfishness and pride. This is why Jesus used infancy as the symbol of both purity and simplicity.

    Seen from a spiritual perspective, this comparison might seem completely unfair. After all, the spirit of a child may be very old and, on returning to the physical realm, might bring with it imperfections it hasn't been able to resolve during its past lives. (As we know, only spirits that have reached perfection can offer an example of true purity.) From the point of view of our present life, however, the comparison is exact because a child, who hasn't yet had opportunities to reveal any improper tendencies, presents us with an image of innocence. Jesus makes it clear, in any event, that the kingdom of heaven isn't meant for children per se, but for those who resemble the image we have of the child.

4.   Yet, we might ask, since the spirit of a child has lived before, why doesn't it show itself as it really is right from birth? Everything in

God's work is full of wisdom. A child needs special care that only a mother's tenderness can give it—tenderness that is aroused in the mother by the child's frailty and innocence. For a mother, her child is always an angel—an attitude that ensures her continuing concern for it. For if, in place of the child's innocent ways, she saw toughness in its character or found it had adult ideas, she would be disinclined to offer it the same quality of care—particularly if she happened to glimpse its past.

As is natural, the rate of intellectual activity must be compatible with the physical development of the body. The brain would be strained if the spirit functioned at peak level, a difficulty sometimes observed in highly gifted children. For this reason, prior to incarnating, the spirit gradually loses self-awareness. Its senses slowly dim and go into a seemingly latent state. This state is temporary, but necessary in order to dull memories that may interfere with its life program.[1] The accomplishments of the spirit are never lost, however. In every incarnation, the spirit is reborn with a more solid foundation, both moral and intellectual, and sustained by the intuitions that stem from knowledge already acquired.

After birth, as the child grows up, she gradually recovers the essence of her ideas, memories, and impulses. During the first years, the spirit is truly in a state of innocence, since the elements that form its true character remain dormant. During this period of semi-dormancy, the senses are more receptive to the impressions that can shape the person's character and help her progress. In this early phase, the child is easier for the parents to educate.

The spirit, then, wears for a period of time the gown of innocence; and Jesus was right when, despite the many previous lives experienced by every child, He took a child as the symbol of purity and simplicity.

SINNING BY MEANS OF THOUGHT; ADULTERY

5.   *"You have heard that it was said, 'Do not commit adultery.' But I tell you that anyone who looks at a woman lustfully has already committed adultery with her in his heart."*

(Matthew, 5: 27-28)

---

[1] *Translator's Note: For an extended discussion see Allan Kardec's* The Spirits' Book, *chapter XI, "The Return to the Body," question 344-360.*

6. The word adultery should not be understood in its limited sense (marital infidelity) but in a more general one. Jesus used it frequently to indicate wrongdoing, sin, and every type of bad thought, as in this passage: "If anyone is ashamed of me and my words in this adulterous and sinful generation, the Son of Man will be ashamed of him when he comes in his Father's glory with the holy angels."[2]

    Since true purity is both a matter of behavior and thought, the person who has a pure heart doesn't even think of evil. Jesus, in other words, condemns wrongdoing even in thought, because it is a sign of inner imperfection.

7. Do we suffer consequences if we have a bad thought even if we don't act on the thought?

    At this point let's make an important distinction. As the soul advances along its evolutionary path, it slowly grows in awareness as it willingly works at shedding its imperfections.

    All unclean thoughts result from the flaws of the soul. But where the soul has a strong desire to change itself, such a thought becomes an opportunity for growth when the spirit actively chooses not to act on that thought. Here is a positive movement on the part of the soul to change. In this way the soul strengthens its resistance to temptations, and having resisted, feels more sure and content in its victory. By contrast, a person without such resolve may not act on this thought only for lack of the right opportunity. In this case, the person will be just as guilty as if he or she had actually committed the act.

    To sum up: For the person who doesn't even consider doing wrong, a degree of progress has already occurred; for the person who feels the urge but battles it, progress is in the process of realization; for the person who indulges in the thought and dreams up ways of satisfying it, the evil still exists in all its strength. In the first, the work has been done; in the last, it hasn't even begun. But Divine Justice takes into account all these nuances when assessing individual responsibility for acts and thoughts.

TRUE PURITY; UNWASHED HANDS

8.   *Then some Pharisees and teachers of the law came to Jesus from Jerusalem and asked, "Why do your disciples break the tradition of the elders? They don't wash their hands before they eat!"*

---

[2] *Translator's Note: Mark 8:38*

Jesus replied, "And why do you break the command of God for the sake of your tradition? For God said, 'Honor your father and mother' and 'Anyone who curses his father or mother must be put to death.' But you say that if a man says to his father or mother, 'Whatever help you might otherwise have received from me is a gift devoted to God,' he is not to 'honor his father' with it. Thus you nullify the word of God for the sake of your tradition.[3] You hypocrites! Isaiah was right when he prophesied about you: 'These people honor me with their lips, but their hearts are far from me. They worship me in vain; their teachings are but rules taught by men.'"

Jesus called the crowd to him and said, "Listen and understand. What goes into a man's mouth does not make him 'unclean,' but what comes out of his mouth, that is what make him 'unclean.'"

Then the disciples came to him and asked, "Do you know that the Pharisees were offended when they heard this?"

He replied, "Every plant that my heavenly Father has not planted will be pulled up by the roots. Leave them; they are blind guides. If a blind man leads a blind man, both will fall into a pit."

(Matthew, 15: 1-14, see also Mark, 7: 5-23)

9.   *When Jesus had finished speaking, a Pharisee invited him to eat with him; so he went in and reclined at the table. But the Pharisee, noticing that Jesus did not first wash before the meal, was surprised.*

Then the Lord said to him, "Now then, you Pharisees clean the outside of the cup and dish, but inside you are full of greed and wickedness. You foolish people! Did not the one who made the outside make the inside also?"

(Luke, 11: 37-40)

10. During Jesus' era, the Jews had become fervent observers of the man-made rules of the religious code, to the point of making its observance a matter of conscience and becoming increasingly neglectful of the Divine commandments. The original purpose and meaning of the rules became lost for them in complicated forms of ritual. And since it was much easier to practice these outward forms of formal religion than to bring about real moral reform—to wash their hands rather than cleanse their hearts, so to speak—they deluded themselves into believing that conformity to minor regulations was all they needed to satisfy God. Since they had been taught that God only demanded this of them, they

---

[3] *Translator's Note: "An irresponsible Jewish son could formally dedicate to God, i.e., to the temple, his earnings that otherwise would have gone for the support of his parents. The money, however, did not necessarily have to go for religious purposes." Adapted from the* NIV Study Bible, *1995, note 7:11, page 1504.*

naturally stayed the same, from a moral perspective, as they had always been. For this reason, the prophet said: "Their reverence of me is worthless; the lessons they teach are nothing but human commandments."

Unfortunately, many present-day Christians behave in much the same way as the ancient Jews. Christ's moral teachings have been demoted to second place. Many Christians believe that external acts of worship can assure salvation better than one's moral transformation. It's to these human-made additions to God's Law that Jesus refers when He says, "Any plant my heavenly Father has not planted will be pulled out by the roots."

The purpose of religion is to lead humanity toward God. This final aim can only be reached through a profound transformation of the soul. Any religion that doesn't make human beings better than they are at present fails in its purpose. We can also positively say that any religious belief that supports human beings in their wrong-doing is either flawed at the core or has had its principles misconstrued. This is exactly what has happened to religions where the form has become more important than the substance. Belief in the value of ritual acts is meaningless if it doesn't stop violence, cheating, stealing, lying, slander, and the abuse of others in all its forms. Such religions never create godly men and women, only people who are superstitious, hypocritical, and fanatical.

The appearance of purity isn't enough; above everything else, you must have a pure heart.

OFFENSES: "IF YOUR HAND OR YOUR FOOT CAUSES YOU TO SIN, CUT IT OFF AND THROW IT AWAY"

11.   *"But if anyone causes one of these little ones who believe in me to sin, it would be better for him to have a large millstone hung around his neck and to be drowned in the depths of the sea.*

"Woe to the world because of the things that cause people to sin! Such things must come, but woe to the man through whom they come! If your hand or your foot causes you to sin, cut it off and throw it away. It is better for you to enter life maimed or crippled than to have two hands or two feet and be thrown into eternal fire. And if your eye causes you to sin, gouge it out and throw it away. It is better for you to enter life with one eye than to have two eyes and be thrown into the fire of hell.

"See that you do not look down on one of these little ones. For I tell you that their angels in heaven always see the face of my Father in heaven."

(Matthew, 18: 6-11)

12. As it is usually used, the word *offense*[4] is any action that goes counter to moral standards or social norms. Invariably, it implies a certain amount of public disapproval. But the offense itself is not so much in the action as in the repercussions it causes. It is a fact that many people care foremost and only for their public reputation. They fear that their moral failures will be discovered, but care little about the baseness of their soul if they can keep their failures secret. For them, this alone is enough to soothe their conscience. They are, as Jesus said: "...whitewashed tombs, which look beautiful on the outside but on the inside are full of dead men's bones and everything unclean."[5]

    In its Gospel sense, *offense* (which Christ uses repeatedly) has a much more general meaning, which explains why its uses are so often misunderstood. An offense, in this sense, refers not only to something that hurts the feelings and integrity of another person but also to everything that results from human imperfection, especially every bad action of one individual against another, whether public or not. An offense, in other words, is the direct result of poor moral development.

13. Jesus said that offenses must exist on earth. He said so because our imperfections still incline us to enjoy wrongdoing, just as bad trees tend to produce bad fruits. From these words we must realize that wrongdoing comes about because our nature is still frail, not because doing wrong is ever necessary.

14. Jesus also added, "Such things (sins) must come." Humanity undergoes its process of purification as it comes to realize that it is the first victim of its own misdeeds. That is how it will eventually conclude that wrongdoing serves no useful purpose. Tired of dwelling on the bad, mankind will seek goodness. Thus, having to react to each other's vices is a correction for some and a test for others. This is how the Divine Planner brings good out of evil, and how humanity learns to use wrongs for its growth.

15. One might say, of course, that evil is a necessity, that it will last forever (since its disappearance would deprive Providence of a powerful means to correct the guilty), and that trying to improve humanity is of no use. However, note that if there were no wrongdoers there would be no need for correction. Indeed, let's

---

[4] *Translator's Note: In the French Scripture the word used is 'scandal'. Other English manuscripts use sin, offense, or scandal. We adopted the word 'offense' because it conforms better to the argument.*

[5] *Translator's Note: Matthew 23:27.*

suppose that humanity is transformed, that it is composed only of good men and women. No one, in this case, thinks of doing his or her neighbor wrong; everyone is happy to be good. This, in fact, is the condition found on advanced realms where evil has been banished. It is also what will actually happen here on earth when we've made enough progress. Yet we must remember that in this great universal concert, new planets are being formed. Many will be populated by spirits in early stages of development and serve occasionally as correction centers for the rebellious ones who, for their persistence in doing wrong, are no longer fit for life in happier, more advanced worlds.

16. "Woe to the world because of the things that cause people to sin!" That is to say, wrong is always wrong, and the person who does wrong will be accountable for it, even though the action may have indirectly served as an instrument of correction for another. For instance, an ungrateful child may represent an opportunity for reparation for parents who were once ungrateful children themselves and who made their own parents suffer. Now they experience what they made their parents go through. It is the penalty they pay. Yet these circumstances don't excuse the child's behavior, and eventually he or she too will experience a comparable run of events, either in their own children or in some other way.

17. "If your hand or your foot causes you to sin, cut it off and throw it away." This is a very strong statement, and it would be absurd to take it literally. It should be understood to mean that we must destroy anything in us that might cause offense—that is to say, all the bad. We can do this by rooting out all our impure thoughts and base desires. Further, we can interpret the statement as meaning that it is preferable for a person to have a hand cut off rather than use it to do harm, or (to extend the metaphor) to lose one's sight rather than allow it to become a stimulant of vicious thoughts. Those of us who take the trouble to consider the allegorical meaning of His words know that Jesus never said anything absurd. Still, many of His words can't be adequately understood without a key to decipher them. It is this key that the Spiritist Doctrine offers us.

SPIRIT TEACHINGS

LET THE CHILDREN COME TO ME

18. ■ Christ said, "Let the children come to me." These words, profound and yet simple, invite not just children but all souls who find themselves hopeless and strong-armed by adversities. Jesus also calls to the immature in spirit, to the morally frail, and the debased. He had nothing, in fact, to teach the children because their underdeveloped intellect would make it impossible to comprehend a superior order of ideas and standard of behavior.

Jesus wanted human beings to surrender to Him with confidence, just as tiny tots give themselves up to their mothers. Then He could place their souls under His tender and delicate influence.

You should know that Jesus was the flame that brought light into the darkness. He was the light of dawn that announced the sunrise. It was Jesus who first proclaimed the principles that the Spiritist Doctrine defends today, which should in turn attract to Him, not children especially, but all people of good will. This attraction has already had a dynamic beginning. As a result, your approach can no longer be one of unthinking belief and mechanical obedience. Rather, humanity must begin to pursue a reasoned understanding of the Law, which, through its intelligent design, reveals its universality.

Dearly beloved, the time has come in which statements that seem quite wrong will be properly explained and emerge as truths. It is our mission, as spirits, to teach you the proper meaning of the parables and show you the strong correspondences that exist between old notions and this fresh perspective on Christ's teaching. In truth we tell you that these great revelations will open up new horizons and that the teachings of the higher spirits will shine brilliantly, as the sun shines on the mountain top. ■ —John the Evangelist (Paris, 1863).

19. ■ Let the little children come to us for we have the milk that will strengthen the weak. Let the frightened and the feeble, and those in need of help and consolation, come to us. Let the ignorant come: We can enlighten them. Let the sufferers, the sick and unfortunate, come to us: We will share with them the great remedy that will ease all their hurts and reveal the secret that will cure their innermost wounds. And what is this great and soothing balm, friends, that is so powerful that it can heal all the wounds of the heart? It is love and compassion. If you have this divine

flame, you don't need to be afraid of anything. Rather, every moment of your life you will say, "Dear God, I pray that Your Will be done and not mine; if You see fit to test me through pains and trials, bless that test, since it's for my own good. If it pleases You, God, have mercy on my weakness, and give me whatever happiness my heart has earned—and, once again, give Your blessing. Yet don't let love merely lie sleeping in my soul; make it rise up constantly until it becomes a witness of my thankfulness."

If you have love, you have the most precious thing on earth. You possess "the pearl of great value" that nothing—not hatred or persecution—can take away from you. If you have love, your treasure will be in a place where the worms and the rust can't attack it, since you will have rid yourselves of everything that could mar the purity of your soul. Every day you will feel the pull of matter diminish, and like a bird in the sky that no longer remembers the earth, you will continually rise up until your soul, full of exhilaration, fills itself with true life in the bosom of God. ■ —A Spirit Guide (Bordeaux, 1861).

BLESSED ARE THE BLIND[6]

20. ■ My good friends, why did you call me? Do you want me to put my hands on this poor sufferer and cure her? What a hard plight hers is! She has lost her sight and is now in total darkness. Poor child! Let her pray and have faith. I don't know how to perform miracles if God doesn't will them. All the cures I've brought about, and that you have heard of, are due to God alone. In your suffering, then, always lift up your eyes to heaven and say from the bottom of your hearts, "Almighty, cure me, but cause my frail soul to cure itself before You cure my body; let my flesh suffer, if necessary, so that my soul can rise up to Your bosom with the same purity it had when You created it." After this prayer, my friends, which God always hears, you will gain new strength and courage, and hopefully the cure you have asked for, as a reward for your fortitude.

Since today I'm in an assembly that is devoted primarily to study, I will tell you that people who experience a life of blindness should consider themselves fortunate, as far as their spiritual purification is concerned. I would remind you that Christ said it is better to pluck out your eye if it leads you astray, better to throw it away than let it to become a reason for catastrophe.

---

[6] *This communication was given in response to an appeal of a blind person, in whose name the spirit of J. B. Vianney, a parish priest of Ars, was evoked.*

There are many people in this world who will one day find themselves in absolute darkness and will curse the time they saw the daylight. Oh yes, you are lucky if you realize that, as part of your purification, you have lost your sight. At least your eyes won't cause you to offend or bring about your downfall. You can live the full life of the soul. You can, indeed, see more clearly than people with earthly vision. Always, when God lets me restore light to the eyes of one of you, I say to myself, "Dear soul, why don't you appreciate all the delights of contemplation and love the treasures of meditation? If you did, you wouldn't ask to live in a world of coarse and aggressive images, much bleaker than anything you glimpse in your blindness."

Bless you, the blind, who want to live with God in your hearts. You are fortunate indeed—more so than all others. You can sense the perfect joy, and join the angelic souls on journeys that even the most illuminated of earth can't glimpse. Human eyes, when open, always create for the soul the risk of a stumble; when shut, they may open your inner path to God. Believe me, my good and dear friends, blindness is often the true light of the heart, whereas sight is frequently an angel of darkness that leads to spiritual death.

And now, a few words directed to you, my dear friend. Have hope and courage, and hold fast to your faith. If I were to say, "My child, your eyes will open," you would be filled with joy. But who knows if your joy wouldn't be the cause of a great loss? Trust the good Father Who gives us joys, and allows us our sadness. I will do everything I can for you; but, on your side, you must pray, and even more important, meditate on the things I've told you.

Before I leave, I give my blessing to everyone gathered together here. ■ — J.B. Vianney, parish priest of Ars (Paris, 1863).

21.   *Comment:* When a particular form of suffering doesn't result from actions in this life, its cause must be in a previous one. Those hardships that appear totally random are nothing more than the working out of Divine Justice. Divine Justice is not capricious; it designs every trying circumstance so that it may correct an existing imperfection. As the ultimate source of mercy, God places a veil over our past. But at the same time, we are alerted to the rule "all who draw the sword will die by the sword."[7] In other words, each of us will suffer the conse-

---

[7] *Translator's Note: Matthew 26:52 and Genesis 9:6 "Whoever sheds the blood of man, by man shall his blood be shed."*

quences of our own misdeeds. If someone is impaired visually, it may be because sight caused his or her downfall in another life or because this person caused someone else to lose their sight. The condition may also have come about through excessive work that the now-blind person imposed on others, or through ill treatment, thoughtlessness, negligence, etc. In these cases the person responsible always undergoes the penalty caused by his or her actions. Sometimes the visual impairment could well have been a choice made by the spirit who regrets a wrong done. In such cases, we see a direct application of Jesus' words: "And if your eye causes you to sin, gouge it out and throw it away."[8, 9]

---

[8] *Translator's Note: Matthew 18:9*

[9] *Translator's Note: The issue of "choice of trials" is also addressed in* The Spirits' Book, *where it is pointed out that souls might opt for a particular experience, e.g., visual impairment, as a way to learn a certain set of lessons for self, family, or community. (Chapter X, "Spirit Life," question 258 - 273)*

Chapter 9

Blessed Are the Meek and the Peacemakers

SCRIPTURES AND COMMENTARY

INSULTS AND VIOLENCE

1. *"Blessed are the meek, for they will inherit the earth."*

(Matthew, 5: 5)

2. *"Blessed are the peacemakers, for they will be called sons of God."*

(Matthew, 5: 9)

3. *"You have heard that it was said to the people long ago, 'Do not murder, and anyone who murders will be subject to judgment.' But I tell you that anyone who is angry with his brother will be subject to judgment. Again, anyone who says to his brother, 'Raca,' is answerable to the Sanhedrin. But anyone who says, 'You fool!' will be in danger of the fire of hell."*

(Matthew, 5: 21-22)

4. In these words, Jesus makes meekness, prudence, gentleness, kindness, and patience essential principles of the Law; through them He implicitly condemns, excluding by them, violence, anger, and all insulting expressions toward others. Among the Jews, for example, Raca was an expression of contempt; it meant "a worthless person" and the user accompanied it by spitting in an exaggerated manner and turning the head to one side. As in the scripture above, Jesus goes so far as to threaten with hellfire anyone who insults a brother.

   In this, as in all other cases, the intention of the speaker either heightens or lessens the offense. But why should a simple word be seen as something so serious that it would meet with the most severe disapproval from Jesus? The reason is that every offensive word expresses an attitude that violates the laws of love and compassion, which should preside over all human relationships and maintain harmony among individuals. When we use these words, we uphold the spirit of hatred; and we undermine the value of compassion and fellowship. To sum up, we should avoid them because, next to submission to God, love for your neighbor is the highest duty of all Christians.

5.   But what did Jesus mean by the words "Blessed are the meek, for they will inherit the earth," especially when He had recommended that we give up all worldly goods for heaven? It is clear that while awaiting these heavenly riches, we need the earth on which to live. Jesus is only recommending that we not give more importance to worldly goods than to spiritual ones. With this, He also implied that, until now, worldly goods have been owned and controlled by the violent at the expense of the meek and peaceful, who often lack even the basics of life, while the violent live surrounded by plenty. Jesus promises that justice will be done on "earth as it is in heaven" because the meek, too, are God's children. Indeed, when love and compassion become the foundation for human law, selfishness will no longer exist; the strong and violent will no longer exploit and crush the meek and peaceful. According to the Law of Progress and the promise made by Jesus, this will be the condition of human relationships on earth when it rids itself of its evil-natured souls. The earth will then have ascended to a more advanced and happier condition.

SPIRIT TEACHINGS

AFFABILITY AND KINDNESS

6.   ■ Good will toward your fellow human beings, the result of loving your neighbor, reveals itself in the form of warmth and kindness. Don't imagine, however, that you can always trust appearances. Education and worldly experience can give someone a thin veneer of courteousness that very much looks like these qualities. In fact, many people who seem to be good-natured are only wearing masks, as some people wear expensive clothes, to cover up moral shortcomings. The world is full of these people. They have a smile on their lips but poison in their hearts. They appear mild as long as nothing upsets them; but provoke them a little and they bite. They are eloquent and golden-tongued when they speak with you face to face; behind your back, the same tongues turn into poison darts.

In this same category, we place those who, while appearing kind and gentle to the outside world, act as virtual tyrants in their homes and jobs, making their families and subordinates suffer because of their pride and dictatorial attitudes. Often such people are trying to compensate for the lack of power they feel elsewhere. They don't dare to impose their authority on strangers (who would quickly put them in their place), so they settle for being feared by those who aren't in a position to challenge them. It boosts their sense of pride to say "I give the orders here and I'm obeyed." But they rarely think that they could add "and I am detested."

To have milk and honey flowing from your lips isn't enough. Your heart has to correspond with the feelings you express or you're simply being a hypocrite. On the other hand, people whose friendliness and mildness are not a mere pretense never find themselves leading contradictory lives because they're the same both in society and in private. They know that, even though it might be possible to deceive people, no one can deceive God. ■ —Lazarus (Paris, 1861).

PATIENCE

7.   ■ Suffering is often a blessing. When you suffer, don't let yourself become discouraged; rather, be accepting of the Divine Will, which, through the pain of this world, prepares the way for your glory in the greater life.

You must nurture patience, because it may also be an expression of love and compassion, as taught by Christ. There are many different ways of expressing compassion—giving money to the poor, for example, is one of the easiest ways. There's one kind of compassion, though, that is much harder to exercise and consequently offers a greater merit—to forgive those people who cause your suffering and strain your patience.

We're well aware of how difficult life can be. It is composed of so many little difficulties that seem like pinpricks but that, repeated often enough, end up hurting badly. Still, if you look carefully at the duties you've been called to fulfill and at the resources and support you've received, you have to admit that the number of blessings is far greater than the number of pains. Raise up your eyes to the sky, then, with abundant hope. If you do, your burdens will seem much lighter than when you walk disheartened, with downcast eyes.

Courage, friends! Christ is your model. He suffered far more than any of you, although He had nothing of which to purify Himself, unlike those of you who have to make up for your past and so strengthen yourselves for the future. Be patient; be Christians! This last word summarizes everything. ■ —A Spiritual Friend (Havre, 1862).

OBEDIENCE AND FORTITUDE

8. ■ Jesus constantly teaches fortitude and obedience to the Law, two virtues that go alongside gentleness and mildness of character. Unfortunately, many have mistaken such teaching to be the negation of will and self-determination. In fact, obedience is the consent of your reason; resignation, the consent of your heart. Both are active forces; both help shoulder the burdens necessary to your purification. Often those who are short of them, give themselves up to anger and quit their obligations. Indeed, the cowardly person can no more have fortitude than the proud and selfish can accept the Law. By contrast, Jesus was the very personification of obedience and fortitude, qualities which were much despised by society. He came to earth at a time when the dissolution of values had started to corrode Roman society, and He came to show to a dispirited human culture the benefits of renouncing an overly materialistic, self-centered life.

Every stage of social development is identified by a dominant quality that propels it forward or a vice that restrains its progress. The quality of this current generation is its intellectual activity, its vice is its moral indifference. More than the sporadic insights of a few geniuses whose discoveries are well ahead of their times, intellectual activity refers here to the concerted efforts of society in general toward a goal possibly less dazzling, but more typical of the intellectual elevation of the era.

Surrender then to the forward impetus that is given to your souls. Embrace the great Law of Progress, which is the motto of your generation. As for those who are either too complacent or aren't open to new understanding, they are the unfortunate ones. Sooner or later, their attitude will be changed by those who inspire the progress of humanity; their rebelliousness will be checked by means of the double action of brake and spur, when necessary. Eventually, their resistance will wear out. In the meantime those who are mild and gentle will be blessed, because they are more receptive to new teachings. ■ — Lazare (Paris, 1863).

ANGER

9.   ■ Pride leads you to think that you are better than you really are and to dismiss any comparison with others that might reflect poorly on you. How superior you are to your fellow human beings—in spirit, social position, even in personal qualities! Or so you like to believe. Consequently, the least parallel between yourself and someone else irritates and annoys you. And then you have a fit of anger.

Your bouts of rage make you resemble savages since they take away all your self-control and reason. Their origin, if you look for it, will nearly always be found in hurt pride. It will, most likely, be pride hurt by a dissenting opinion that causes you to reject, angrily, reasonable comments about a problem and to dismiss solutions to it suggested by wiser heads. Even irritations, which originate from trivial issues, take on a magnitude directly related to the importance you attach to your own personality, before which—you make it clear—others have to give way.

In your outbursts of anger, you strike out at everything, even break things that are in your way, as if they had refused to yield to you. But if you could see yourself objectively in these moments, your temper would either scare you or make you think, "I'm simply ridiculous." Imagine, too, the impression you make on other people. In reality, these tendencies turn you into pitiful beings, and even if it's merely out of self-respect, you should make a concerted effort to overcome them.

Furthermore, anger can't solve any problem; it can even harm your health to the point where it puts your life at risk. In becoming violently angry, you essentially become your first victim. However, the chief reason that you should want to restrain this type of behavior is the distress it causes the people around you. If you have a heart, your rages are bound to be a source of guilt for you—for having made the people you love suffer. And you continually run the risk that in one of your explosions you'll do something you will deeply regret for the rest of your life—a terrible burden for your conscience to bear.

Anger doesn't mean that you don't have good qualities; but it can stop you from doing good, and it may lead you into great evil. These two facts alone should be enough for human beings to make the necessary effort to overcome this emotion. And Spiritists have an additional motive to conquer it—it is contrary to love and to the humbleness of heart that should characterize every Christian. ■ — A Guardian Spirit (Bordeaux, 1863).

10. ■ Because people wrongly believe that their nature can't be changed, they often consider themselves relieved of the responsibility of trying to correct their faults. This applies especially to faults that they willingly indulge in—their pursuit of pleasure—or that would require a great deal of persistence and inner strength to eliminate. This is why, for example, people who are prone to angry outbursts usually blame an "uncontrollable temper" for their pattern of behavior. Instead of admitting their guilt, they point to some physiological cause of their anger, and in this way shift the blame for their problem onto God—still another result of the pride that is at the heart of human imperfections.

Unquestionably, some people are more likely to commit violent acts than others, just as some muscles are more flexible and more capable of acts of strength. But don't think that the real cause lies in their physical constitution. You can rest assured that a peaceful spirit, even in a strong, muscular body, will always be peaceful. But a violent spirit, even when it occupies a feeble body, won't be any milder; its anger will simply take on a different form. One is characterized by self-control, the other is given to uncontrolled outbursts.

It isn't the body that causes raging anger or any other vice. All the higher qualities, and all the lower ones, come from the spirit. If not, where would merit and responsibility lie? The person who has a physical deformity can't do anything to remedy that situation because his spirit lacks the power to correct it. What he can change are his internal impulses—when, that is, the desire to change is strong enough. And don't doubt that the power of such desire is nearly unlimited—as you can see when you look at the truly miraculous transformations in people's lives that happen around you daily. It is important to realize that human beings are only controlled by their vices because they want to be. People who really want to free themselves can always do it. If this weren't so, the Law of Progress wouldn't exist. ■ —Hahnemann (Paris, 1863).

Chapter 10

Blessed Are the Merciful

SCRIPTURES AND COMMENTARY

FORGIVE OTHERS SO THAT GOD MAY FORGIVE YOU

1. *"Blessed are the merciful, for they will be shown mercy."*

    (Matthew, 5: 7)

2. *"For if you forgive men when they sin against you, your heavenly Father will also forgive you. But if you do not forgive men their sins, your Father will not forgive your sins."*

    (Matthew, 6: 14-15)

3. *"If your brother sins against you, go and show him his fault, just between the two of you. If he listens to you, you have won your brother over."*

    Then Peter came to Jesus and asked, "Lord, how many times shall I forgive my brother when he sins against me? Up to seven times?" Jesus answered, "I tell you, not seven times, but seventy-seven times."

    (Matthew, 18: 15, 21-22)

4. Forgiveness goes hand in hand with mildness, since an unforgiving person can't be either mild or level-headed. Forgiveness fuses together the ability to forget and the willingness to pardon offenses. It is a sign of the advancement of the soul, just as hate and rancor are the marks of an unevolved soul. While the former is calm, has sweetness of temperament, and is full of compassion, the latter is bitter and full of resentment.

    People who claim they can't forgive are unfortunate indeed. Their inability to forgive may go unnoticed by their fellow human beings, but not by God. And how will they be able to ask God to forgive their own failings when they were so hard on those of others? Doesn't Jesus teach us that our mercy should be unlimited? He says that we must forgive our brothers and sisters not merely seven times, but seventy-seven times.

There are, however, two different ways of forgiving. The first way is noble, truly generous, and devoid of hidden intentions. It delicately avoids hurting the feelings of the offending person, even when his or her acts can't be justified. In the second way, the offended (or supposedly offended) person, in subtle ways, humiliates the offender, weighing him down with a forgiveness that incites animosity instead of peace. If he extends his hand to the offender, the gesture isn't prompted by genuine good will, but by a desire to show off, a way of saying to other people, "Look how generous I am!" Under these circumstances a real reconciliation between offender and offended is impossible. No generosity is involved, only an attempt to satisfy pride. In every argument, the person who shows him- or herself to be the more conciliatory—who shows more selflessness, understanding, and real generosity of soul—invariably wins the hearts of all.

RECONCILIATION WITH ENEMIES

5.   *"Settle matters quickly with your adversary who is taking you to court. Do it while you are still with him on the way, or he may hand you over to the judge, and the judge may hand you over to the officer, and you may be thrown into prison. I tell you the truth, you will not get out until you have paid the last penny."*

(Matthew, 5: 25-26)

6.   In the act of forgiveness, as in acts of goodness generally, there is both a spiritual and a material effect. As we know, death doesn't free us from our enemies. In the afterlife, a revengeful spirit frequently pursues with considerable hatred any other spirit against whom it bears resentment. From this we learn that the proverb "The poison dies with the beast" is mistaken when applied to human beings. In the spirit world, a revenge-bent spirit may wait until the subject of its hate is in a physical body. There, its victim is not as free as in the spirit realm and can be more easily tormented and hurt in her dearest interests and affections. Such a situation is behind most cases of spiritual oppression, especially the more difficult ones, such as spiritual bondage and possession.[1] The disturbed or possessed person is almost always the victim of a vengeance that finds its cause in conduct prior to the

---

[1] *Translator's Note: The French original used the word 'obsession' in this context, which in the nineteenth century conveyed the notion of 'the hostile action of an evil spirit besetting any one' (Oxford English Dictionary). Nonetheless, according to the OED such usage of the word obsession has become obsolete in contemporary*

Footnote continued on next page

present life. Divine Justice lets such things occur as a way either of correcting a past wrong or admonishing a person for heartless and unforgiving ways. In the interest of lasting inner peace, then, it is important that each person amend the wrong done to others and forgive all enemies, thus clearing away in this life every ill-feeling and every cause of hostility toward another. In this way we turn an enemy in this world into a friend in the afterlife. At least with this effort we are on the right side of the Law. And God, we can be certain, won't allow anyone who acts with forgiveness to fall victim to a vengeful soul.

Thus, when Jesus tells us to reconcile with our enemies as soon as possible, He isn't merely concerned with patching up quarrels during our earthly life; He is encouraging us to avoid having our quarrels spill over into future lives. As He said, "…you will not get out until you have paid the last penny"—that is to say, not until God's Justice has been completely satisfied.

THE OFFERING MOST PLEASING TO GOD

7.   *"Therefore, if you are offering your gift at the altar and there remember that your brother has something against you, leave your gift there in front of the altar. First go and be reconciled to your brother; then come and offer your gift."*

(Matthew, 5: 23-24)

8.   With the words "… go and be reconciled to your brother; then come and offer your gift," Jesus teaches us that the offering that most pleases God is giving up our personal resentments. He tells us also that before seeking forgiveness of our wrongs from the Father, we must redeem ourselves before those we have offended. Only when our hearts are free of taint will our offering be pleasing to God. Jesus explains this precept in the material sense

---

Footnote continued from previous page

English, so, instead, in this translation we used the terms 'spiritual disturbance' and 'spiritual oppression.' We believe such terminology better preserves the original meaning and intent of the French text. (In modern day usage the word 'obsession' is commonly understood in the psychological realm as 'an idea or image that repeatedly intrudes upon the mind of a person against his will and is usually distressing [in psychoanalytic theory, attributed to the subconscious effect of a repressed emotion or experience]).

According to Spiritist studies, many of the abnormal conditions catalogued by psychology and psychiatry, have a spiritual component, in addition to their recognized organic causes. This spiritual element is often explained as part of the notion of 'spiritual oppression.'

of offering gifts because Jews in those days offered sacrifices; thus, He chose words that conformed to the custom of the time. The true Christian person, however, doesn't offer material gifts to God; the offering is of a spiritual nature—a fact that lends the precept even more strength. The Christian offers God a clean soul. Accordingly, on entering God's temple, we should leave any feelings of hate and resentment outside, especially thoughts of hostility towards our fellow human beings.

Only under these conditions will the angelic beings take our prayers and place them before God, the Eternal. This is what Jesus meant when He told us to "…leave the gift in front of the altar. First go and be reconciled to your brother; then come and offer your gift."

THE PLANK IN THE EYE

9.   *"Why do you look at the speck of sawdust in your brother's eye and pay no attention to the plank in your own eye? How can you say to your brother, 'Let me take the speck out of your eye,' when all the time there is a plank in your own eye? You hypocrite, first take the plank out of your own eye, and then you will see clearly to remove the speck from your brother's eye."*

(Matthew, 7: 3-5)

10. One of our worst habits is noticing the defects of others before we see our own. But if we are to attain discernment, we must start from within, looking at ourselves as in a mirror, with honesty and like an outside observer. We should ask what we'd think if we saw someone doing what we do.

Invariably it is pride that blinds us to our flaws, both moral and physical. This attitude is a violation of the law of love. True love goes hand in hand with humbleness of heart and tolerance. Love that consents to arrogance of heart is a contradiction in terms: These two feelings negate each other. After all, how can a person so conceited as to think herself superior to others be self-less enough to notice the good qualities in them? In her mind, to highlight the good qualities of another is to eclipse herself, while to denigrate another is a way to raise herself. Pride is a source of many vices, but it is also a force that represses many virtues. Unfortunately, in pride we can find the motive and basis for a multitude of human actions, which is why Jesus—who recognized pride as the chief obstacle to human progress—fought so hard against it.

DO NOT JUDGE OR YOU TOO WILL BE JUDGED.
LET THE ONE WHO IS WITHOUT SIN BE THE FIRST TO THROW A STONE.

11.   *"Do not judge or you too will be judged. For in the same way you judge others, you will be judged, and with the measure you use, it will be measured to you."*

(Matthew, 7: 1-2)

12.   *The teachers of the law and the Pharisees brought in a woman caught in adultery. They made her stand before the group and said to Jesus, "Teacher, this woman was caught in the act of adultery. In the Law Moses commanded us to stone such women. Now what do you say?" They were using this question as a trap, in order to have a basis for accusing him.*

But Jesus bent down and started to write on the ground with his finger. When they kept on questioning him, he straightened up and said to them, "If any one of you is without sin, let him be the first to throw a stone at her." Again he stooped down and wrote on the ground.

At this, those who heard began to go away one at a time, the older ones first, until only Jesus was left, with the woman still standing there. Jesus straightened up and asked her, "Woman, where are they? Has no one condemned you?"

"No one, sir," she said.

"Then neither do I condemn you," Jesus declared. "Go now and leave your life of sin."

(John, 8: 3-11)

13. With the sentence "If any one of you is without sin, let him be the first to throw a stone at her," Jesus makes tolerance a duty toward others, for the simple reason that all of us stand in need of it ourselves. Jesus also teaches that we should never judge others more severely than we judge ourselves, nor condemn in someone else what we condone in ourselves. Before criticizing another person for a fault, let us first see if that same censure could be applied to us.

Criticism can be aimed at someone for two reasons: to put an end to wrongdoing and to discredit someone. There is absolutely no excuse for the second; its motivation can only be spite and meanness. The first, though, can be praiseworthy. In certain cases, it even becomes a duty since good can result from it. Without a healthy dose of criticism to counter it, the evil in society would never be brought under control. Further, isn't it the duty of each of us to help our fellow human beings progress? Thus, we shouldn't take the principle "Do not judge or you too will be judged" in its most literal sense, which would be wholly unhealthy. We should note the spirit of these words, which gives life to an important concept. Jesus did not mean to discourage being critical of what is evil. Far from it, He Himself gave examples of this in clear terms. His real point is that the right to blame rests with the moral authority of the person who passes judgment. If the person is guilty of what she condemns in someone else, she loses her moral authority and ruins her ability to correct the wrong.

In addition, our inner being refuses respect and obedience to any person, who, while invested with some kind of authority, violates the very same principles he is to uphold. In the eyes of God, no legitimate authority exists, except that which arises from the practice of goodness. This also is emphasized in Jesus' words.

SPIRIT TEACHINGS

FORGIVING OFFENSES

14. ■ How many times must I forgive my brothers and sisters? Not just seven times, but seventy-seven times. Here is one teaching of Jesus that should most impress your intelligence and speak most loudly to your hearts. Consider also the words in the Lord's prayer—so simple, so concise, yet so brimming with aspiration. You discover there the same message. Jesus, Who personified all virtues, answers Peter: You must forgive without limit; you must forgive each offense as many times as it is done to you; your brothers and sisters on earth must be taught that it is forgetfulness of self that makes a person invulnerable to attack, misbehaviors, and insults. Your heart must be mild and humble without measuring out your gentleness. In short, you must do whatever you wish God to do for you. Doesn't God frequently forgive you? God doesn't keep count of the number of times the Divine Justice has descended upon you to forgive your shortcomings.

Pay attention to Jesus' reply to Peter, and as Peter did, apply it to yourselves. Forgive freely. Be tolerant, charitable, generous; be lavish with your love. Give and you will receive. Forgive and you will be forgiven. Be meek and you will be raised up. Be humble and you will have a seat at the Maker's right hand.

Dearly beloved, study and ponder among yourselves these words. I speak by inspiration from the One Who, from the heights of heavenly splendor, cares about you and continues with love the thankless task that began nineteen centuries ago. Forgive your fellow human beings as you would have them forgive you. If their acts cause you personal harm, this is just one more motive for you to be tolerant toward them, since the merit in forgiveness is in direct proportion to the seriousness of the wrongdoing. There is little merit in only overlooking the errors that cause nothing more than simple scratches.

Spiritists, don't forget that forgiving wrongdoing should never be an empty expression, either by word or deed. Since you call yourselves Spiritists, be Spiritists with all your might. Forget the wrongs that have been committed against you and think of only one thing: the good you can do. Those who follow this path mustn't stray from it even in thought, for God knows your thoughts and you are responsible for them. Take care, then, to eliminate all vindictive feelings from your heart. Again, what lies at the bottom of your hearts is known to God. You will live happily indeed if you can go to sleep each and every night saying, "I have nothing against my neighbor." ■ —Simon (Bordeaux, 1862).

15. ■ To forgive your enemies is to become deserving of forgiveness yourself. To forgive friends is to show true friendship. To be able to forgive offenses is to show that you are better than you once were. So, friends, forgive others that you may be forgiven. For if you are hard, demanding, unbending, and treat even minor offenses severely, how can you expect God to forget that every day you stand in even greater need of mercy yourself?

Those who say "I will never forgive" are unfortunate: They only condemn themselves by such an attitude. If you honestly search deeply within, you may find that the aggressor in many instances is really you. In the dispute that began as a small spat and ended in a broken relationship, who knows if you didn't give the first blow, if you didn't say harsh, offending words or otherwise conduct yourself unreasonably? No doubt the other person, by letting him- or herself be easily drawn into the argument, lost the high ground. This is only another reason for being tolerant, for not putting yourself in a position where you deserve the blame you ascribe to someone else.

But let's concede, for the moment, that in a given circumstance you really were the offended person. Who can say that you haven't simply poisoned the situation further by reacting with contempt or that your reaction turned an incident that could have easily been forgotten into a serious quarrel? If preventing the escalation of this situation depended on you and you did nothing to prevent it, you truly are responsible. Finally, let's concede that your conduct was completely without blemish. In this case you would gain even greater merit by being lenient.

Still, there are two very different ways of forgiving—one proceeds from the lips, the other from the heart. Many people will say to the offending person "I forgive you," but inside they are glad when something unfortunate happens to that person and will remark that he or she has only gotten what they deserved. Many others will say "I forgive you," and then add quickly, "but I'll never be reconciled with you, and I never want to see you again in my life!" Is this forgiveness according to the Gospel? Not at all. True forgiveness—Christian forgiveness—blots out the past. This is the only type of forgiveness which is taken into account, since the All-Knowing is not convinced by mere words or pretense. God listens to the innermost recesses of your hearts, and to your most secret thoughts. Absolute and unconditional forgiveness of all offenses is the distinguishing trait of great souls. Resentment is always a sign of lack of spiritual progress. Don't forget, that true pardon is demonstrated in actual deeds, not words. ▨ — Paul, the Apostle (Lyon, 1861).

TOLERANCE

16. ▨ Spiritists, today we would like to talk about tolerance, that pleasant brotherly feeling that each of you should hold toward other people, but which all too often is little in evidence. Tolerance takes no notice of the defects of others; or if it does, it refrains from talking about or disclosing them. To the contrary, tolerance tries to keep those defects that it alone knows about out of the sight of others. Moreover, if ill-disposed people do discover someone else's defects, tolerance always has a ready and plausible explanation for mitigating these defects. We don't mean here the kind of excuse that only seems to gloss over the fault while in fact making it more obvious.

Tolerance never dwells on the defects of others unless it's to offer help, and even then will try to do it in the most gentle manner. Tolerance never makes shocking statements or reproaches anyone; instead, it offers advice, usually in a tactful way.

When you criticize, what conclusion should the objective person ideally come to? That you are not guilty of the same thing yourself, that you are worthier than the other person! We ask every human being, "When will you judge your own hearts, thoughts and actions first, and stop worrying about what your brothers and sisters are doing? When will you look critically only at yourselves?"

Be critical of yourselves, tolerant toward others. Be mindful of the One Who has the final word, Who sees the innermost movements of your heart and forgives many, many times the faults you condemn, and condemns at times the ones you condone. Our Maker knows the motive behind every action. Those who so bitterly point at the misdeed of a fellow human being may, in the eyes of God, be guilty of even more harmful things.

Always be tolerant, friends, for tolerance draws in peace and harmony. Intolerance only drains energy, drives people apart, and causes hard feelings. ■ —Joseph, a Guardian Spirit (Bordeaux, 1863).

17. ■ Be tolerant toward others' faults, whatever they are. Don't judge severely any actions but your own. Then God will be lenient toward you as you have been toward others.

Support the strong of character and encourage them to keep going. Strengthen the frail and show them the love of God, Who takes into account even the smallest degree of regret for a misguided act. Help everyone see the Angel of Repentance, who stretches out her white wings over humanity's shortcomings, as if she wanted God not to see them. Acknowledge Infinite Mercy, and never fail to say to God through thought and, above all, through actions, "Forgive us our debts, as we also have forgiven our debtors."[2] Understand the meaning of these sublime words fully. Not only is their literal sense admirable, so is the guidance they contain.

What do you ask for when you seek God's forgiveness? Do you simply ask God to forget your transgressions? Note that this leaves you with nothing, for while God's forgetfulness of your error might spare you from suffering the consequences, you have done nothing to forestall a recurrence of your faults. You cannot expect God to reward you for the good you haven't done, or the wrong you haven't committed. But when you ask God to forgive your transgressions, ask also God's favor for the strength not to repeat them. Plead for the courage to start on a new path, one illuminated by surrender and love, where you can grace your repentance with a sincere desire to repair your wrongs.

By the same token, when you forgive someone, don't be satisfied with merely throwing a veil of forgetfulness over that person's wrongdoing. That veil, in most cases, is going to be trans-

---

[2] *Translator's Note: Matthew 6:12.*

parent to you anyway. Rather, wrap your forgiveness in love. Do for your brother or sister what you want God to do for you. In other words, substitute the anger that soils with the love that cleanses. Exemplify through your conduct the tireless compassion taught by Jesus. Spread love as He did during His journey on earth, and as He continues to do from the realm open only to the perceptions of the soul. Follow His divine example. Walk in His footsteps: they will lead you to a refuge that offers rest after the struggle. Carry your own cross. Even when facing pain, be courageous and tread your own Calvary. At the summit, you will find perfect glory. ■ —John, Bishop of Bordeaux (1862).

18. ■ Dear friends, be critical of yourselves, but always tolerant of others' weaknesses. This is the practice of a saintly compassion, a way of life which, unfortunately, not enough people embrace. Everyone has negative tendencies to overcome, faults to correct, and bad habits to change. Everyone has a burden to get rid of before climbing the mountain called Progress. Why, then, do you seem to have an extra sense that lets you spot your neighbor's faults but blinds you when it comes to your own?

When will you stop taking notice of the small speck in your brother's or sister's eye, and instead, pay attention to the plank in your own? This plank is what blinds you and causes you to move from one failure to another. Believe what we, your spiritual kindred, are telling you. Every man and woman, proud enough to think of him- or herself as superior in virtue and merit to their brothers and sisters, is foolish and will be held accountable by Divine Justice. In its true character, compassion is always modest and mild. It doesn't dwell on a person's defects but strives to rouse better qualities. The human heart may still be a pit of passions, but hidden in its innermost recesses are the seeds of good, the life force of the spirit.

The Spiritist Doctrine is a source of blessings and comfort. Those who know it and who benefit from the uplifting teachings that are delivered from God's messengers, are indeed happy. For them, the pathway is illuminated. Along it, they can read the signposts that point them to the final goal of the journey. The signs call for putting love into action, for loving with all one's heart, for loving others like self. In short, we should extend unconditional love to everyone, and to God above all, for in our love for God we find a synthesis of all our responsibilities as human beings. For this reason, the practice of love is God's supreme Law. ■ — Dufetre, Bishop of Nevers (Bordeaux).

19. ▨ Since no one is perfect, should we conclude that nobody has the right to be critical of other people?

Certainly not, since each of you should be working for the progress of everyone else, and especially of those who've been placed in your care. But when you do criticize, do it in moderation, trying your best to be helpful. Don't do it, as frequently happens, because you take a secret pleasure in berating someone. If this is your motive, your criticism will simply be an instance of malice. When you have to make a critical observation, do so in a way consistent with the law of love, being as considerate as possible. Be careful, too, that the criticism you levy at someone else can't also be directed at you. You should determine first whether or not you deserve the very censure you plan to give. ▨ —Saint Louis (Paris, 1860).

20. ▨ Is it wrong to notice others' imperfections when this doesn't benefit them, even though you don't disclose anything about them?

Everything depends on your intention. Certainly you aren't prohibited from seeing wrong where it exists. It would be very inopportune to see only good everywhere, as such an illusion would hinder your progress. The mistake occurs when you use your observation in such a way that harms your neighbor and needlessly discredits him or her in the eyes of others. This is even more objectionable when you do it simply to give vent to your spite or to get satisfaction from finding fault with others. It is not inappropriate, however, to analyze someone else's imperfections as a means of furthering your own improvement, that is, to study their failings as long as nothing about the person is disclosed. This is the method of a thoughtful person, who, by observing individual cases, is able to better understand human behavior. ▨ —Saint Louis (Paris, 1860).

21. ▨ Are there times when it's right to disclose the wrongdoing of others?

This is a very delicate question. Answering it requires that we reason from a space of genuine love. If a person's faults only harm him- or herself, there's no use in spreading word of them. If, however, these shortcoming might harm others, the interests of the majority outweigh those of a single person. According to circumstances, it may even become a duty to expose hypocrisy and lies, just as it is preferable that one person fall than for many to become his or her victims. In such cases, you have to weigh the total sum of the advantages and disadvantages. ▨ —Saint Louis (Paris, 1860).

Chapter 11

Love Your Neighbor As Yourself

SCRIPTURES AND COMMENTARY

THE GREATEST COMMANDMENT

1. *Hearing that Jesus had silenced the Sadducees, the Pharisees got together. One of them, an expert in the law, tested him with this question: "Teacher, which is the greatest commandment in the Law?"*

Jesus replied: "'Love the Lord your God with all your heart and with all your soul and with all your mind.' This is the first and greatest commandment.

"And the second is like it: 'Love your neighbor as yourself.' All the Law and the Prophets hang on these two commandments."

(Matthew, 22: 34-40)

2. *"So in everything, do to others what you would have them do to you, for this sums up the Law and the Prophets."*

(Matthew, 7: 12)

"Do to others as you would have them do to you."

(Luke, 6: 31)

3. *"Therefore, the kingdom of heaven is like a king who wanted to settle accounts with his servants. As he began the settlement, a man who owed him ten thousand talents was brought to him. Since he was not able to pay, the master ordered that he and his wife and his children and all that he had be sold to repay the debt.*

"The servant fell on his knees before him. 'Be patient with me' he begged, 'and I will pay back everything.' The servant's master took pity on him, canceled the debt and let him go.

"But when that servant went out, he found one of his fellow servants who owed him a hundred denarii. He grabbed him and began to choke him. 'Pay back what you owe me!' he demanded.

"His fellow servant fell to his knees and begged him, 'Be patient with me, and I will pay you back.'

"But he refused. Instead, he went off and had the man thrown into prison until he could pay the debt. When the other servants saw what had happened, they were greatly distressed and went and told their master every-thing that had happened.

"Then the master called the servant in. 'You wicked servant,' he said, 'I canceled all that debt of yours because you begged me to. Shouldn't you have had mercy on your fellow servant just as I had on you?' In anger his master turned him over to the jailers to be tortured, until he should pay back all he owed.

"This is how my heavenly Father will treat each of you unless you forgive your brother from your heart."

(Matthew, 18: 23-35)

4. The commandments "Love your neighbor as yourself" and "Do to others what you would have them do to you" define love in its most complete form, because they sum up all our obligations toward others. Nor can we find more effective guidance than that contained in the principle that we should do to others what we would have them do to us. What right do we have, after all, to expect that other people behave better than we do ourselves, that they be more tolerant, kinder, more attentive to us than we are to them?

As we embrace these precepts, we are working practically at overcoming our own selfishness. And eventually, when we adopt these commandments as a rule of conduct and apply them to all our human institutions, we'll begin to understand true brother-hood. Only then will it become possible for peace and justice to rule on the planet. When this happens, the world won't know the hatred and conflict it experiences now—only unity, harmony, and mutual kindness.

GIVE TO CAESAR WHAT IS CAESAR'S, AND TO GOD WHAT IS GOD'S.

5.   *Then the Pharisees went out and laid plans to trap him in his words. They sent their disciples to him along with the Herodians. "Teacher," they said, "we know you are a man of integrity and that you teach the way of God in accordance with the truth. You aren't swayed by men, because you pay no attention to who they are. Tell us then, what is your opinion? Is it right to pay taxes to Caesar or not?"*

But Jesus, knowing their evil intent, said, "You hypocrites, why are you trying to trap me? Show me the coin used for paying the tax." They brought him a denarius, and he asked them, "Whose portrait is this? And whose inscription?"

"Caesar's," they replied.

Then he said to them, "Give to Caesar what is Caesar's, and to God what is God's."

When they heard this, they were amazed. So they left him and went away.

(Matthew, 22: 15-22; Mark, 12: 13-17)

6. The question the Pharisees asked Jesus was prompted by Jewish hatred of the Roman tax, and the fact that the Jews had turned paying this tax into a religious question. A large, well-organized party had arisen to oppose the tax, and it made sure that payment remained an irritant in the body politic. If this weren't true, the question to Jesus, "Is it right to pay taxes to Caesar or not?" wouldn't have made sense. It was, essentially, a trap set by people who expected the reply to antagonize either the Roman authority or the dissident Jews. But Jesus, "who knew their evil intent," avoided the trap and gave the Pharisees a lesson in justice by declaring that they should give to each what each was due.

7. We shouldn't, however, understand the words "Give to Caesar what is Caesar's" in a narrow or absolute sense. As Jesus always did in his teachings, he summarized here a general principle, and used a particular situation to give the principle a form that would be both practical and memorable. This principle grows naturally out of his earlier statement that we should act toward others as we would have others act toward us. Further, it condemns every sort of abuse that one person might inflict on another, and any violation of the interests of others. It commands that we respect the rights of every person, just as we want everyone to respect ours. It also extends our obligations beyond separate individuals to include our families, society, and authority.

SPIRIT TEACHINGS

THE LAW OF LOVE

8. ■ Love sums up the complete doctrine of Jesus, for it is the most sublime human sentiment.

Sentiments themselves are a result of the transformation of instincts as human progress follows its course. At the very beginning of evolution, humans had only instincts. In the next stage they became capable of sensations. Finally, with more intellectual progress and greater spiritual refinement, humans reached a level at which they were capable of genuine emotions.

Now, as we have said, the finest and highest emotion is love—not love in the common sense of the word (that is, romantic love), but love as an inner sun that, at its burning center, concentrates the soul's highest aspirations and its essential divinity. The law of love substitutes for individualism the reconnection of all beings. It eliminates social ills. Consequently, those who transcend their physical nature and come to love wholeheartedly all who face suffering, are blessed. Indeed, they are blessed, for their love of others makes their own spiritual and physical challenges appear trivial. Their step is light and they live as if they were outside and beyond themselves. This is why, when Jesus pronounced the divine word "love," the ancient world trembled and the martyrs, enraptured with new hope, walked fearlessly to meet death in the Roman circus.

The Spiritist Doctrine, in its turn, has come to announce the second word in the divine lexicon. Now pay attention, because this word, "reincarnation," sets free at last, the life that people thought to put away under a gravestone. It represents the final triumph over death, and reveals to an astonished humanity its legitimate heritage. Death is no longer a dark road into domains of anguish. Rather, it is a joyful flight toward a liberated, transformed self. For centuries, the belief had been that blood redeemed the human spirit. Now it is the spirit that redeems human life from the bondage of matter.

We have said already that, at the beginning, human beings were predominantly governed by their instincts. Therefore, if your character is dominated by instincts, you remain closer to the starting point than to the goal. Reaching this goal requires that you transcend the instincts, bringing to light your more noble thoughts and feelings. You can perfect the latter by overcoming your tendency to live only for the material world.

In many of your instincts you will also find the seeds of higher feelings. Instincts bring with them the drive toward progress; they are like the acorn that hides within itself a great oak tree.

Individuals dominated by their passions, then, are in earlier stages of evolvement. They change very reluctantly, and only slowly come out of their shell. The spirit, you must understand, needs to be cultivated as you would cultivate a pasture. All your spiritual wealth in the future depends on the work of cultivation you are doing now. More than any of your material achievements, this is the work that will take you to glorious heights. As you come to understand the law of love, you will begin to experience the sweet delights of the soul. These delights are preludes to your heavenly happiness. ■—Lazarus (Paris, 1862).

9. ■ Love is a divine essence, and all of you, from first to last, have a spark of its sacred fire in your hearts. It is a well-known and consistently proven fact that even the most abject, the most worthless, the most criminal persons are capable of deep affection for a living being or even an object. Such affection is usually unwavering and often reaches a condition of sublimity.

I purposely stress living beings and objects because there are people whose hearts overflow with love, but who bestow most of it on material things—toys, really—and animals, to the exclusion of human beings. These people are misanthropists of a sort, seemingly bitter about humanity and stubbornly resistant to the natural inclination of their soul, which is to look for love and nurturing from the human beings around them. In doing so, they reduce the love force to a mere impulse.

No matter what they do, though, they won't suffocate the love that God planted in every heart at the moment of creation. This seed will develop and grow, along with the spirit's moral sense and intelligence. At times it may be repressed by selfishness; but it will ultimately blossom, for it is the source of the qualities that produce lasting affections and that help you tread the rugged and arid pathways of human existence.

There are people who reject reincarnation because they believe that others will meddle in or steal away relationships they jealously feel are theirs alone. Poor brothers and sisters! Their misguided feelings have made them selfish. They've limited their love to their own little circle of friends and relatives, and are indifferent to anyone else. But to practice the law of love as God intended, they have to learn, step by step, to love all their fellow human beings without distinction. This will be a long and difficult achievement, but they will get there. It is God's Will. Realize, then, that the law of love is the first and most important precept of this new doctrine. One day it will eliminate selfishness in all its forms—whether at the personal, the family, the group, or the national level.

Jesus told you "Love your neighbor as yourself." Who is that "neighbor"? Should love be confined to your family, your immediate associates, your country? No. "Neighbor" is the whole of humanity. On more advanced realms, mutual and unconditional love unites and inspires the spirits. Your plane, destined to make

considerable progress soon and witness great social transformation, will also see its inhabitants embrace the practice of this great
law, which is, in essence, a reflection of the Divine.

The result of putting the law of love into practice will be the
moral advancement of the human race and the potential for true
happiness during the earthly life. Even the most stubborn and
vicious personalities will reform when they see the benefits of
treating others as they want to be treated and doing all the good
within their power.

Don't believe, then, that the human heart is indifferent and
harsh. Despite everything, it always gives in to true love. Love is
an irresistible force that revives and fertilizes the latent virtues
hidden away in every heart. Eventually, as your earth grows from
a place of trials and purification, this sacred fire of love will be
widespread. Then you will see ample manifestations of charity,
humility, patience, altruism, selflessness, dedication to others, and
sacrifice—all the offspring of true love—practiced everywhere. So
don't tire of meditating on the words of John the Evangelist. As
perhaps you know, when sickness and old age forced him to stop
preaching, he limited himself to simply repeating these gentle
words: "My children, you must love one another."

Beloved brethren, make good use of these lessons. They are difficult to put into practice, but your soul will benefit handsomely
from them. Believe me when I tell you to love one another, and
make a sublime effort to do so. When you succeed, you will see
earth transformed into a Paradise, where peace-loving spirits
will come to renew themselves. ■ —Fénelon (Bordeaux, 1861).

10. ■ Esteemed fellow students, on behalf of the loving spirits present at this moment, I say to you, "Love so that you will be loved."
This thought is so completely just and fitting that you'll find in it
all that brings comfort and ease in your daily trials. Better still, by
practicing it, you will elevate yourselves so far above material
consciousness that you'll become spiritualised even before you
leave your earthly bodies. Since the study of the Spiritist
Doctrine helps you understand the future, you can be sure of one
thing: You are progressing toward God and the fulfillment of the
innermost aspirations of your soul. This is why you must elevate
yourselves sufficiently beyond the grasp of matter before you
pass judgment on anybody. Do not reproach anyone before first
raising a thought toward the Merciful Father.

To love, in the true sense of the word, is to be loyal, honest, and
conscientious in applying to your life the principle "Do to others

what you would have them do to you." Love requires you to become aware of the life around you and to search for the inner meaning behind the pain of your fellow human beings, allowing you to help them in their distress. It's to consider the great human family as your own—because you all will meet again at some future time, in more advanced realms. Remember, they are children of the same Loving Father and, like you, are destined to infinite progress. Don't deny your fellow men and women what God has generously given you. After all, in their place, you would be happy if they met your needs in the same generous manner. Always have a word of comfort and hope for people who suffer. In this way, you will be all compassion and love.

Believe that the wise precept "Love greatly so as to be greatly loved" will open up the way. These are revolutionary words; and by following them you'll find yourselves on a sure and steady path.

Those of you who listen to these words, you are much better now than you were a hundred years ago. You've changed so much for your own good that you can willingly accept a host of new ideas about freedom and brotherhood that you would have rejected then. Without doubt, in another hundred years or so, you'll accept just as easily ideas that you don't comprehend today.

Today, the Spiritist movement has taken a great step forward. You can see how quickly ideas of justice and renewal, both constants in spirit teachings, have been accepted by educated people. These ideas accord with the spiritual in people's lives. The soil was well prepared with the ideas of progress fostered in the past century.

As everything flows in the natural order under Providence's guidance, every beneficial lesson will be repeated and reinforced until we truly love one another. In this way, individuals will learn discernment, and join hands with their brothers and sisters everywhere. All will come together in understanding and love to eliminate injustice and the causes of misunderstanding among people.

The ideal of transformation, so well presented in *The Spirits' Book*, will produce amazing miracles in the upcoming century. It will lead to the establishment of harmony among all the physical and spiritual interests of humanity. This will be brought about through a fuller understanding of the precept "Love greatly so as to be greatly loved." ■ —Samson, a member of the Spiritist Society of Paris (1863).

SELFISHNESS

11. ■ Selfishness is a plague. It is an obstacle to moral progress, and
must disappear from earth. The Spiritist Doctrine has the task of
helping to ensure that earth ascends to a higher stage. Therefore,
selfishness is the target on which all Spiritists should train their
sights, summoning up all their strength and courage.

We say "courage" because people need more of it to achieve
victory over themselves rather than over others. Each of you
should use all your strength in the fight against your own selfishness, recognizing that this monster has devoured many minds.
This offspring of pride is at the root of all earth's miseries.
Selfishness, to put it briefly, is the enemy of love and thus the
greatest barrier to human happiness.

Jesus was the example of love; Pontius Pilate an example of
selfishness. As Jesus was about to begin undertaking the holy stations of His martyrdom on the cross, Pilate washed his hands of
the affair, saying, "What does it matter to me!" He even said to
the Jews, "This is a just man, so why do you want to crucify
Him?" Yet he allowed Jesus to be led to His martyrdom.

It's because of this endless battle between love and selfishness
(which invades the human heart like a disease) that Christianity
still hasn't completed its mission. The higher spirits, however, are
now inspiring you, as you are the new apostles of the faith. On
your shoulders rests the responsibility for helping to eliminate
this evil, and by doing so, to clear away the obstacles to the practice of Christianity in its full force. Once selfishness is banished,
earth will become a better place, and a more advanced dwelling
in the celestial system. The time is approaching for humanity to
put on the nuptial robe—but before this can happen, selfishness
must be rooted out of human hearts. ■ —Emmanuel (Paris, 1861).

12. ■ If human beings loved each other with genuine love, true compassion would be better practiced. For this to happen, you must
shed the plated armor that covers your heart and let that heart
become sensitive to others' sufferings. Coldness smothers the
sentiments of the heart. Christ, you will notice, never avoided or
rebuffed anyone who came looking for Him, no matter who they
were. He helped the adulterous woman and the criminal, and
had no thought that His reputation might suffer as a result. When
will you take Him as your model for action? If love ruled on
earth, the evil ones wouldn't prevail. They would fade away in
shame; they would hide themselves. Everywhere they went, they

would feel out of place. This is how evil will one day simply disappear, and you can be quite sure that this will happen.

Begin by being examples yourselves. Be compassionate to everyone without distinction, and try not to pay attention to people who show contempt for you. Leave justice to God, Who separates the wheat from the chaff every day.

Selfishness is a denial of love. Yet without love, human society would find no rest. To take the matter a step further, nothing would be safe. For if selfishness and pride dominated—and they go hand in hand—life would be a race in which the winners would always be the most cunning. It would be a war of personal interests in which the holiest and most delicate feelings would be trampled underfoot, and even family ties would go unrespected. ■ —Pascal (Sens, 1862).

FAITH AND CHARITY

13. ■ Beloved children, a short time ago we told you that love without faith isn't enough to maintain a social order capable of affording a continuous sense of happiness. We might add that compassion without faith isn't possible. It is true that you can find generous impulses in people without faith, but true compassion can only come from selfless dedication and the absence of personal interest, qualities that only faith is able to inspire. Further, a powerful faith is an abundant source of courage and endurance to carry the cross of earthly life.

Yes, children, the pleasure-lovers and self-seekers fool themselves about their purpose when they try to justify putting all their energies into succeeding on earth. God created you to be happy in Eternity; of that there is no doubt. But for this to happen, you must experience life on earth, which serves the purpose of facilitating your moral improvement.

Your experiences in the physical realm are designed to help you acquire happiness with greater ease. Life offers countless opportunities to practice love. In addition to the ordinary struggles of the journey, the diversity of tendencies, needs, and views among you is another means for self-improvement as it presents countless occasions for love and compassion. In the face of such diversity, it is only through mutual acceptance and some sacrifice that harmony is achieved.

Still, you would be correct to say that humanity is meant to be happy on earth—if you added this proviso: Happiness is to be sought in goodness, not in material pleasures. The history of Christianity tells of martyrs going happily to their deaths. Today, Christians no longer need to face torture and death to affirm their faith; but you do need to sacrifice all selfishness, pride, and vanity. If you are inspired by love and sustained by faith, you will triumph. ■ —A Guardian Spirit (Cracow, 1861).

LOVE TOWARD CRIMINALS

14. ■ True love is one of the most sublime principles of the Divine Code. Among those who espouse this principle in their lives, only complete brotherhood should exist. Your love must include even those who succumb to a life of crime. They are also children of God. If they repent of their wrongs, God will extend forgiveness and mercy to them as willingly as God does to you when you violate the Divine Laws. Consider, too, that, in many instances, you may be more reprehensible and guiltier than those you consider undeserving of your forgiveness or sympathy. They may not know God as you do and so less will be expected of them than of you.

Friends, never make an absolute judgment. The condemnation you pronounce against someone today may be applied to you no less severely in the future. Rest assured that you too will need all the leniency you can get for your own mistakes, which pile up almost daily. Do you realize that many actions, which are wrongs in the eyes of the Pure One, are not considered even minor offenses in the world?

True love for others doesn't consist in simply making monetary contributions to the needy, giving handouts, or even offering comforting words along with your gifts. God expects much more from you. Sublime love, as Jesus taught it, also consists in constant generosity regarding all things pertaining to your neighbor. Your love should even embrace those who solely believe in giving alms. When true love blossoms in their lives, how beautiful will be the words of love, faith, and courage they will help raise to the Lord.

The time is near, we repeat, when true brotherhood will reign on earth—a time in which the teachings of Christ will guide human relations. These laws will both set limits of behavior and nurture hope; eventually, they'll lead all souls to the blissful realms. Love one another, then, as children of the one God. Do not discriminate against the less fortunate, and never despise anyone, because you are all equal before the Loving Father. As for hideous criminals, their presence among you is allowed in order to serve as learning experiences. In the future—when humanity turns to the Divine Laws for guidance—such experiences will no longer be needed, and all corrupt and violent souls will be steered to other realms which better correspond with their tendencies.

Nevertheless, it is your duty to help individuals of this kind with your prayers; that is true love. It isn't your place to say of a criminal, "He is despicable and ought to be wiped off the face of the earth. The death penalty is much too good for the likes of him." This is hardly the way to talk!

Consider the model we all should be striving to imitate—Jesus. What would He have said if He found one of these unfortunate people beside Him? Wouldn't Jesus take pity on him, look at him as a sick, miserable soul and extend a helping hand to him? Now, you may not be able to do the same thing—yet. But at least you can pray for him and help uplift his spirit during the time he has left on earth. If you pray with earnestness, you may perhaps touch him and call him to repent. He is your "neighbor" every bit as much as the more honorable and righteous persons in your society. His soul may have strayed and become rebellious, but his soul was created for the same reason as your own—to be perfected. Help him, then, to get out of the fix he has fallen into and pray for him. ■ —Elizabeth of France (Havre, 1862).

15. ■ Someone's life is in danger. In order to save that person, we must risk our lives. However, the endangered person is a criminal who, on escaping from this situation, may well commit other crimes. Despite these facts, should we still risk our own lives to save the criminal's?

This is a very serious question that arises naturally in the mind. I'll address it from the standpoint of my present understanding.

Should you risk your life for a criminal?

Devotion is blind. Just as you are expected to rescue an enemy soldier, you should also rescue an enemy of society—that is to say, a criminal. Do you suppose that, in such a case, it's only from death that you hurry to save these hapless persons? You may well be rescuing them from their errors of the past!

Imagine that in those fleeting moments on the brink of existence, the criminal is able to review his past, or rather, his past plays itself out before his eyes. Perhaps if his death occurred now, it would come prematurely, and his next life would be many times more painful. Quickly, then, rush to offer help! Spiritists should be the first to give help in this situation, the first to snatch the person from this terrible end. Then, instead of someone who might have died full of hatred, he may live on in order to learn thankfulness. In any event, don't stop to wonder what he will or won't do—just save him. By this act you are honoring the voice of your heart which tells you: "You can save him, therefore do save him!" ■ —Lamennais (Paris, 1862).

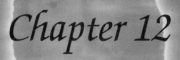

Chapter 12

Love Your Enemies

SCRIPTURES AND COMMENTARY

RETURN GOODNESS FOR EVIL

1.   *"You have heard that it was said, 'Love your neighbor and hate your enemy.' But I tell you: Love your enemies and pray for those who persecute you, that you may be sons of your Father in heaven. He causes his sun to rise on the evil and the good, and sends rain on the righteous and the unrighteous. If you love those who love you, what reward will you get? Are not even the tax collectors doing that? And if you greet only your brothers, what are you doing more than others? Do not even pagans do that?"*

(Matthew, 5: 43-47)

   "For I tell you that unless your righteousness surpasses that of the Pharisees and the teachers of the law, you will certainly not enter the kingdom of heaven."

(Matthew, 5: 20)

2.   *"If you love those who love you, what credit is that to you? Even 'sinners' love those who love them. And if you do good to those who are good to you, what credit is that to you? Even 'sinners' do that. And if you lend to those from whom you expect repayment, what credit is that to you? Even 'sinners' lend to 'sinners,' expecting to be repaid in full. But love your enemies, do good to them, and lend to them without expecting to get anything back. Then your reward will be great, and you will be sons of the Most High, because he is kind to the ungrateful and wicked. Be merciful, just as your Father is merciful."*

(Luke, 6: 32-36)

3.   If the first principle of the law of love is to love our neighbors, then to love our enemies is that principle's highest application, because it represents the greatest victory over our self-centeredness and pride.

   Usually, however, there's a misunderstanding about the meaning of the word "love" in this context. Jesus didn't mean that we should have the same fondness for an enemy as we have for a brother, sister, or friend. Affection assumes trust, and you can't place confidence in someone who's hostile to you. Nor can you show open friendship to a person who'll most likely abuse it. People lacking confidence in each other simply aren't going to share affection in the same way as those with compatible ideas. No one takes the same pleasure in the company of an enemy as in the company of a friend. Such a feeling (or its absence) is the result of a physical law—the blending of similar energies and the repulsion of opposing ones.

A malicious thought sets up a vibrating current that produces an unpleasant impression. A good thought, by contrast, surrounds the receiver with a very agreeable energy. This is the reason we experience such different sensations when we're near a friend as opposed to an enemy. To love our enemy, then, can't mean that we should feel the same liking for both friends and enemies. This false idea—that we should consider the two equally in our affections—would make Jesus' precept difficult, if not impossible, to put into practice. Actually, the problem is due to the limitations of human language, which sometimes requires us to use a single word to express different degrees of the same feeling. Thus, it is necessary to use reason and common sense to establish and interpret the meaning according to the context.

Loving one's enemies doesn't mean showing an unnatural affection—meeting an enemy makes our heart beat in an entirely different way from the way it beats on meeting a friend. What the phrase does mean is that we shouldn't hate, bear rancor toward, or desire revenge against, an enemy. It means that we forgive, sincerely and without conditions, the evil they've done us. It means that we don't place obstacles in the way of a reconciliation. Instead of wishing for something bad to happen to them, we genuinely wish them well. Loving one's enemies is to feel gladness, instead of regret, when good things come their way. It is to help them when they are in need and refrain from words or acts that might harm them. Finally, it is to return good for evil without the intention of humiliating the enemy. Anyone who can conduct him- or herself in this way fulfills the conditions of the commandment "Love your enemies."

4. To unbelievers—people who think the present life is all there is—loving your enemy is contrary to common sense. To them, an enemy is a nuisance, a disturber of their peace of mind from whom they can be freed, they think, only by the enemy's death.

From this, the desire for revenge arises easily. Such people aren't interested in forgiving, unless it's to show off in the eyes of the world. In some cases they even consider the act of forgiveness to be a sign of weakness unworthy of them. And if they don't succeed in getting revenge, they'll continue to hold grudges and harbor secret desires to hurt the other person.

To believers—and, above all, to Spiritists—the situation appears very different because their vision extends beyond the past and into the future, between which the present life is no more than a point in time. They know that this is a planet of trials and that meeting wrongdoing and wicked people is to be expected. They know the wrong they encounter constitutes a test they must endure. From this elevated perspective, reverses in life are easier to accept and less bitter—whether they originate with other people or from material concerns. As they learn not to complain about their trials, they are equally expected not to complain about those who become instruments of their sorrows. Instead of bemoaning, they thank God for being put to the test and for providing the opportunity to prove their patience and fortitude. This attitude will naturally help them be more forgiving. They also realize that the more generous in their forgiving they are, the more they will grow as human beings in their own eyes, effectively putting themselves beyond reach of their enemies' darts.

On earth, people of high status tend not to be offended by the remarks of those beneath them. In the moral province, the same holds true of people who've risen above the materialism of many of their brothers and sisters. They realize that hatred and bitterness will only degrade and lower them. They know, too, that in order to stand taller than their adversaries, their souls must, by comparison, be able to love more intensely, be nobler and more generous.

INVISIBLE ENEMIES

5. Spiritists have still other reasons for being tolerant of their enemies. First, they know that wrongdoing isn't a permanent characteristic of the human condition but arises from a state of imperfection, and that one day wrongdoers will realize their mistakes and turn toward the good—much like children who, growing toward adulthood, learn to steer themselves in the right direction.

Spiritists also know that the death of an enemy is a liberation only from the enemy's physical presence. An enemy can conceivably act on hatred even from the spirit realm. Thus, from the spirit realm, a vengeful individual may continue to pursue a victim and go as far as tormenting her during a new incarnation. Through long observation of personal cases and the study of the principles that govern the interaction between the two realms, the Spiritist Doctrine shows how radically wrong the expression "drown hate in blood" really is. Blood only feeds hate. What the Doctrine offers instead is a positive reason, and a practical motivation, for extending forgiveness to others and for following Christ's commandment, "Love your enemies." For there is no heart so hardened that genuine goodness doesn't touch it, even if imperceptibly in some cases. At the very least, acts of generosity dissuade vindictiveness, and may even turn an enemy into a friend, here or in the hereafter. On the other hand, aggression only inflames an enemy, whose actions then become the conduit through which Divine Justice works to correct the unforgiving heart.

6. It follows, then, that a person's enemies may be found both among people on earth and among souls in the hereafter. One way enemies in the invisible world reveal themselves, and their hostility to us, is through so-called spiritual oppression and possession. Nevertheless, like other life challenges, these situations can actually help us in our spiritual progress if we face them with courage and fortitude. Spiritual oppressions and possessions result from the unevolved nature of our planet. If there were no wicked people on earth, there wouldn't be inferior spirits on it either. Consequently, if we are to be generous and tolerant to our earthly adversaries, we should be no less so to those in the spirit realm.

    In ancient times, live human sacrifices were offered to appease rancorous gods. These gods were, in fact, no more than unevolved spirits who, in later times, reappeared as devils in other belief systems. The Spiritist Doctrine shows us that such devils were merely the souls of base individuals who still clung to their earthly passions. Such souls can only be appeased by the sacrifice of our hatred, and by our offering of love. Love will not only put an end to their vicious practices, but it will also put them back on the right path—in itself a practical contribution to their spiritual progress. The precept, Love your enemies, then, isn't limited to the earthly environment and the present life; rather, it is an article of form in the universal code of solidarity and brotherhood.

IF SOMEONE STRIKES YOU ON THE RIGHT CHEEK, TURN TO HIM THE OTHER ALSO

7.   *"You have heard that it was said, 'Eye for eye, and tooth for tooth.'*

But I tell you, Do not resist an evil person. If someone strikes you on the right cheek, turn to him the other also. And if someone wants to sue you and take your tunic, let him have your cloak as well. If someone forces you to go one mile, go with him two miles. Give to the one who asks you, and do not turn away from the one who wants to borrow from you."

(Matthew, 5: 38-42)

8. What the world mistakenly calls "a point of honor" breeds a kind of tense sensitivity that has roots in pride and an inflated sense of self. This sensitivity very often leads an individual to return one injury or offense for another. For such people, whose moral sense still can't rise above their earthly passions, these revengeful acts are what justice is about. It was for this reason that the Mosaic law decreed that there should be an "eye for an eye" and a "tooth for a tooth"—a decree in keeping with the level of consciousness in Moses' era. When Christ came, however, He taught us to return good for evil. And He said more: "Offer no resistance to the wicked," and He added, "If someone strikes you on the right cheek, turn to him the other also." This teaching impresses the proud as cowardly; they simply fail to understand that it takes more courage to rise above an insult than it does to get revenge for it. The vision of such persons goes no further than the present.

Should we, then, take Jesus' precept about turning the other cheek literally? The answer is no—no more than we take literally the precept that tells us to gouge and throw away one of our eyes when it is a cause of sin.[1] Following His teaching to the letter, in this case, would mean the end of all restraints, including legal ones; it would leave the field open for wrongdoers, who would have nothing to fear from their actions. Furthermore, if nothing was done to restrain the wrongdoers' aggressions, good people would soon become no more than their victims. But the instinct of self-preservation prevents us from offering ourselves up for assassination. Jesus' precept doesn't mean that self-defense is forbidden; rather, it condemns vengeance. In saying that we should offer the other cheek, Jesus is merely telling us in another way that we mustn't repay evil with evil and that we are to accept with calmness the situations that help subdue our pride. There is greater merit in receiving an offense than in giving it, in enduring an injustice patiently than in inflicting it, in being deceived than in being a deceiver, in being ruined than in causing ruin. This precept also includes the condemnation of all fighting and confrontations, which are nothing more than veiled expressions of pride.

---

[1] *Translator's Note: Matthew 18:9.*

Only faith in the future life and the Justice of God, Who never lets wrongdoing pass without correction, will give us the strength to bear up patiently under blows to our interests and our self-respect. This is why we constantly repeat how important it is to consider the future. The more we can raise our thoughts above this material life, the less we will be hurt by the things of this world.

SPIRIT TEACHINGS

REVENGE

9.   ■ Revenge is one of the last of the old, barbaric tendencies the human race has to discard in its upward progress. It is, like the duel, a reminder of the uncivilized habits that marked humanity at the beginning of the Christian era. The spirit of revenge is a sure sign of an unevolved state, both in those who harbor it and those who (from the spirit realm) inspire it. Friends, revenge should never find a resonance in the heart of anyone who proclaims him- or herself a Spiritist. You are well aware that to avenge yourself goes entirely against Christ's precept "Forgive your enemies," and that the person who refuses to forgive is not only no Spiritist, but no Christian. In addition, revenge is so harmful a feeling that it often goes hand in hand with falsehood and baseness. The person blinded by a desire for vengeance rarely acts in the open. When he has the upper hand, he'll savage the person whose mere sight stirs up his anger and hate. More often than not, however, he clothes himself in hypocrisy, hiding the intentions he harbors in the heart. He carries out his plans in roundabout ways, secretly watches the unsuspecting enemy, and goes about laying his harmful snares. When the moment is right, he will, so to speak, put the poison in the cup.

Where hatred of the vengeful person doesn't quite go so far, he'll target his victim's honor and relationships. Without hesitating, he'll use slander and false allegations in his attacks, and watch them gain momentum as they move along the social grapevine. Thus, when his victim goes to a place where his slander has been whispered, she's shocked to see cold faces where before she was received with friendship and warmth. She'll be even more surprised when, instead of stretching out their hands, people now refuse to shake her hand. The final blow comes when she discovers that even best friends and relatives start avoiding her. Cowards who take their revenge in this way are a hundred times guiltier than the ones that insult their enemies face to face.

Do away, then, with all these primitive tendencies; they're the practices of a bygone era. Today, those claiming the right to seek revenge aren't worthy of taking part in the vanguard of spirits who hold as their motto, "Without love there is no salvation!" It's hard to imagine a member of this great Spiritist family who would dare, in the future, to give in to the impulse of revenge rather than forgiveness. ■ —Jules Olivier (Paris, 1862).

HATE

10. ■ Love one another and you will be happy. Above everything else, consider carefully the need to love people who inspire indifference, hatred, and contempt in you. Christ, Who is your model, gave a perfect example of this kind of devotion to others. Missionary of love that He was, He loved so much that He gave His very blood and life for love. Of course, to love people who insult and abuse you is a painful sacrifice, but it's precisely this sacrifice that raises you above them. If you were to hate them as they hate you, you wouldn't be any worthier than they. Yet loving them is the Immaculate Host, wrapped in sweet fragrances, that you offer up to God on the altar of your hearts. Even though the law of Love requires that each of you love all your brothers and sisters without distinction, it doesn't shield your heart from their wickedness. This is the most anguishing of trials—one which I know all too well, having experienced it during my last journey on earth. But the All-Knowing Father is always aware and will correct everyone who ignores the law of love. Dear children, don't forget that love draws you nearer to God while hate drives you away from the Divine. ■ —Fénelon (Bordeaux, 1861).

DUELING[2]

11. ■ Think of outstanding individuals as those who consider life merely as a journey that leads to a determined goal. They don't allow themselves to be distracted from the objective, and attach little importance to the briars and thorns that hurt along the way. They realize that taking a detour to avenge an offense is to retreat from the battles of life. It is to waste precious time from duties. Before God, seeking revenge is always a crime. It would be a

---

[2] *Translator's Note: Duel: a private fight between two persons, using deadly weapons. Duels did not occur in the ancient world. Modern duels arose in the*

Footnote continued on next page

crime and ridiculous nonsense among you, too, if your under-standing wasn't so distorted by misconceptions and prejudices.

As your own laws recognize, to kill someone by dueling is a crime. Under no circumstances does someone have the right to make an attempt on another person's life. Beyond earthly law, it is a crime by the standards of Divine Justice. In this case more than any other, you act as a judge for your own cause. Remember, you will be forgiven only to the extent that you forgive others. Through forgiveness you draw closer to the Divine, and merci-fulness goes hand in hand with inner strength. But as long as even one drop of human blood is shed by another human being, the true kingdom of God—the time when peace and love will for-ever banish hatred, dissension, and wars—will fail to take root on this planet. When it finally does happen, the word duel (and by extension, all violent confrontations) will exist in your lan-guage only as a vague and distant reminder of a past that is long gone. Then no rivalry will exist among human beings—except, that is, for the noble desire of serving more and giving more. ■
—Adolf, Bishop of Argel (Marmande, 1861).

12. ■ In some cases, dueling in its traditional form is undoubtedly a proof of physical courage, of a certain disdain for life. But in the end, as with suicide, it's always a sign of moral frailty. The sui-cide doesn't have the courage to face life's difficulties; the duelist can't swallow a personal insult. Yet Christ has said, concerning this matter of settling scores, that there is more honor and value in presenting your left cheek to someone who has hit you on the right. In Gethsemane, remember, He said to Peter, "Put your sword back in its place, for all who draw the sword will die by the sword."[3] Isn't this, to extend the logic, a condemnation of the act of dueling? In fact, children, what kind of courage comes from a violent nature, from a choleric and raging temper, that leads a person to shout and yell at the slightest offense? Very lit-tle worth can exist in someone who thinks that only blood can

---

Footnote continued from previous page

Teutonic countries, in the Middle Ages, when legal, judicial combat was used to decide controversies, such as guilt for crimes and ownership of disputed land. Dueling was extremely popular in France, England, Germany, and in the U.S. Dueling eventually became socially and legally unacceptable and has disappeared with the advent of modern society. Nevertheless, the following comments illumi-nate many aspects of our duty to nurture harmonious personal relationships in our daily lives.

[3] *Translator's Note: Matthew 26:52.*

make up for even a small insult. Such a person should tremble. His conscience, in a voice welling up from the depths of his heart, will persist in saying, "Cain! Cain! What have you done to your brother?"[4] He'll answer that he had to spill blood in order to save his honor. And his conscience will reply, "You only thought about saving your honor before society for the rest of your earthly life. You never once thought to save it before God."

Unfortunate fool! How much blood should Christ demand to make up for the abuse He suffered? He was violated by a crown of thorns and the lances of soldiers, nailed to die on a cross (reserved for the lowliest criminals), and made to undergo mockery and derision throughout His final agony. And yet has He demanded any reparation for these offenses and for many others? No. The Lamb's last cry was a plea to God to have mercy on His tormentors. Be like Him! Forgive and pray for those who offend you.

Friends, remember the precept "Love one another" and practice it. Then you can answer every hateful blow with a smile, every insult hurled at you with forgiveness. No doubt the world will turn on you in these moments and call you cowards. But lift up your heads and show how little afraid you are to wear your crown of thorns, as Christ wore His. Let the world know that you refuse to be an accessory to a murder currently justified by outlandish ideas of honor—ideas that have their origin in pride and self-conceit. When creating human beings, God didn't give them the right of life and death over each other. This was left to Nature alone, for purposes of reconstruction and reorganization. You don't have the right even to take your own lives. Thus the duelist, in coming before God, will—like the suicide—be marked by blood. For both, the Supreme Judge will prescribe long and difficult corrections. Consider, in this context, that this is the same Divine Law that calls to task even those who treat their fellow human beings with spite. Think, then, how much more exacting the correction will be for people who come into the Divine Presence with the blood of their brothers and sisters on their hands! ■ —Saint Augustine (Paris, 1862).

13. ■ The duel, in the Middle Age called "God's Judgment," is one of those barbaric customs still present in society. What if you saw arguments settled by plunging rivals into boiling hot water or making them endure contact with red hot iron, with the winner

---

[4] *Translator's Note: Genesis 4:10.*

being the one who held up better under the test? Wouldn't you consider such customs utterly insane? Yet dueling is far worse than this. For the skilled duelist, well aware of his power, the duel amounts to little more than cold, premeditated murder. For his opponent, virtually sure to be killed because of his inexperience and lack of skill, it's a sort of planned self-murder. Now, we know that sometimes, to avoid legal consequences, opponents entrust the solution to the luck of the draw to decide who will survive. But this is really going back under a different name to the Middle Age's notion of God's Judgment, except, we remind you, that in those times human beings were far less guilty because their understanding was limited. The very use of the phrase "God's Judgment" tells us that theirs was a naive faith, based on the idea that the Justice of God would never let the innocent die. But a duel goes beyond the old tests of God's Judgment. It makes use of deadly force, and very often, it is the offended one who perishes.

We ask, then: When will such baseless conceit, such empty egotism and wild arrogance, be replaced by true Christian love of your fellow human beings and by humbleness—both of which Christ decreed and of which He himself set the greatest example? Only when this happens will you see the grotesque misconceptions that still govern most human behavior disappear. The laws are powerless to curb such conduct. It is not possible to forbid wrongs and legislate goodness. Human behavior will only change when a love for goodness and an aversion for wrongdoing truly take root in the human heart. ■ —A Guardian Spirit (Bordeaux, 1861).

14. ■ "What will people say about me," you often ask, "if I don't respond in kind to a provocation, or if I don't seek reparation for an offense?" While the foolish and closed-minded may criticize you, the sensible person, who is guided by reason and a moral sense, will say that you've acted with true wisdom. Think for a moment. Because of a word—sometimes said unthinkingly, without any intention of insulting you—your pride is hurt. In your anger, you respond harshly and sometimes a fight starts. Before you get to this point, stop and ask yourself if you're behaving like a Christian. Ask, too, what your responsibility will be to society if, in your anger, you end up taking the life of one of its members. Think of your remorse at taking a husband away from a wife, a son away from a mother, a father away from his children, and the means of support away from a family. True, someone who

wrongs you should be held accountable in some way. But it's far more honorable for that person to freely take responsibility and make amends than to settle matters in a confrontation that ultimately exposes the life of the very person who was wronged.

As for the wronged person, it is true that some situations bring great suffering either to yourself or to your loved ones. In such instances, it isn't simply a matter of hurt pride: Your heart is aching, you experience poignant anguish. This is a time, however, when a confrontation is more than unwise. What good will come from exposing your life further to someone who has already shown himself capable of anything? If you were to kill him, would the injuries you suffered cease to afflict you? Spilling blood doesn't change the facts. If the offense had no merit, wouldn't it be better to commit it to the care of time, and if it had any merit, to bury it in silence? After all is said and done, you are left only with the satisfaction of revenge. Unfortunately, it's sorry satisfaction, for it will kindle bitter regrets later. And where is redress when the offended person is the one who loses his life?

When love finally becomes the guiding rule for human behavior, all acts and words will be summed up in this precept: "Do to others what you would have them do to you." When this rule comes into full effect, all causes of discord will disappear and with them physical acts of revenge and wars, the latter being simply duels between nations. ■ —François Xavier (Bordeaux, 1861).

15. ■ Oh men and women of earth, joyous guardians of a treasure, who for an insulting word, or a slight, are willing to risk a life— your own or a foe's—that only belongs to God! We tell you, You are a hundred times guiltier than the thief who is driven by greed and sometimes by desperation, to break into a house intending to rob it and ends up killing someone who tries to stop him. In the case of the burglar, we're usually dealing with an uneducated person whose notions of right and wrong are sometimes ill-formed. But the duelist, as a rule, belongs to the more cultured classes. The thief kills brutally, the duelist kills with method, with refinement, and for this reason society forgives him. But we would add that the duelist is infinitely more guilty than the unfortunate person who gives in to the desire for revenge and takes someone's life in a moment of rage. The duelist doesn't have the heat of the moment as an excuse, because between the moment of insult and the moment of reparation, there has been ample time for reflection. The duelist acts coldly, with premeditation, studying and calculating everything in order to be sure of

killing his opponent. True, he risks his own life, which is what redeems him in the eyes of the public, who only see it as an act of courage and disregard for life. But is there really any courage involved when someone is proven to be more skilled?

The duel is a reminder of uncivilized times when the law was "Might makes right." It will disappear when you come to appreciate better what honor really means, and to the extent that you consolidate your faith in a future life. ■ —Saint Augustine (Bordeaux, 1861).

Comments: As time goes by, dueling becomes more and more rare. At the time of this writing, this unfortunate event may still occur, but the number of duels has declined greatly compared with days gone by. In the old days a man couldn't leave his house without anticipating a quarrel, and so always took the necessary precautions. Carrying a weapon, either openly or concealed, was a custom among people in those days.

The elimination of this practice shows a softening of human customs. It is interesting to follow the progress from periods in which the knight wouldn't set out on his horse without his armor and spear, to later periods when a sword at the waist was worn simply as an ornament. Another indication of the change in customs is that, while duels were once held in the middle of a street before a crowd more than eager to make room for the two combatants to fight, today such confrontations take place in secret. Today, the death of a human being is something that causes emotion in society at large. In the past, no one took notice of it. The Spiritist Doctrine has come to help eliminate these last barbaric vestiges. It will do so by awakening men and women to love and brotherhood.

Chapter 13

Do Not Let Your Left Hand Know What Your Right Hand Is Doing

SCRIPTURES AND COMMENTARY

DOING GOOD WITHOUT SHOWING OFF

1.   *"Be careful not to do your 'acts of righteousness' before men, to be seen by them. If you do, you will have no reward from your Father in heaven.*

"So when you give to the needy, do not announce it with trumpets, as the hypocrites do in the synagogues and on the streets, to be honored by men. I tell you the truth, they have received their reward in full. But when you give to the needy, do not let your left hand know what your right hand is doing, so that your giving may be in secret. Then your Father, who sees what is done in secret, will reward you."

(Matthew, 6: 1-4)

2.   *When he came down from the mountainside, large crowds followed him. A man with leprosy came and knelt before him and said, "Lord, if you are willing, you can make me clean."*

Jesus reached out his hand and touched the man. "I am willing," he said. "Be clean!" Immediately he was cured of his leprosy. Then Jesus said to him, "See that you don't tell anyone. But go, show yourself to the priest and offer the gift Moses commanded, as a testimony to them."

(Matthew, 8: 1-4)

3.   Doing good without making a show of it has considerable merit. The merit is even greater when we give anonymously. Such giving is a mark of greater moral development and demonstrates that in order to see things from a higher level than the average person, we must first detach from the present life and identify ourselves with the future. In other words, we must place ourselves above society's judgment and praise, and seek the

approval of God alone. If we defer to society's opinions, we are demonstrating that we place more faith in it than in Our Maker and value the present life more than the future one—or even that we do not believe in the future life. We may deny this is so, but the proof of our beliefs is in our acts.

Many people give only in the expectation that the receiver will proclaim their generosity from the rooftops. Others publicly give huge sums of money, but wouldn't part with a penny if their philanthropy had to be anonymous. This is why Jesus said, "Those who do good to be honored by men, have already received their reward in full." People who do good as a way of seeking glory on earth have already received their recompense; God owes them nothing. The only thing left for them is correction for their pride.

"Do not let your left hand know what your right hand is doing" is an image that admirably sums up modest giving. But true modesty in giving is not always practiced, and there are many instances in which only an imitation of modesty is shown. Some people, for instance, appear to hide the hand that gives; yet they also take great care to leave a small portion visible, all the time looking around to see if anyone has noticed their attempts to hide their gifts. This is disgraceful, a parody of Christ's precept. But if human society thinks of these recognition-seeking givers with reservations, consider how God must view them. They, too, have already received their reward on earth. We witness their giving; they enjoy great satisfaction from our taking notice of their generosity, and that will be their sole reward.

And what reward will there be for someone who makes his or her gifts a burden to the receiver? These givers demand that those on the receiving end somehow bear witness to their generosity; and they reveal all the sacrifices they had to make on behalf of their protegés. In this case, there isn't even an earthly reward, since this kind of giver forfeits the satisfaction of hearing his or her name blessed. This is the first punishment of pride. Such people will eventually realize that while the gift was of help, the tears it momentarily stopped will, instead of rising to heaven, fall back on the needy's heart as salt on a wound. They will have no merit in giving, because their motivation is uncharitable. The beneficial value of their actions is like that of counterfeit money, which is ultimately worthless.

Doing good without ostentation is meritorious both because it relieves a material need and because it shows compassion. Above all else, it is considerate of the feelings of the person helped, and, when appropriate, is willing to convert alms into work opportunities. It goes to great lengths not to hurt the needy's self-esteem, and to protect human dignity. In contrast, when help is no more than almsgiving, receiving alms may be mortifying to the needy. True charity is nothing like that. It acts in subtle ways; it is even inventive in concealing its actions; it avoids any appearance, no matter how small, of arrogance because it knows not to add mental anguish to the pain already caused by want. True charity can always find kind and loving words that will put those in need at ease in its presence, knowing that lack of compassion only adds pain to material want. Finally, true charity rises to the level of the sublime when the giver finds a way of being indebted to the person being helped. This is what Christ means by the words "Do not let your left hand know what your right hand is doing."

HIDDEN MISFORTUNES

4. When great calamities occur, human charitableness comes to the fore, and we see generous efforts to help repair the damages. But along with these very visible public disasters, there are also millions of private ones that go unnoticed, for many people suffer them in silence. These out-of-the-way and hidden misfortunes are the ones the truly compassionate discover and aid without needing to be asked.

Who is this woman with the distinctive air? She is simply dressed, although well-cared for, and accompanied by a young girl dressed with equal modesty. Together, the two enter a sordid-looking house, and from the respect they are shown as they enter, it is obvious that the lady is well-known here. Where is she going now? Up to the garret. There, surrounded by her young children, rests a mother. On the arrival of the two outsiders, happiness springs to life in the gaunt faces of the children. They know the woman has come to ease their pains. She has brought everything they need, offering her aid with kind and comforting words—thus permitting her charges, who aren't professional beggars in any sense, to accept the gifts without embarrassment. The father of the family is in the hospital at the moment, and the mother has found that she can't provide life's necessities with her work. But, by the grace of this good woman, her children no longer feel cold or hungry. The older ones go to school well clothed; the infants continue to nurse at their mother's breasts, which won't go dry now. If a member of the family becomes ill, she will take care that the person's needs are attended to. Later, she will go from this garret room to the hospital, to take the father small comforts and put his mind at rest about his family.

At the corner of the road a vehicle is waiting. Inside it are all the supplies intended for her various charges, which the distinctive woman visits one after the other. Not once, though, does she ask what their religion is or what their opinions are; she considers them to be her brothers and sisters, children of the same God. Once she finishes her rounds she can honestly say to herself, "My day has started off well." What is her name? Where does she come from? No one knows. To the needy her name is not important; in their eyes she is the very picture of a consoling angel. Each night a host of blessings rise up to the heavens in her name from Catholics, Jews, and Protestants alike.

And why does she wear such modest clothing? Because she doesn't want to insult the misery of the poor with her luxury. Why does she take her daughter? So the daughter too can learn how to practice charity. This young woman wishes to give in the same way as her mother. But, then, her mother says, "What can you give, daughter, when you have nothing of your own? If I give you something of mine to give away, the merit really won't belong to you; it's just me doing the giving in a different guise. What good does that kind of giving do? No, it isn't fitting for you. So, instead, when I visit the sick you will help me treat them. To give care to someone else is to give something of yourself. Don't you think that this is good enough to start with? Nothing, really, could be easier. You can begin by learning to make useful articles and clothes for the children. In this way you can give something of yourself that's real and needed." This is how this truly Christian mother prepares her daughter to practice the virtues Christ taught. Is she a Spiritist? What does it matter?

In her own home, this lady is a woman of the world; her position requires it of her. Her friends don't know anything about her charitable activity; she doesn't want approval from any source other than God and her own conscience. One day, however, something unexpected happens. One of her charges comes to her door, selling handmade goods. The woman recognizes her and wants to praise her as a benefactor. But the lady tells her, "Be silent and tell no one!" Jesus spoke in just this way.

THE WIDOW'S MITE

5.   *Jesus sat down opposite the place where the offerings were put and watched the crowd putting their money into the temple treasury. Many rich*

people threw in large amounts. But a poor widow came and put in two very small copper coins, worth only a fraction of a penny.

Calling his disciples to him, Jesus said, "I tell you the truth, this poor widow has put more into the treasury than all the others. They all gave out of their wealth; but she, out of her poverty, put in everything—all she had to live on."

(Mark, 12: 41-44)

As he looked up, Jesus saw the rich putting their gifts into the temple treasury. He also saw a poor widow put in two very small copper coins. "I tell you the truth," he said, "this poor widow has put in more than all the others. All these people gave their gifts out of their wealth; but she out of her poverty put in all she had to live on."

(Luke, 21: 1-4)

6. Many people deplore the fact that they can't do all the good they would like because of their limited financial resources. If only they were rich, they say, they would put all their funds to good use. The expression of such aims is, no doubt, praiseworthy, and in some cases even sincere. But in many others, these aims aren't devoid of self-interest. For instance, some people, while quite willing to do good for others, would like to begin that practice by doing good for themselves, by giving themselves a few more pleasures or the enjoyment of goods they couldn't formerly afford. After these expenditures, they are very ready to use their left-over wealth to help the poor. However, this desire—possibly subconscious but which they would have to face if they really searched the depths of their hearts—cancels out any merit their announced intentions might have. The truly charitable think of others before thinking of themselves. The truth is, if such people really wanted to reach the sublime in their giving, they would look to their work for the resources necessary to realize their generous impulses; they would use all their strength, intelligence, and other talents. In so doing they would be offering the kind of sacrifice the Eternal One finds most pleasing. Unfortunately, most of us live out our lives concocting ways and means of getting rich as quickly and easily as possible. We run after some foolish daydream, like discovering a buried treasure, or hope for that lucky one-in-a-million chance, or look forward to the possibility of an unexpected inheritance, etc. What can be said, too, about people who expect to find spiritual guides to help in realizing these ends? They don't know or understand the sacred ends of the Spiritist Doctrine, and even less about the mission of the illuminated spirits the Creator permits to communi-

cate with humanity. Consequently, they find themselves braving disappointments of every sort.[1]

People whose intentions truly are without self-interest have to comfort themselves with the realization that it's impossible to do all the good they would like. But they should remember, too, the mite of the poor. When people give while sacrificing their own needs, it weighs more on the divine scales than the gold of the rich; they give in plenty of all they have. Undoubtedly, it would be sublime to help the poverty-stricken on a large scale. But if this is not possible, one has to be willing to do what little can be done. Further, tears can't be dried only with money. The lack of money is no excuse for not reaching out to those in need. Anyone who really wants to help his or her fellow beings will find thousands of ways of doing it. If you look for them they will appear, in one form or another. There isn't anyone in full command of their faculties who can't help someone else—for example, by offering encouragement, by soothing both physical and psychological suffering, or by doing some other useful work. Money may be in short supply. But don't all of us have time, work, and hours of repose to spare that we can use to help others? This, too, is like the giving of the poor, the widow's mite.

TO INVITE THE POOR AND THE CRIPPLED

7.   *Then Jesus said to his host, "When you give a luncheon or dinner, do not invite your friends, your brothers or relatives, or your rich neighbors; if you do, they may invite you back and so you will be repaid. But when you give a banquet, invite the poor, the crippled, the lame, the blind, and you will be blessed. Although they cannot repay you, you will be repaid at the resurrection of the righteous."*

When one of those at the table with him heard this, he said to Jesus, "Blessed is the man who will eat at the feast in the kingdom of God."

(Luke, 14: 12-15)

8.   Jesus tells us that when we prepare a feast we shouldn't invite our friends and relations but the poor and handicapped. Taken literally, these words seem absurd. But if we understand their spiritual meaning, they are sublime. Jesus couldn't have meant for us to invite the beggars from the streets to join us around our tables instead of our friends. His language, you must recall, was almost always figurative because the people of His era couldn't understand delicate shades of thought. Thus, He found that He

---

[1] *See Allan Kardec,* The Medium's Book, *Part II, items 294-95.*

needed to use strong words that would produce images that had impact. Nevertheless, He made the essence of His thought clear in this sentence "…you will be blessed. Although they cannot repay you…." This means that we shouldn't do good because we expect a reward; we should do good for its own sake. In saying "Invite the poor to your banquet…," Jesus was using a striking comparison. By the word "banquet" we should understand that He is talking about participation in the abundance we generally enjoy, not an actual meal.

Yet Jesus' advice can also be employed in a more literal sense. How many of you often invite to dinner people who'll talk well about your hospitality to others and invite you to their dinners? Why can't you also invite over friends and relatives who are less fortunate than yourselves? Don't we all have several of them in our lives? Yet in this way you can extend your kindness without appearing to do so. Remember this: Even without inviting the sightless and the handicapped, you can put Jesus' teachings into practice, i.e., doing good without showing off, and striving to blend it with sincere cordiality.

SPIRIT TEACHINGS

MATERIAL CHARITY AND MORAL CHARITY

9. ■ "Love one another and do to others what you would have them do to you." The fundamental principles of all religions and moral systems are contained in these two precepts. If you obeyed them in this world, you would achieve perfection. I'll go even further: With their practice, there would be no more poverty because all the poor people would be fed and clothed from the abundance of the rich. Nor would poor women be seen dragging pitiful little children along the unlit and grimy streets where I last lived.

Oh you, who are well off today, consider this. Help to the best of your ability everyone who is less fortunate than you. Give, so that the Sustainer will one day reward the good you've done. Give, and on leaving your material body behind, you will be greeted by a host of grateful spirits who will welcome you at the threshold of a happier world. If only you could experience the joy I felt when, on reaching the world beyond, I found waiting the spirits I had been given to serve during my last life!

Love your neighbors as you would love yourself—because you know now that, in rejecting even one unfortunate person, you may be sending away a brother, father, or friends from other times. If this turns out to be the case, imagine how truly terrible you will feel when you recognize that person again on reaching the spirit world.

I want you to understand exactly what moral charity is. It is something that all of you can practice. It costs you nothing, but it is difficult to put into practice. Moral charity consists in being tolerant and understanding toward each other, attitudes that unfortunately are not in excess supply on your unevolved planet yet. Believe me, there is great moral charity in listening, with your mouth shut, when someone perhaps not so well prepared is speaking, or in being deaf to the mocking words of people who are used to deriding others, or in forgiving the scornful smiles of haughty people, who often judge themselves better than they truly are. In fact, in the spiritual life, the real life, persons of this kind may be far below you. Your merit in these situations actually comes not from humbleness but from the understanding with which you excuse the base qualities of others. This is what moral charity is.

Still, this kind of charity doesn't exclude the other. Seek by any means to avoid degrading your fellow human beings. Remember what I have told you: If you rebuff a needy person, you may perhaps be rejecting a soul you once loved, who now temporarily finds itself in a position less fortunate than yours. I have met in the spirit world one of those destitute on earth whom I had the chance to help more than once, and now she is the one whom I seek for help myself.

Jesus said we are all brothers and sisters. Always think of this before rebuffing a beggar or a sick person. So long. Please, think of those who suffer and pray for them. ■ —Sister Rosalie (Paris, 1860).

10. ■ Dear friends, we have heard many of you say, "How can I practice charity when I can scarcely provide the necessities of life for myself?"

Friends, there are thousands of ways of giving. You can do it through thoughts, words, and deeds. Through thought, you can pray for the unfortunate ones who passed on without the light of awareness; a prayer from the heart will comfort them. Through words, you can make a point of always saying a good word to those you see daily. And to those who carry anger and bitterness and curse God for their suffering, you can say, "I was like you once; I also suffered and felt downtrodden, but I discovered the Spiritist Doctrine and now I have peace within." To the old who tell you, "It is useless; I'm now at the end of my journey. I will die as I have lived," you may say, "God shows equal justice to everyone; remember the workers who earned their reward at the last hour." To children who've been corrupted by their environment and prowl about, already prey to the lowest temptations, you may say, "God watches over you, my children." Never get tired of repeating these gentle words to them. One day they'll take root in their minds and, instead of drifting through life as criminals and wastrels, they'll become men and women. This, too, is moral charity.

Some of you will say, "Bosh! There are so many of us here on earth that God can't possibly see each one of us." Listen carefully, friends. When you are on the top of a mountain, don't you see the millions of grains of sand that cover it? This is the way God views you. Like the sand that is allowed to go where the wind blows, God allows you your free will so that you can do as you want. But there is a condition: God has put a vigilant spark in you called conscience. Listen to it because it will give you good advice. Sometimes, sad to say, you manage to numb it. You welcome into your life negative forces, and then conscience goes silent. But you can be certain as soon as you begin to have even a little regret, your rejected conscience will make itself heard. So listen to it, probe it, and you will be amazed by the uplifting guidance you will obtain.

Friends, to every new regiment, the general always offers a banner. To you I offer this precept of Christ as your watchword, "Love one another." Observe this precept, let everyone unite under this flag, and you will find happiness and strength. ■ — A Guardian Spirit (Lyon, 1860).

DOING GOOD

11. ■ The act of doing good in this world, friends, will give you the purest and sweetest delights. It will gladden your heart, which will not be disturbed either by regret or indifference. If only you could understand something of the grandeur and gentleness that mark the generosity of beautiful souls intent on doing good! Theirs is a feeling that causes them to look at the person in need as their equal, and makes them willing even to offer their own clothes if necessary to help a fellow human being. If only you could have as your single occupation making other people

happy! No worldly pleasure can ever compare to the joy of serving as an instrument of God in bringing aid and hope to families that have known only bitterness and want. It cannot compare to witnessing a downcast face suddenly glow with hope because there is now bread on the table and because a tearful child, still too young to understand the harshness of life, will no longer cry, saying "I'm hungry!" These words no longer tear into parental hearts like daggers. Oh! If you could only imagine how delightful it can be to see happiness spring back where there was nothing but desperation just a while ago. Be aware of your responsibility toward your fellow human beings. Go face the material misfortunes, but battle also the hidden miseries of the soul that are the most painful of all. Dearly beloved brethren, go, remembering these words of our Savior: "Whatever you did for one of the least of these brothers of mine, you did for me."[2]

Compassionate love, charity: mighty words that sum up all the virtues. You have the task of leading the peoples of earth toward happiness. When they embrace you they will start preparing for themselves a future of joy, and you will become their solace during their journey on earth. Through you they will enjoy a foretaste of the joys reserved for them in the heart of God. Love—celestial virtue—you gave me the only true moments of joy during my earthly journey. Beloved friends, sojourners on earth, I hope that my words reach your souls, and that you trust this advice: "It is in love for others alone that you will find peace of heart, contentment for the soul, and the balm for life's sorrows." Remember that, whenever you're on the point of blaming God, you must cast your eyes around and make an effort to see all the miseries waiting to be relieved—the children without families, the old who don't have a friendly hand to clasp when death visits. There is so much good waiting to be done! Beloved, don't complain. On the contrary, give thanks to God, and lavish compassion, understanding, and aid on anyone who suffers alone. You will reap sweet rewards on earth, and later. Only God can fully describe the blissfulness that awaits you beyond this life! ∎
—Adolf, Bishop of Argel (Bordeaux, 1861).

12. ∎ Be kind and compassionate, for this is the key to heaven. Remember that unfailing bliss hinges on this precept: "Love one another." The soul can't rise to a higher spiritual realm except through dedication to other human beings. And it will never attain inner peace and happiness except through the practice of

---

[2] *Translator's Note: Matthew 25:40.*

true charity. Be kind and supportive; root out the scourge known as selfishness. As you do it, you'll see new pathways to lasting happiness open before you. Besides, which of you hasn't felt your heart beat faster, and a rush of warm emotions, on account of an act of extraordinary devotion or of some truly generous work? If only you would acquire the taste for the pleasure that stems from a good deed, you would always stay on the route of spiritual progress. Good examples aren't lacking; what is rare is people willing to follow them. Your own history is rich in memories of such great men and women.

Didn't Jesus tell you everything concerning the virtues of love and compassion? Why set aside His teaching, then? Why close your ears to His sublime words, and your hearts to His inspiring lessons? I very much hope that you accept with greater faith and trust His message in the Gospel. Unfortunately, many of you have chosen to disregard this book and consider it to be obsolete, or simply a compilation of hollow words. And for this reason, you've relegated this admirable code to the dust. Many of your present-day ills come from your conscious rejection of this great summary of the Divine Laws. Please, go back to those scintillating pages that tell of Jesus' devotion and meditate on them.

If you are strong, prepare yourselves for the work that lies ahead. If your condition is feeble, let your kindness and faith be your best weapons. Become more enthusiastic and more constant in spreading this new doctrine. The loving Father allows us, the spirits, to communicate with you only as a way of stimulating your resolve and your virtue. And if you truly want to fulfill your highest purposes, God's help and your own free will will be enough for every need, for, to tell the truth, spiritual communication is intended only for those of you whose eyes are closed and who have unruly hearts.

Love is the fundamental virtue. All earthly virtues are based on it, and lacking it, none of the others can exist. Without love, there is no hope for a better fate and no interest in a moral plan of life. Without love, faith is null, since faith is the radiant power that makes a loving soul brilliant. On every sphere of life, love is the anchor of salvation, the purest emanation of life, God's own essence shared with His children. How is it that so often we fail to recognize this gift? What heart, having known this divine emotion, would still be so hardened so as to reject and drive it away? Where is the soul, spark of the Almighty, so dull of sentiments that it rejects the sweet caress that is love?

Personally, I can't presume to speak of my own efforts on earth, because spirits have their modesty, too. But I genuinely believe the work I began during my incarnate life is the kind that will most contribute to easing the burden of the less fortunate. I frequently see spirits who, having asked, are given the work of continuing my task as their mission in life. I see them, these generous and beloved sisters,[3] committed to their divine ministry. I see them practicing the virtues I recommended with the kind of joy that can only come from dedication and sacrifice. It is my great good fortune to see how their condition is honored, how they are protected and esteemed in the mission they perform. Like them, unite yourselves—you women and men of character—so that you can continue to spread works of love. You will find your reward in the very exercise of this virtue. Through it, you will experience the joys of heaven even in the present life. So be united, and love one another as Jesus recommended. So be it! ■ —Saint Vincent de Paul (Paris, 1858).

13. ■ I am the virtue you call Charity, I am the main path that leads to God. Come along with me. I am the virtue toward which everyone should be striving.

This morning I went on my usual rounds; now I come to you sad at heart and say: Friends! How many sorrows and tears there are—and how much has to be done to dry those tears. In vain, this morning, I tried to console the poor mothers, whispering in their ears, "Courage! There are good souls watching over you. Have patience—you won't be abandoned. God lives, and loves you. You are among His chosen ones." They seemed to hear me and turned their startled eyes in my direction. But I could read in the appearance of their bodies—those tyrants of the spirit—that they were hungry. And so even if my words brought a little serenity to their hearts, they couldn't ease the gnawing in their stomachs. I repeated, "Courage! Courage!" Then one poor mother, still very young, held her infant up with outstretched arms, as if asking me for protection for her child, who couldn't find enough nourishment in her milk-dry breasts.

Elsewhere I saw destitute old people, unable to work, without shelter, and prey to every kind of suffering and hardship. They were ashamed of their misery, had never begged, and so lacked the courage to ask for pity from others. My heart burst with compassion, and I, who could give nothing, became a beggar of sorts,

---

[3] *Translator's Note: Reference to the sisters of the order Daughters of Charity.*

seeking help for them, going from place to place in order to stimulate positive action and inspire good thoughts in generous and compassionate hearts. This is what I have come here to tell you. Out there are people living in poverty. They have no bread, their stoves have no heat, their beds are without blankets. I won't tell you what you should do; I leave the initiative to your own kindly hearts. If I were to tell you how to act, you would have no merit. I say only that I am Charity and I point my hands toward your suffering brothers and sisters.

But if I ask of you, I also give and give generously. I invite you to a great banquet where I will unveil a bountiful tree that will keep you nourished and sheltered. You will see how heavy it is with flowers and fruit. Gather all the fruits of this magnificent tree, which is called Good-Doing, and in place of the leaves and fruit you have taken away, I will fasten to it all the good deeds you've practiced. And I will take this tree to God, Who will make it full again, for the tree of Good-Doing knows no limits. Come along with me, friends, and let me count you among the followers of my banner! Don't be afraid. I will show you the path of redemption, for I am the virtue you call charity. ■ —Carita, martyred in Rome (Lyon, 1861).[4]

14. ■ There are various ways of being charitable that go far beyond giving handouts. There is indeed a considerable difference between handouts and true charitableness. Handouts are useful sometimes because they give immediate help to the poor. Yet this kind of giving may be humiliating and awkward, both to giver and receiver. By contrast, true charitableness connects giver and receiver at a different level, and giving is disguised in ways that protect the receiver's esteem. It's possible, too, to be charitable even to friends and relations, simply by being tolerant of them, forgiving their failings, and taking care not to hurt their self-respect. You, Spiritists, can also be charitable in the way you behave toward people who think differently from you, and by the way you inform them about our ideas without offending them or attacking their convictions. In addition, you can invite them lovingly to your meetings, where they can better inform their opinion and where we can touch their hearts. All this is just one aspect of charity.

---

[4] *Translator's Note: Carita should be understood as a personification, as an individual who stands forth, not in her own person, but rather in the guise of Charity, and who does this in order to express the essence of charity.*

But be mindful, too, of the material wants of the needy, the dis-inherited of this world. They will be victorious in the eyes of the Eternal One if they undergo their suffering without complaint, and that may depend on you. You will understand what I mean by the following example.

We've had the opportunity of observing, several times each week, a meeting of women of all ages. We see them almost as sisters. What do they do? They are working—quickly, very quickly, their fingers being nimble and skilled. We see a glow on their faces and note how their hearts all beat as one. But what is all this effort for, you ask? Winter is near, and winter can be very hard on the poor. During the year, the poor are not able to set aside all they need for the coming cold, and many have already pawned most of their belongings. Now the needy mothers are anxious and often cry when they think about their children, who'll go cold and hungry during the long season ahead. But God has inspired women of more means, who have joined together—to make clothes for the needy little ones!

As the snow arrives, covering everything in its way, you'll probably feel tempted to say—as many people do when they suffer—that God is not fair. But, look, a person sent by those generous women, true servants of the poor, comes to your door with their gifts. Yes, it is for you that they were working, and their compassion now will turn your grumblings into words of praise. Indeed, in the hearts of those who suffer much, love follows close behind anger.

As they sew clothes, I notice the waves of encouragement they receive from evolved spirits everywhere. The menfolk of the group to which these generous women belong also take part in their endeavor, helping to ease the work by readings, which are pleasant to all. As a reward for everyone's enthusiasm, and each individual in particular, we spirits promise to bring these hard-working laborers good clients, who will pay in the form of blessings—which is the only currency acceptable in heaven. We also assure them, without fear of error, that this currency will never be lacking for any one of them. ■ —Carita (Lyon, 1861).

15. ■ Dear friends, every day I hear some of you say, "I'm broke, I can't afford giving charity." And yet each day I also see how intolerant you are toward each other. You forgive nothing; you set yourselves up as severe judges, not considering if you would like to be treated the same way. But isn't tolerance a form of charity? If this is the kind of charity you can afford—so be it, but be

generous in its exercise. And as for charity in its material aspect, we would like to tell you a story from the spirit world.

Two men had just died, and God was heard to say that while these men had been alive, all their good deeds had been placed in two separate sacks, which would be weighed on their death. When the men passed over, God sent word for them to bring their sacks. One sack, God found, was crammed full—bulky and resounding with all the precious metal it contained. The other was so small and thin you could see the few coins it contained showing through the cloth. Each man recognized his own sack: "This is mine," said the first one, "I recognize it; I was rich and gave away a great deal." The other man said, "This one is mine. I always lived with scant means and, alas, had very little to give." But what a surprise the men had when their sacks were put on the scales, because the bulky one became light in weight and the small one showed itself to be heavy—so much so that it lifted the first sack high in the air.

Then God spoke to the rich man: "It is true that you gave much. But you did it simply to display your wealth and see your name in a prominent place in the temples of pride. In giving, you never actually deprived yourself of anything. Go to the left and be satisfied that the handouts you gave count for something, however small." Next God spoke to the poor man: "You gave very little, but each one of your coins, now on these scales, represents a sacrifice for you. Even if you didn't give much materially, you were charitable in the true sense of the word; and the best thing is that you gave of yourself naturally, without thinking about whether your deeds would be put into your merit account. You were invariably tolerant and never critical of colleagues; on the contrary, you showed understanding for their actions. Go to the right and you'll receive your reward." ■ —A Guardian Spirit (Lyon, 1861).

16. ■ The woman of means who has no need to work could easily spend a few hours a day helping her fellow human beings. Using some extra money, she could buy clothes for the poor, who shiver from cold. With her delicate hands, she could make warm clothing or help a mother-to-be clothe her newborn child. Her own children may have to do without some frills and fancies, but at least a poor child will have something to keep it warm. By helping the needy, this woman labors in the vineyard of the Lord.

Even those of you who struggle to make ends meet, who don't have anything in extra supply, can, if you feel love for your brothers and sisters, give from what you have. Give a few hours of your time. If you are skilled with your hands, you could make some of the remarkable handicrafts that always attract the well-off. Sell the product of your extra work, and you will be in a position to provide your share in alleviating a brother's or sister's plight. You might have fewer luxuries, but you'll be providing shoes to the barefoot.

Then there are the women who've dedicated their lives to God. To you, we say: Keep working at your undertakings. Be careful, however, that you don't use your talents simply to decorate chapels or call attention to your abilities and zeal. You should, rather, work in such a way that the product of your work is helpful to your brothers and sisters before God. The poor are God's dearly beloved children, so to work for them is to glorify God. Aid the needy with the same spirit with which God "gives sustenance to the birds in the sky." Trade the gold and silver threads you use to embroider for food and clothes for people who have none. If you do this, your work will be blessed.

As for those of you who are more endowed, give of your talents, your inspirations, your hearts. God will richly bless you. You, poets and writers, who are only read by the worldly, satisfy the leisure of these persons, yes. But also dedicate some of the proceeds of your works to help charitable causes. Likewise, painters, sculptors, and artists of all kinds—use your gift to benefit your fellow beings. Your repute will be no less and you will help to ease suffering.

Everyone can give! Whatever your social standing, you will always find that you have something you can share with another. From whatever God has given you, you owe a part to those who are less fortunate; for certainly, if you were in their place, you would welcome somebody else's kindness. Your earthly wealth may be a little less as a result. But think how much more your heavenly treasure will increase. It is here, in this realm, that you will reap by a hundredfold what you have sown on earth in helping others. ■ — Jean (Bordeaux, 1861).

COMPASSION

17. ■ Compassion is a quality that brings you the company of angels. It is the sister to charity, and together they lead you to God. In the face of the pain and suffering of your fellow human beings, let compassion move your hearts. If you cry for their suf-

fering, your tears are a soothing balm on their wounds. And as you lend them help, what a joy to see hope and confidence returning to them! For certain, this joy is not without a tinge of pain, the pain of seeing a fellow human being in a dire situation. Moreover, the joy of caring may not give the thrills of worldly pleasures, but neither does it cause any of the disappointments that such pleasures leave in their wake. Compassion has a gentle quality that enlivens the soul. Compassion, when heartfelt, pours from love—the kind of love which pours from selfless dedication. That same dedication, which leads to forgetting the self, inspires you to give your all to helping the less fortunate. This concern for the less fortunate is a virtue, one to which Jesus gave witness and which He made the cornerstone of His sublime doctrine. When the pure essence of His doctrine is understood and embraced by everyone, the world will at last become a happy place, and harmony, peace, and love will reign.

Feelings of compassion are the most important element of your spiritual progress because they help subdue your pride and selfishness. They predispose you toward humbleness of heart, goodness, and the love of others. Compassion is the feeling that moves you deeply inside whenever you see the suffering of a fellow human being; it is what persuades you to lend a helping hand, and what brings tears of sympathy to your eyes. Never stifle this emotion in your heart; it is heaven-born. Don't walk on by, like the hard and selfish, who turn away from the afflicted because the sight of their hardship upsets their cheerful lives. Instead, be fearful of remaining indifferent when you could be of help. Inner peace, bought at the price of a guilty indifference, resembles the tranquillity of the Dead Sea: It may be all calm on the surface, but at the bottom lies a vast hidden mass of stagnation and rot.

Compassion is far from causing the disturbance and inconvenience of which selfish people are so afraid. It may be true that, on first coming into contact with others' misfortunes and looking into your own heart, you may experience a profound anguish that vibrates through your whole being, troubling you considerably. But the feeling of reward is immense when you are able to rekindle hope and courage in someone who, in utter despair, yearns for the touch of a loving hand, and more especially, when you see her eyes raised to heaven in tears of thankfulness for the comfort and support received in her hour of need. Yes, compassion is the sad yet celestial forerunner of love, the feeling that prepares the way and gives real meaning to your good deeds. ■
—Michael (Bordeaux, 1862).

ABANDONED CHILDREN

18. ■ Brothers and sisters, you should love all the abandoned children. If you could only know how sad it is to be alone and abandoned, especially at a very young age. These children are an opportunity for you to love them as parents. To protect someone who's been cast aside, to keep children from hunger and cold, to minister to their soul, guiding them straight, is an act of divine love. Indeed, to care for an abandoned child is to please God, since it shows that you understand and practice the Divine Law. Think, too, of the possibility that the child you are helping may once have been someone dear to you in a previous life, and that if you could remember it, you would now see your beneficial act as a duty rather than an act of charitableness.

In this way, every suffering soul is your brother or sister and has a right to your help. This shouldn't, however, be the kind of help that hurts one's self-respect, nor the kind of handout that burns the hand that receives it. Unfortunately, to receive help hurts, and many times persons receiving it would refuse it if their only other options weren't sickness and misery. So when you give, do it with sensitivity; and along with the benefits you offer, give the most precious of all—a kind word, a loving gesture, a friendly smile. Don't be patronizing—it only turns the dagger of suffering in the receiver's heart and causes more bleeding. Consider, too, that by doing good, you're working for your own benefit as well as for those you love. ■ —A Spiritual Friend (Paris, 1860).

GOOD ACTS REWARDED BY THANKLESSNESS

19. ■ What should we think of people who, after seeing their good deeds met with ungratefulness, decide to stop giving altogether for fear of meeting more unappreciative persons?

Such people are much more selfish than charitable. They do good simply to get the recognition that goes along with it. Clearly, they don't act with disinterest—and only when an act of goodness is done with genuine disinterest is it acceptable to God. Such people have much pride and so play the part of good-doers because they enjoy the submissiveness they hear in the receivers' expressions of gratitude. But listen: If you look for your reward on earth for the good you do there, you won't receive it in heaven. God does, however, esteem anyone who acts without the thought of an earthly reward.

You should always help the weak, and do it realizing beforehand that you may not get any thanks for your help. You can be sure, though, that if the person you help forgets, God will credit your good deed even more than if that individual had showed his or her appreciation. If occasionally God allows your goodness to be paid with thanklessness, it's primarily to test your perseverance in the practice of goodness.

In addition, a generous act, although momentarily forgotten, may produce good fruits in the future. It is a seed, at any rate, that will germinate with time. Unfortunately, you usually never see anything but the present, and all too often you focus on yourselves and not on others. But, in time, your acts of kindness will soften the hardest heart. Your gifts may be forgotten on earth, but when the beneficiary soul sheds its earthly garment, the memory of its ungratefulness becomes a sore. The soul will deplore its lack of gratitude and will seek ways of redressing its debt in a future opportunity. In many cases, it will even seek a future life of dedication to its former benefactor. In this way, without even realizing it, you will have contributed to the moral progress of that spirit. And you yourself will come to recognize the truth in the words, "A good deed is never lost." At the same time, you'll also have worked for yourself, since you'll have earned merit for having done good, and done it without self-interest and without having your disposition sapped by disappointments.

Friends, if you knew all the ties that link your present life to your previous ones, and could see at a glance the web of relationships that join everyone together for the purpose of mutual progress, you would admire even more the wisdom and goodness of the Creator Who allows each of us to live many lives so that one day we will be able to come into the presence of the Divine. ■ —A Protecting Guide (Senns, 1862).

20. ■ Is benevolence rightly employed when reserved primarily for persons who have the same opinions, beliefs, or belong to the same group as we do?

No. It is exactly this sectarian notion that has to be eliminated, because all human beings are brothers and sisters. The true Christian sees brothers and sisters in all and doesn't stop to ask about someone's beliefs or opinions before offering help. Would a Christian be obeying the precepts of Jesus Christ, Who told you to love even your enemies, if he or she were to turn away an unfortunate person just because the person held different beliefs? Hardly. Help without inquiring about their beliefs because, if they have other views, this may be just the means that will bring them to appreciate yours. By rejecting them because of their beliefs, you'll cause them to hate religion even more. ■ —Saint Louis (Paris, 1860).

Chapter 14

Honor Your Father and Your Mother

SCRIPTURES AND COMMENTARY

1.   *"Which commandments?" The man inquired.*

     Jesus replied, "Do not murder, do not commit adultery, do not steal, do not give false testimony, honor your father and mother, and 'love your neighbor as yourself.'"

(Mark, 10: 19; Luke, 18: 20; Matthew, 19: 18-19)

2.   *"Honor your father and your mother so that you may live long in the land the Lord your God is giving you."*

(Decalogue, Exodus, 20: 12)

FILIAL DEVOTION

3.   The commandment "Honor your father and your mother" is an application of the universal law of love for our fellow human beings, since an inability to love our mothers and fathers points to a lack of ability to love anyone at all. But where parents are concerned, the word honor contains an additional obligation— filial devotion. The Lord wants to show us that respect, caring, and deference should be joined to love. Together, these qualities require each person to carry out the duties of the love of neighbors in an even stricter sense when our parents are concerned. These duties naturally extend to persons who take the place of a mother or father, and whose merit is much greater since their selfless dedication is less a moral obligation. Serious consequences await those who violate this precept.

    Honoring our mothers and fathers means not only respecting them but also helping them meet their needs, providing for their security and well being in old age, and surrounding them with care—just as they did for us during our childhood. Above all, sincere devotion is demonstrated when our parents have scarce means. Unfortunately, this command of Jesus isn't often well kept, especially when we start congratulating ourselves on the good we're doing while we furnish our parents with only the barest necessities—giving them just enough to keep them from starving, but sacrificing nothing ourselves.

Nor is the commandment well kept when, to save them from homelessness, we give our parents the worst rooms in the house and reserve the best and most comfortable ones for ourselves. In many instances, the parents are lucky when even this much isn't done with ill will or when they are not asked to pay for their room by taking up the day-to-day chores of running their sons' and daughters' households. Should elderly, fragile parents really have to serve their younger and stronger children? Did the mother of these children make them pay for the milk she fed them? Did she tote up the sleepless nights she spent sitting up with them when they were sick? Did she keep a record of the struggles she went through to guarantee they would be taken care of? No. As adult children we owe our parents far more than bare necessities; we owe them, according to our own ability to give, all the extras, as well as thoughtfulness and loving care, which are nothing more than interest on what we ourselves received, and the payment of a sacred debt of gratitude. This is the only expression of filial devotion that pleases God.

Woe to those who neglect the parents who nurtured them in their infancy and who, in giving them physical life, also nurtured their moral identity, and many times incurred great privations to ensure the well-being of their children. Woe indeed to the ungrateful, for he or she will suffer ungratefulness and abandonment as well. They'll be hurt in their most cherished affections (sometimes even in the present life, but certainly in a future one), which will bring on them the same suffering they caused others.

It's true that some parents neglect their duty and aren't everything they should be to their children. But only God is competent to judge these matters, not the children, who may have asked to be born to such parents as a trial. Consider, too, that if the law of love requires that we repay evil with goodness, be tolerant of others' flaws, say nothing bad about our neighbors, forget and forgive our grudges, and love even our enemies, it must demand much more of us in our relationships with our parents. Consequently, in matters having to do with parents, we should take as our guide to conduct all the principles of Jesus concerning other fellow human beings. We should be aware, as well, that the same behavior that is reproachable when directed toward strangers, is far more so when directed toward those who are close to us. And we should remember that an act that might only be a minor offense in the first case, will be considered a serious violation in the second, because it unites the offense of uncharitableness with that of ungratefulness.

4.   According to the Bible, God said, "Honor your father and your mother so that you may live long in the land the Lord your God is giving you." Why was the earthly life promised as a reward and not the heavenly one? The explanation lies in the words "that God is giving you." These were omitted in some versions of the Ten Commandments, and the result has been a distortion in meaning for the entire passage. To understand these words precisely, we must first go back to the situation and the ideas existing among the Jewish people at the time the Ten Commandments were given. The early Jews still couldn't fully understand the concept of a future life; their horizons did not extend beyond the physical. They had to be impressed more by what they saw than by what they couldn't see. So God spoke to them in a language they could easily understand, as one would do with a child, putting the words in a perspective that would satisfy them. At the time, they were still in the desert. The land God planned to give them was the Promised Land, the object of their deepest desires. They wished for nothing more, and God said that they would live there for a long time. That is, they would possess the land for a long time if they kept the Divine commandments.

Now, by Jesus' time, Jewish ideas of the future had advanced considerably. The time had come for them to receive nourishment that was less material, so Jesus began to teach them about spiritual life by saying, "My kingdom is not of this world."[1] With these words, the Promised Land stopped being a material one and was transformed into a spiritual Homeland. This is why, when we are called on to keep the commandment "Honor your father and your mother," it isn't this world that is promised, but a spiritual one.

WHO IS MY MOTHER AND WHO ARE MY BROTHERS?

5.   *While Jesus was still talking to the crowd, his mother and brothers stood outside, wanting to speak to him. Someone told him, "Your mother and brothers are standing outside, wanting to speak to you."*

---

[1] *Translator's Note: John 18:36.*

He replied to him, "Who is my mother, and who are my brothers?" Pointing to his disciples, he said, "Here are my mother and my brothers. For whoever does the will of my Father in heaven is my brother and sister and mother."

(Mark, 3: 31-35; Matthew, 12: 46-50).

6. Some of these words appear quite extraordinary coming from Jesus, seeming to contradict the unchanging goodness and tenderness that were His. Indeed, many an adversary latched on to words such as these to argue that He contradicted Himself. It's undeniable, though, that His doctrine has as its basic principle, as its cornerstone, the laws of charity and love. Is it possible that He would destroy on one side what He had built up on the other? Our answer can only lead us to one conclusion: that if certain propositions attributed to Jesus contradict the fundamental principle of His doctrine, we must understand these words either to have been wrongly recorded, wrongly understood, or never spoken by Him at all.

7. Not surprisingly, people are amazed when reading this passage that Jesus shows so much indifference towards His relatives and, in a way, rejects even His mother.

    Concerning His brothers, we know they didn't much care for Him. They were spirits who had evolved very little and didn't understand His mission. They considered His ways eccentric and His teaching didn't touch them. Not one of His siblings became His disciple. It was said that they shared, at least to some extent, the same mistaken ideas about Jesus as His enemies. It is well known that whenever He was with His siblings He was treated more as a stranger than as a brother. John tells us quite clearly, "For even his own brothers did not believe in him!"[2]

    As for His mother, no one can deny her tenderness for her son. However, it is possible that she may not have fully understood the scope of her son's mission; there are no accounts, for instance, that she was one of His followers or that she testified for Him, as did John the Baptist. Her predominant feature always was her motherly care for Jesus. Still, to suppose that Jesus denied His mother is to misjudge His character. Such a denial couldn't have been seriously made by someone who said, "Honor your father and your mother." We must, then, look elsewhere for the full meaning of His words, which were almost always veiled in allegorical form. It can only be surmised that Jesus, Who never lost

---

[2] *Translator's Note: John 7:5.*

an opportunity to teach, took advantage of the moment and the arrival of His family to show clearly the difference that exists between physical and spiritual kinship.

PHYSICAL AND SPIRITUAL KINSHIP

8. Blood ties don't necessarily create bonds between spirits. The body comes from the body. The spirit, however, doesn't come from the spirit, since the spirit existed before the formation of the body. The parents don't create the spirit of the child. They simply supply its material wrapping—although it's their duty to help with the intellectual and moral development of their child in order to further its progress.

Spirits incarnated in the same family, especially as close relations, are, more often than not, congenial. For the most part, their mutual affection in this life has roots in past existences. But such spirits can also be complete strangers to each other. Or they may act coolly toward each other because of some past dislike that is translated, on earth, into mutual antagonism. And here, the antagonism they feel for each other may become, in itself, a form of corrective trial.

Real family ties have nothing to do with blood. Instead they are ties based on empathy and the affinity of ideas developed before, during, and after their incarnations. As a result, two people born of different parents may be more like brothers or sisters than if they were related by blood. These people will attract each other, seek each other out, and feel happy together. On the other hand, two blood brothers or sisters may reject each other, something we often see. This is a moral issue the Spiritist Doctrine can resolve through the principle of reincarnation.[3]

In a way, there are two basic types of families: those whose members have spiritual ties and those whose members share solely physical ties. In the first case, the ties are long-lasting and strengthen with their progress; they also carry over into the spirit world by way of the diverse journeys of the soul. In the second case, the ties are as fragile as the physical body itself; they die with it and, in many instances, wither even while still in the physical realm. This was what Jesus was trying to make His disciples understand when He said, "Here are my mother and my brothers (by spiritual ties). For whoever does the will of my Father in heaven is my brother and sister and mother."

---

[3] *See also Chapter 4, item 2.*

Mark's narrative clearly reveals the hostility that Jesus' brothers felt toward Him. The same passage also tells us that they intended to take Jesus with them, using as their excuse that He was out of his mind. He was well aware of their feelings against Him, however, and it is understandable that when He heard of their arrival, He took the opportunity to speak in spiritual terms, referring to His disciples as His true brothers and sisters. That His mother came with His brothers in no way implies that Jesus was generalizing here to the point that He identified her as someone who had no meaning to Him spiritually or that she deserved only His indifference. He demonstrated the opposite on many other occasions.

SPIRIT TEACHINGS

CHILDREN'S UNGRATEFULNESS AND FAMILY TIES

9.   ■ Ungratefulness is the fruit of selfishness and a disgusting notion for an honest heart. A child's ingratitude toward its parents is especially sad. It's from this particular perspective that we are going to consider the causes and effects of ungratefulness. Here, as in other situations, the Spiritist Doctrine can shed light on one of the greatest problems of the human heart.

When spirits leave the earthly realm, they take with them their qualities and passions and go on either to actively improve in the spirit world or to remain more or less stationary until choosing to embrace the light again. Among the latter, some return to the spirit world with raging hates and an insatiable desire for revenge. The more conscious among them are able to see a glimpse of the truth and realize the consequences of their hatred. This awareness, in turn, leads spirits to make better resolutions for the future. Gradually, they discover that the path to God requires only one password: love. Spirits also learn that love requires forgiveness of offenses and injury, and that love cannot flourish in hearts where there is hatred. For other spirits, though, animosity reemerges at the mere sight of a person they hated on earth. These spirits rebel against the idea of forgiving, or the notion of any affection for somebody who may have usurped their fortune, destroyed their honor, or their family. They are shaken to the core. Distraught, they waver in a torrent of conflicting feelings. If good prevails, they will beseech God's assistance, and the good spirits will sustain them through their ordeal—meeting an enemy—with their heads held high.

Eventually, after years of reflection and prayer, the spirit decides that it would be beneficial to join the family of those for whom it had so much hatred. It will then beseech Divine Providence for an opportunity to return to the physical realm to pursue its purposes. How will it fare in the new family? This will depend solely on its determination to carry out the good resolutions it made in the spirit world. The constant contact with those it previously hated constitutes a difficult test for the soul, one that many can't bear if their resolve is not strong. Thus, the strength of its resolutions will make it love or hate its next of kin. This, then, is the explanation for the inexplicable aversions and instinctive rejections you often notice among certain children. In actual fact, there is nothing in the present life that could have caused such antipathy; to find its real cause you must reach back into the past.

Spiritists, realize the importance of humankind. You must recognize that when a body is created, the soul that incarnates in it has come from the spirit world with only one purpose: spiritual advancement. Make this clear to yourselves, accept your responsibility, and use all your love to bring this soul nearer to God. This is the mission with which you have been entrusted and for which you will receive a just reward if you fulfill it well. The care and education you give to this child will help in its improvement and future well-being. Remember that God will ask every mother and father, "What have you done with the child who was entrusted to you?" If the child went astray because of something you did or failed to do, your greatest punishment will be to see it suffer among other rebellious spirits, knowing that its future happiness rested at one time in your hands. Then, feeling pangs of guilt, you will ask for a way of redeeming your failings. You will ask for another incarnation for both of you, when you will strive to surround the spirit of that child with the type of loving care that truly enlightens the soul. In the end, it is you who will be surrounded by love, love that emanates from a truly grateful soul.

Don't give up on a child who rejects a parent, or treats a parent with ingratitude. It is not by chance that the child is this way, nor is it an accident that the child is under your care. Such reactions often reveal a dim intuition of the past, from which fact we can conclude that one or the other—the parent or the child—may have hated or harmed the other in the past. In fact, the current life may offer a great opportunity for forgiveness or for redress. Parents, embrace the child who vexes you and say to yourself,

"One of us is guilty!" Make yourselves worthy of the supreme joys of parenting by teaching your children that they are on earth in order to perfect themselves, to love, and to make their lives a blessing to others. Be aware, however, that there are many parents who, instead of educating their children to counter those inborn tendencies carried over from their previous lives, actually encourage these tendencies through their feebleness of character or lack of care. Later on, they will have their hearts torn apart by the ungratefulness of their children, and that in itself will start their purification, even in this life.

Still, parenting isn't a task as hard as it might seem. It doesn't require the wisdom of the world. Everyone, whether uneducated or highly learned, can carry out this duty. The Spiritist Doctrine has come primarily to help by illuminating the causes of the imperfections in the human soul.

The good and bad tendencies a child reveals early on have roots in previous lives. This finding is, of itself, deserving of serious study. Clearly, the root of all bad tendencies can be found in selfishness and pride. So be on the lookout for the least sign that will reveal the existence of these tendencies, and attack them before they take deeper root in the child. Do as the good gardener does: Cut off all the defective shoots as soon as they appear on the tree. If you allow selfishness and pride to develop, you shouldn't be surprised, later on, when you are rewarded by ungratefulness.

Where parents have done everything possible for the moral progress of their children, even if unsuccessfully, they have nothing to reproach themselves for and their consciences can rest easy. For the pain that naturally results from the fruitlessness of their efforts, God has in store a great, an immense, consolation: the assurance that this interlude is really only a short delay. They will be able to finish the work they've already begun in another lifetime, and one day their ungrateful children will reward them with love.[4]

God never gives anyone a challenge greater than the strength of the person who asked for it. Rather, God only allows a soul to undertake a trial that it can complete successfully. If the result is failure, the cause doesn't lie in lack of conditions, but more likely in lack of will power. There are many individuals who, instead of resisting their base inclinations, actually indulge in them.

---

[4] *See also Chapter 13, item 19.*

Unfortunately, these revelers will find that their current behavior will only bring them tears and sorrow in future lives.

But never cease to admire the unbounding goodness of God, Who never bolts the door to repentance. The day will come when the wrongdoer, tired of suffering and with his or her pride finally humbled, will see that God is holding the door open to receive the prodigal child back home. Listen carefully, now, to what I am going to tell you: the most difficult trials almost always indicate the end of the suffering and a certain perfecting of the spirit, as long as you accept them with all your thoughts focused on God. These are, in fact, defining moments that your spirit should take care not to waste through moaning and complaining; otherwise, the fruits of the experience will be lost and you'll have to start all over again. Instead of complaining about your difficulties, thank God for the opportunity to be a real life winner. Then when you leave earth's turbulent environment and enter into the spirit world, you'll be received like a soldier returning in glory from a battle well fought.

The hardest of all trials to endure are the ones that affect the heart. A person who can courageously put up with physical pain and the struggles of making ends meet often gives in under the burden of emotional grief, especially those that arise at home, such as the ungratefulness of family members. This is suffering of a particularly harsh kind. But there is nothing that can strengthen the soul more than the understanding of the causes of such trials. Even where there are wounds of a longstanding nature, you can be sure that they will have an end, because no one is destined to suffer indefinitely. Besides, what can be more comforting, more revitalizing, than the idea that the length of your suffering depends solely on your doing away with the negative qualities within you? But to be able to do this, you can't confine your vision exclusively to this world or to this lifetime. You must lift yourself so that you can see the infinity of both the past and future. When this happens, God's everlasting Justice will become apparent, and you will find the answers to what were once the greatest paradoxes of earthly life. The many wounds you received will seem like simple scratches. When you glance at the whole of life, your family ties will reveal themselves in their true light. You'll no longer see only the fragile blood ties that join various members of a family together, but also the enduring bonds of the spirit—bonds that perpetuate themselves as the spirit progresses, bonds that grow stronger, not weaker, with reincarnation.

In the spirit world, spirits with similar inclinations, similar moral advancement, and with long-cultivated ties of affection often form groupings. These same spirits, when incarnated on earth, tend to gravitate to each other as they did in the spirit realm. That is how strong family ties on earth come to develop. If, in their journey, members of the group are temporarily separated, they will seek each other later on, happy for the new progress they have made. But since they cannot work exclusively for their own benefit, Providence lets less advanced spirits incarnate among them so that these can receive guidance and find role models that will help inspire them on their own path. Sometimes these less evolved spirits may cause great upset for the others. This ends up constituting trials for the latter, and a mission of love to be fulfilled. So receive these less developed spirits as your brothers and sisters; help them and afterwards, in the spirit world, the reunited family will rejoice in having helped redeem one stray soul—who in its turn, may help redeem others in the future. ■ —Saint Augustine (Paris, 1862).

Chapter 15

Without Love There Is No Salvation

SCRIPTURES AND COMMENTARY

WHAT THE SOUL NEEDS IN ORDER TO BE SAVED; THE PARABLE OF THE GOOD SAMARITAN

1.   *"When the Son of Man comes in his glory, and all the angels with him, he will sit on his throne in heavenly glory. All the nations will be gathered before him, and he will separate the people one from another as a shepherd separates the sheep from the goats. He will put the sheep on his right and the goats on his left.*

"Then the King will say to those on his right, 'Come, you who are blessed by my Father; take your inheritance, the kingdom prepared for you since the creation of the world. For I was hungry and you gave me something to eat, I was thirsty and you gave me something to drink, I was a stranger and you invited me in, I needed clothes and you clothed me, I was sick and you looked after me, I was in prison and you came to visit me.'

"Then the righteous will answer him. 'Lord, when did we see you hungry and feed you, or thirsty and give you something to drink? When did we see you a stranger and invite you in, or needing clothes and clothe you? When did we see you sick or in prison and go to visit you?'

"The King will reply, 'I tell you the truth, whatever you did for one of the least of these brothers of mine, you did for me.'

"Then he will say to those on his left, 'Depart from me, you who are cursed, into the eternal fire prepared for the devil and his angels. For I was hungry and you gave me nothing to eat, I was thirsty and you gave me nothing to drink, I was a stranger and you did not invite me in, I needed clothes and you did not clothe me, I was sick and in prison and you did not look after me.'

"They also will answer, 'Lord, when did we see you hungry or thirsty or a stranger or needing clothes or sick or in prison, and did not help you?'

"He will reply, 'I tell you the truth, whatever you did not do for one of the least of these, you did not do for me.'

"Then they will go away to eternal punishment, but the righteous to eternal life."

(Matthew, 25: 31-46)

2.   On one occasion an expert in the law stood up to test Jesus. *"Teacher,"* he asked, *"what must I do to inherit eternal life?"*

"What is written in the Law?" He replied, "How do you read it?"

He answered: "'Love the Lord your God with all your heart and with all your soul and with all your strength and with all your mind'; and, 'Love your neighbor as yourself.'"

"You have answered correctly," Jesus replied. "Do this and you will live."

But he wanted to justify himself, so he asked Jesus, "And who is my neighbor?"

In reply Jesus said: "A man was going down from Jerusalem to Jericho, when he fell into the hands of robbers. They stripped him of his clothes, beat him and went away, leaving him half dead. A priest happened to be going down the same road, and when he saw the man, he passed by on the other side. So too, a Levite, when he came to the place and saw him, passed by on the other side. But a Samaritan, as he traveled, came where the man was; and when he saw him, he took pity on him. He went to him and bandaged his wounds, pouring on oil and wine. Then he put the man on his own donkey, took him to an inn and took care of him. The next day he took out two silver coins and gave them to the innkeeper. 'Look after him,' he said, 'and when I return, I will reimburse you for any extra expense you may have.'

"Which of these three do you think was a neighbor to the man who fell into the hands of robbers?"

The expert in the law replied, "The one who had mercy on him."

Jesus told him, "Go and do likewise."

(Luke, 10: 25-37)

3.   All Christ's moral teaching can be summed up in the practice of love and humbleness, the two virtues opposite to selfishness and pride. Jesus consistently identified these virtues as ones leading to eternal happiness. In the Beatitudes, He said that the poor in spirit—that is to say, the humble—are blessed because the kingdom of heaven will be theirs. He said, too, blessed are those who have pure hearts; blessed are the gentle and the peacemakers; blessed are the merciful. He taught us that we should love our neighbors as we love ourselves, act toward others as we would have them act toward us, love our enemies, forgive all offenses if we want to be forgiven, do good without making a display of our

goodness, and judge ourselves before we judge others. In all these precepts, we see love and humbleness, the two qualities Jesus never stopped advocating and for which He stands as an example. He never stopped fighting against pride and selfishness. Nor did He limit himself simply to encouraging love: He told us, in very clear and explicit terms, that it was the absolute condition for future happiness.

Concerning Jesus' description of the Last Judgment here, we must separate, as in many other cases, the actual message from the form or allegory. The people to whom Jesus spoke still couldn't fully grasp questions that were entirely spiritual, and knowing this, He provided them with material images that would both grab their attention and impress them. In other words, to make sure that they understood Him, Jesus kept closely to the form in which ideas of that era appeared, realizing that the real meaning of these ideas, which could not be immediately and clearly explained, would emerge in the future. Yet even here, side by side with the figurative parts of His explanation, He emphasizes one feature—the happiness reserved for the just and the unhappiness waiting for wrongdoers.

What then will that Last Judgment consist of? What will the indictment be based on? Will the Judge ask if the person being examined has fulfilled this or that formality, if he or she has observed this or that ritual? No. Only one question will be asked: "Have you practiced the law of love?" Then, according to the answer, the Supreme Judge will make a decision: "Go to the right, all of you who've helped your brothers and sisters. Go to the left, all of you who've been hardhearted." Will there be a question about the orthodoxy of someone's faith or about the particular way in which someone practiced it? No. Jesus placed the Samaritan, who was considered a heretic then but showed love to a fellow human being, above the devout religious, who lacked love. Therefore, Jesus doesn't consider love to be merely one of the conditions for salvation, but the only condition. If there were others to be met, Jesus would have emphasized them. Instead, He put love in the first place because it implicitly includes all the other virtues—humbleness, kindness, generosity, tolerance, justice, etc.—and because it's the absolute antithesis of pride and selfishness.

THE GREATEST OF THE COMMANDMENTS

4.   *Hearing that Jesus had silenced the Sadducees, the Pharisees got together. One of them, an expert in the law, tested him with this question: "Teacher, which is the greatest commandment in the Law?"*

Jesus replied: "'Love the Lord your God with all your heart and with all your soul and with all your mind.' This is the first and greatest commandment. And the second is like it: 'Love your neighbor as yourself.' All the Law and the Prophets hang on these two commandments."

(Matthew, 22: 34-40)

5. Love and humbleness: These are the only path to salvation. Their opposites, selfishness and pride, invariably lead to ruin. This principle is expressed most precisely in these words: "Love the Lord your God with all your heart and with all your soul and with all your mind, and love your neighbor as yourself. All the Law and the Prophets hang on these two commandments." And so that no one would misunderstand the meaning of our love for God and our neighbor, He stressed that "the second is like it." In other words, it isn't possible to truly love God without loving your neighbor, or to love your neighbor without loving God. Thus, whatever you do against your neighbor, you do against God. The love of God assumes the practice of love toward our neighbor. All our human obligations can be summed up in this one maxim: "Without love, there is no salvation."

THE NEED FOR CHARITY ACCORDING TO PAUL THE APOSTLE

6. *If I speak in the tongues of men and of angels, but have not love, I am only a resounding gong or a clanging cymbal. If I have the gift of prophecy and can fathom all mysteries and all knowledge, and if I have a faith that can move mountains, but have not love, I am nothing. If I give all I possess to the poor and surrender my body to the flames, but have not love, I gain nothing.*

Love is patient, love is kind. It does not envy, it does not boast, it is not proud. It is not rude, it is not self-seeking, it is not easily angered, it keeps no records of wrongs. Love does not delight in evil but rejoices with the truth. It always protects, always trusts, always hopes, always perseveres.

And now these three remain: faith, hope and love. But the greatest of these is love.

(Paul: I Corinthians, 13: 1-7, 13)

7. Paul fully understood the importance of love when he said that even if he had the ability to "speak in the tongues of men and of angels" and "the gift of prophecy to fathom all mysteries and all knowledge," and even if he had "a faith that can move mountains," if he had "not love, he would gain nothing." Paul also notes that among faith, hope, and love, "the greatest of these is love." Quite clearly Paul places love above even faith. Why?

Because love is within everyone's reach, from the least educated to the most learned, from the poorest person to the richest. And because it is independent of particular beliefs.

But Paul does even more: He defines true love by showing that it doesn't consist only in doing good deeds, but contains within itself all the higher qualities of the heart, particularly kindness and generosity toward our fellow human beings.

WITHOUT THE CHURCH THERE IS NO SALVATION; WITHOUT TRUTH THERE IS NO SALVATION

8. The precept "Without love there is no salvation" is based on a universal principle. It opens the door to blissfulness for all God's children. By contrast, the dogma "Without the church there is no salvation" doesn't rest on a fundamental faith in God or the immortality of the soul, a belief common to all religions, but on a special faith in a particular belief system. Far from bringing God's children together, the idea that only one particular religion offers salvation separates them. Such a notion is exclusive and absolute. Instead of encouraging love of others, it feeds on and condones dissension, in which the members of each denomination consider members of the others eternally damned, even though these members might be their relations or friends. Further, ignoring the fact that we all have the same rights beyond the grave, some seek to separate people according to their faith even in their last place of repose.[1] The precept "Without love there is no salvation" sanctifies the principle of equality before God and freedom of conscience. Under this precept, men and women accept each other as brothers and sisters (no matter how differently they worship), hold up their hands, and pray for each other. The dictum "Without the church there is no salvation" fosters division, mutual hatred, and persecution. In such a climate, the father doesn't pray for his son, or the son for the father, or a friend for another friend, since all of them believe that the others are damned without recourse. This dogmatic approach stands against the teaching of Christ and the tenets of the Gospel.

9. "Without truth there is no salvation" is really the equivalent of saying, "Without the church there is no salvation." Both statements are exclusive of others, since every denomination claims that it alone has the truth. Yet who can honestly believe that he or

---

[1] *Translator's note: The author refers to the old Roman Catholic Church practice of prohibiting the burial of violent criminals, heretics (i.e., non-Catholics), and suicides in ordinary cemeteries, which were considered consecrated grounds.*

she has a grasp of the whole truth when our knowledge is constantly expanding and our ideas changing every day as a result? Only spirits of the most elevated rank can claim to know absolute truth. We on earth can make no such claim because human beings here are still too limited. We can aspire only to relative truth, one that is in keeping with our level of progress. If God had made the realization of absolute truth a condition for future happiness, He would have had to condemn us all. Yet everyone can practice love. The Spiritist Doctrine, in agreement with the Gospel, holds that everyone can have salvation; it contends that salvation exists independent of particular beliefs, provided that God's Laws are observed. It doesn't say that without the Spiritist Doctrine there is no salvation, just as it doesn't pretend to teach all truth. It doesn't say, "Without truth there is no salvation," knowing full well that this precept serves only to foster division and perpetuate dissension.

SPIRIT TEACHINGS

WITHOUT LOVE THERE IS NO SALVATION

10. ■ Children, in the precept "Without love there is no salvation," you find the destiny of humanity, both on earth and in heaven— on earth, because once everyone is gathered beneath this banner, human beings will live in peace; in heaven, because everyone who's practiced love will find grace in God's eyes. This precept is the heavenly light, the beacon that will lead humanity out of life's desert and put it on the right path to the Promised Land. It shines in heaven as a halo around the head of saintly figures, and on earth it's engraved on the hearts of all those to whom Jesus will say, "Go to the right and receive the blessing of God." They will be known by the radiant aura of love that surrounds them.

Nothing captures Jesus' ideas more precisely or so well sums up humanity's obligations as this divine precept. The Spiritist Doctrine could find no better way to affirm its roots than to adopt this precept as its highest rule, since it typifies the purest essence of the Christian experience. No one will ever go wrong embracing love as a norm for life. Dedicate yourselves, then, to understanding the real meaning behind these words. Discover for yourselves all the many ways you can practice love. Let love govern all your actions and your conscience will be your guide, not only steering you away from wrongdoing, but also sustaining you on the path of righteousness. For it is not sufficient to do no wrong, one must actively do good. Doing good necessitates a conscious act of will, while in the view of some, indifference is enough to do no wrong.

Friends, praise God for the lights of the Spiritist Doctrine. Obviously, salvation is not only for those who follow it, but it will make you into better Christians because it helps you to understand Christ. Make every effort to live it, so that your fellow human beings, seeing you do so, will recognize that the true Spiritist and the true Christian are one and the same. Everyone who is loving and charitable is a disciple of Jesus, regardless of the profession of faith. ■ —Paul, the Apostle (Paris, 1860).

Chapter 16

It Is Not Possible to Serve Both God and Money

SCRIPTURES AND COMMENTARY

THE SALVATION OF THE RICH

1.   *"No servant can serve two masters. Either he will hate the one and love the other, or he will be devoted to the one and despise the other. You cannot serve both God and Money."*

(Luke, 16: 13)

2.   *Now a man came up to Jesus and asked, "Teacher, what good thing must I do to get eternal life?"*

"Why do you ask me about what is good?" Jesus replied. "There is only One who is good. If you want to enter life, obey the commandments."

"Which ones?" the man inquired.

Jesus replied, "'Do not murder, do not commit adultery, do not steal, do not give false testimony, honor your father and mother,' and 'love your neighbor as yourself.'"

"All these I have kept," the young man said. "What do I still lack?"

Jesus answered, "If you want to be perfect, go, sell your possessions and give to the poor, and you will have treasure in heaven. Then come, follow me."

When the young man heard this, he went away sad, because he had great wealth.

Then Jesus said to his disciples, "I tell you the truth, it is hard for a rich man to enter the kindgom of heaven. Again I tell you, it is easier for a camel to go through the eye of a needle than for a rich man to enter the kingdom of God."

(Matthew, 19: 16-24; Luke, 18: 18-25; Mark, 10: 17-25)

A WARNING AGAINST GREED

3.   *Someone in the crowd said to him, "Teacher, tell my brother to divide the inheritance with me."*

Jesus replied, "Man, who appointed me a judge or an arbiter between you?" Then he said to them, "Watch out! Be on your guard against all kinds of greed; a man's life does not consist in the abundance of his possessions."

And he told them this parable: "The ground of a certain rich man produced a good crop. He thought to himself, 'What shall I do? I have no place to store my crops.'

"Then he said, 'This is what I'll do. I will tear down my barns and build bigger ones, and there I will store all my grain and my goods. And I'll say to myself, "You have plenty of good things laid up for many years. Take life easy; eat, drink and be merry."'

"But God said to him, 'You fool! This very night your life will be demanded from you. Then who will get what you have prepared for yourself?'

"This is how it will be with anyone who stores up things for himself but is not rich toward God."

(Luke, 12: 13-21)

JESUS IN THE HOUSE OF ZACCHAEUS

4.   *Jesus entered Jericho and was passing through. A man was there by the name of Zacchaeus; he was a chief tax collector and was wealthy. He wanted to see who Jesus was, but being a short man he could not, because of the crowd. So he ran ahead and climbed a sycamore-fig tree to see him, since Jesus was coming that way.*

When Jesus reached the spot, he looked up and said to him, "Zacchaeus, come down immediately. I must stay at your house today." So he came down at once and welcomed him gladly.

All the people saw this and began to mutter, "He has gone to be the guest of a 'sinner.'"

But Zacchaeus stood up and said to the Lord, "Look, Lord! Here and now I give half of my possessions to the poor, and if I have cheated anybody out of anything, I will pay back four times the amount."

Jesus said to him, "Today salvation has come to this house, because this man, too, is a son of Abraham. For the Son of Man came to seek and to save what was lost."

(Luke, 19: 1-10)

THE PARABLE OF THE BAD RICH MAN

5.   *"There was a rich man who was dressed in purple and fine linen and lived in luxury every day. At his gate was laid a beggar named Lazarus, covered with sores and longing to eat what fell from the rich man's table. Even the dogs came and licked his sores.*

"The time came when the beggar died and the angels carried him to Abraham's side. The rich man also died and was buried. In hell, where he was in torment, he looked up and saw Abraham far away, with Lazarus by his side. So he called to him, 'Father Abraham, have pity on me and send Lazarus to dip the tip of his finger in water and cool my tongue, because I am in agony in this fire.'

"But Abraham replied, 'Son, remember that in your lifetime you received your good things, while Lazarus received bad things, but now he is comforted here and you are in agony. And besides all this, between us and you a great chasm has been fixed, so that those who want to go from here to you cannot, nor can anyone cross over from there to us.'

"He answered, 'Then I beg you, father, send Lazarus to my father's house, for I have five brothers. Let him warn them, so that they will not also come to this place of torment.'

"Abraham replied, 'They have Moses and the Prophets; let them listen to them.'

"'No, father Abraham,' he said, 'but if someone from the dead goes to them, they will repent.'

"He said to him, 'If they do not listen to Moses and the Prophets, they will not be convinced even if someone rises from the dead.'"

(Luke, 16: 19-31)

THE PARABLE OF THE TALENTS

6.   *"Again, it will be like a man going on a journey, who called his servants and entrusted his property to them. To one he gave five talents of money, to another two talents, and to another one talent, each according to his ability. Then he went on his journey. The man who had received the five talents went at once and put his money to work and gained five more. So also, the one with the two talents gained two more. But the man who had received the one talent went off, dug a hole in the ground and hid his master's money.*

"After a long time the master of those servants returned and settled accounts with them. The man who had received the five talents brought the other five. 'Master,' he said, 'you entrusted me with five talents. See, I have gained five more.'

"His master replied, 'Well done, good and faithful servant! You have been faithful with a few things; I will will put you in charge of many things. Come and share your master's happiness!'

"The man with the two talents also came. 'Master,' he said, 'you entrusted me with two talents; see, I have gained two more.'

"His master replied, 'Well done, good and faithful servant! You have been faithful with a few things; I will put you in charge of many things. Come and share your master's happiness!'

"Then the man who had received the one talent came. 'Master,' he said, 'I knew that you are a hard man, harvesting where you have not sown and gathering where you have not scattered seed. So I was afraid and went out and hid your talent in the ground. See, here is what belongs to you.'

"His master replied, 'You wicked, lazy servant! So you knew that I harvest where I have not sown and gather where I have not scattered seed? Well then, you should have put my money on deposit with the bankers, so that when I returned I would have received it back with interest.

"'Take the talent from him and give it to the one who has the ten talents. For everyone who has will be given more, and he will have an abundance. Whoever does not have, even what he has will be taken from him. And throw that worthless servant outside, into the darkness, where there will be weeping and gnashing of teeth.'"

(Matthew, 25: 14-30)

THE WISE USE OF WEALTH

7. If wealth were an impossible obstacle to salvation—and this is a possible interpretation of some of Jesus' words when taken in their literal rather than spiritual sense—then, in giving us wealth, God would be presenting certain people with the instrument of their own ruin, against which they would have no defense. This idea is clearly contrary to reason. Surely, wealth can be a treacherous trial because of the temptations it stirs up and the fascination it holds. And it often is a trial more dangerous than the trial of poverty. At times, our wealth is like a potent elixir that excites our pride, selfishness, and lust. It often is the strongest tie binding us to this earth and diverting our thoughts from all that is heavenly. Wealth can be so intoxicating that it's not uncommon for someone who goes from poor to rich to quickly forget his or her humble beginnings, including the relations who stayed behind. It is as if the newly rich have become desensitized, selfish, and vain. Nevertheless, just because wealth makes the jour-

ney more challenging, we shouldn't conclude that it makes salvation impossible or that it can't be a means of salvation when properly used. It's very much like certain substances that have the power to heal when they're taken in correct dosages and used with discernment, but can kill when used incorrectly.

When Jesus told the young man who asked how he could receive eternal life, "Go, sell your possessions and give to the poor...then come, follow me," He was not proclaiming an absolute principle, i.e., that everyone should get rid of all earthly possessions, nor was He saying that this was the only price of salvation. He did mean to show that attachment to worldly goods is a hurdle to salvation. The young man in this case considered himself to be free from further effort because he had observed certain commandments, and so he rejected the idea of parting with his goods. His desire for eternal life did not go as far as being able to make such a sacrifice.

What Jesus proposed to him was a test to uncover the depth of his motivation. In the eyes of the world he could be a perfectly honest man—someone who never harmed anyone, never spoke ill of his neighbor, never appeared vain or proud, and who always honored his mother and father. Still, he didn't have true love, because for all his good qualities, he was incapable of sacrificing his own comforts for the sake of others. This is what Jesus wanted to show. Here He reaffirmed the principle "Without love there is no salvation."

If we were to take these words at face value, we would have to say that wealth should be abolished because it's detrimental to our future happiness and because it's a source of considerable evil on earth. We would also have to condemn any form of work, since work is a means of gain and accumulation of wealth. This is absurd for it would reduce us to a very primitive level of existence. For this very reason, this line of thinking is wrong; it contradicts a natural law, the Law of Progress.[1]

If wealth stirs up so many wicked passions and causes so many evils and crimes, it isn't wealth itself we should blame but ourselves, because we misuse it, as we misuse many of God's gifts. By misuse we constantly turn things that could help us into things that harm us, a sorry consequence of the still undeveloped state of our world. To sum up, if wealth were only a wellspring

---

[1] *Translator's Note: For a more comprehensive explanation see Allan Kardec's* The Spirits' Book, *Chapter 23, "The Law of Progress."*

of trouble, God wouldn't have allowed it on earth. In the end, it's up to us to use wealth to manifest good, realizing that even if it isn't an important element in our moral betterment, it is unquestionably a powerful stimulus to our intellectual progress.

Indeed, it's part of our mission on earth to work to improve the conditions of life in this world. It's up to us to reclaim earth, make it a healthy place to live, and develop it so that one day it will be able to support all the population that its vast area can hold. To feed earth's growing population will require greater production; if one country can't produce enough, then food must be imported from elsewhere. For this reason, good relationships among the peoples of earth are vitally necessary. In order to make these relations easier, we should work to eliminate the barriers that separate countries by making possible clear and swift communications across the globe.

Progress is the work of time. Raw materials had to be extracted from deep within the earth: Science has afforded us the means to do so. To further the work of progress, financial resources were also needed, and just as necessity has fostered the development of science, it has given rise to the accumulation of wealth. All these challenges lead to our intellectual advancement. Although such intellectual gains were initially motivated by the sole satisfaction of our physical needs, one day they will help us master all the great spiritual and moral truths. We can infer, then, that no great work—no organized economic activity, cultural progress, or research—can be carried on without sufficient resources. With good reason we should consider wealth an element of progress.

THE UNEQUAL DISTRIBUTION OF WEALTH

8. The unequal distribution of wealth is a problem we will not resolve as long as we only consider the present life. The first question it presents is, "Why aren't we all equally affluent?" The simple answer is that we aren't all equally intelligent, active, and hardworking enough to acquire wealth, or levelheaded and careful enough to keep it. Moreover, it's mathematically demonstrable that wealth divided equally would give each person only a small and insufficient amount. Suppose this division were actually made. In a short time, the balance would be broken because of the diversity in human traits and aptitudes. Even if it really could be done and made to last, with each person having just enough to live on, we would see an unfortunate result—the end of all the great works that contribute to progress and the well-

being of humanity.² Finally, if each person were provided the indispensable things of life, there would be no wants to push people to make discoveries or begin useful enterprises. So if Providence has allowed the concentration of wealth in certain areas, it's because that wealth can be increased from those points in great enough quantities to meet human needs.

But if this is so, we can reasonably ask, why are some people endowed with wealth who aren't capable of making it bear fruit for the good of everyone? The answer gives us still another proof of God's wisdom and goodness. By giving us free will, God intends that we learn to distinguish between right and wrong through our individual experience, and to practice good entirely through our own effort and choice. God doesn't lead us in a deterministic manner toward good or evil; that would reduce us to passive beings who, like the lower animals, can't be held responsible for their actions.

Wealth is a way of testing our moral strength. But since it's also a powerful means of bringing about progress, it can't remain unproductive over long periods of time; therefore Providence constantly sees that it moves around. Each of us possesses it sooner or later, so that we can train ourselves in how to use it wisely and demonstrate the uses we've learned to put it to. We have to realize though that, first, it would be physically impossible for all of us to be wealthy at once and, second, even if it were possible, nobody would work and the improvement of the planet would be jeopardized. If you aren't wealthy today, you most likely have been already or you'll have wealth at some future time, perhaps in another lifetime. And if you do have it now, there's no guarantee that you'll have it tomorrow. Thus, there are rich and poor people in the world because Providence sees that we all must work for a living. In addition, the lack of means is, for some, a test of patience and fortitude. Wealth is, for others, a test of charitableness and the spirit of self-giving.

It's with good reason, then, that people who put their wealth to bad use and are motivated by greed, deserve criticism. The situation makes us wonder what kind of justice there is when

² *Translator's Note: The communist ideology came the closest to this utopian ideal. The philosophical foundation of Communism was first established in 1848 by the Communist Manifesto of Karl Marx and Friedrich Engels. The communist experiment in the former Soviet Union started in 1917 and lasted for about 70 years. As anticipated by the spirits here, such a system was bound to fail. The socialist experiment finally folded in 1989 with the dissolution of the Soviet Union.*

wealth is given to people of this kind. And indeed, if each of us had only one life, nothing could justify such arbitrary distribution of earthly goods. Yet when we focus not only on the present life but on the sum of all our lifetimes, we realize that everything is in fair balance. From this perspective, the poor have no grounds for blaming Providence for their situation, just as they have no grounds for envying the well-off—who, in their turn, have no cause to think especially well of themselves because of what they own.

Those who misuse their wealth may disguise their actions under the cover of the law but can't conceal what goes on in their hearts. Human laws are continuously changing, but their abuse leads to harsh consequences. The cause of most abuses is pride and self-centeredness. Only when we are governed by the law of love will abuses of this kind finally come to an end.

SPIRIT TEACHINGS

TRUE PROPERTY

9.   ▪ The only true property you can own is what you can take with you when you leave this world. What you find on coming to earth, and what you leave on departing it, you can enjoy only while you are here. Thus, strictly speaking, you do not have property rights over the things you are forced to leave behind, but the right to their temporary use. Of what does true property consist? Nothing that the body can use but everything that serves the soul—such as intelligence, knowledge, and moral qualities. This is what you bring and take with you. It is what no one can take away, and it will be even more useful to you in the next realm. It's your responsibility to be richer on departing than you were on arriving in this world, because your future depends entirely on the qualities you gain in the present life. Think, if you will, of travelers to a far-off country. These travelers put in their luggage only things they'll need in that country; they don't worry about what they can't use. Be like those travelers in regard to your future life and provide yourselves only with that which will benefit you there.

Take the analogy a step further. The traveler who arrives at a hotel is only given a good room when he or she is able to pay for it. People with fewer resources have to make do with something less comfortable. And if they don't have anything at all, they have to content themselves with sleeping on a cot. The same applies to you on your arrival in the spirit world. What you own will determine where you will go. And you can't pay with money. You will never be asked how much you had on earth, or what social position you filled, or whether you were a prince or a laborer. Instead, you'll be asked what you've brought with you. Your worldly goods and titles can't be appraised, only the total sum of good qualities you've acquired.

Seen from this aspect, it's possible that the laborer may be far richer than the prince. The prince may claim that, prior to his death, his entry into the heavenly realm was paid for—but the claim won't do him any good. The only reply he'll hear is that no one can buy a place here; it must be earned by each person and by means of doing good for others. Earthly money may buy land, houses, or palaces; but in our world everything is paid for through the qualities of the soul. Are you rich in these qualities? Then you're welcome to go to one of the higher realms, where bliss awaits you. But if you are poor in them, you have to go to the lower, less accommodating places, where you'll be treated according to what you own in true property. ■ —Pascal (Geneva, 1860).

10. ■ Earthly goods belong to God, Whose wishes determine how they're distributed; human beings are granted the right of use only. They are mere custodians of those goods. Their rights are so tenuous that reversals of fortune sometimes occur when they are least expected, and financial wealth vanishes from the hands of even those who thought they had the most solid rights to it.

Some might argue that it is easy to understand that we are only custodians and not true owners of our worldly possessions but, they would say, this is not the case when wealth has been acquired through our own hard work. Without a doubt, wealth gained honestly is legitimate, by which we mean gained without wronging anyone, since you will have to give an account of any ill-gotten gains. Nevertheless, it remains true that even wealth acquired honestly cannot be taken with you after death. At times, even the care you take to bequeath it to your descendants ends up going nowhere. This may occur because wealth was not in Providence's design for your loved ones, and against such designs there is no recourse. It is also true that you can't use and abuse it at will without having to account for it. Your wealth may well be God's recompense to you during your present existence for your effort, courage, and endurance. However, if you use it only to indulge your pride and your senses, or if it causes you to fail, you would have been better off never to have had it. When you act in this way, what you've gained on one hand, you've lost on the other, and any merit for your work is canceled out. When you leave earth, you will be treated as if you had already enjoyed your reward. ■ —M., A Guardian Spirit (Brussels, 1861).

THE PROPER USE OF WEALTH

11. ■ You can't serve both God and Money. Some of you, it's true, are dominated by the love of money and would sell your souls to be wealthy. But, while wealth may raise your status among your peers and allow you to indulge in many pleasures, beware! You can't serve both God and Money. If you feel that the appetites of the flesh dominate your mind, get rid of this bondage as fast as you can, for one day the Just One will say to you: "What did you do with the wealth I entrusted to you, unfaithful steward? This wonderful instrument of good works has been squandered in the exclusive pursuit of your own desires!"

What's the best way to use wealth? If you look to the words "love one another" you'll find your answer. For people who love their neighbors, these words define a course of action already; they know that the use of wealth that pleases God most is charity—not the cold, selfish charity that hands out the leftovers from a golden lifestyle, but charity that is full of love, that goes out of its way to seek the unfortunate and helps them without causing humiliation. If you are well-off, share what you have in excess. Go even further—share something that you consider important to you. But always give wisely. Don't turn your back on people for fear that they may be conning you; instead, seek ways to address the source of their ills. First, do what you can to ease their immediate pain, then examine their true needs to see if a job lead, a friendly bit of advice, or even a simple expression of care wouldn't be a more effective way of helping than simply handing over money. Lavish your love of God, of work, of your fellow human beings, upon others in a spirit of grace. Invest your riches in a fund that will never fail you and will always produce interest, a good deeds fund. Lastly, recall that intellectual wealth, too, should serve you in the same way that economic wealth does. Share your knowledge freely, and scatter the treasure of your love over your brothers and sisters so that they will bear fruits. ■ —Cheverus (Bordeaux, 1861).

12. ▪ When I think of how short life is, I'm painfully reminded of how constantly preoccupied with material well-being you on earth are. At the same time, you give little time or significance to your moral improvement, even though this is what really matters in Eternity. You put so much effort into your material well-being, one would think that you're dealing with a question of enormous importance for humanity. But in most cases, this work is no more than an attempt to satisfy exaggerated needs, to please vanity, to surrender to indulgence. You cause yourselves so much pain, heartache, and stress. Think of all the sleepless nights you spend trying to find a way to get more money when you often already have more than enough.

As a crowning blindness, you often find people who are so enamored of money (and the lifestyle it affords) that they will subject themselves to long and tiring workdays, and afterwards boast about the life of sacrifice and merit they lead—as if they weren't really working for themselves but others. How very foolish you can be! Do you really think that the care and effort you put into amassing more money will count for much when you are solely motivated by selfishness and greed, especially when you neglect your own spiritual future and the duties of fraternity that are part of life in society? Your thoughts have been centered on the well-being of your physical bodies. For the sake of the body, which will die, you've woefully neglected your spirit, which will live forever. This is how that spoiled and flattered lord, your body, comes to rule over you; it dominates your soul, making you its slave. Can this possibly be the reason God granted you life? ▪ —A Guardian Spirit (Krakow, 1861).

13. ▪ Since every person is a custodian for the property Providence has placed in his or her hands, a strict accounting of how those assets were employed will naturally take place. The sign of inapt usage is the use of money for the exclusive satisfaction of personal wants; the sign of good usage is any use that brings benefits to others. The merit here is proportional to the sacrifice. Consider that giving money is only one way of putting wealth to good use. Employed in this way it helps to ease poverty, quell hunger, and provide shelter and warmth to the homeless. Even more imperative and noteworthy than easing poverty, though, is the duty of preventing poverty in the first place. This, above all, is the true mission of the great fortunes of the world, which can be mobilized to create all sorts of work opportunities. The good that comes from such use is not diminished by profits legitimately

earned. The jobs these profits create help people to gain skills and enhance their sense of dignity. They earn their living and no longer have to experience the humiliation that comes with receiving handouts.

Your wealth should be like a spring of running water; that is, it should spread life and well-being wherever it goes. We say, then, to wealthy men and women—use your wealth following the Lord's inspiration and your heart will be the first to drink from that spring. Instead of the pleasures of the selfish that only leave behind an empty heart, you will reap in this life the purest bliss of the soul. Your name will be praised on earth; and when you leave earth, the Maker will say to you, as in the parable of the talents, "Well done, good and faithful servant!…Come and share your master's happiness!" In the parable, the servant who buried the money his master entrusted to him represents the miserly— people in whose hands wealth always remains unproductive.

Meanwhile, if Jesus spoke primarily in terms of handouts, it was because in His time and place, the kinds of productive activities that we know today (the wealth which can serve the general good) didn't exist. To all who have something to give, be it little or much, I would also say this: Give handouts only when it's necessary; but whenever possible, convert your money into wages so that the person who receives it feels dignified. ■ — Fénelon (Argel, 1860).

DETACHMENT FROM WORLDLY POSSESSIONS

14. ■ Brothers, sisters, and friends, I come with a small contribution to encourage you along the pathway to self-improvement on which you're now entering. We are all dependent on one another. Thus, it's only possible to achieve spiritual renewal by means of a sincere and affectionate partnership between spirits and incarnate beings.

Attachment to worldly possessions is one of the greatest obstacles to moral and spiritual improvement. This fixation exhausts your ability to act lovingly. Let's be honest with each other: Isn't money really a mixed blessing? When your coffers are full, don't you still feel an emptiness in your hearts? Hidden at the bottom of this splendid basket of flowers, isn't there often a snake? I understand the satisfaction you feel, and quite justifiably, when you earn your fortune through honorable and persistent work. But from this satisfaction, which is natural and blessed, to the all-absorbing attachment I am talking about here—one that para-lyzes the heart's better impulses—there is a large gap. This gap is almost as wide as the one that separates the acts of the miser from those of the extravagant. Between these two extremes, God places true charitableness, the holy virtue that inspires the rich to give without making a show of giving, so that the poor can receive without feeling debased.

But whether you inherited your fortune or earned it, there's something you should never forget: Everything comes from God and everything goes back to God. Nothing belongs to you on this earth—not even your own physical body (death strips you of that as it does of every earthly thing). You shouldn't fool yourselves, then. You're merely the trustees of your possessions, not the owners. God has only loaned these things to you, and they have to be returned. Moreover, they're only loaned to you on the con-dition that at least the surplus will be shared with people who can't provide for themselves.

Assume that one of your friends lends you a certain sum of money. You make a point of conscientiously repaying the loan, and you are grateful to your friend. Now, this is exactly the posi-tion of the well-off person. God is the Friend who lends you rich-es, and wants nothing more in return than love and recognition of the loan. However, God does expect that, in turn, the affluent man or woman will share some of this loan with the needy, who are no less the children of God than the affluent.

Often, unfortunately, the gifts of God stir up a burning and uncontrollable greed in you. Have you ever stopped to think, on becoming overly attached to your holdings (something just as perishable and temporary as you are), that you'll have to account one day for what God has given you? Have you forgotten that your wealth indicates that you've accepted a ministry of service on earth, that you've been called on to be good administrators of these resources? Isn't it logical to conclude that when you use what God has entrusted to you solely for your own benefit, you are being unfaithful trustees? And what will be the outcome of this willing neglect of your responsibility? Death, unbending and tireless, will rip away the veil you've been hiding behind and force you to give an account to the Friend you've forgotten and Who, at that moment, stands before your conscience as Judge.

Don't fool yourselves by trying to present your selfishness under the guise of virtue—it won't work. And it's just as useless to refer to your stinginess as "economy and foresight" or pretend that your excesses, which primarily benefit you, are really acts of generosity. For example, the parents who abstain from giving to charity, economize, and amass a considerable amount of money in order to leave their children, as they put it, with enough money so that they'll never know poverty. This is reasonable and parent-like, I agree, and no one can criticize them for it. But is this the only motive behind their actions? Doesn't it often represent an excuse before their own conscience to justify their personal attachment to worldly goods through the claim of leaving a large inheritance? And even if parental love is their only motive, is this any reason to totally forget their brothers and sisters before God? When they've already amassed more than enough, will they really be leaving their children to lives of poverty if they have just a little less? By acting in this way, they are, in reality, giving their children a lesson in selfishness and hardening their hearts—a lesson that will cause their love for their neighbors to wither away. Mothers and fathers, you are under a delusion if you think this is the way to earn your children's affection. By teaching them to be selfish with others, you're only teaching them to be selfish with you, too.

People who've worked hard all their lives and accumulated material things by the sweat of their brow are often heard to say that one appreciates the value of money better when one works for it. This is very true. Well, then—those who declare they know the full value of money have all the more reason for being charitable. Their merit will be greater than that of someone who was born to wealth and didn't know the value of hard work. On the other hand, if those self-made people, who remember well their own sufferings and trials, are selfish and heartless toward the poor, they'll be guiltier than the hardhearted person who was born wealthy. Why? Because the more you know from your own experience about the hidden distress of not having enough to make ends meet, the greater your desire should be to help others.

Unfortunately, the well-to-do often exhibit a trait as strong as their attachment to money, arrogant pride. Frequently, you'll see a moneyed person bedazzling someone who's seeking their help, with tales of their successes and abilities. In the end, rather than offer help, they often say, "Work hard, as I did." Of course, according to this way of thinking, God's Providence played no role in their becoming wealthy; they alone take the credit for it. Their pride has blinded and deafened them. Despite having intelligence and talent, they still don't understand that their atop-the-world position is fragile, and that Providence may change it at a moment's notice.

Squandering wealth is scarcely a demonstration of detachment from worldly goods either. It is, rather, a sign of carelessness and indifference. Human beings, as the trustees of these goods, have as little right to squander their wealth as they do to keep it solely for themselves. Profligate use of money is not the same as true generosity; indeed, it is often a form of selfishness. For example, someone who spends money hand over fist in order to satisfy a whim may well be unwilling to give even a penny to someone in need.

Being truly detached from worldly goods means appreciating them according to their real value, knowing how to use them for the benefit of others and not just yourself, refusing to sacrifice your interest in a future life because of them, and being able to part with them without a murmur when the Divine Will so determines. Should unforeseeable circumstances reduce you to the condition of Job, say, as he did, "The Lord gave and the Lord has taken away; may the name of the Lord be praised."[3] This is real detachment. Above all, accept the design of Providence and trust God Who, having given and taken away, may see fit in the future to restore everything you lost. Resist, with all your might, feeling sorry for yourself or falling into desperation—these attitudes paralyze your will. When life deals you a blow, never forget that alongside the most devastating trial, there will always be support and solace from God. Most importantly, consider that there are things far more precious than any you will find on earth: This thought will help you to have the strength to move on. Remember that the less attached you are to something, the less sensitive you will be to its loss. The person who holds on to material things is like a child who sees only the moment; the person who achieves detachment is like the wise adult who sees the more important things in life and understands fully the prophetic words of the Savior: "My kingdom is not of this world."[4]

God doesn't require people to give up what they own—this would only condemn them to voluntary poverty and quickly make them burdens to society. To proceed in this way is to misunderstand the true meaning of detachment from worldly goods. It is selfishness of another kind, since individuals who act on this idea exempt themselves from the responsibility of putting their money to good uses. Providence gives wealth to people who have the ability to administer it for the benefit of society. The person with money has been given a mission—a mission rich with mean-

---

[3] *Translator's Note: Job 1:21.*

[4] *Translator's Note: John 18:36.*

ing for others, as well as for him- or herself. To reject wealth, which is a gift of Providence, is to reject the benefits of the good it can do—that is, when it is administered with good judgment. By knowing how to do without it when you don't have it, how to use it properly when you get it, and how to give it up when that becomes necessary, you are proceeding according to God's wishes. Let us hope, then, that if you are one of those people who've come into what is called in the world "good fortune," you will be able to say, "My Lord, you have entrusted me with a new mission; give me the strength to fulfill it according to your wishes."

Friends, this is the sum of what I wanted to share with you about living with detachment. I would summarize it by saying: Know how to be content with only a little. If you don't have much, don't envy the rich, because money isn't necessarily happiness. If you're a person of means, don't forget that your money has only been entrusted to you and that you'll have to account for the way you used it, just as on earth you will have to account for an investment that you're responsible for. Don't be an unfaithful trustee, using your money only to satisfy your own vanity and sensuality. Don't think you have the right to dispose of a loan as if it were a gift entirely for your own benefit. If you don't know how to honor the loan, don't ask for wealth—you are not ready for it. And remember that the person who shares of abundance settles a loan received from God. ■ —Lacordaire (Constantine, 1863).

15. ■ Does the principle which says that human beings are only the trustees of the goods in their possession take away their right to leave that wealth to their descendants?

No, they have a perfect right to leave to their loved ones what they enjoyed during life. But this right is always subject, in the last instance, to the Will of God, Who can prevent the descendants from getting or at least enjoying their inheritance. This is the reason so many apparently solid fortunes collapse. The wealthy person's plan may be powerless when it comes to keeping a fortune in the hands of descendants. This fact, however, doesn't take away someone's right to transfer the loan received from God, since God can take it away whenever circumstances warrant. ■ —Saint Louis (Paris, 1860).

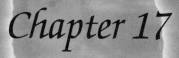

Chapter 17

Be Perfect

SCRIPTURES AND COMMENTARY

CHARACTERISTICS OF PERFECTION

1. *"But I tell you, Love your enemies and pray for those who persecute you."*

   "If you love those who love you, what reward will you get? Are not even the tax collectors doing that? And if you greet only your brothers, what are you doing more than others? Do not even pagans do that? Be perfect, therefore, as your heavenly Father is perfect."

   (Matthew, 5: 44, 46-48)

2. Since God is infinitely perfect in all things, the commandment "Be perfect, therefore, as your heavenly Father is perfect" would assume, if taken literally, that we can reach a state of absolute perfection. But if we could become as perfect as God, we could also become God's equal—obviously an impossibility. The people Jesus spoke to, however, didn't understand this nuance, so that He limited Himself to the presentation of a model and told them to strive to conform to it. We have to understand these words, then, as referring to a relative perfection, which human beings can achieve and through which they most nearly approach the Divine. At this point, we might logically ask, What does this perfection consist of? Jesus gives us the answer: By loving one's enemies, in doing good to those who hate us, in praying for those who persecute us. In this way He showed that the essence of perfection is love in the fullest sense of that word, since the practice of love implies the practice of all the other virtues.[1]

---

[1] *Translator's Note: The word in the French original is* charité, *which is explicitly characterized by A. Kardec as charity in its most inclusive meaning [*charité dans sa plus large acception*]. Throughout the book, the word* charité *is employed to express Christian love in its purest reflection of the Greek word agape. In the English language, and particularly in religious usage, the word "love" has been substituted in all instances in the* Revised Version of the New Testament *(published in 1811).*

Footnote continued on next page

If we observe the results of our vices and even simple character flaws, we see that there isn't one that doesn't more or less mar
our ability to love, since all of them begin in selfishness and
pride, which are love's very negation. This is because everything
that overinflates our ego destroys, or at least weakens, the elements of true love, i.e., doing good, being tolerant, showing selfless dedication and devotion to others. This love of our fellow
human beings, extending even to love of our enemies, can't go
together with those very attitudes that negate it. Having such
love is, for this reason, always an indication of how advanced we
actually are. We have to conclude that the degree to which we are
perfect is in direct relation to how far we can extend our love. It
was for this reason that Jesus, having given His disciples the
rules of the most sublime love, said to them, "Be perfect, as your
heavenly Father is perfect."

THE GOOD PERSON

3.   Truly good people comply with the laws of justice, love, and
charity in their purest form. When such people examine their
consciences regarding their actions, they ask themselves if they
have violated any of these laws—if they've done any wrong, or
done all the good it was possible to do, if they've willingly neglected opportunities to be of service, or given anyone cause to
complain of them, and finally, if they've done to others everything they would want done to themselves.

Good people place their faith in God, in Divine Goodness,
Justice, and Wisdom. They know that without God's permission
nothing can happen, so in all things they submit themselves to
God's Will. The good also have faith in the future, which is the
primary reason they put spiritual possessions before worldly
ones. They know that all life's struggles—its pains and disappointments—are either purification trials or atonements, and
they accept them without protest. Moreover, they do good for the

Footnote continued from previous page

Confirmation of this usage appears in the translation of Paul's words, "If I speak in the tongues of men and of angels, but have not love…" [1 Corinthians 13:2] which, in Romance languages, might correspond to charity. For consistency, when the orig-inal French employed the word charité it has been translated as love, except in the few circumstances where the meaning was 'acts or works of charity to the poor.' This decision is also motivated by the fact that the predominant meaning of the word charity in the United States is: (a) actions for the needy, or (b) charitable institu-tion. The Oxford English Dictionary was followed in the determination of the best use and meaning for each occurrence.

sake of goodness, without expecting to be rewarded for their actions. They repay wrong-doing with good, defend the weak against abuses of the strong, and are always willing to sacrifice their own interests in the cause of justice. Their satisfaction arises from the many benefits they spread, the services they render, the happiness they promote, the tears they dry, and the comfort they offer the suffering. Their first impulse is to think of others before themselves and to look after others' interests before considering their own. By contrast, the selfish always calculate the advantages and losses that arise from a generous action.

Good people are always just, humane, and kindhearted towards others; and because they see all men and women as brothers and sisters, they don't make distinctions based on race or creed. They respect the convictions of other people and never disapprove of someone because that person happens to think differently. Love guides them in every case. They know that people who speak evil of others, who hurt others' feelings by giving free reign to their arrogance and disdain, who don't think twice before causing others unnecessary pain, fall very short of their duty to love their neighbor and aren't deserving of God's Mercy.

Good people don't nourish feelings of bitterness or hatred, and they don't nurture thoughts of revenge. Instead they follow the example of Jesus, forgiving and forgetting wrongs and only remembering the good they've received. They know that we're forgiven ourselves only to the extent that we forgive others. The good are tolerant of others' frailties since, as they know, they often need tolerance themselves; they recall Christ's words: "If any one of you is without sin, let him be the first to throw a stone at her."[2] Nor do they take pleasure in focusing on flaws in other peoples' characters or in calling attention to such flaws. Whenever the occasion demands, they will always try to find good qualities in someone as a way of lessening the bad ones. Good people study their own imperfections and constantly battle against them, using all their strength so that tomorrow they can say that they're just a little better than they were yesterday.

Good people never emphasize the importance of their own selves or their talents at the expense of others. On the contrary, they take every opportunity to highlight whatever is good and useful in other people. They aren't snobbish if they have money or other personal advantages. Everything they've been given,

[2] *Translator's Note: John 8:7.*

they realize, can be taken away. They use, but don't abuse, their worldly goods because they recognize that they have these things only on deposit and will have to give a full account of them. Also, they know that the worst use their money can be put to is the sole satisfaction of their own lust.

When good people find themselves in positions of authority over others, they treat them with kindness and respect, because before God everyone is equal. They use their authority to lift up the morale of their subordinates, and will never crush anyone to indulge their pride. They avoid anything that might cause a subordinate position to be more stressful than is necessary. On the other hand, when they are in a subordinate position, they fully appreciate their duties and conscientiously fulfill them.[3]

Finally, good people always respect the rights of their fellow human beings—as guaranteed by the Laws of Nature—just as they want their own rights respected.

These aren't all the qualities that distinguish the good person, but anyone who tries diligently to possess them will find him or herself on the road that leads to all the rest.

THE GOOD SPIRITIST

4.   The Spiritist Doctrine—when properly understood and deeply and sincerely felt—leads to all the results just mentioned. These qualities characterize the true Spiritist as much as they do the true Christian—which should cause no surprise since these are one and the same. Further, the Spiritist Doctrine has set up no new moral code. It does, though, make it easier for us to understand and practice Christ's moral system by offering to those who are uncertain about their convictions an unshakable and enlightened faith.

Many people who accept the reality of communication with the spirit realm don't really understand the moral consequences and implications of this possibility. Or if they do understand them, they don't apply these lessons to their own lives. How can we explain this fact? Is it because the doctrine isn't clear? No, it doesn't have any of the allegories or symbolism that could lead to differences in interpretation. Its clarity is the source of its strength. It speaks directly to human reason, and its fundamental principle is the practice of love. It has nothing mysterious, and its followers don't possess any secrets that they hide from other people.

---

[3] *See also Chapter 17, item 9.*

Do you have to have superior intelligence to understand it? No, there are people of considerable mental ability who don't grasp it at all, while many others of ordinary intelligence, even young people, see the meaning of its most complex points with great exactness. This proves that while the so-called tangible part of Spiritist thought only requires eyes that can observe a phenomenon, the essential part demands a certain degree of sensitivity—a certain maturity—that's independent of age and educational level because it's unique to the progress of the soul.

Nevertheless, for some Spiritist individuals, material ties are still too strong for them to let go of worldly things. A kind of mist surrounds their minds and prevents them from comprehending the infinite future. They find it difficult to break away from their habits, and curb their appetites. They seem unable to comprehend that there is something better than their present. They believe in the existence of spirit as a simple fact. Such belief, however, changes few or none of their inclinations. They see a small ray of light, but this isn't enough to guide them or instill aspirations that would allow them to overcome their tendencies. They get far more excited by spirit phenomena than the moral principles of the doctrine, which they find trivial and dull. All they are interested in, usually, is asking the spirits to reveal new secrets, never considering that they might not be worthy yet of penetrating God's mysteries. These are the imperfect Spiritists, the ones who've stood still by the wayside or who've turned away from their faithful friends because they were faced with the need for self-reform. Perhaps they prefer to keep in step with people who share their inclinations and prejudices. Still, accepting some of the fundamental principles of the doctrine is the first step, and this will make it easier for them to take a second step in a future life.

Those who can be called true and sincere Spiritists already enjoy a slightly higher level of moral progress. Their souls command their physical bodies, allowing them a clearer perception of the future. Spiritist principles, which leave many unmoved, stir their innermost aspirations and make their faith unshakable. They are like the musician who is touched by hearing a few chords that a less musical person would identify only as sound. In addition, true Spiritists can be recognized by their moral transformation and by the efforts they make to overcome their bad traits. Imperfect Spiritists may be content with a limited horizon, but the sincere ones, who know that better things exist, try in every way to raise themselves above earthly temptations and always succeed when their desire is strong and true.

THE PARABLE OF THE SOWER

5.   *That same day, Jesus went out of the house and sat by the lake. Such large crowds gathered around him that he got into a boat and sat in it, while all the people stood on the shore. Then he told them many things in parables, saying, "A farmer went out to sow his seed. As he was scattering the seed, some fell along the path, and the birds came and ate it up. Some fell on rocky places, where it did not have much soil. It sprang up quickly, because the soil was shallow. But when the sun came up, the plants were scorched, and they withered because they had no root. Other seed fell among thorns, which grew up and choked the plants. Still other seed fell on good soil, where it produced a crop—a hundred, sixty or thirty times what was sown. He who has ears, let him hear."*

(Matthew, 13: 1-9)

*   "Listen then to what the parable of the sower means. When anyone hears the message about the kingdom and does not understand it, the evil one comes and snatches away what was sown in his heart. This is the seed sown along the path. The one who received the seed that fell on rocky places is the man who hears the word and at once receives it with joy. But since he has no root, he lasts only a short time. When trouble or persecution comes because of the word, he quickly falls away. The one who received the seed that fell among the thorns is the man who hears the word, but the worries of this life and the deceitfulness of wealth choke it, making it unfruitful. But the one who received the seed that fell on good soil is the man who hears the word and understands it. He produces a crop, yielding a hundred, sixty or thirty times what was sown."*

(Matthew, 13: 18-23)

6.   The parable of the sower represents the various ways we can make use of Gospel teachings. There are so many people who see in these precepts nothing more than dead words; in their case, Jesus' teachings are like seeds that fall on stony ground, fail to take root, and so produce no fruit.

We can justly apply the parable to the different kinds of Spiritists among us. In it we find symbolized the Spiritists who are primarily attracted by phenomena, who seek only to satisfy their curiosity, and who fail to learn anything of worth from them. The parable also brings to mind those Spiritists who find the brilliance of spirit communication interesting only as long as it satisfies their imaginations and who continue to be just as cold and indifferent as before. Then there are the ones who consider the spirits' advice very good and admirable but only apply it to others—never to themselves. Finally, we find in the parable those Spiritists for whom the teachings are like seeds that have fallen on good soil, and that produce fine fruit.

SPIRIT TEACHINGS

DUTY

7.   ■ Duty is a moral obligation, first to the self and then to others. Duty is a fundamental law of life. It is expressed in the smallest and in the most elevated human actions. I speak here, you must understand, only of moral duty—rather than the obligations owed, for instance, to your profession.

Duty is one of the most difficult attributes to act on because it is often in conflict with personal interests and desires of the heart. Its victories have no witnesses; its defeats go unnoticed. As such, duty is, in essence, a matter of free will. The conscience acts as the guardian of virtue as well as its caretaker, but frequently it is powerless against the deceptions of desire.

Duty, if you attend to it faithfully, lifts you up spiritually. But, you will ask, is it possible to define duty with any precision? Where does duty begin? Where does it end? I will say that your duty begins precisely at the point where the peace and happiness of your neighbor is threatened by your actions; it ends at that point beyond which you wouldn't like anyone to cross, with respect to yourself.

God has created everyone equal where suffering is concerned. Tall and short, ignorant and educated alike, suffer for identical reasons, i.e., to understand the depth of pain human actions can cause. The same is not true of goodness, whose expressions are more varied and complex. Do understand that equality in the face of pain is part of the Divine Plan. God wants everyone, informed by experience, to stop doing wrong and hiding behind excuses of not knowing its consequences.

Duty is a practical expression of all moral theories. It is the bravery of the soul that withstands the struggles of life. Duty is both austere and resilient, adaptable to the knottiest complexities and yet inflexible before temptation. Those who fulfill their duty show that they love God above all things, and their fellow human beings more than themselves. Duty is simultaneously judge and slave of its own cause.

Duty is the most beautiful laurel in the grove of reason. Reason nurtures the sense of duty, much as a mother nurses her child. You should love duty not because it spares you from the wrongs of life—no one escapes those—but because it gives your soul vigor, which it needs in order to grow.

The sense of duty grows and shines forth in increasingly more elevated forms as humanity progresses. Your obligation toward God has no end. You must ultimately express in yourself the most sublime virtues, for this is the aim of God, Who will not settle for an unfinished picture. God expects all the beauty of your soul to shine in all its grandeur. ■ —Lazarus (Paris, 1863).

VIRTUE

8. ■ Virtue, at its highest level, combines all the essential qualities that make up a good person: generosity, charitableness, industriousness, temperance, and modesty. Unfortunately, on earth these virtues are nearly always accompanied by moral flaws in other areas that tarnish or deaden them. This is why people who bask in the praises of their own virtues aren't really virtuous—they lack one of the highest qualities, modesty. At the same time, they reveal one of the worst flaws, haughtiness. True virtue doesn't make a show of itself, and when it is divined, it moves quietly offstage. Saint Vincent de Paul[4] was virtuous. The dignified priest of Ars[5] was virtuous. So are a good many other people the world doesn't know about—but they are known to God. None of these good people are aware of the fact that they are virtuous. Rather, they're carried along by their saintly inspirations. They practice goodness with abandonment and complete forgetfulness of self.

Children, it is to virtue, understood and practiced correctly, that I call you. Dedicate yourselves wholeheartedly to it—it's truly a Christian and a Spiritist ideal. Further rid your hearts of pride, vanity, and self-seeking: These mar the otherwise beautiful qualities in you. Do not be like people who set themselves up as models, the ones who blow their own horns to anyone who'll listen about all the good qualities they have. Their showy kind of virtue almost always covers a mass of little defects and sheer meanness.

In principle, people who praise themselves and erect statues to their own virtues cancel out any merit they might actually have had. And what about those whose only goal is appearing to be

[4] *Translator's Note: see Biographical Sketches.*
[5] *Translator's Note: see Biographical Sketches.*

what they are not? Of course, when individuals do good, they may have a natural feeling of satisfaction in their hearts. Yet the moment that satisfaction comes out into the open for the purpose of gaining praise, it deteriorates into love for the self above all others.

To all of you whom the rays of the Spiritist faith have reinvigorated and who know just how far from perfection humanity is, I say: Never give yourselves up to this weakness. Virtue is a blessing and I desire it for all sincere Spiritists. But take this as a warning: It's better to have fewer virtues and be modest than have many and be proud. It was through blind pride that various societies lost themselves through the ages. By becoming more humble they'll one day redeem themselves. ■ —François Nicolas Madeleine (Paris, 1863).

SUPERIORS AND SUBORDINATES

9.   ■ Authority, like wealth, is delegated: People who receive it will eventually have to give an account of what they did with it. Don't think, either, that it's given just so that some people can relish the fleeting pleasures of commanding others, or that it's a right or privilege of some kind, as most powerful people on earth seem to believe. Providence constantly proves that authority is intended neither as a pleasure nor a right by occasionally taking it away. If authority was an exclusive privilege of the person who exercised it, it would never be transferred to someone else. No one can say that something really belongs to him or her if it can be taken away without their consent. Providence grants positions of authority either as a trial or mission, and may revoke the charge when circumstances warrant.

People who are entrusted with authority—from bosses over workers to the monarchs over subjects—should never forget that they have souls in their charge, and will have to answer for the good and bad guidance they give. The mistakes their subordinates make, the vices they surrender to because of the poor guidance they have received (or because their superiors set bad examples), will carry consequences for the people in positions of authority. In the same way, the reward for leading their subordinates on an upright path will also come back to those in authority. Recall that every person on earth has a mission, some greater than others; but whatever form it takes, it's always designed to further love in the world. You thus fail in your mission when you betray this Providential design.

If Divine Justice asks the rich person, "What have you done with the money that was given to you so that you could make it bear fruit for all around you?" it will also ask people with authority, "What have you done with your authority? What wrongs have you prevented? How much progress have you fostered? If you were given subordinates, it wasn't so you could turn them into servants to cater to your whims and your greed. You were given power and trust over people so that you could protect them and inspire them to climb upward to God."

Leaders who keep Christ's words don't look down on those below them because they know that social distinctions don't exist before God. The Spiritist Doctrine shows that people who obey orders today may have already given orders in the past, or that they may come to be leaders in the future, at which time they'll be treated in the same way as they have treated others.

Further, if superiors have duties to perform, subordinates also have duties that are no less important. If subordinates are also inspired by the Spiritist Doctrine, their conscience will tell them, in no uncertain terms, that they aren't exempt from carrying out their duties even if their superiors don't carry out theirs. They know that you don't repay one wrong with another and that the failings of higher-ups don't authorize the ones beneath them to do wrong. If they find their positions difficult, they'll acknowledge that this may be deserved since they probably abused authority they had in the past and are now experiencing some of the grief they caused others. If they try but are unable to find a better position, the doctrine inspires fortitude in them, reminding them that the situation is a test of their mildness of heart, which is a quality necessary for their progress. This conviction guides them in their conduct; it leads them to behave as they wish subordinates would behave toward them if they were in authority. As a result, they're more diligent in their jobs because they understand that negligence in their work causes a loss to their employer who expects their best effort. In short, they're guided by their sense of duty, which is enhanced by their faith and the knowledge that every deviation from the straight and narrow path will create a debt that must be repaid sooner or later. ■ — François Nicholas Madeleine (Paris, 1863).

THE WORLDLY PERSON

10. ■ A feeling of compassion should always move the hearts of people who gather together under the Lord's banner to seek the

inspiration of their spirit guides. Cleanse your hearts, then. Clear your minds of mundane thoughts. Raise up your souls toward those spirit friends whose inspiration you seek. Once they feel your devoted commitment toward them, they will shower your hearts with seeds that will germinate and produce the fruits of love and justice.

Don't think, however, that in constantly advising you to pray and meditate, I want you to lead the lives of mystics outside of the very social order where you are expected to live. No—you are to live with the people of your time, just like everybody else is expected to. Fulfill the demands of modern life, even allowing yourselves the little indulgences of the times, but do so with a pure heart and reverence.

You are called on to be in contact with people of diverse characters and natures. Make it a goal never to hurt anyone. Always be happy and joyful, but may your happiness be one that comes from a clear conscience, and your joy be that of a people who are going to inherit heaven and who are counting the days until they receive their inheritance.

Virtue doesn't mean having a hard, gloomy appearance. It doesn't mean that you have to deny yourselves or others the pleasures the human condition rightly allows. All you need do is to acknowledge the Giver of life in your spirit. All you need do is to lift a thought to God at the beginning of every undertaking, asking from your hearts for God's protection and for inspiration as you work, and God's blessings once the work is over. Whenever you do anything at all, let your thoughts soar to the Supreme Source. And never do anything without sanctifying it with a thought toward God.

Perfection, Christ said, can only be found by practicing unconditional love, and this applies to all, regardless of social condition, from the lowest to the highest. If you live in isolation, you deprive yourself of opportunities to share love. The only way you will find to practice it is through contact with your fellow human beings; indeed, it's often in the heat of life's struggles that you find valuable opportunities to demonstrate your love. To isolate yourselves is to become cut off entirely from your most powerful means of perfecting your souls. In only having to think of the self, you come to lead the life of a selfish person.[6]

---

[6] *See also Chapter 5, item 26*

Finally, don't imagine that to be in contact with us, to meet the expectations of God, you have to wear a hair shirt and cover yourselves with ashes.[7] This is not the way. Be happy within the compass of human needs. But in this happiness, never allow a thought or an act that could offend God, or cause a shadow to fall across the faces of those who love and guide you. God is love and blesses all who love with devotion. ■ —A Guardian Spirit (Bordeaux, 1863).

LOOK AFTER BOTH BODY AND SPIRIT

11. ■ Do you need to mortify the body in order to reach moral perfection? In answering this question, I turn to elementary principles. First, I begin by showing you the importance of taking good care of the body because its health or sickness has a significant influence on the soul. The soul is, after all, a sort of prisoner of the flesh; and if the soul is to function, prance, and rejoice in freedom (albeit relative), the body must be sound, alert, and vigorous. Consider the following situation. Suppose that both body and soul are in perfect condition: What should you do to maintain the balance between their very differing aptitudes and needs?

Two systems have arisen with supposed answers to this situation: the system of the ascetics, who want to chastise and subdue the body; and the system of the materialists, who glorify the body and want to annihilate the soul. These are, in fact, two forms of violence and one is about as foolish as the other. Between these two perspectives is a large and indifferent mass of people. They lack both conviction and passion, they are tepid in love and stingy in pleasures. Ask yourself, then, Where is the wisdom in any of this? Where is the science of living? No where at all. But don't doubt for a moment that this great problem would remain unsolved if the Spiritist Doctrine hadn't come to help the researchers and to demonstrate the real relationship between the body and soul—to show them that, since the two are absolutely necessary to each other, both body and soul have to be looked after.

Love your soul, but also take care of your body, which is the instrument of the soul. Not to pay attention to its needs is to ignore the Laws of Nature, which is akin to ignoring God. Don't blame your body, either, for failings that happen only because you misuse your free will and for which the body is about as

---

[7] *Translator's Note: It refers to historic self-mortification practices employed to express repentance for one's sins.*

responsible as a misguided horse is for the accidents it causes. Besides, will you be more perfect if, in chastising your body, you don't become less selfish, less arrogant, more loving toward your neighbors? No, this isn't the way to perfection, which can only be found in the betterment of the spirit. When it comes to your lower tendencies, subdue and slight them; indeed, reform them in the forge of your good resolutions. This is the way to make your soul responsive to the Divine Will. This is the one and only way to perfection. ■ —Georges, A Guardian Spirit (Paris, 1863).

Chapter 18

Many Are Invited, but Few Are Chosen

SCRIPTURES AND COMMENTARY

THE PARABLE OF THE WEDDING BANQUET

1.   *Jesus spoke to them again in parables, saying: "The kingdom of heaven is like a king who prepared a wedding banquet for his son. He sent his servants to those who had been invited to the banquet to tell them to come, but they refused to come.*

"Then he sent some more servants and said, 'Tell those who have been invited that I have prepared my dinner: My oxen and fattened cattle have been butchered, and everything is ready. Come to the wedding banquet.'

"But they paid no attention and went off—one to his field, another to his business. The rest seized his servants, mistreated them and killed them. The king was enraged. He sent his army and destroyed those murderers and burned their city.

"Then he said to his servants, 'The wedding banquet is ready, but those I invited did not deserve to come. Go to the street corners and invite to the banquet anyone you find.' So the servants went out into the streets and gathered all the people they could find, both good and bad, and the wedding hall was filled with guests.

"But when the king came in to see the guests, he noticed a man there who was not wearing wedding clothes. 'Friend,' he asked, 'how did you get in here without wedding clothes?' The man was speechless.

"Then the king told the attendants, 'Tie him hand and foot, and throw him outside, into the darkness, where there will be weeping and gnashing of teeth.'

"For many are invited, but few are chosen."

(*Matthew, 22: 1-14*)

2.   Unbelievers laugh at this parable and consider it naive and art-less. They can't understand how so many problems could attend going to a feast or why the guests would refuse the invitation, even to the point of murdering the messengers sent by the king to invite them. "Beyond doubt," the skeptics will say, "parables are figurative, but it really isn't necessary to go so far outside the limits of plausibility."

The same criticism could be made of allegories, and all creative fables, before you cut through their wrappings and uncover their hidden meaning. Jesus based his allegories on everyday events and customs, and adapted these to the habits and character of the people He talked to. Most of His allegories were aimed at open-ing the minds of the masses to the idea of spiritual life. Thus, their meaning is nonsensical only for those who don't consider Jesus' perspective.

In this parable, Jesus compares the kingdom of heaven, where everything is happiness and bliss, to a feast. When He speaks of the first guests to be invited, He's alluding to the Hebrews, the earliest people to know God's Law. The servants sent by the king represent the prophets who came to tell the Hebrews how to fol-low the road to true happiness. In the parable, the servants are slaughtered; similarly, the Hebrews, who paid little attention to the prophets and disregarded their warnings, massacred many prophets. Finally, the would-be guests who declined the invita-tion, saying they had to look after their pastures and businesses, symbolize the worldly. Absorbed in the matters of the world, these people are indifferent to heavenly matters.

The Jews of Jesus' time believed that their nation would gain supremacy over all other nations. Didn't God, they reasoned, promise Abraham that his posterity would cover the face of the earth? But as always, they considered the form of the prophet's words rather than their substance, and took them as predictions of actual material dominance.

Before Christ came, the peoples of earth—except, that is, for the Jews—were idol worshippers and believers in many gods. If a few insightful individuals among them entertained the idea of one God, that idea was strictly a personal belief. Nowhere else was this idea accepted as a fundamental truth, except perhaps by a few initiates who hid their knowledge behind a veil of mystery that made it inaccessible to the masses. The Jewish people were the first to practice monotheism publicly; and it was to the Jews that God gave the Law, first through Moses and later through

Jesus. From the tiny land of Israel, the light, destined to spread throughout the world, shot out. In time, it would triumph over paganism, and it gave Abraham a spiritual posterity as numerous as the stars in the sky.[1] Nevertheless, even as they rejected idol worship, the Jews neglected the moral implications of the Law, finding it easier to cling to exterior (ceremonial) forms of worship. Social unrest had reached a dangerous point; the subjugated nation was torn by numerous factions, divided by sectarian strife; disbelief had begun to creep into the Temple. It was at this point that Jesus came to call on the Jews to keep the Law and open up new horizons to a future life. But while they were the first to be invited to the great banquet of universal faith, they rejected the words of this Celestial Messenger.

That was how the Jewish people failed to enjoy the benefits of being the first invited to the banquet.

It would be unfair, however, to blame an entire people for this state of affairs. The responsibility rests mostly with the Pharisees and Sadducees. The arrogance and fanaticism of the former, along with the unbelief of the latter, did great harm to the Jewish nation. They were primarily the ones Jesus identified as the guests who refused to appear at the wedding feast. Jesus added that when the king heard of their refusal, he told his servants to go to the street corners and invite to the banquet anyone they found, good and bad alike. In this way, Jesus intended that the Word should be preached to all other peoples, both pagans and idol worshippers, who, on accepting it, would be admitted to the feast in place of the first-invited guests.

But to take part in this celestial banquet, it isn't enough to be invited, or to say you're a Christian, or simply to sit at the table. Before anything else, it's essential—an express condition, in fact—that we are clothed in the nuptial tunic, that is to say, that we are pure in heart and observe the spirit of the Law. The Law is contained in these words: "Without love there is no salvation." Many hear this divine word; very few keep it and make good use of it. Thus, few become worthy enough to enter into the kingdom of heaven. This is why Jesus said, "Many are invited, but few are chosen."

---

[1] *Translator's Note: Genesis 22:17.*

THE NARROW DOOR

3.   *"Enter through the narrow gate. For wide is the gate and broad is the road that leads to destruction, and many enter through it. But small is the gate and narrow the road that leads to life, and only a few find it."*

(Matthew, 7: 13-14)

4.   *Someone asked him, "Lord, are only a few people going to be saved?"*

He said to them, "Make every effort to enter through the narrow door, because many, I tell you, will try to enter and will not be able to. Once the owner of the house gets up and closes the door, you will stand outside knocking and pleading, 'Sir, open the door for us.'

"But he will answer, 'I don't know you or where you come from.'

"Then you will say, 'We ate and drank with you, and you taught in our streets.'

"But he will reply, 'I don't know you or where you come from. Away from me, all you evildoers!'

"There will be weeping there, and gnashing of teeth, when you see Abraham, Isaac and Jacob and all the prophets in the kingdom of God, but you yourselves thrown out. People will come from east and west and north and south, and will take their places at the feast in the kingdom of God. Indeed there are those who are last who will be first, and first who will be last."

(Luke, 13: 23-30)

5.   The door to damnation is wide because the number of base passions is so large and the majority prefer to tread such a path. The door to salvation is narrow because to go through it we have to overcome our lower tendencies, which means that we must exert enormous control over ourselves. Few of us have the courage to undertake this kind of effort—a situation that finds expression in the precept "Many are invited, but few are chosen."

This is the condition in which human beings on earth find themselves. Earth is a world of trials and purifications; its dominant trait, consequently, is imperfection. Only when the planet is transformed will the most frequently followed path be the one to goodness. Thus, we should understand Christ's words in relative, not in absolute terms. If the present condition of earth was permanent, God would have condemned most of humankind to doom. This hypothesis, however, is inadmissible because God, as we recognize, is all justice and all kindness.

Yet if humankind as a group is a castaway on earth, and if the soul has had no other corporeal existences but the present one, we must ask what human beings have done to deserve such an unhappy state of affairs, both now and in the future? Why are so many hurdles placed before us? If the soul's destiny is determined immediately and permanently after death, why is the door so narrow that only a few can enter through it? In fact, if there was only one existence, human beings would always be at odds with themselves and God's justice. But once we accept that the soul has lived many lives and that there are many worlds, our spiritual horizons spread out. This perspective illuminates the obscurest points of religious faith. The present, the future, and the past of the soul become unified, and we will at last understand the depth, truth, and wisdom of Christ's words.

NOT EVERYONE WHO SAYS LORD! LORD! WILL ENTER THE KINGDOM OF HEAVEN

6.   *"Not everyone who says to me, 'Lord, Lord,' will enter the kingdom of heaven, but only he who does the will of my Father who is in heaven. Many will say to me on that day, 'Lord, Lord, did we not prophesy in your name, and in your name drive out demons and perform many miracles?' Then I will tell them plainly, 'I never knew you. Away from me evildoers!'"*

(Matthew, 7: 21-23)

7.   *"Therefore everyone who hears these words of mine and puts them into practice is like a wise man who built his house on the rock. The rain came down, the streams rose, and the winds blew and beat against that house; yet it did not fall, because it had its foundation on the rock. But everyone who hears these words of mine and does not put them into practice is like a foolish man who built his house on sand. The rain came down, the streams rose, and the winds blew and beat against that house, and it fell with a great crash."*

(Matthew, 7: 24-27, and Luke, 6: 46-49)

8.   *"Anyone who breaks one of the least of these commandments and teaches others to do the same will be called least in the kingdom of heaven, but whoever practices and teaches these commands will be called great in the kingdom of heaven."*

(Matthew, 5: 19)

9.   Everyone who recognizes Jesus' mission says; "Lord! Lord!" But what good does it do for people to say "Master" or "Lord" when they don't follow Jesus' precepts? Can we really call people Christians who make public acts of devotion and at the same time abandon themselves to the arms of pride, selfishness, greed, and all the other dark human impulses? Are people who spend their days in prayer but show themselves to be no better, no more charitable, no more tolerant toward their fellow human beings,

really his disciples? No. Like the Pharisees, they may have prayer on their lips but not in their hearts. They may impress others with their show, but not God. It's useless for them to say to Jesus, "Lord, Lord, did we not prophesy in your name, and in your name drive out demons and perform many miracles? ... Didn't we eat and drink with you, and didn't you teach in our street?" He'll answer such questions by saying, "I don't know who you are—go away from me. You do terrible things: You deny with your acts what you say with your lips, you slander your neighbor, you rob widows, and commit adultery. Go away from me. Your hearts are full of hate and bitterness. You spill the blood of your brothers and sisters in My name, you cause tears instead of drying them. For you, there will be weeping and gnashing of teeth, because the kingdom of heaven is only for the gentle, the humble, the charitable. Don't expect to bend Divine Justice with all your prayers or the number of times you kneel. The only path that will lead you to grace in His sight is the sincere practice of the law of love and charity."

The words of Jesus are eternal because they are the truth. And they aren't only a safe conduct to celestial life, but a promise of peace, harmony, and stability in earthly affairs. This is why institutions—political, social, or religious—that rely on them will stay as firmly grounded and unshakable as the house built on rock. Humanity will respect these institutions because in them human beings find fulfillment for their lives. The institutions that violate the words of Jesus are like houses built on the sand—the wind of renewal and the river of progress will eventually sweep them away.

MUCH WILL BE ASKED OF HIM WHO RECEIVES MUCH

10.   *"The servant who knows his master's will and does not get ready or does not do what his master wants will be beaten with many blows. But the one who does not know and does things deserving punishment will be beaten with few blows. From everyone who has been given much, much will be demanded; and from the one who has been entrusted with much, much more will be asked."*

(Luke, 12: 47-48)

11.   *Jesus said: "For judgment I have come into this world, so that the blind will see and those who see will become blind."*

Some Pharisees who were with him heard him say this and asked, "What? Are we blind too?"

Jesus said, "If you were blind, you would not be guilty of sin; but now that you claim you can see, your guilt remains."

(John, 9: 39-41)

12. These precepts apply even more specifically to Spiritist teachings. Anyone who knows Christ's precepts but doesn't keep them is guilty beyond question. But the Gospel is known only in Christian religions, and within them, many people don't read it regularly, and among those who read it, many don't understand it well. As a result, Jesus' words remain foreign to most men and women the world over.

The spirits come now to reveal the teachings of Jesus following a variety of perspectives. They develop and comment on them in order to put them within the reach of all. Every person—educated and uneducated, believer and unbeliever, Christian and non-Christian—can have access to them because the spirits communicate these truths everywhere. Therefore, no one who receives them, either directly or through the go-between of a medium, can claim to be ignorant of their significance. It's no longer possible to offer excuses based on a lack of awareness or the teachings' obscure allegorical meaning. Consequently, people who don't take advantage of these views and interpretations to better themselves, who think of them only as novel or entertaining, or who keep their hearts cold to them, are guilty. So, too, are those who don't become more useful, less proud, less selfish, less attached to material things, and who act no better toward their neighbors. These are indeed more guilty because they, more than others, have better means of finding the truth.

As for sensitives (mediums) who receive virtue-inspiring communications but continue doing wrong, they're even more likely to suffer because they often write their own sentence. If they weren't blinded by pride, they'd realize that the spirit guides are first and foremost speaking to them. But instead of taking to heart the lessons dictated by spirit guides—with their assistance or the assistance of other mediums—their one concern is to apply the lessons to others. In this way they confirm the words of Jesus, "Why do you look at the speck of sawdust in your brother's eye and pay no attention to the plank in your own eye?"[2]

In the sentence "If you were blind, you would not be guilty of sin," Jesus wanted to point out that the degree of responsibility is in direct relationship to the person's level of awareness. Thus, the

---

[2] *Translator's Note: Matthew 7:3. See also Chapter 10, item 9.*

Pharisees, who claimed to be the most enlightened people in Israel—and indeed were—became more reprehensible before God than the uneducated folk. The same applies today.

As such, much is expected from those who embrace the Spiritist Doctrine because they've been given much; and those who put it to good use will be given a great deal more.

The first thought of sincere Spiritists should be to find out if something in the counseling given by illuminated spirits also applies to them. In this way, the Spiritist Doctrine helps to multiply the number of the ones who are invited; and, because it strengthens faith, it helps to multiply the number of the chosen.

SPIRIT TEACHINGS

WHOEVER HAS WILL BE GIVEN MORE

13.   *The disciples came to him and asked, "Why do you speak to the people in parables?"*

He replied, "The knowledge of the secrets of the kingdom of heaven has been given to you, but not to them. Whoever has will be given more, and he will have an abundance. Whoever does not have, even what he has will be taken from him. This is why I speak to them in parables: Though seeing, they do not see; though hearing, they do not hear or understand.

"In them is fulfilled the prophecy of Isaiah, 'You will be ever hearing but never understanding; you will be ever seeing but never perceiving.'"

(Matthew, 13: 10-14)

14.   *"Consider carefully what you hear," he continued. "With the measure you use, it will be measured to you—and even more. Whoever has will be given more; whoever does not have, even what he has will be taken from him."*

(Mark, 4: 24-25)

15. ■ "Whoever has will be given more; whoever does not have, even what he has will be taken from him." I invite you to reflect on these great teachings, which often seem so paradoxical. "Whoever has" refers to people who know the meaning of the divine word. They've gained this knowledge only because they've striven to be worthy of it and because God, Who is merciful and loving, strengthens the efforts of anyone who inclines toward goodness. Their sustained efforts and unwavering persistence bring upon them the blessings of God. These people are

like magnets, attracting to themselves the best sources of inspiration and progress, the abundant grace that makes them strong enough to scale the sacred mountain, at the top of which they'll find rest after their labor.

"Whoever does not have, even what he has will be taken from him." This is the figurative counterpoint to the first part of the phrase, not a literal one. Consider that God doesn't take back the good once it's given. Oh! Blind and deaf humanity! Please, open your minds and your hearts; see with the eyes of your spirit and listen with your souls. Above all, don't misinterpret so grossly and unjustly the words of the One Who makes the Justice of God shine brilliantly before you. No, it isn't God who takes away from the one who has little—it's the soul itself, by its wastefulness and carelessness; it doesn't know how to preserve, nurture, and grow the gift of love that it's been given.

The son who doesn't cultivate the fields his father has left him will soon see them covered with weeds. Is the father, then, taking away a harvest the son didn't look after? No, he isn't. If the seeds that would have produced the crop die because of the son's neglect, can the son rightfully blame his father because they didn't produce anything? He cannot. Instead of blaming his loss on the father who actually gave him a field ready for cultivation, the son should complain to the real instigator of his problems—himself. Only after that, and armed with new energy and true regret for his mistake, can he go out to do the hard work ahead. Through sheer will power, he plows the hard land, sustained by heartfelt repentance and hope. Then he can sow the good seeds he has separated, and water them with his love and compassion. Then God, the God of love and compassion, will give him more of that which he already has. And he will see his efforts crowned with success; one grain will produce a hundred, another a thousand. So take courage, workers! Take up your harrows and your plows; work with your hearts; tear out the weeds; sow the good seed the Lord has given you and the dew of love will cause the fruits to grow. ■ —A Spiritual Friend (Bordeaux, 1862).

CHRISTIANS ARE RECOGNIZABLE BY THEIR WORKS

16. ■ "Not everyone who says to me, 'Lord, Lord,' will enter the kingdom of heaven, but only he who does the will of my Father who is in heaven."

Everyone who rejects the Spiritist Doctrine as the work of the devil should ponder these words of the Master. Listen closely, the time to unlock their real meaning has come.

Is it enough to wear the livery of the Lord to be considered His faithful servant?[3] Is it enough to say simply "I am a Christian" to be a real follower of Christ? If you're looking for real Christians, you'll recognize them by their works. "A good tree cannot bear bad fruit, and a bad tree cannot bear good fruit. Every tree that does not bear good fruit is cut down and thrown into the fire."[4] These are Jesus' words. Understand them well, disciples of Christ! Christianity is a mighty tree; its leafy branches provide shade to parts of the world, although at the moment it doesn't give shelter to everyone who looks for shade. But what kind of fruits should the tree of Christianity bear? From this Tree of Life come the fruits of spiritual life, hope, and faith. Christianity, as it has done for centuries, continues to inspire sublime virtues everywhere. But very few pick the fruits! The tree is fertile, but sadly, the gardeners of the Christian tree have often done a poor job. They have tried to shape it to reflect their own ideas and to justify their own needs. They pruned it, abridged it, mutilated it, and soon enough many of its branches stopped producing. Though the tree itself has never produced bad fruits, some of its branches now produce no fruit at all—they have become sterile. Now, when a hungry voyager of life seeks rest under its shade and reaches for the fruits of hope, which sustain with strength and courage, he finds only the same bleak barrenness that often precedes the storm season. In vain he looks for fruits. Only dry leaves fall at his feet. Human hands have so tampered with the Tree that they have scorched its leaves.

Dearly beloved, open your hearts and ears. Nurture the Tree of Life; its fruits give eternal life. The One who planted it urges you to treat it with love so that you will see it produce its divine fruits abundantly. Keep it just as it was when Christ gave it to you. It wants to cast its immense shade over the earth, so don't mutilate it or cut its branches. Let its hearty fruits fall abundantly so they can satisfy the hungry travelers who want to reach the end of their journey. Don't amass these fruits and then simply let them rot in a hidden place where they will benefit no one.

---

[3] *Translator's Note: The reference here is to the dress (usually distinguished by color) worn by the servants of one house or master.*

[4] *Translator's Note: Matthew 7:18-19.*

"Many are invited, but few are chosen." This is because some people try to monopolize the Bread of Life, just as there are people who hoard bread at the expense of others. Don't be one of them. The Tree produces good fruits and it must produce them for everyone. So go find the downtrodden, lead them under the leafy branches of the Tree of Life, and share its shade with them. "Do people pick grapes from thornbushes?"[5] Brothers and sisters, turn away from those who call you only to show you the thornbushes along the way. Instead, follow the ones who lead you under the shade of the Tree of Life.

The Divine Savior, who is just to the highest degree, said (and His words will never die), "Not everyone who says to me, 'Lord, Lord,' will enter the kingdom of heaven, but only he who does the will of my Father who is in heaven."

May the Lord of Grace bless you; may the Lord of Light illuminate you. May the Tree of Life offer you its abundant fruits. Trust and pray. ■ —Simeon (Bordeaux, 1863).

---

[5] *Translator's Note: Matthew 7:16.*

Chapter 19

Faith Moves Mountains

SCRIPTURE AND COMMENTARY

THE POWER OF FAITH

1.   *When they came to the crowd, a man approached Jesus and knelt before him. "Lord, have mercy on my son," he said. "He has seizures and is suffering greatly. He often falls into the fire or into the water. I brought him to your disciples, but they could not heal him."*

"O unbelieving and perverse generation," Jesus replied, "how long shall I stay with you? How long shall I put up with you? Bring the boy here to me." Jesus rebuked the demon, and it came out of the boy, and he was healed from that moment.

Then the disciples came to Jesus in private and asked, "Why couldn't we drive it out?"

He replied, "Because you have so little faith. I tell you the truth, if you have faith as small as a mustard seed, you can say to this mountain, 'Move from here to there' and it will move. Nothing will be impossible for you."

(Matthew, 17: 14-20)

2.   Confidence in our own strength lets us do things (in the material sense) that we couldn't undertake if we doubted ourselves. Here, however, we'd like to concentrate solely on the moral meaning of Jesus' words. The mountains faith can move are life's obstacles: the difficulties, the resistances, the ill will, the barriers confronting us even in the pursuit of the noblest ventures—in short, everything we have to face as members of the human community. Prejudices, routines, material interests, selfishness, the blindness of fanaticism, the passions that exaggerate pride are only a few of the mountains that block our way in the process of working for our progress. When our faith is robust we find in ourselves the strength, determination, and resources to overcome

such barriers, whether they are large or small. Wavering faith, by contrast, breeds hesitation and the kind of tentativeness our opponents quickly exploit. People don't strive to win because they don't believe they can win.

3. Another commonly understood meaning of faith is "confidence in bringing something about and the certainty of reaching a specific goal." Faith gives us the clarity of mind that lets us visualize our goal and the means of attaining it. Thus, people who have faith move forward with a sense of absolute security. Whether as defined here or in the above, faith can help us realize great things.

    Faith, when real and sincere, is always calm. Because it is supported by reason and an understanding of life, it teaches us patience and gives us the assurance that we'll eventually grasp what we reach for. A wavering faith, though, senses its own weakness. And if it's motivated by personal interest, it may turn into hostility on the assumption that aggression can make up for a lack of strength. Yet calmness during the struggle is always a sign of strength and confidence, just as violence indicates weakness and self-doubt.

4. Here we should be careful not to confuse faith with an unwarranted presumption. True faith is linked to meekness of spirit. People who have it place more confidence in God than in themselves. They know they're simply instruments of the Divine Will and can't do anything without God—which is why the good spirits come to help them. A bold, exaggerated self-assurance is the opposite. It displays arrogance more than faith, and sooner or later this arrogance is punished by failure and disappointment.

5. The power of faith can be shown in a direct and special manner by magnetic action. Through the intermediary of faith, human beings act on the universal principle; faith transforms its properties and gives it, so to speak, an irresistible force.[1] Consequently, anyone who joins healing energy to a strong faith can, purely by focusing his or her will on love, produce the phenomenon of healing and the events that in ancient times were called "miracles" but were nothing more than the consequences of a Law of Nature. This is why Jesus said to his apostles that if they didn't cure it was because they lacked faith.

---

[1] *Translator's Note: Universal principle in modern scientific language may be interpreted as the force that sustains the fundamental fields of nature. For a more detailed explanation see Allan Kardec's* The Spirits Book, *2003, AKES, Philadelphia (PA), p. 9.*

RELIGIOUS FAITH; THE STATE OF UNSHAKABLE FAITH

6.   From the theological perspective, faith consists in belief in particular principles, around which the various religions have formed.
All religions have their articles of faith, and on this basis, religious faith may be considered either blind or rational. Blind faith
examines nothing. It accepts truth and falsehood without critical
examination. For this reason, it is constantly clashing with reason
and hard evidence. Taken to the extreme it produces fanaticism.
But when based on erroneous principles, sooner or later blind
faith collapses. Only faith that is based on truth lasts into the
future. This kind of faith has nothing to fear from scientific
progress; it knows that what is true in the dark is also true in the
light. Still, religions tend to affirm (to their faithful) that they
have sole and exclusive possession of the truth. Unfortunately,
this can only happen if blind faith is demanded from believers.
But to impose blind faith on a point of belief is to confess that the
correctness of that point cannot be deduced from reasoning.

7.   It's often said that you can't dictate to people what they should
believe in. Many blame an experience of this type of behavior for
the fact that they themselves have no faith. Unquestionably, faith
can't be dictated. Even more certainly, faith can't be imposed. It
can only be acquired, and we should add that no one is intrinsi-
cally unsuited to possess it, even the most skeptical of persons.
(Here we're speaking of faith in basic spiritual truths, not of any
particular belief.) Yet faith doesn't seek people out; people have
to seek out faith, and if they search sincerely they'll inevitably
find it. You can be sure that people who say, "There's nothing I'd
like more than to believe, but I can't," are only saying this with
their lips, not their hearts, because they close their eyes and ears
to the call of faith. In reality, the evidence of basic spiritual truths
is all around them. So why do they refuse to recognize it? For
some, the problem is apathy; for others, the fear of feeling compelled to change their habits. For the great majority, it's their
pride which refuses to acknowledge the existence of a superior
power before which they would have to show reverence.

In some people faith appears to be inborn and only needs the
proper spark to unfold completely. This ease in absorbing spiritual truths is an evident sign of previous progress. Others have
difficulty absorbing the truths of the spirit, a no less evident sign
that their natures are still unevolved. The former bring with them
at their rebirth the intuition of what they learned previously.
Their spiritual education is closer to completion. The latter still

have much to learn. Their education is still to come, but come it will; and if it isn't completed in this lifetime, it will be in another.

The resistance of unbelievers is almost always due less to themselves than to the way ideas and information have been presented to them. Faith needs a foundation that provides a complete intellectual understanding of what we're asked to believe. Nowadays it isn't enough to see in order to believe. Understanding is vital, because blind faith is no longer acceptable in this century. Indeed, it is blind, dogmatic faith that produces the greatest number of unbelievers today. Such faith tries to impose itself; it demands that we surrender the most precious prerogatives of the human soul—rationality and free will. It is principally against this kind of faith that unbelievers rebel, proving the truth of the view that faith can't be dictated. Further, blind faith, in denying the need of any evidence, leaves the spirit feeling empty and so breeds doubt. A rational faith, based on facts and logic, leaves no doubts. Discerning believers believe because they have certainty, and no one can be certain unless they understand. That is why a rational faith doesn't have to fear the facts. For the only unshakable faith is that which can withstand reason, face to face, at every stage in humankind's development.

This is the situation that the Spiritist Doctrine will bring about, and it will do so wherever it doesn't encounter bigoted and prejudiced opposition.

THE PARABLE OF THE DRY FIG TREE

8.   *The next day as they were leaving Bethany, Jesus was hungry. Seeing in the distance a fig tree in leaf, he went to find out if it had any fruit. When he reached it, he found nothing but leaves, because it was not the season for figs. Then he said to the tree, "May no one ever eat fruit from you again." And his disciples heard him say it.*

In the morning, as they went along, they saw the fig tree withered from the roots. Peter remembered and said to Jesus, "Rabbi, look! The fig tree you cursed has withered!"

"Have faith in God," Jesus answered, "I tell you the truth, if anyone says to this mountain, 'Go, throw yourself into the sea,' and does not doubt in his heart but believes that what he says will happen, it will be done for him."

(Mark, 11: 12-14, 20-23)

9.   The dried up fig tree is a symbol for people who maintain the appearance of good-heartedness but don't produce anything

worthwhile. They're like the preachers who have more style than substance. Their words have a superficial polish that pleases our ears. But on closer examination, we realize that they've offered nothing of significance to our hearts. After listening to them, we wonder what we have gained.

The dried fig tree also symbolizes all those persons who could be useful but aren't, as well as all the utopias, the futile philosophies, the doctrines without solid foundations. In the majority of these cases, what's lacking most is true faith, productive faith, the kind of faith that stirs the heart—in a word, the faith that moves mountains. Such people and belief systems are like trees that are covered with leaves but fail to bear fruit. This is why Jesus condemns them to sterility, knowing the day will come when they'll find themselves dry down to the roots. Of all the doctrines and philosophical systems, the ones that have produced no good for humanity will be reduced to nothing. And all those persons who've deliberately led a purposeless life, who've failed to put into action the resources at hand, will be treated like the fig tree that has dried up.

10. It's instructive here to mention mediums, the spirits' interpreters, who offer the physical means by which the spirits communicate their teachings. Mediums are beneficiaries of this gift for a reason. In these days of social renewal, they have a special duty to perform. They are to be like fruitful trees, destined to provide spiritual nourishment for their brothers and sisters. This is why their numbers are now multiplying: There must be an abundance of spiritual food. This is why sensitive individuals can be found everywhere, in all countries, in every social class, among rich and poor, notables and laborers, so nobody is disenfranchised, and every human being is called. However, if mediums turn this precious gift away from the goals of Providence, if they use it for frivolous or harmful ends, put it at the service of mundane interests, foster corrupted fruits, refuse to use their gift to benefit others (employing it, instead, for their own profit), they will be like the sterile fig tree. God will take away their gift, that seed they don't know how to cultivate, because it has become useless in their hands. He will then let them follow their path in the company of like-minded, unenlightened spirits.

SPIRIT TEACHINGS

FAITH, THE MOTHER OF HOPE AND LOVE

11. ■ To be worthwhile, faith must be constantly active and never dulled by inaction. Faith is the mother of all the virtues leading up to God, and its duty is to keep close watch over the development of its offspring. From faith come hope and love—virtues that, together with faith, form an inseparable trinity. Isn't it faith that helps you hope for the realization of the Lord's promises? How could you have such hope if faith didn't exist? And isn't it faith that sustains love? If you didn't have faith, how would you express gratitude to God and show the full extent of your love.

Faith is the inspiration that awakens humanity's noblest impulses and impels it toward the good. Faith is also the base of all spiritual renewal. Consequently, this base must be soundly built. Doubt, if harbored, will cleave through the base and imperil the building sitting on it. You must build your faith on solid foundations. Thus, nurture your faith to be stronger than the futile arguments of critics and firm enough to withstand the ridicule of unbelievers.

Sincere faith is infectious and captivating. It touches the soul of people who lack it and even those who rebuff it. It inspires persuasive words that touch the heart—as opposed to feigned faith, which only uses high sounding words and leaves listeners cold and indifferent. Teach through the example of your faith and you will infect everyone. Teach through the example of your works and you will demonstrate the merit of faith. Teach through an unshakeable hope and everyone will see the courage that empowers you to brave even the hardest of life's challenges.

Have faith! Let yourself be enraptured by all its beauty and goodness, its purity and rationality. Don't accept a faith that can't stand up to reason, for that faith is an offspring of mental blindness. Love God, but know well why you love God. Believe in God's promises, but have a clear understanding of why you believe in them. Listen to our advice, but convince yourself of the ends we point you to, and the means we suggest by which you can reach them. Trust and be patient, without ever losing heart: Miracles are the works of faith. ■ —Joseph, a Guardian Spirit (Bordeaux, 1862).

HUMAN AND DIVINE FAITH

12. ■ In human beings, faith is an inborn feeling about their future destiny. It's the intuitive realization that they have in themselves enormous abilities, though in a latent state, which they are expected to make blossom and grow through the action of their will.

Until the present time, faith has only been understood in its religious sense because Christ extolled it as a powerful lever and because He has been seen only as the head of a religion. But Christ, Who performed material miracles, showed human beings through these miracles what they could do if they had faith—that is to say, the will to desire and the conviction that this desire will be fulfilled.

Didn't the apostles also perform miracles by following His example? And what were these miracles except the natural effects of causes that weren't understood in those days—that can be explained in great part now and totally understood through studying the principles of the Spiritist Doctrine and physical magnetism.[2]

Faith is either human or Divine, depending on whether human beings use their talents to satisfy their earthly needs or their heavenly and future aspirations. A talented person who throws him- or herself into realizing a great undertaking will succeed if sustained by a strong faith. Faith gives that inner conviction, a powerful certainty that he or she is bound to reach the end visualized. The good man or woman who believes in a heavenly future and wants to fill life with beautiful and noble actions (con-

---

[2] *Translator's Note: Physical magnetism, related to properties of "animal magnetism," a system of healing proposed by Franz Anton Mesmer (1733-1815) in* De Planetarium Influxu *(1766). According to Mesmer, we are immersed in a fluid that is universal and continuous through which celestial bodies, the earth, and animated bodies mutually influence each other. This influence manifests itself in the human body through properties analogous to those of the magnet and can be communicated, changed, destroyed, and reinforced. Modern physics helps us understand this fundamental idea through the concept of fields of energy. Accordingly, living forms constituted of atoms, cells, organs, and bodies would be a complex system of hierarchical fields. If one conceives an ill person as being in less than an optimal energy state, then a transfer of energy from a person with a surplus could help accomplish healing. Mesmer's concept of a universal fluid is analogous to the Spiritist Doctrine's Cosmic Principle discussed in* The Spirits *Book, question 27. This is the essence of the concept of physical magnetism espoused by Allan Kardec. Dr. Dolores Kruger, Ph.D. and Professor of Nursing, New York University, is a modern pioneer researcher in this area, now renamed Therapeutic Touch.*

fident that happiness awaits) draws on faith for the necessary power to do so, and through faith accomplishes miracles of love, devotion, and self-denial. Finally, faith is a powerful instrument to help us correct any negative impulses of the soul.

Physical magnetism is one of the greatest proofs of the power of faith when put into action. It is through faith that it cures and produces the unique physical healing that in other times was called a miracle.

I repeat: Faith is both human and Divine. If all souls could be convinced of the force they have within, and if they genuinely wanted to place their will at the service of this force, they too could produce these so-called miracles, which are nothing more than the development of human gifts. ■ —A Guardian Spirit (Paris, 1863).

Chapter 20

Workers of the Last Hour

SCRIPTURE AND COMMENTARY

WORKERS OF THE LAST HOUR

1.   *"For the kingdom of heaven is like a landowner who went out early in the morning to hire men to work in his vineyard. He agreed to pay them a denarius for the day and sent them into his vineyard.*

"About the third hour he went out and saw others standing in the marketplace doing nothing. He told them, 'You also go and work in my vineyard, and I will pay you whatever is right.' So they went.

"He went out again about the sixth hour and the ninth hour and did the same thing. About the eleventh hour he went out and found still others standing around. He asked them, 'Why have you been standing here all day long doing nothing?'

"'Because no one has hired us,' they answered.

"He said to them, 'You also go and work in my vineyard.'

"When evening came, the owner of the vineyard said to his foreman, 'Call the workers and pay them their wages, beginning with the last ones hired and going on to the first.'

"The workers who were hired about the eleventh hour came and each received a denarius. So when those came who were hired first, they expected to receive more. But each one of them also received a denarius. When they received it, they began to grumble against the landowner. 'These men who were hired last worked only one hour,' they said, 'and you have made them equal to us who have borne the burden of work and the heat of the day.'

"But he answered one of them, 'Friend, I am not being unfair to you. Didn't you agree to work for a denarius? Take your pay and go. I want to

give the man who was hired last the same as I gave you. Don't I have the right to do what I want with my own money? Or are you envious because I am generous?'

"So the last will be first, and the first will be last."

(Matthew, 20: 1-16) [1]

SPIRIT TEACHINGS

THE LAST WILL BE FIRST

2. ■ The workers of the last hour have a right to their wages as long as they've willingly made themselves available to their employer and their lateness in taking up work hasn't been due to laziness or lack of will. They're entitled to wages because from daybreak they've eagerly waited for the opportunity to work. They've been diligent, even if there was nothing for them to do.

And what of workers who refuse to work during the day? Of those who say, "Wait a minute, all this rest suits me. I'll think about today's wages when the last hour comes. In the meantime why should I care about an employer I don't know and who doesn't care about me? The later the better!" These people, friends, will never receive the wages of work, only of laziness.

Finally, what can be said of individuals who, rather than simply do nothing, use the hours of their workday to engage in shameful acts? These are the ones who curse God, spill the blood of their brothers and sisters, stir up trouble in families, cause the ruin of trusting people, take advantage of the innocent—in short, the ones who feed on the depravities of human nature. What will become of them? Will it be enough to say at the last hour, "Master, I've used my time badly. Take me on until the end of the day. I'll do some of the work, though I know it will only be a small portion of my share. Won't you please give me the wages of a good worker?"

"No!" The Lord will say to them, "I don't have any work for you right now. You've wasted your time; you've forgotten what you learned. You can't work any longer in my vineyard. You'll have to start your learning all over again. But when you've changed your attitude for the better, come to me again and I'll open up to you my vast fields, where you can work at any time."

[1] *See also the Parable of the Wedding Feast, Chapter 19, item 1.*

Good Spiritists, dearly beloved, you are all workers of the last hour. It is pure presumption to think otherwise, to claim that "I began work at dawn and will work until nightfall." All of you came when you were called to this incarnation—some earlier, some later. But for how many centuries have you been called to the divine vineyard without any desire on your part to enter it? Now you have a chance to earn a wage. Make good use of the time that's left, and never forget that your life, however long it appears to be, is only a fleeting moment in the immensity of time that is Eternity. ■ —Constantine, a Guardian Spirit (Bordeaux, 1863).

3. ■ Jesus liked the simplicity of symbols. In His figurative language, the workers who arrived at the first hour were Moses, the prophets, and all those who blazed the trail of spiritual progress. Throughout the ages, others—the apostles, the martyrs, the founders of the Church, the sages, the philosophers, and finally the Spiritists—have continued this work.

And, just as announced by the Messiah, those who come latest will receive the same pay as the early workers. In a way, their pay will be even greater, since they will profit from all the contributions of their predecessors. Here, as in every form of knowledge, each generation builds on previous ones. Any great feat is by nature a collective event—a fundamental solidarity of life that God blesses. Now, many of the early workers are again living in the physical realm, or will be doing so soon, in order to complete the endeavors they began in the past. More than one famous leader, more than one sage, more than one servant of Christ, more than one missionary of Christian ideals can be found among Spiritists today. Only now they're more enlightened, more advanced, than they were; and they no longer work at the base but at the apex of the structure. They will receive their wages according to the merit of their work.

The august doctrine of reincarnation reveals in precise terms the spiritual unity of human life. When called on to give an account of its earthly obligations, the soul realizes the connections between its different journeys on earth and sees that its task is only temporarily interrupted, that the work has to continue. With this, the spirit experiences a sense of unity with the concerns of every member of the human family throughout time. It is then that the spirit, strengthened by this realization, resumes its learning on earth. So none of you, workers of the first and last hours whose eyes are fully open to the profound Justice of God, should ever complain about your fate, but praise the loving God.

This is one of the true meanings of this parable. As all Jesus' parables to the people did, it contains elements of the future that awaits us, and reveals the magnificent unity—in all its forms and from every aspect—that harmonizes all things in the Universe and the common purpose that joins all present beings to the past and the future. ■ —Heinrich Heine (Paris, 1863).

THE MISSION OF THE SPIRITISTS

4.   ■ Don't you already hear the sounds of the tempest that will sweep away the old world and crush into oblivion all earth's wickedness? Ah, praise God, all of you who've put your faith in God's sovereign Justice. New apostles of a belief revealed by superior, prophetic voices—go forward to spread this new doctrine of reincarnation and the continuous progress of the soul, which is entirely based on how well or badly you fulfill your earthly mission and endure the trials of life.

Don't be afraid! Tongues of fire are above your heads.[2] Oh, devoted Spiritists, you are the chosen ones today! Go and sing the Good News to the world. The time has come for you to give of yourselves, to take time off from your labors and leisure in order to serve—so go and tell everyone! Enlightened spirits are with you.

Most certainly you'll speak to people who don't want to hear the Voice of God because it demands that they live their lives more selflessly. You'll preach disinterestedness to the greedy, self-restraint to the sinful, gentleness to domestic tyrants and to despots! Your words will be lost, I know. But it doesn't matter. For the land to produce fruits, it will be necessary to water the soil with the sweat of your brow, and work it tirelessly with the harrow and plow of the Gospel. So go and sing it to the world!

To you men and women of good faith, conscious that there are more advanced realms in infinite space, throw yourselves into the crusade against injustice and wrongdoing! Go—halt the worship of the golden calf that seems more widespread every day. Your tongues will be freed, no matter how well prepared and sophisticated you think you are. You will speak as no speaker has

---

[2] *Translator's Note: 'Tongues of fire' a reference to Acts 2:3-4 ["They (the disciples) saw what seemed to be tongues of fire that separated and came to rest on each of them. All of them were filled with the Holy Spirit and began to speak in other tongues as the Spirit enabled them."]*

ever spoken. Go then and preach. The ones who listen (with their souls) will gladly take in your words of comfort, good fellowship, hope, and peace.

The ambushes your enemies have set for you along the pathway won't matter. Only wolves fall into wolf traps, and the Shepherd knows how to defend the sheep from those who sacrifice to hatred.

Go—you who are great before God and more blessed than Saint Thomas, for you believe without demanding proofs and accept spirit phenomena even without producing it yourselves. Go—the Divine Spirit is guiding you.

March forward, soldiers of faith! The army of unbelievers will vanish before you as quickly as dew at the first rays of the sun.

Jesus said that faith moves mountains. But heavier than the heaviest mountain are the moral flaws and vices lodged in the hearts of human beings. Have courage, then. Go and help eradicate this mountain of moral corruption so that future generations will know it only as a legend, as you know dimly of the times that existed before the pagan civilizations.

Ethical and philosophical upheavals will be produced everywhere on the globe. The hour approaches when the divine light will spread itself over both the physical and spiritual worlds. ■

THE WORKERS OF THE LORD

5.   ■ The time is near when the things that have been announced for humanity's transformation will be complete. All of you who've worked in the field of the Lord without self-interest and with no other motive than love will be blessed! You will be paid a hundred times more for your working days than you expected. You will be blessed, having said to your fellow human beings, "Let's work together and unite our efforts so that when the Lord comes, He'll find His work finished." To you the Lord will say, "Come to me, you who've been good servants, who knew how to silence your rivalries and discords so that no harm should come to the work!"

But those who've stirred up trouble and delayed the time of the harvest will be unfortunate indeed. The tempest will come and they'll be swept away by its force! They'll cry out, "Mercy! Mercy!" But the Lord will say to them, "How can you ask for mercy when you showed no mercy to anyone else, when you refused to offer a helping hand, trampling on the weak instead of giving them a hand up? How can you plead for mercy when you looked for your reward in earthly pleasures and the satisfaction of your pride? You've already received your reward, just as you wanted it. There's nothing more to ask for. heavenly rewards are for those who haven't looked for their payment in earthly things."

Providence is now preparing a count of the faithful servants. Already God has taken note of those people who only seem to be devout, and will prevent them from stealing the wages of courageous servants. To the latter, who do not draw back from the challenge, God will entrust critical positions in the great work of spiritual transformation to which the Spiritist Doctrine will contribute. These words will be fulfilled: "The last will be first, and the first will be last." ■ —The Spirit of truth (Paris, 1862).

Chapter 21

False Christs and False Prophets Will Appear

SCRIPTURE AND COMMENTARY

A TREE IS KNOWN BY ITS FRUITS

1.   *"No good tree bears bad fruit, nor does a bad tree bear good fruit. Each tree is recognized by its own fruit. People do not pick figs from thornbushes, or grapes from briers. The good man brings good things out of the good stored up in his heart, and the evil man brings evil things out of the evil stored up in his heart. For out of the overflow of his heart his mouth speaks."*

(Luke, 6: 43-45)

2.   *"Watch out for false prophets. They come to you in sheep's clothing, but inwardly they are ferocious wolves. By their fruit you will recognize them. Do people pick grapes from thornbushes, or figs from thistles? Likewise every good tree bears good fruit, but a bad tree bears bad fruit. A good tree cannot bear bad fruit, and a bad tree cannot bear good fruit. Every tree that does not bear good fruit is cut down and thrown into the fire. Thus, by their fruit you will recognize them."*

(Matthew, 7: 15-20)

3.   *Jesus answered: "Watch out that no one deceives you. For many will come in my name, claiming, 'I am the Christ,' and will deceive many."*

"And many false prophets will appear and deceive many people. Because of the increase of wickedness, the love of most will grow cold, but he who stands firm to the end will be saved."

"At that time if anyone says to you, 'Look, here is the Christ!' or, 'There he is!' do not believe it. For false Christs and false prophets will appear and perform great signs and miracles to deceive even the elect—if that were possible."

(Matthew, 24: 4-5, 11-12, 23-24)

THE MISSION OF THE PROPHETS

4. The gift of revealing the future is generally credited to the prophets; thus, the words "prophecy" and "prediction" have come to have the same meaning. But as it is used in the Gospel, "prophet" has a wider significance. It is the name given to everyone God sends us with the express mission of teaching humanity and revealing what was previously unknown and mysterious about our spiritual life. A person, then, can be a prophet without making predictions. Such was the understanding of the Jews at the time of Jesus, as shown by that passage in Matthew where Jesus is taken before Caiaphas, the high priest, in whose presence the teachers of the law and the elders had assembled. After spitting in Jesus' face, they strike him with their hands, saying, "Prophesy to us, Christ. Who hit you?"[1]

    It's also true that there were prophets who could see into the future, whether through intuition or revelations from Providence, and who made predictions about things to come. When their prophecies came true, people naturally started to consider the gift of predicting the future to be one of the signs of the prophet.

SIGNS AND MIRACLES OF THE FALSE PROPHETS

5. "False Christs and false prophets will appear and perform great signs and miracles to deceive even the elect—if that were possible." These words of Jesus give us the true meaning of the word miracle. In the standard theological interpretation, miracles are exceptional phenomena occurring outside the Laws of Nature. These laws are the exclusive work of God, Who can revoke them if necessary. But simple good sense tells us that God would never give immature, often ill-meaning beings powers equal to divine power—and certainly wouldn't give such beings the right to undo what God has done. This is definitely not what Jesus is referring to in this passage. Again, taking the traditional interpretation at face value, we could say that if ill-intentioned spirits had the power to work miracles capable of deceiving even the elect, then they would be able to do what God does. Miracles, accordingly, would no longer be the exclusive domain of God's messengers and would be worthless as a sign of God's power since nothing would distinguish the miracles of the upright from those of

---

[1] *Translator's Note: Matthew 26:68.*

the devil. This being so, we must look for a more rational explanation of Jesus' words.

To the uneducated, any phenomenon without an apparent cause becomes something supernatural, marvelous, miraculous. Find the cause, though, and, soon enough, people will accept that the phenomenon, no matter how extraordinary it seems, is nothing more than the application of a natural law. In this way the circle of supernatural events grows smaller as scientific knowledge widens. Thus, we find throughout history, men and women who have used certain kinds of knowledge to further their own ambitions, self-interests, and desire for power. They have used it to create images of themselves as possessors of supposedly superhuman powers or to claim divine missions. These are the false Christs and false prophets. However, with the growth of (scientific) knowledge, the credibility of these persons has begun to wither, and their numbers go on diminishing.

The simple fact is that being able to perform acts that pass among some as miracles doesn't in any way constitute a sign of a divine mission. The phenomena may result from acquired knowledge that anyone can learn, or come from some special gift that has nothing to do with one's worthiness or unworthiness. True prophets are recognized by their morals and their moral outlook.

DON'T BELIEVE ALL THE SPIRITS

6. *"Dear friends, do not believe every spirit, but test the spirits to see whether they are from God, because many false prophets have gone out into the world."*

(1 John, 4: 1)

7. Far from condoning false Christs and false prophets, as some people like to suggest, the phenomena on which Spiritist thought rests deal them a death blow. Don't ask the Spiritist Doctrine for supernatural signs or miracles: It positively declares that it doesn't perform them. Just as physics, chemistry, astronomy, and geology reveal the laws of the physical world, the Spiritist Doctrine reveals unknown laws of another kind. These laws govern the relationships between the physical and spiritual worlds, and they are every bit as natural as the ones that concern the physical sciences. Indeed, by explaining the laws that govern a class of phenomena that have been inexplicable until now, the Doctrine destroys what remains of the miraculous. Consequently, people who are tempted to exploit these phenom-

ena for personal gain—pretending, for example, that they're messengers from God—won't be allowed to abuse the public's credulity for long and will quickly be unmasked. As we've already said, the phenomena by themselves don't prove anything. A true mission is attested to by its moral effects, and these can't be produced by just anyone.

To sum up, we find here one of the benefits of the development of the Spiritist Doctrine: In scrutinizing the causes of certain phenomena, it raises the veil that has kept them in the domain of the wondrous and mysterious. Of course, people who prefer the darkness to the light have every interest in fighting against this progress. But truth is like the sun: It breaks through even the thickest clouds.

The Spiritist Doctrine also reveals a far more dangerous aspect of false Christs and false prophets. This aspect doesn't concern human beings, but discarnate spirits. In the spirit realm there are many beings who have left earth but have not given up their deceiving, hypocritical, proud, pseudo-intellectual ways. Many of them adopt distinguished names to hide behind in an attempt to give credence to their own strange and foolish ideas. Before the mediumistic process was adequately explained, they acted in less open ways, e.g., by means of inspiration and deep trances, clairvoyance and clairaudience. A great many of them have, in various periods (and above all in recent years) passed themselves off as some of the old prophets, Christ, the Mother Mary, even God. John warns against these spirits when he says, "Dear friends, do not believe every spirit, but test the spirits to see whether they are from God, because many false prophets have gone out into the world."[2] The Spiritist Doctrine offers us the means for evaluating spirits when it precisely describes the traits of good spirits, traits which are invariably moral and never related to the phenomenon per se.[3] It is in regard to distinguishing good and bad spirits from each other that we can understand these words of Jesus: "A good tree cannot bear bad fruit, and a bad tree cannot bear good fruit." Spirits must be judged by the quality of their works over time, just as a tree is judged by its fruits.

---

[2] *Translator's Note: 1 John 4:1*

[3] *For a discussion of the way spirits can be identified, see* The Medium's Book, *Part II, starting at Chapter 24.*

SPIRIT TEACHINGS

FALSE PROPHETS

8. ■ Wherever someone says, "Christ is here," don't go in. To the contrary, be on your guard, because false prophets exist in great number. You are aware when the leaves of the fig tree are fading. Don't you see its many shoots waiting for the time when the tree will flower? Jesus told you that you would know the tree by its fruit. If the fruit is bitter you already know the tree is evil. But if the fruit is sweet and healthy you can say, "Nothing that's pure can come from something bad."

Brothers and sisters, judge by the works. Examine the works. If the people who tell you they have divine powers reveal signs of a mission of a high order—that is to say, if they have Christian and eternal virtues of the highest order (charity, love, tolerance, goodness that unites all hearts)—and if in supporting their words they act in ways that accord with these virtues, you can say to yourself and others, "These are true messengers of God."

But distrust smooth words. Distrust the modern Scribes and Pharisees, for whom worship is a public performance. Distrust people who claim to have a monopoly on the truth!

Christ is not among these people. The people He sends to preach His sacred doctrine, and renew His peoples' will, follow His example above everything else. They will, above all, be gentle and have humble hearts. Those who, through their examples and teachings, guide humanity away from the tortuous path of doom will essentially be modest and humble of heart. So whenever you see a self-proclaimed prophet who shows even an atom of pride, run away from him or her as you would from an infectious disease. Remember, people bear the stamp of their spiritual worth or lack of it on their brow, and more especially in their actions.

Go, then, beloved children. Move without hesitation or second thoughts along the sacred route you've undertaken. Go without fear. Carefully turn away from everything that might block your path in your march toward the eternal goal. Travelers, it will not be long before the shadows and pains of the journey will dissipate. Open up your hearts to this sweet doctrine that comes to show you the Eternal Laws and to satisfy every desire of your souls regarding the unknown. Indeed, you may have already discerned a faint figure passing before you in your dreams, one that in its fleetingness has enchanted your soul, though it has never found a way into your mind. Beloved, perhaps you now realize that your old notion of death is dying, giving way to a radiant angel you can now see clearly: the angel of reunion, who assures you that you will see your dear ones again. All of you who've fulfilled your earthly tasks well have nothing more to fear from Divine Justice, since God, the wise Parent, always forgives children who've strayed when they cry out for mercy. You must always continue to advance. Let your motto be "Progress, Continuing Progress in All Things," until finally you reach the happy end of your journey, where everyone who went before you is waiting. ■ —Louis (Bordeaux, 1861).

CHARACTERISTICS OF THE TRUE PROPHET

9.   ■ Beware of false prophets. This warning is helpful in every era, but especially in times of transition, like the present one, when the world undergoes a profound transformation. In such times, many ambitious and scheming persons will promote themselves as reformers and messiahs. Be on guard against them, and realize that it's the duty of every honest person to unmask them. How can you identify them? Here are some signs to look for:

The command of an army is only confided to a capable general. Do you think God has less insight in giving out leadership roles than human beings? You can be sure that God only gives important missions to spirits who are able to carry them out. Great missions are heavy burdens: They crush anyone who isn't strong enough to shoulder them. As in other aspects of life, the teacher must know more than the student. To lead humanity's moral and intellectual progress requires men and women of superior intelligence and moral convictions. This is why only advanced spirits, who have honed these qualities in other lifetimes, are chosen for such tasks. If these spirits aren't superior to the society in which they act, their actions will bear no fruit.

You can conclude, then, that the true missionaries of God affirm their missions through their uprightness, their virtues, their generosity of spirit, and through the transforming impact of their actions. You should also consider the opposite possibility. If, in their character, virtue, and intelligence, people who claim to be God's missionaries demonstrate that they are less than what they claim to be, or less than the persons under whose names they present themselves, you should realize that they're only poor charlatans who can't imitate their own models.

For the most part, true missionaries of God aren't aware of their status. They perform their missions of service through the strength of their characters, seconded by a subtle but powerful inspiration that guides them toward, but doesn't predetermine, the achievement of their goals. In short, true prophets are revealed by their actions and are discovered by others; false prophets declare themselves to be messengers of God. The first are humble and modest, the second are full of themselves, speak arrogantly, and, like all liars, always seem to be afraid that no one will believe them.

In the past, impostors have passed themselves off as apostles of Christ, and even as Christ Himself. Embarrassingly enough, they've come across many people gullible enough to believe in their lies. But a little thought about the matter will open the eyes of even the blindest person.

If Christ were to reincarnate on earth, He'd show all his spiritual qualities and virtues—anything less would imply that He had somehow degenerated, a foolish idea. Just as you can rightly say that even if one of God's qualities were taken away, God wouldn't be God, so you can say that even if one of Christ's virtues were lacking, He wouldn't be Christ. The question is, Do the people who claim to be Christ have all His virtues? Observe these people, scrutinize their ideas and actions, and you'll see that, beyond anything else, they lack the distinctive qualities of Christ, His love and humbleness of heart, and are filled with qualities Christ never had, such as greed and pride. Further, the numbers just don't add up. At this moment in various countries around the globe, there are many self-proclaimed Christs, just as there are many Elijahs, Saint Johns, and Saint Peters. Clearly, it's impossible for all of these claims to be true. These people are, in fact, only characters who exploit others' gullibility and find it convenient to live at their followers' expense.

Beware, then, of false prophets, especially at a time of renewal like the present. At such a time, there will be many impostors who say they're sent by God. By doing so, they try to satisfy their egos here on earth, but you can be sure that they'll meet with an austere justice. ■ —Erastus (Paris 1862).

THE FALSE PROPHETS OF THE SPIRIT WORLD

10. ■ False prophets aren't found only among human beings. You'll find them in even greater numbers in the spirit realm where

some spirits are still full of egotism. These spirits pose as being all love and compassion, but under this guise they try to sow confusion and hold back the spiritual emancipation of humanity. Through their mediums, they propose senseless ideas. In order to make a stronger impression, as well as give their theories more weight, they often appropriate false identities, unscrupulously claiming names that are revered on earth.

Their ideas breed antagonism among groups, and foster distrust and separation. The existence of such a climate is enough to expose them. Acting in this way, the effects of their proclamations provide the first clear proof that they aren't who they claim to be. We should add that people who fall for a hoax on this scale are blind indeed.

There are many other ways of recognizing the false prophets of the spirit world. For example, the category of spirits they claim to belong to must comprise spirits who are not only highly moral, but also eminently rational. Put their ideas to the test of reason and good sense and see what you have left. Whenever a spirit proposes to address the ills of humanity or to achieve its transformation by advancing a harebrained scheme—something utopian, impractical or ridiculous—and whenever that spirit's arguments contradict even basic scientific principles, you can be sure that it is lacking in both knowledge and truth.

While a few people may be unable to discern the truth, the good sense of the majority is often a reliable guide. Whenever two ideas contradict each other, you can find the value inherent in both by determining which one produces the greater echo and sympathy in the human mind and heart. It's illogical—is it not?—to suppose that a body of ideas that steadily loses supporters is more truthful than one that continually gains them. God wants the truth to reach everyone and hasn't confined it to a narrow circle but made it appear in all places, so that the light shines wherever ignorance has residence.

You should also reject, without hesitation, all communications from spirits that are presented as the sole and final authority about a matter but that produce separation and isolation. Almost always, such spirits are conceited and mediocre beings. They bewitch the weak of mind and naïve people by inflating their egos with exaggerated praise. They are the power seekers who, in their earthly lives, were insensitive tyrants either in the public arena or in their own homes. Even after death, they continue looking for victims over whom they can tyrannize.

In general, beware of any communications that have a mystical and extraordinary character about them or demand that you perform bizarre acts and ceremonies. In all of these cases, there is always a legitimate motive for suspicion.

You can be certain that when a new spiritual principle is to be revealed to humanity, the revelation will be simultaneously communicated to all serious groups that have trustworthy mediums at hand. It won't be revealed to one group to the exclusion of others. In addition, no one can be a clear channel if he or she is beset by, or under the influence of, ill-meaning spirits.[4] Such influence is very evident when a medium claims to receive communications solely from one spirit, no matter how elevated the spirit pretends to be. Consequently, mediums and groups who believe that they are privileged because they alone receive certain communications, or who adopt superstitious practices, are unquestionably under negative influences. This is particularly true when the intervening spirit parades under a name we all should honor, respect, and never tarnish.

If you submit all the facts and communications received from a spirit to the test of reason and logic, you will discover that it's easy to reject errors and absurd ideas. Where you to suspect that a single medium is deluded, or a group is unperceptive, examine carefully what's occurring elsewhere. Seek validation in the accumulated knowledge already at your disposal, in the moral authority of leading members of other Spiritist groups, or in the teachings received by mediums of recognized integrity and proven ability to interact with noble spirits. In this way, you'll be able to correct any falsehoods and misleading ideas that come from false or ill-meaning spirits. ■ —Erastus, a disciple of Paul, the Apostle. (Paris, 1862).[5]

JEREMIAH AND THE FALSE PROPHETS

11.   ■ *This is what the Lord Almighty says: "Do not listen to what the prophets are prophesying to you; they fill you with false hopes. They speak visions from their own minds, not from the mouth of the Lord. They keep saying to those who despise me, 'The Lord says: You will have peace.' And to all who follow the stubbornness of their hearts they say, 'No harm will come to you.' But which of them has stood in the council of the Lord to see or to hear his word? Who has listened and heard his word?*

---

[4] *Translator's Note: See Chapter 10, footnote 1.*

[5] *See also: (a) Introduction, section 2, Universal Control: The Ultimate Authority, and, (b) Allan Kardec's The Mediums' Book, Chapter 23, "Obsession."*

"I did not send these prophets, yet they have run with their message; I did not speak to them, yet they have prophesied.

"I have heard what the prophets say who prophesy lies in my name. They say, 'I had a dream! I had a dream!' How long will this continue in the hearts of these lying prophets, who prophesy the delusions of their own minds?

"When these people, or a prophet or a priest, ask you, 'What is the oracle of the Lord?' say to them, 'What oracle? I will forsake you, declares the Lord.'"[6]

(Jeremiah, 23: 16-18, 21, 25-26, 33)

12. Friends, I would like to talk to you about a passage from the prophet Jeremiah. Speaking to Jeremiah, God said, "They speak visions from their own minds." These words clearly show that even in those times charlatans and fanatics were already misusing and exploiting the gift of prophesy. They abused the simple, near- ly blind, faith of the people, predicting good and much-desired events—for money. This kind of fraud was widespread in the Jewish nation, and it's easy to understand why people, in their ignorance, had a hard time distinguishing good prophets from bad: They were always being duped by pseudo-prophets, who were simply the impostors and religious extremists of their era.

There's nothing more significant than these words: "I did not send these prophets, yet they have run with their message; I did not speak to them, yet they have prophesied." Later God says, "I have heard what the prophets say who prophesy lies in my name. They say, 'I had a dream! I had a dream!'" Here Jeremiah illustrates one ruse false prophets employed to gain the trust of the unaware, who, taking their words at face value, never thought to question the truth of these dreams and visions. They considered the explanations of these "prophets" quite plausible and often invited them to speak.

Consistent with Jeremiah's words is the excellent advice of the Apostle John, who said, "Dear friends, do not believe every spir- it, but test the spirits to see whether they are from God."[7] The rea- son for the test is that some among the invisible spirits take pleas- ure in deluding you if they get the chance. The deluded ones are, as we know, mediums who don't take the necessary precautions.

---

[6] *Translator's Note: The NIV Bible utilizes the word 'oracle' which is an alterna- tive translation to the Hebrew word. Other bibles, including that used by Allan Kardec, employ 'burden' which would imply 'a burdensome message from the Lord.' NIV Bible, 1995, note 23:33, p. 1156.*

[7] *Translator's Note: 1 John 4:1*

This is unquestionably one of the greatest stumbling blocks people encounter, especially those new to the Spiritist Doctrine, and it brings many to grief. For them it's a test and they'll be able to work their way through it only by exercising considerable caution. Before anything else, then, learn to distinguish good from bad spirits so that you, in your turn, won't become a false prophet yourself. ■ —Luoz, a Guardian Spirit (Carlsruhe, 1861).

Chapter 22

Whom God Has Joined Together, Let No Man Put Apart

SCRIPTURE AND COMMENTARY

CAN A MARRIAGE BE DISSOLVED?

1. *Some Pharisees came to him to test him. They asked, "Is it lawful for a man to divorce his wife for any and every reason?"*

"Haven't you read," he replied, "that at the beginning the Creator 'made them male and female,' and said, 'For this reason a man will leave his father and mother and be united to his wife, and the two will become one flesh'? So they are no longer two, but one. Therefore what God has joined together, let man not separate."

"Why then," they asked, "did Moses command that a man give his wife a certificate of divorce and send her away?"

Jesus replied, "Moses permitted you to divorce your wives because your hearts were hard. But it was not this way from the beginning. I tell you that anyone who divorces his wife, except for marital unfaithfulness, and marries another woman commits adultery."

(Matthew, 19: 3-9)

2. Everything human is subject to change. The only unchanging things are those that emanate directly from God. Thus, while the laws of nature are the same at all times and in all countries, human laws vary according to times, places, and intellectual progress. What is of a divine order in marriage is the union of the sexes, so that the replenishment of the population might be sustained. But the conditions that regulate this union are so human in their makeup that in the whole world, even the Christian part of it, there are no two countries where the laws governing unions are exactly the same and where, over time, these laws don't undergo amendment. What is legitimate according to the civil

laws of one country during one particular time may very well constitute adultery in another country and at another time. This is because the civil law aims at regulating individual interests that can vary considerably depending on local customs and requirements. For example, in some countries only religious marriages are recognized; in others, a civil marriage is required as well; in others, a civil marriage by itself is sufficient.

3. Now, along with the natural law pertaining to the physical union of the sexes and reproduction, which is of a divine order and applicable to all living beings, there is another divine law, equally unchanging but pertaining chiefly to the moral realm: the law of love. Providence wants human beings to unite not only through the ties of the flesh, but those of the soul. In this way the mutual caring and affection between a husband and wife can be passed on to their children, as lessons in love. Together the two of them, not just one, are expected to love and care for their children and help them progress.

One might wonder, however, whether it is genuinely the law of love that shapes the lives of most ordinary couples. In many cases the answer is No. All too often, what sustains the marriage is not the mutual affection that binds one to the other—those feelings have long been shattered. What then are these couples really looking for in marriage? Rather than the joys of the heart, many see it as a way of furthering their own egos, of ostentation, of satisfying their greed, and other purely material interests. As long as these interests are well served, the marriage suits them well. Well-lined pockets, people say, make any match a good one, for they are supposed to assure the couple's happiness

Yet neither civil laws nor the obligations these place on marriage partners can replace the law of love. If a marriage is not governed by love it will fall apart no matter how binding the marriage contract. Where the vows taken at the altar are simply recited as an empty formula, they make a sham of matrimony. Here we have the seeds of dysfunctional marriages, and sometimes of tragic ends, a double disgrace couples could avoid if, in their lives together, they didn't neglect the one condition that gives divine sanction to their union: the law of love. When God said, "And the two will become one flesh," and Jesus added, "Therefore, what God has joined together, let man not separate," we should understand their words as referring to marriages consummated according to God's unchanging Law and not according to human laws, which are changing in nature.

4. Do we really need the civil law then? Should we go back to marriage as it existed in the state of nature? Certainly not. The purpose of civil law is to regulate social relationships and family interests in such a way that the two coincide with the requirements of society. The civil law is both useful and necessary, varying though it often is. It must also be farsighted because today's human beings cannot live like their primitive predecessors. Further, there is nothing—absolutely nothing—that prevents us from shaping the civil codes to reflect the Divine Laws. It is only the stubbornness of misconceived notions of social interest that impede the enactment of laws inspired by the Divine Code. Fortunately, the hold of these laws is waning and a more illuminated understanding is emerging. Such notions will disappear completely with moral progress, which will open humanity's eyes to many wrongs, including the failings and even crimes that come from marriages based solely on material interests. One day society will ask if it's really more humane, more charitable, more ethical to chain together people who can't live with each other than it is to give them their freedom, and whether marriages that can't be ended don't actually increase the number of adulterous relationships.[1]

DIVORCE

5. Divorce is a human law whose purpose is legally to separate people who are separated in fact already. It's not against God's law; it only corrects what human beings have done and it only applies in cases where Divine Law wasn't taken into account in the first place. If divorce were contrary to God's Law, those church leaders who, in the name of religion granted it more than once, would have to be considered betrayers of a trust. In these cases the betrayal would

---

[1] *Translator's Note: The status of divorce varies, often depending on the country's prevailing religious beliefs. Among Roman Catholics throughout the world, the traditional attiude is that a true marriage is indissoluble by legal means. In countries where Protestantism is dominant, the doctrine that marriage is indissoluble has been rejected. However, modern political theories generally maintain that marriage is preeminently a civil contract and therefore is subject to dissolution. For historical reference, until 1857 in Britain, freedom to remarry could only be obtained by an act of Parliament following a separation decree given by an ecclesiastical court on the basis of some wrong such as adultery or abandonment. In France, the 1809 Civil Code recognized marriage as a civil contract, and divorce as a possibility. In the United States of America, all the states had divorce statutes prior to the Revolution (1776). In most countries divorce was granted only on the grounds of adultery, cruelty, desertion, or bigamy.*

have been double since the Church only had worldly interests in mind and not the satisfaction of the law of love.[2]

Even Jesus didn't sanction the idea that a marriage should never be dissolved. Didn't He say, "Moses permitted you to divorce your wives because your hearts were hard"? In other words, since the time of Moses, the need for separation has been recognized whenever marriage isn't motivated solely by mutual love. Nevertheless, Jesus added that "it was not this way from the beginning." Here He refers to the early times, before these were contaminated by selfishness and pride, when people lived more in accordance with Divine Law, and the union of two beings was based on sincere affection and not on vain or greedy motives. It is in these types of union that divorce has no place.

Jesus goes even further and specifies a case in which divorce is justified: that of marital infidelity.[2] Marital unfaithfulness, of course, doesn't exist where there is a sincere and shared affection. It's also true that Jesus forbade a man to marry a repudiated woman. But we must consider here the customs and character of the people at a period when the Mosaic law decreed that adultery was punishable by stoning to death. Jesus wanted to abolish this barbaric custom, so He had to find a substitute penalty. He found it in the disgrace that would come from the prohibition of a second marriage. In a sense it was the substitution of one civil law for another. But like all laws of this kind, it had to pass the test of time.

---

[2] *Translator's Note: Matthew 5:31-32.*

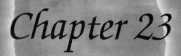

Chapter 23

Strange Lessons

SCRIPTURE AND COMMENTARY

ON HATING ONE'S FATHER AND MOTHER

1. *Large crowds were travelling with Jesus, and turning to them he said: "If anyone comes to me and does not hate his father and mother, his wife and children, his brothers and sisters—yes, even his own life—he cannot be my disciple. And anyone who does not carry his cross and follow me cannot be my disciple.*

   "In the same way, any of you who does not give up everything he has cannot be my disciple."

   (Luke, 14: 25-27, 33)

2. *"Anyone who loves his father or mother more than me is not worthy of me; anyone who loves his son or daughter more than me is not worthy of me."*

   (Matthew, 10: 37)

3. Sometimes certain words credited to Jesus, though very few, stand in marked contrast to His normal manner of speaking. When this happens, we sensibly lay aside their literal meaning so as to preserve the sublime nature of His teachings. We must remember that the Gospels were written after Christ's death— none of the Evangelists wrote while He was alive—and so we can reasonably assume that in places the writings fail to give full expression to the depth of His thoughts; or, just as likely, that the original meaning has undergone some change as the Gospels were translated from one language to another. In the latter case, it's enough for a small error to occur only once to have it repeated over and over in new versions of a manuscript. This often happens, we know, in passing down historical facts.

   The word hate in Luke's phrase "If anyone comes to me and does not hate his father and mother, his wife and children, his brothers and sisters " is a case in point. Ordinarily no one would even think of attributing this statement to Jesus. Accordingly, arguing or justifying it on the basis of its literal meaning seems beside the point. For such a discussion to occur, we would first have to know if Jesus actually used the expression, and if He did, whether the idiom in which hate was used conveyed the same meaning to its first hearers as it does to us. For an example of the differences that can arise, consider this passage from John: "The man who loves his life will lose it, while the man who hates his life in this world will keep it for eternal life."[1] Here there is no doubt that Jesus did not attach the same meaning to these words as we do.

The Hebrew of biblical times wasn't a language rich in expression, and it contained many words that, according to context, had quite different meanings. Look, for instance, at the word used in Genesis to describe the separate phases of Creation. This word can mean "a period of time," and also simply "the length of a day." Later, it came to be translated to mean only the length of a day, and so we have the belief that the world was created in a period lasting six times twenty-four hours. There was also a word in Hebrew that meant both camel and rope, since ropes were made of camel hair. This double meaning is why we find the word incorrectly translated as "camel" in the allegory of the eye of the needle (See also Chapter 16, item 2).

In addition to linguistics proper, we ought to pay close attention to the customs and character of a people, because these can exert an enormous influence over the nature of their language. Without this knowledge, the actual meanings of some words will often escape us. The same term, in passing from one language to another, may add to or lose its original force. In one case, it might communicate insults and curses; in another, it might not have any importance at all. Everything depends on the idea the word evokes in that particular culture. Even in the same language, words can change their meaning over time. Thus, a rigorously literal translation doesn't always express a writer's thoughts exactly. To maintain the true meaning, it becomes necessary at times to use analogous terms or even paraphrases that correspond to the original idea, rather than directly corresponding words.

You'll find that these comments are especially useful in interpreting the Scriptures, and in particular the Gospels. If the culture

---

[1] *Translator's Note: John 12:25.*

in which Jesus lived isn't taken into account, misunderstandings about the meaning of certain expressions and facts become inevitable, since our general tendency is always to imagine that other people think just as we do.[2] In any case, we need to rid ourselves of the idea that the term hate in Luke's passage has anything to do with its modern meaning. This meaning, clearly, is contrary to the true message found in the rest of Jesus' teachings.[3]

LEAVE FATHER, MOTHER AND CHILDREN

4. *"And everyone who has left houses or brothers or sisters or father or mother or children or fields for my sake will receive a hundred times as much and will inherit eternal life."*

(Matthew, 19: 29)

5. *Peter said to him, "We have left all we had to follow you!"*

"I tell you the truth," Jesus said to them, "no one who has left home or wife or brothers or parents or children for the sake of the kingdom of God will fail to receive many times as much in this age and, in the age to come, eternal life."

(Luke, 18: 28-30)

6. *Still another said, "I will follow you, Lord; but first let me go back and say good-by to my family."*

Jesus replied, "No one who puts his hand to the plow and looks back is fit for service in the kingdom of God."

(Luke, 9: 61-62)

7. Without arguing about the definitions of words, let's look at the critical idea in this text. It is, quite obviously, that the interests of the future life should come before every other human interest and consideration. This notion agrees completely with the substance of Jesus' teaching. The contrary idea, repudiating one's family, is in clear contradiction to His message.

Isn't this idea similar to what motivates people to abandon family and property to defend their country? Do we ever criticize people for leaving their parents, brothers and sisters, wives and children to defend their homeland? Quite the opposite, we think more of them because they've been able to give up the comfort of

---

[2] *Translator's Note: The author refers to the phenomenon known as ethnocentrism, i.e., a tendency to view one's group as more important and the basis for understanding other cultures.*

[3] *See also Chapter 14, item 5 and following.*

their homes and the enjoyments of social life in order to perform their duty. Some duties obviously are greater than others. For example, isn't a daughter expected to leave her parents and follow her husband? The world presents us with plenty of situations in which difficult separations are necessary. But the ties of love and affection aren't at all weakened by them. Distance doesn't lessen the esteem for our parents or the love the parents have for their children. Even if we take these words literally—with the exception of the word hate—we find that they don't contradict the commandment that we honor our fathers and mothers, or that our parents love us. This is even more true when the words are understood in their spiritual sense.

In the end, making use of hyperbole, Jesus makes clear how important it is that we concern ourselves with the future life. The image of separation, furthermore, would have been less shocking then, since, for reasons of culture, family ties weren't as strong as they are in more developed societies. With social progress, ties of affection, which in earlier societies tended to be weaker, become stronger. Nevertheless, separation is still a necessary element in human life. Without it, families and races would degenerate; both require the intermingling of different strains. This is a Law of Nature, which is as much in the interests of moral progress as it is of physical progress.

Here we've considered the matter entirely from an earthly perspective. The Spiritist Doctrine, however, allows us a higher vantage point. It shows us that the real ties of affection aren't of the flesh but of the spirit. It also tells us that these ties don't fade with physical separation, not even at the death of the body. In fact, they become stronger in the spirit life as the spirit grows purer. This realization is a source of great strength in our life struggles.[4]

LET THE DEAD BURY THEIR OWN DEAD

8.   *He said to another man, "Follow me."*

    But the man replied, "Lord, first let me go and bury my father."

    Jesus said to him, "Let the dead bury their own dead, but you go and proclaim the kingdom of God."

(Luke, 9: 59-60)

9.   What can the words "Let the dead bury their own dead" mean? If we interpret them in light of the commentary above—i.e., in

---

[4] *See Chapter 4, item 18; and Chapter 14, item 8.*

terms of the linguistic and cultural circumstances that gave rise to them, we realize that they can't be taken as a criticism of people who believed it was the duty of children to bury their parents. They must, then, have a deeper meaning. It is, in fact, a meaning that can only be made apparent by a more complete knowledge of spirit life.

In the spirit world we live our true life; it is there that our souls are in their normal life. The sojourn in the physical realm is always a transitory state. Compared to the splendor of spirit life, it is the earthly journey that resembles conventional notions of death. For the spirit, the physical body is really no more than a gross covering that binds it to the earth, and of which it is happy to be free. The respect we give the dead, then, isn't inspired by the physical envelope but our sentiments for the departed soul. The deference we pay to the body is in many ways akin to the emotions we attach to the keepsakes, mementos, pictures, and other personal items that belonged to the departed. This is what the man in this passage couldn't understand for himself. Jesus reminded him not to worry about the body; to think of the spirit first; to go and teach others about God's kingdom; and to tell humanity that its true home isn't found on earth but in heaven, because the true life only exists there.

I HAVE NOT COME TO BRING PEACE, BUT DISSENSION

10.   *"Do not suppose that I have come to bring peace to the earth. I did not come to bring peace to the earth. I did not come to bring peace, but a sword. For I have come to turn a man against his father, a daughter against her mother, a daughter-in-law against her mother-in-law—a man's enemies will be the members of his own household."*

(Matthew, 10: 34-36)

11.   *"I have come to bring fire on the earth, and how I wish it were already kindled! But I have a baptism to undergo, and how distressed I am until it is completed! Do you think I came to bring peace on earth? No, I tell you, but division. From now on there will be five in one family divided against each other, three against two and two against three. They will be divided, father against son and son against father, mother against daughter and daughter against mother, mother-in-law against daughter-in-law and daughter-in-law against mother-in-law."*

(Luke, 12: 49-53)

12. Could Jesus, Who personifies gentleness and goodness and Who constantly preaches in the Gospels that we are to love our neigh-

bors, have literally meant, "I did not come to bring peace, but a sword. For I have come to turn a man against his father, a daughter against her mother, a daughter-in-law against her mother-in-law—a man's enemies will be the members of his own household." and "I have come to bring fire on the earth, and how I wish it were already kindled!" Don't these verses seem blatantly to contradict His teaching? In crediting Him with language suitable to a bloody and brutal conqueror, don't we blaspheme Him? No. His words are neither blasphemous nor contradictory. He spoke them, and they testify to His great wisdom. They are, however, a little ambiguous, and so misunderstandings have arisen over their true meaning. Taken literally, they would transform His mission, which was about peace, into one of agitation and confrontation. But this is nonsense and our good sense rejects it, since we know that Jesus couldn't contradict Himself.[5]

13. Every new idea inevitably meets opposition. Not one has ever taken hold in the human mind without a fight. And the more important its anticipated results are, the greater is the resistance it will face. If the idea is based on weak principles, if it's seen as unimportant, no one will feel threatened. People will let it go by, knowing that it lacks a life of its own. If it's true, however, and built on a solid basis, if it seems to have a future, something forewarns its opponents that it represents a danger to them and to the order of things they're committed to uphold. Then they'll rise up and battle against it and its followers.

We can measure the importance of a new idea, then, by the intensity of emotion it arouses, the fury of the opposition it incites, and the persistent anger its opponents feel.

14. Jesus proclaimed a doctrine that undermined the very basis of the abuses on which the Pharisees, teachers of the law, and priests of His time, lived. As a result, they had him put to death, believing that by killing the man they were killing the idea. But the idea survived because it was true. It spread everywhere, for that was the plan of Providence. From a small and obscure town in Judea, it succeeded in placing its standard in the very capital of the pagan world, i.e., Rome. It did so in the face of its fiercest enemies, people who had great interests at stake and who fought against it because it undermined centuries old beliefs, which they upheld more out of self-interest than personal conviction. In Rome, its followers faced an incredible struggle, and many gave their lives in

---

[5] *See Chapter 19, item 6.*

sacrifice. But the idea continued to grow and triumph because, being true, it was greater than the ideas it replaced.

15. Christianity, it's worth noting, laid roots and grew at a time when Roman paganism was waning, sapped by an incipient rationalism. Though widely practiced, paganism was purely a matter of form; faith and conviction had been replaced by a form of worship that was sustained purely by self-interest. People who are motivated by self-interest are reluctant to deal with objective evidence. As contrary arguments become more decisive and as the truth of new ideas becomes more demonstrable, the supporters of the old ways grow increasingly defensive. They can well see where they may be wrong, but this knowledge doesn't stop them: Need for truthful conviction isn't yet part of their souls. What they fear most is the light that may free the blind. While the old ideas serve their purposes, they hold on to them and fight for them.

Didn't Socrates teach a doctrine that was similar, to a degree, to Christ's? Why weren't his ideas embraced by the people of his time, one of the most intellectually advanced peoples on the planet? The truth is that the times weren't right for his ideas to take hold. Socrates sowed his seed on unplowed land. In his time, paganism was still a force. Christ, on the other hand, carried out his mission in a more favorable era. It's true that not everyone was able to grasp the meaning of Jesus' ideas, but there was already a predisposition to accept them. They filled the spiritual emptiness that conventional beliefs could no longer serve. As such, Socrates and Plato opened up the way and prepared the soil, i.e., predisposed the human soul.[6]

16. Unfortunately, the followers of the new doctrine couldn't always agree on the meaning of Jesus' words, embedded as that doctrine often was in allegories and figures of speech. As a result, a number of sects quickly developed, each of which claimed exclusive ownership of the truth—which is to say, the true and only interpretation of His words. More than eighteen centuries have passed and the rifts are still unpatched. People have lost sight of the most important of Jesus' precepts, the cornerstone of His mission, and an explicit condition for salvation: that we should show solidarity, good fellowship, and love toward each other. Instead they have assailed each other and at times taken to unthinking violence. The powerful crushed the weak in cruel blood baths,

---

[6] *See the Introduction, item 4, "Socrates and Plato, the Forerunners of Christian Ideas and of the Spiritist Doctrine."*

and through torture and fire. Thus, the Christians, victorious over paganism, went from being the persecuted to becoming persecutors. They planted the cross, standard of the Lamb of God, in the non-Christian world, but they did it with fire and the sword. It is a fact that the religious wars brought about some of the cruelest battles, and produced more victims than most political wars.[7] No other event in history has produced so many acts of atrocity and barbarity.

But can we blame Christ's doctrine for this situation? Clearly not. Christianity condemns all forms of violence. Did Jesus ever tell His disciples to kill, massacre, or burn people who didn't believe as they did? On the contrary, He always reminded them that all of us are brothers and sisters, that God is supremely merciful, that we should love both our neighbors and our enemies, and that we should do good to people who persecute us. He also said that those who live by the sword will die by the sword. The responsibility for these horrors, then, doesn't lie with the doctrine of Jesus. It rests with those who adulterated its principles, and turned it into an instrument to satisfy their own desires, completely disregarding Christ's own words when He said, "My kingdom is not of this world."[8]

In His great wisdom, Jesus had foreseen these events. He knew they were inevitable because they resulted from the unevolved nature of human beings—a nature that can't be transformed overnight. So, during all these centuries, Christianity had to go through this long and severe test. It had to show its strength and demonstrate that, despite the evils committed in its name, it could remain holy and uncontaminated. This has never been a matter of dispute. Those who corrupted and abused Christian ideals are liable. To each act of intolerance, we can safely say that if Christianity were better understood and more widely practiced, this would never happen.

17. When Jesus said, "I did not come to bring peace, but a sword," the thought behind His words was this: "Don't believe that my

---

[7] *Translator's Note: The author refers to the Crusades, a so-called holy war waged by European Christians against the Moslems for the recovery and protection of the Holy Sepulcher in Jerusalem. Four major crusades were launched in the period 1095 - 1291 under the inspiration of the Roman Church. The first one was lead by Pope Urban, the other ones by European noblemen. They left immense destruction and devastation everywhere they passed in Europe and produced terrible atrocities in the Moslem world.*

[8] *Translator's Note: John 18:36.*

doctrine will be established peacefully. It will bring many bloody battles and my name will be used as an excuse for them. Humanity won't have understood me and won't want to understand. Brothers and sisters, separated by their different convictions, will draw swords against each other, and dissension will rule in the families divided by different faiths. Yet, just as you set fire to a field in order to destroy the weeds, I've come to bring fire to the earth in order to purify it of its errors and prejudices. And I'm impatient for this fire to spread; for in that way the purification will be that much quicker.

"From this conflict, you should know, truth will rise triumphant. War will be followed by peace, hatred by universal brotherhood, the darkness of fanaticism by the light of a reasoned faith. When the field is prepared I will send you a Comforter, the Spirit of truth, and it will set aright all your views about life. In other words, the more discerning among you will analyze the meaning of my words and finally understand them. And when they do, they will put an end to the destruction which has so divided God's children. Finally, tired of the endless confrontations and the devastation they leave in the hearts of families, human beings will realize where their true interests lie, both in this world and the next. They will find out where the friends and the enemies of their peace really are. Then they'll gather under one banner, that of Love, and the true meaning of all things will be reestablished on earth in accordance with the principles I've defended."

18. The Spiritist Doctrine has come, as announced, to help fulfill Christ's promises. In order for this to happen, though, the vices of the human soul must be eradicated. As Jesus had to do Himself, the Spiritist Doctrine has to confront the hostilities of arrogance, greed, selfishness, and fanaticism. These forces, preparing their last defenses, throw up all kinds of barriers and persecutions along the way. So the Spiritist Doctrine, too, has to fight. But the time for physical battles and bloody atrocities is passed. The battles from now on will take place in the realm of ideas, and the time of our own engagement approaches fast. The first battles lasted for centuries; these will last much less, because the light is starting to shine not from one but from numerous points of the globe, and it will very soon bring awareness to people everywhere.

19. We should understand that Jesus' words in these verses refer to the opposition His doctrine would stir up, the temporary conflicts it would create, the fights it would have to take up before

being finally established. In many ways, this is analogous to what happened to the Hebrews before they entered the Promised Land. Hence, we shouldn't see in Jesus' words in this passage a prearranged plan to sow disorder and conflict. The evil results from the human condition, never from Jesus. He was like the doctor who comes to cure and whose medicine produces a beneficial crisis in the sick.

Chapter 24

Do Not Light a Lamp and Put It Under a Bowl

SCRIPTURE AND COMMENTARY

THE LIGHT UNDER A BOWL; WHY JESUS SPOKE IN PARABLES

1.   *"Neither do people light a lamp and put it under a bowl. Instead they put it on its stand, and it gives light to everyone in the house."*

(Matthew, 5: 15)

2.   *"No one lights a lamp and hides it in a jar or puts it under a bed. Instead, he puts it on a stand, so that those who come in can see the light. For there is nothing hidden that will not be disclosed, and nothing concealed that will not be known or brought out into the open."*

(Luke, 8: 16-17)

3.   *The disciples came to him and asked, "Why do you speak to the people in parables?"*

He replied, "The knowledge of the secrets of the kingdom of heaven has been given to you, but not to them. Whoever has will be given more, and he will have an abundance. Whoever does not have, even what he has will be taken from him. This is why I speak to them in parables:

"Though seeing, they do not see; though hearing, they do not hear or understand.

"In them is fulfilled the prophecy of Isaiah:

"'You will be ever hearing but never understanding; you will be ever seeing but never perceiving.

"For this people's heart has become calloused; they hardly hear with their ears and they have closed their eyes. Otherwise they might see with their eyes, hear with their ears, understand with their hearts and turn, and I would heal them.'"

(Matthew, 13: 10-15)

4.   It may seem odd to hear Jesus say that the light shouldn't be covered up or hidden. He Himself constantly hid the meaning of His own words behind allegories, which obviously not everybody understood. He explained this apparent contradiction by telling His disciples that He spoke to people in parables because they weren't yet ready to understand certain things. He added that people could see, hear, listen, and still not understand His ideas. It would have served no purpose, then, to have told them everything. Jesus noted that He did tell more to His disciples because they could understand what others still regarded as mysteries. But to the people of His time, Jesus spoke as you would to children whose thought processes haven't matured. It is in this context that we should look for the real meaning behind Jesus' words when He said that "No one lights a lamp and hides it in a jar or puts it under a bed. Instead, he puts it on a stand, so that those who come in can see the light." These words don't mean that all things are to be revealed indiscriminately but, rather, that the speaker should consider the timeliness of the revelation. Teaching should always be appropriate to the level of the students; otherwise, instead of illuminating, too dazzling a light will blind them.

     As one generation succeeds another, humanity goes from the stage of infancy to youth and then to maturity, much as we experience these stages in our lives. Each thing has its own proper time. To use another analogy: If you sow a seed out of season, it won't take root. But what good sense keeps veiled in a certain period will come to light later when people reach the proper level of development. Then, feeling the burden of their own unawareness, human beings will start an earnest search for the living light. For this, God has given us intelligence so that we can reason and lead ourselves in the affairs of earth and heaven. As our intellect grows, it becomes all the more important not to place our lamp under a bowl. Without the light of reason faith will grow feeble.[1]

5.   Providence is wise and careful enough to reveal truths gradually. These truths are only communicated as humanity shows itself mature enough to receive them. Providence doesn't hide truth under a bowl—doesn't conceal it from humankind—but stands always ready to deal it out. Yet very often the exceptional human beings who first discern a revealed truth conceal it from the common folk in order to maintain their ascendancy over them. These are the persons who really place the light under a bowl. Similarly,

---

[1] *See Chapter 19, item 7.*

many religions have their mysteries—dogmatic points of faith that followers are forbidden to examine critically. But while these religions rigidify with time, science and knowledge advance steadily and pierce the numerous sacred mysteries. Growing more mature, humanity is finally able to see into the heart of the matter and refuses to accept those articles of faith that are contrary to observed facts.

Absolute mysteries can't exist and Jesus was right when He said that there is no secret that won't eventually be known. One day everything that's now hidden will be uncovered. What we still don't understand will become clear in more advanced realms where the extent of our purification will be progressively greater. By contrast, we still live here on earth as if we were trying to find our way in the midst of a thick fog.

6. One might wonder how people could benefit from Jesus' many parables since the real meaning of these was often beyond their understanding. Here, it is important to note first that Jesus spoke in parables only when his teachings were fairly abstract in nature. When it came to declaring that love toward our neighbors and humbleness of heart were the fundamental conditions for salvation, Jesus was perfectly clear and explicit, leaving no room for ambiguity in His statements. Indeed, He could not have done otherwise: These were, after all, rules of conduct that everyone had to understand in order to practice the faith. He made this essential point when he told the crowd simply, "Do this and you will live."[2] When it came to more complex matters, Jesus revealed His thoughts only to His disciples, who were more morally and intellectually advanced than others and so could be introduced to knowledge of more abstract truths. This is also one reason why He said, "Whoever has will be given more, and he will have an abundance." [3]

Still, He wasn't specific on many points even with the apostles and, in some areas, reserved a complete understanding for later times. It was these areas that led to so many different interpretations of His teachings. Nevertheless, science on one hand and the postulates of the Spiritist Doctrine on the other have helped shed light on a new class of natural laws, making transparent the more profound meaning of Jesus' words.

7. Today the Spiritist Doctrine is casting light on a great number of obscure points. However, it doesn't do so indiscriminately. When

---

[2] *Translator's Note: Luke 10:28*

[3] *Translator's Note: Matthew 13:12. See Chapter 18, item 15.*

the enlightened spirits share new ideas, they act with admirable good sense. They have only gradually and prudently introduced the ideas that now form the Doctrine, and they will reveal other principles when the time is right to make them common knowledge. Why? If they'd presented the complete Doctrine right from the start, fewer people would have been inclined to accept it, and the ones who weren't prepared would have felt overwhelmed by it, thereby harming the spread of the Doctrine. If the spirits still haven't told us everything, it isn't because the Doctrine holds mysteries that only a privileged few are given to know, or because the "lamp must be under a bowl," but because there is a time for everything.[4] The enlightened spirits allow time for each idea to mature and spread before presenting another and for circumstances to prepare the stage for the assimilation of new ideas.

DO NOT GO AMONG THE GENTILES

8.   *These twelve Jesus sent out with the following instructions: "Do not go among the Gentiles or enter any town of the Samaritans. Go rather to the lost sheep of Israel. As you go, preach this message, 'The kingdom of heaven is near.'"*

(Matthew, 10: 5-7)

9.   On many occasions Jesus shows us that His vision wasn't confined only to the Jewish people but embraced all humanity. Further, if He told His apostles not to "go among the Gentiles" (pagans), it wasn't that he didn't care for their conversion—such an attitude wouldn't be in keeping with His ministry of love. He told them so because the Jewish people already believed in the existence of only one God, and were also waiting for a Messiah. In other words, they had been prepared by the laws of Moses and the Prophets to accept His word. With the pagans, even the basics weren't in place, and the apostles would have had to do everything, a task they weren't prepared yet to undertake. This is why He told them, "Go rather to the lost sheep of Israel"[5]—that is, go and sow in lands that are already cleared. Jesus knew that the conversion of the Gentiles would occur at a later date. Indeed, the apostles did, later on, plant the cross in the very heart of paganism, i.e., Rome.

----

[4] *Translator's Note: Ecclesiastes 3:1 ["There is a time for everything, and a season for every activity under heaven."]*

[5] *Translator's Note: Matthew 10:6*

10. We can also apply Jesus' words to the followers and missionaries of the Spiritist Doctrine. Today, those who systematically refuse to accept the Doctrine, the skeptics and mockers, and those who see it as a menace to their interests, are to Spiritists what the Gentiles were to the early disciples. So, if we are to follow the apostles' example, let's make our first believers among people of good will, who are seeking the light. Go where you'll find fertile soil, for their numbers are high. Let's not waste our time with people who don't want to see or hear. In most cases, we would only manage to inflate their egos by giving them so much attention trying to win them over. It's better to open the eyes of a hundred blind people who want to see than insist on awakening one person who prefers the darkness. By concentrating your efforts on the first group, you'll find that it's possible to more quickly multiply the number of people who'll actively support the Spiritist cause. Leave the others alone, not out of indifference for them but for a principle of respect. Eventually, the time will come when open discussion and the weight of popular opinion will prevail. They will then gradually come to voluntarily accept these principles naturally on their own. Let's keep in mind that some ideas, like seeds, can't germinate out of season or on ground that hasn't been prepared. So, on the whole, it's better to wait for the right time and spend your energies on the ones that germinate first. To insist on rushing those seeds that are not ready, is to risk killing them off and losing them altogether.

In Jesus' time, most ideas were shaped by the narrow and material concerns of the people. Everything was limited and local in nature. The house of Israel was a small nation, and the Gentiles lived in small communities scattered in the surrounding lands. Today ideas have a more spiritual and universal scope and no one society can claim that the new light is exclusively its own. The light has no barriers; its focal point is everywhere because all human beings are brothers and sisters. The Gentiles are no longer a group; they represent only a point of view that is found everywhere, but that will, little by little, be overcome by the truth, as Christianity triumphed over paganism. Only the battles aren't fought any longer with swords, but with the force of ideas.

THE HEALTHY DO NOT NEED A DOCTOR

11. *While Jesus was having dinner at Matthew's house, many tax collectors and "sinners" came and ate with him and his disciples. When the Pharisees saw this, they asked his disciples, "Why does your teacher eat with tax collectors and 'sinners'?"*

On hearing this, Jesus said, "It is not the healthy who need a doctor, but the sick."

(Matthew, 9: 10-12)

12. Jesus addressed Himself especially to the needy and disadvantaged, who most required His comfort. He spoke particularly, too, to the blind (in spirit) who, humbly and in good faith, asked Him for a new vision. He didn't address Himself to the proud or to people who believed they had all the knowledge they needed and wanted no more.[6]

This dialogue, like so many others in the Gospel, finds a fitting application in Spiritist activities. Sometimes people are surprised to find that mediumship is given to individuals who don't seem to be worthy of it and are capable of misusing it. It's such a precious gift, the objection goes, that it should only be conferred on the most worthy individuals.

In the first place, we should say that mediumship is an organic faculty that anyone can demonstrate. In this, it's like the ability to see, hear, and speak. Like these faculties, it can be abused, according to our free will. What if speech had only been given to people who expressed wholesome ideas? The majority on earth would be speech impaired! But Providence has endowed us with these faculties and the freedom to use them as we see fit. Remember, though, that Providence holds us responsible for the consequences of their use.

Second, if the ability to communicate with spirits were only given to truly worthy persons, what kind of people would dare say they have it? And where do we draw the line between worthiness and unworthiness? The gift of mediumship is given without distinction so that the spirits can bring awareness to people in all walks of life—to all classes, to rich and poor; to the righteous to strengthen their goodness, to the vile to correct them. Aren't vicious people similar to sick ones who need a doctor? God, Who doesn't want sinners to die in sin, doesn't deny them the help that can pull them out of their spiritual morass! The good spirits come to help them, to give them positive advice of a kind that will impress the weak among them in a more forceful manner. God, being all kindness, has put the light directly in their hands as a way of sparing them an arduous search. Aren't they, then, more reprehensible when they ignore the spirits'

---

[6] *See the items titled "Publicans" and "Tax Collectors" in the Introduction.*

advice? Can they use ignorance as an excuse when they've seen, written, heard, and spoken their own censure? Further, if they misuse the gift of mediumship, they will suffer the consequences in the form of loss or impairment of the faculty. In the latter case, ill-meaning spirits may come onto the scene with their trickery and disturbing influence, adding to the real anguish that sooner or later afflicts those who make themselves unworthy of truly serving Providence's designs, who allow pride and selfishness to harden their hearts.

Mediumship doesn't necessarily mean that a medium will have constant relations with superior spirits. It's simply an ability to serve as a channel, more or less clear, to spirits in general. A good medium, then, isn't someone who finds communicating with spirits easy, but a person who is compatible with, and is normally assisted by, noble spirits.

THE COURAGE OF FAITH

13.   *"Whoever acknowledges me before men, I will also acknowledge him before my Father in heaven. But whoever disowns me before men, I will disown him before my Father in heaven."*

(Matthew, 10: 32-33)

14.   *"If anyone is ashamed of me and of my words, the Son of man will be ashamed of him when he comes in his glory and in the glory of the Father and of the holy angels."*

(Luke, 9: 26)

15. Humanity has always admired people who have the courage of their convictions. To proclaim your ideas openly, especially if they go against popular beliefs, is willingly to withstand opposition, sarcasm, personal attacks, and even injury. In such willingness there is always merit. But the merit, in this as in every instance, depends largely on the circumstances and the importance of the end result. To waver in your beliefs in the face of opposition shows weakness of character. In some, cases it is an act of cowardice as great as that of a soldier deserting the battlefield.

Jesus denounced this kind of cowardice. From the point of view of His doctrine, He said that if anyone was ashamed of His words, He would be ashamed of them. He also promised that He would disown the person who denied Him and would acknowledge before God in heaven only those people who publicly acknowledged Him on earth. In other words, people who are afraid of being known as disciples of truth aren't worthy of being admitted into the kingdom of truth. By giving in to this fear, they miss the strength that faith fosters. They turn it into a selfish faith, something they keep to themselves and hide because they're afraid that others' attitudes might cause them difficulties in this world. Meanwhile, people who put truth above every material interest and openly proclaim it are working for the future, both their own and that of others.

16. Followers of the Spiritist Doctrine will find that the courage of conviction applies very much to their case because the Doctrine they profess is nothing more than the development and application of the Gospel's teachings. Christ's words above fit them well. What they plant on earth will be harvested in the spirit world. It is there that we gather the fruits of moral courage or weak convictions.

TAKE UP YOUR CROSS; WHOEVER WANTS TO SAVE HIS LIFE WILL LOSE IT

17.   *"Blessed are you when men hate you, when they exclude you and insult you and reject your name as evil, because of the Son of Man. Rejoice in that day and leap for joy, because great is your reward in heaven. For that is how their fathers treated the prophets."*

(Luke, 6: 22-23)

18.   *Then he called the crowd to him along with his disciples and said: "If anyone would come after me, he must deny himself and take up his cross and follow me. For whoever wants to save his life will lose it, but whoever loses his life for me and for the gospel will save it. What good is it for a man to gain the whole world, yet forfeit his soul?"*

(Mark, 8: 34-36. Also Luke, 9: 23-25; Matthew, 10: 39; John, 12: 25)

19. Jesus told us to rejoice when we are hated and persecuted because of Him since our reward will be in heaven. We should understand the meaning of these words as follows: Consider yourself blessed when your fellow human beings, through their ill will toward you, give you the chance to prove the sincerity of your faith, since what they do against you will only result in your benefit. Pity them in their blindness, but don't curse them.

He also told us that if we want to follow Him, we should take up our own cross. In other words, we should face the trials and hardships our faith may bring with courage. We should realize that people who try to save their lives and their property by renouncing Christ will lose the blessings of heaven. On the other hand, the ones who lose everything in this world, even their lives, for the sake of truth, will be richly rewarded in the future life for their courage, perseverance, and self-denial. To those who've sacrificed heavenly treasures for earthly pleasures, Jesus will say: "You have already received your comfort."[7]

---

[7] *Translator's Note: Luke 6:24*

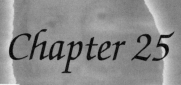

Chapter 25

Seek and You Will Find

SCRIPTURE AND COMMENTARY

IF YOU HELP YOURSELF THEN HEAVEN WILL COME TO YOUR AID

1.   *"Ask and it will be given to you; seek and you will find; knock and the door will be opened to you. For everyone who asks receives; he who seeks finds; and to him who knocks, the door will be opened.*

   "Which of you, if his son asks for bread, will give him a stone? Or if he asks for a fish, will give him a snake? If you, then, though you are evil, know how to give good gifts to your children, how much more will your Father in heaven give good gifts to those who ask him!"

(Matthew, 7: 7-11)

2.   From an earthly perspective, the precept "Seek and you will find" is identical to another well-known expression: "God helps those who help themselves." This is the basis of the Law of Work and consequently the Law of Progress, since progress is the off-spring of work, which puts the force of intelligence into action. During the infancy of the species, human beings used their intel-ligence only to look for food, protect themselves against the ele-ments, and defend themselves against their enemies. But God gave humans something more than the animals—the drive to better themselves. It's this powerful desire that leads us to con-tinuously seek ways to improve our condition, leading us to make new discoveries, invent tools and machines, and advance the sciences. Indeed, scientific progress has provided us with many of the things we lacked. Through such efforts human intel-ligence expands, and moral qualities become more refined. As this happens, the needs of the body eventually become second-ary to those of the spirit—for after attending to their physical needs, humans naturally seek spiritual nourishment. This is how humanity passes from an undeveloped to a civilized state.

But the amount of progress each person makes in a single lifetime is very small—in most cases unnoticeable. How could
humanity progress, then, unless the souls of its members had
lived before and unless they're destined to live again? If the souls
who depart earth daily never returned here, humanity would
constantly have to renew itself at the most elementary level. It
would have to learn and do everything all over again. If that
were the case, human beings would be no more advanced today
than they were when they first appeared on earth: All intellectual work would have to begin again at each person's birth. On the
other hand, returning with a degree of progress already realized,
and acquiring something more with each life, allows the soul to
move gradually from a primitive state to a technological society
and from there to an ethical civilization.

3. If God had excused human beings from doing physical work, our
    limbs would have been much feebler and smaller. If God had
    excused us from intellectual work, our spirits would have
    remained in a state of spiritual infancy, driven by animal-like
    instincts. This is why Providence made work necessary, saying
    "Seek and you will find"; in other words, work and you will pro-
    duce. In this way, we are the product of our own efforts, and have
    the merit for what we have done by ourselves; our reward will
    correspond to our accomplishments.

4. It's because of this principle that the spirits don't intervene in the
    work of scientific research. They don't hand us discoveries or
    inventions that are ready to be put to use. If that were the case,
    all we would have to do is wait for what the spirits place in our
    hands, without having to make any effort or even think. You can
    well imagine that if things were like this, even the laziest person
    could get rich, and the most unprepared human being could
    become erudite with no effort. And both would claim credit for
    things for which they have no merit. No, the spirits don't come
    to spare human beings from the Law of Work, but to show them
    the goal they need to reach and the path that will take them there.
    They say, "Walk and you will get there. You'll find your path lit-
    tered with stones—when you see them, move them out of the
    way. We'll give you the necessary strength if you care to use it."[1]

5. From a moral perspective, Jesus' words mean that if we ask for
    the light that will show us the way, God will give it to us. If we
    ask for strength to resist wrong-doing, we'll receive it. If we ask

---

[1] *See Allan Kardec,* The Medium's Book, *Chapter 26, item 291 and following.*

the good spirits for help, they'll go with us and, like the angel of Tobias,[2] guide us. If we ask for good advice, we will never be denied it; if we knock on His door, He will open it to us. But we have to ask with sincerity, faith, confidence, and fervor. And we should be humble in our asking, avoiding any signs of arrogance; otherwise, we'll be abandoned to ourselves. The failures along the way will then be punishments for our inflated pride.

This is what is meant by the words "Seek and you will find; knock and the door will be opened to you."

LOOK AT THE BIRDS OF THE AIR

6.   *"Do not store up for yourselves treasures on earth, where moth and rust destroy, and where thieves break in and steal. But store up for your-selves treasures in heaven, where moth and rust do not destroy, and where thieves do not break in and steal. For where your treasure is, there your heart will be also.*

"Therefore I tell you, do not worry about your life, what you will eat or drink; or about your body, what you will wear. Is not life more impor-tant than food, and the body more important than clothes? Look at the birds of the air; they do not sow or reap or store away in barns, and yet your heav-enly Father feeds them. Are you not much more valuable than they? Who of you by worrying can add a single hour to his life?

"And why do you worry about clothes? See how the lilies of the field grow. They do not labor or spin. Yet I tell you that not even Solomon in all his splendor was dressed like one of these. If that is how God clothes the grass of the field, which is here today and tomorrow is thrown into the fire, will he not much more clothe you, O you of little faith? So do not worry, saying, 'What shall we eat?' or 'What shall we drink?' or 'What shall we wear?' For the pagans run after all these things, and your heavenly Father knows that you need them. But seek first his kingdom and his righteousness, and all these things will be given to you as well. Therefore do not worry about tomorrow, for tomorrow will worry about itself. Each day has enough trou-ble of its own."

(Matthew, 6: 19-21, 25-34)

7.   Interpreted literally, these words go against all forethought, the need to work, and consequently all progress. With a principle of this kind in place, human beings would be limited to passive waiting, their physical and intellectual power inactive and use-less. If this condition were normal on earth, we would never have

---

[2] *Translator's note. See the Book of Tobit, 5:5.*

left the caves; if it became the law today, we would be living in a state of total idleness. This literal interpretation couldn't have been Jesus' real intention. It contradicts both what He said on other occasions and also the Laws of Nature. God created human beings without clothes or shelter, true; but God also gave us the intelligence to make these necessities ourselves.[3]

We shouldn't view Jesus' words, then, as anything more than a poetical allegory of Providence. Providence never deserts people who put their trust in it; it does require that everyone work his or her fair share. The hand of Providence doesn't always deliver material help; it does inspire ideas on how to resolve our difficulties.[4]

God knows our needs and provides for them. Still, human desires are never totally satisfied, and we don't always know how to be happy with what we have. Simply having the necessities isn't enough; we demand more and more of the superfluous. When that happens, Providence leaves us on our own. So when we grow unhappy, we must recognize that it is often of our own doing and our failure to pay attention to the warning voice of conscience. In such cases Providence lets us suffer the consequences to teach us a lesson for the future.[5]

8.   The earth will produce enough to feed its entire population when we learn how to administer its benefits according to the laws of justice, charity, and love for our neighbors. When solidarity exists among the different peoples in the same way that it does among the communities within a country, temporary surpluses in one region of the globe will be used to reduce temporary scarcities in another. Everyone will have what they need. It will be the case, then, that the wealthy will think of themselves as people who own a great store of seeds. If they share the seeds with others, they'll harvest a hundredfold both for themselves and for the others. If they keep the seeds for their exclusive use or allow their surplus to rot, they'll produce nothing and there won't be enough for everyone else. Seeds that are hoarded in barns are eventually eaten by insects. For this reason Jesus told us not to accumulate treasures on earth because they're perishable, but to accumulate them in heaven where they are eternal. Let us not, then, attach more importance to material possessions than to spiritual ones, and let us know how to sacrifice the first for the second.

---

[3] *See Chapter 14, item 6; and Chapter 25, item 2.*

[4] *See Chapter 27, item 8.*

[5] *See Chapter 5, item 4.*

Love and fraternity aren't decreed under law. If they aren't in our hearts, selfishness will rule. It is the task of the Spiritist Doctrine to see that both take root in the human heart.

DO NOT TAKE ALONG ANY GOLD

9.   *"Do not take along any gold or silver or copper in your belts; take no bag for the journey, or extra tunic, or sandals or a staff; for the worker is worth his keep."*

(Matthew, 10: 9-10)

10.   *"Whatever town or village you enter, search for some worthy person there and stay at his house until you leave. As you enter the home, give it your greeting. If the home is deserving, let your peace rest on it; if it is not, let your peace return to you. If anyone will not welcome you or listen to your words, shake the dust off your feet when you leave that home or town. I tell you the truth, it will be more bearable for Sodom and Gomorrah on the day of judgement than for that town."*

(Matthew, 10: 11-15)

11. At the time Jesus spoke these words, there was nothing unusual about them. They were directed to His apostles as He was sending them out to announce the Glad Tidings for the first time. His words were in keeping with the Middle-Eastern custom of always making a traveler welcome in one's tent. Travelers in those days, however, were very rare, and we must consider that in the modern world the development of travel has created new customs. Nowadays ancient customs of the kind referred to here are observed only in distant countries where progress hasn't yet penetrated. If Jesus were to return today, He couldn't tell His apostles anymore to put themselves on the road without provisions.

Apart from their literal interpretation, these words have a profound moral meaning. Jesus was teaching His disciples to put their entire trust in Providence. Having nothing, they wouldn't inspire greed in their hosts, and they could more easily distinguish the self-interested from the truly charitable. This is why Jesus told them to "search for some worthy person (there) and stay at his house"—in other words, look for someone who is generous enough to lodge a traveler who can't pay, because these are the people who are worthy to hear your words; they will be recognized by their kindness of heart.

As for people who didn't welcome them or pay attention to them, did Jesus tell His disciples to curse them, impose their views on them, or use force and violence to convert them? No, He simply told His disciples to go away and look for people of good will.

Today the Spiritist Doctrine says the same thing to its followers. Don't violate anyone's conscience. Don't force anyone to leave their faith and accept yours. Don't curse people who don't think as you do. Welcome everyone who wants to join you, and leave people who reject your ideas in peace. Remind yourselves of the words of Christ. In the past, heaven was conquered with violence, but today it is gained by mildness of heart. [6]

---

[6] *Translators' Note: Reference to Matthew 11:12 "From the days of John the Baptist until now, the kingdom of heaven has been forcefully advancing, and forceful men lay hold of it." See also Chapter 4, items 10 and 11.*

Chapter 26

Freely You Have Received, Freely Give

SCRIPTURE AND COMMENTARY

THE GIFT OF HEALING

1.   *"Heal the sick, raise the dead, cleanse those who have leprosy, drive out demons. Freely you have received, freely give."*

(Matthew, 10: 8)

2. "Freely you have received, freely give," Jesus told His disciples. With these words He recommended that no one be charged for something that hadn't cost anything in the first place. Now, what the disciples had received freely was the gift of healing the sick and casting out devils (i.e., wrongdoing spirits). God gave these gifts to them in order to ease others' suffering and to spread the faith. So Jesus told the disciples not to commercialize their gifts, i.e., to use them to earn profits or make a living.

PAID PRAYERS

3.   *While all the people were listening, Jesus said to his disciples, "Beware of the teachers of the law. They like to walk around in flowing robes and love to be greeted in the marketplaces and have the most important seats in the synagogues and the places of honor at banquets. They devour widows' houses and for a show make lengthy prayers. Such men will be punished most severely."*

(Luke, 20: 45-47; also Mark, 12: 38-40)

4. Jesus told the people not to charge for their prayers, not to imitate the teachers of the law who devour the homes of widows (that is to say, take over their possessions) by making them pay for long prayers. Prayer is an act of love, an ecstasy of the heart. To charge someone for prayers that we direct to God on their behalf is to turn ourselves into paid go-betweens. The prayers

themselves, in such a case, become merely formulas, their length
dependent on the price someone can pay. There are only two out-
comes: Either God measures blessings by the number of words in
a prayer or God doesn't. Consider this: If God expects lots of
words (in a paid prayer service) then saying short prayers for
people who can't pay is pure lack of love. But if concise prayers
are sufficient, to say long prayers is useless, and by extension, to
charge for them is dishonest.

God doesn't sell benefits; God grants them. So how can someone who isn't an agent of God and can't guarantee good results
charge for a prayer that may come to nothing? The mercy, kindness, and justice of God can't be subordinate to money. Imagine
if, for lack of timely payment, God's mercy, kindness, and justice
were temporarily suspended. This hardly makes sense. Reason,
common sense, and logic tell us that God the Almighty would
never give imperfect beings the right to set a price on Divine
Justice which, like the sun, exists for everyone, rich and poor
alike. It's considered highly unethical, as we know, to traffic for
goodwill, i.e., try to gain the political influence of an earthly
ruler. Can it be any more ethical to negotiate the graces of God,
the Ruler of the Universe?

Still another drawback presented by paid prayer services is
that, in most cases, the people who pay for them consider themselves free of the need to pray personally. Such persons think that
by paying for their prayers they have fulfilled their responsibilities before God. Now we know that what triggers spiritual assistance on our behalf is the sincerity and intensity of our prayers.
But how sincere and intense can someone be who's hired a third
party to pray for him or her? And how fervent in prayer can this
third party be when he or she contracts out the responsibility for
the prayer to someone else, who passes it on to another person,
and so on? Doesn't this really reduce the effectiveness of prayer
to the value of currency?

THE MERCHANTS EXPELLED FROM THE TEMPLE

5.   *On reaching Jerusalem, Jesus entered the temple area and began driv-
ing out those who were buying and selling there. He overturned the tables
of the money changers and the benches of those selling doves, and would not
allow anyone to carry merchandise through the temple courts. And as he
taught them, he said, "Is it not written: 'My house will be called a house of
prayer for all nations'? But you have made it 'a den of robbers.'"*

The chief priests and the teachers of the law heard this and began looking for a way to kill him, for they feared him, because the whole crowd was amazed at his teaching.

(Mark, 11: 15-18; and Matthew, 21: 12-13)

6.	When Jesus expelled the merchants from the temple, He condemned the trading of sacred things in any form whatsoever. God doesn't sell blessings, forgiveness, or the right to enter the kingdom of heaven. Human beings have no right to specify a price for such things.

FREE MEDIUMSHIP

7.	Like the apostles, who were mediums in their own right, the mediums of today receive their gift freely from God. The gift consists in the ability to serve as an interpreter to the spirits who come to impart teaching, to lead people to the pathway of goodness, and to nourish their faith. It isn't right to charge for this gift because the message that mediums convey isn't the result of their own ideas or research or personal work. Note here that God wants the light to reach everyone—not to disenfranchise the poorest of the poor. The poor should never be able to say that they don't have faith because they couldn't pay for it, or that they were denied encouragement and expressions of affection from their departed loved ones because of a lack of money. For this reason, mediumship isn't limited to a privileged few—it is found everywhere. To make someone pay for it is to turn it away from its providential purpose.

8.	People who understand the conditions under which good spirits communicate, who recognize the disgust these spirits feel when confronted by anything that smacks of self-interest, and who know how little it takes to drive these spirits away, can never accept the idea that superior spirits are at the beck and call of the first person who comes along and—at so much per session— claims contact with them. Simple good sense rejects this notion. Isn't it an act of disrespect to call up, for money, highly regarded spirits, or our loved ones? Now, there's no question that a medium can receive communications in this way. But who can really vouch for the genuineness of such messages? Thoughtless, deceitful, mocking spirits—the whole crowd of unevolved and unprincipled ones—always come running, ready to answer any question without regard to the truthfulness of their views. If you want serious answers, begin by posing serious questions. You should also consider the nature of the affinity the medium has with those in the spirit realm. The conditions for enjoying the goodwill of noble spirits are humbleness of heart, devotion, selflessness, and total disinterest, both moral and material.

9.   Besides the ethical question, a second consideration, no less important, comes to mind: the nature of the gift itself. Serious mediumship is not, and never can be, made into a profession. First, from the ethical standpoint, the idea would carry little credibility with people, and second, it would be quickly seen as akin to mere fortune-telling. But there is another obstacle working against it. As a gift, mediumship is basically unstable, elusive, changeable. No one can count on it as something permanent. As an exploitable resource, it is highly uncertain and can fail when most needed. In this respect it differs from a talent acquired through study and work which, because it is the product of one's own efforts, can rightfully be used to one's benefit. But mediumship isn't an art or skill, and no one should consider it as a professional activity. It exists only to the extent that the spirits are willing to cooperate with the medium. If the former aren't present, neither is the mediumship: The potential may still exist, but not the practice. There isn't a medium in the world who can guarantee that he or she will be able to produce a spiritual phenomenon at any given moment.

To exploit mediumship for gain is to rely on something over which one doesn't really have control; to claim the contrary is to deceive the person who's paying for the sitting. What's more, one is not really relying on oneself, but rather on the spirits, the souls of those who have departed the earth and on whose assistance one has put a price. The idea causes instinctive disgust. It was this same kind of trafficking and exploitation by charlatans—along with the ignorance, gullibility, and superstition of the people— that moved Moses to ban communication with the dead. The Spiritist Doctrine, through its understanding of the serious nature of this question, has completely discredited such exploitation and elevated mediumship to the category of a mission.[1]

10.   Mediumship is sacred and should be practiced in a saintly and devout manner. If there's one type of mediumship that demands

---

[1] *See Allan Kardec,* The Mediums' Book, *Part II, Chapter 28; and* heaven and Hell, *Chapter12.*

this attitude more absolutely than the others, it is healing.[2] In the medical world, a physician offers his or her knowledge, often gained at the cost of painful sacrifice. A healing practitioner[3] gives of his or her own energies and sometimes even health. A price can be put on their services. The spiritual-healing medium, however, relays healing energies from the good spirits themselves and so doesn't have the right to charge for them. Remember that Jesus and His apostles, although poor, didn't charge for the cures that were brought about through them.

Persons lacking necessary financial support can earn a living from whatever activity they like—except mediumship. If necessary, they should devote to mediumship only the time they have available after providing for their material needs. For their part, the good spirits will value the devotion and sacrifices of these persons. They will, however, turn away from mediums who intend to use them as stepping stone to earthly gratification.

---

[2] *Translator's Note: This form of healing is akin to the laying-on-of-hands as practiced in the early Christian church. The patient's energy system is replenished with spiritual energies for which the healer serves as conduit while in a deep state of prayer.*

[3] *Translator's Note: In the original, the word magnétiseur (magnetizer) is employed to mean the individual who, without recourse to prayer or faith, possesses the capability to heal by using his own mental or physical energy. This healing method greatly resembles the technique described by Dolores Kruger, Ph.D. in* Therapeutic Touch *(1992). The word was replaced to avoid confusion with alternative techniques based on physical magnetism, i.e., based on the use of magnetic bracelets, collars, etc.*

Chapter 27

Ask and It Will Be Given to You

SCRIPTURES AND COMMENTARY

THE QUALITY OF PRAYERS

1.   *"And when you pray, do not be like the hypocrites, for they love to pray standing in the synagogues and on the street corners to be seen by men. I tell you the truth, they have received their reward in full. But when you pray, go into your room, close the door and pray to your Father, who is unseen. Then your Father, who sees what is done in secret, will reward you. And when you pray, do not keep on babbling like pagans, for they think they will be heard because of their many words. Do not be like them, for your Father knows what you need before you ask him."*

(Matthew, 6: 5-8)

2.   *"And when you stand praying, if you hold anything against anyone, forgive him, so that your Father in heaven may forgive you your sins."*

(Mark, 11: 25-26)

3.   To some who were confident of their own righteousness and looked down on everybody else, Jesus told this parable: *"Two men went up to the temple to pray, one a Pharisee and the other a tax collector. The Pharisee stood up and prayed about himself: 'God, I thank you that I am not like other men—robbers, evildoers, adulterers—or even like this tax collector. I fast twice a week and give a tenth of all I get.'*

"But the tax collector stood at a distance. He would not even look up to heaven, but beat his breast and said, 'God, have mercy on me, a sinner.'

"I tell you that this man, rather than the other, went home justified before God. For everyone who exalts himself will be humbled, and he who humbles himself will be exalted."

(Luke, 18: 9-14)

4.   Jesus clearly defined the quality of prayer. When you pray, he said, you shouldn't draw attention to yourself, but pray in secret. Don't make your prayers overlong. It isn't the number of words that guarantees you a hearing, but their sincerity. If you have anything against another person, forgive him or her before you pray: Prayer that comes from a heart touched by uncharitable feelings isn't pleasing to God. Finally, pray with humility as the tax collector did, not with pride like the Pharisee. Look at the imperfections in your character, not at your good qualities; and if you compare yourself to someone else, look at your own faults first. [1]

5.   *"Therefore I tell you, whatever you ask for in prayer, believe that you have received it, and it will be yours."*

(Mark, 11: 24)

6.   There are people who argue that prayer isn't effective because God knows all our needs and we have no reason to recite them. They add that, since everything in the Universe is linked together by eternal laws, our prayers can't change God's decrees anyway.

We can say, without doubt, that there are natural and unchangeable laws in the Universe that God does not repeal at the whim of an individual. But this is a long way from believing that every life circumstance is preordained by fate. If that were the case, human beings would be passive instruments, devoid of free will and initiative. Thus, in the face of any challenge, our only course would be to bow our heads and make no effort to overcome the situation. Taken to an extreme, we shouldn't even try to protect ourselves from lightning. But God didn't give us reason and intelligence to let them go unused, or a will to discourage us from willing things, or physical energy to have us stay still. We're free to act in one way or the other, both for ourselves and toward others, and the consequences of that freedom depend on what we do or fail to do. Because of our free will, there are events that escape fate without this in any way disrupting the harmony of the universal laws. Compare it, if you will, to the speeding up or slowing down of a clock pendulum—actions that don't repeal the laws of motion on which the movement mechanism is based. Thus, Providence may attend certain prayers without disturbing the laws that govern the whole of life. Ultimately, the response will manifest the will of God.

7.   To conclude from the precept "whatever you ask for in prayer, believe that you have received it, and it will be yours" that we can

---

[1] *See Chapter 10, items 7-8.*

receive anything we want just by asking for it, is illogical. It would be equally unfair to blame Providence in cases where a request isn't answered, since God knows better than we do what is in our own best interest. In a way, God is like a good parent who refuses to give something to a child in the realization that it may not be good for her. Generally, like children, we see only the present moment. If our current suffering is necessary to our future happiness, however, God will let us suffer, just as a surgeon will allow a patient to suffer the pain of a curative procedure.

What God will give us, if we direct our prayers with confidence, is courage, patience, and fortitude. God will also give us ways of resolving situations ourselves with the help of ideas that spirit guides suggest to us. In the end, the merit is ours. God helps those who help themselves. God doesn't help people who simply wait for the help of others and don't use their own abilities. In most cases, unfortunately, what we desire are miracles that require no effort on our part.[2]

8. Let's take an example. A man finds himself lost in the desert. Thirst tortures him terribly. Eventually he faints and falls to the ground. After coming to himself, he asks God for help and waits. No angels, however, come to give him water. Instead, a good spirit inspires him to pick himself up and take one of several paths before him. With the movements of an automaton he gathers all the strength he has left, gets up, starts to walk again, and discovers a stream not far away. The sight of it fills him with new strength. If he is a person of faith he cries, "Thank you, dear God, for the inspiration and for the strength you gave me." If he doesn't have faith, he'll say, "What a good idea I had. A lucky thing— to take the right-hand path instead of the left-hand! Chance is a good guide sometimes! I have to congratulate myself for my courage and for not giving up!"

But, you ask, why didn't the spirit say to him clearly, "Follow that path and you'll find what you need"? Why didn't the spirit show itself? Why not guide the man and support him along the way? Certainly this would have convinced him of the intervention of Providence. But by not receiving direct help, the man learns that each of us must help ourselves and make use of our own strength. Also, by leaving the man unaware of the providential help he is receiving, the man's trust in God and observance of God's Will is put to the test. The man is in the same situation as a child who falls

---

[2] *See Chapter 25, item 1 and following.*

down and, because someone is with him, starts to cry and waits to be picked up. If the same child sees that no one is with him, he'll make the effort and get up by himself. If the angel who accompanied Tobias had said, "I'm sent by God to guide you on your journey and preserve you from danger," Tobias wouldn't have any merit for his actions. He would have entrusted himself to his companion and wouldn't even have had to think. This is why the angel only made itself known after the return.[3]

HOW PRAYER WORKS: THOUGHT TRANSFER

9. Prayer is an invocation. Through prayer we establish a mental relationship with the being we address. A prayer may have the purpose of asking for something, giving thanks, or praising. We may pray for ourselves or for others, for the living or the dead. The prayers we address to God are heard by spirits who are responsible for executing God's Will. The prayers we address to good spirits are referred to God. When someone prays to beings other than God, these beings serve as mediators or intercessors, since nothing can happen outside of God's Will.

10. The Spiritist Doctrine helps us understand the way prayer works by explaining how thought is transferred, both when we raise our thoughts to a being we pray to, or when this being answers our pleas. To understand how this is possible, we should first consider that all beings, in both the physical and spiritual realms, are immersed in the Cosmic Principle[4] that occupies space, just as we on earth are enveloped by the atmosphere. The Cosmic

---

[3] *Translator's note. Tobit 5:4*

Tobit is a book of the Old Testament which tells a story of reward for perseverance in good works. The story is set in Nineveh sometime during the Exile, probably in the latter part of the 8th century B.C. The young Tobias is sent by his blind father Tobit, a pious Israelite, on a long and dangerous journey to Media. In recompense for Tobit's life of goodness and devotion to the Law, God assigns the angel Raphael to care for the youth. The angel takes human appearance under the name Azarias and accompanies Tobias through the entire journey. The angel then guides Tobias to meet and marry Sarah, and to recover the money that his father had left in trust with a friend. Upon his return home, the angel teaches Tobias how to cure his father's blindness. At the end, when Tobias is about to pay Azarias the wage for his work, Azarias finally tells the truth and reveals his true origin and the mission God had entrusted to him.

[4] *Translator's Note: Cosmic Principle, the subtle medium in which the fundamental energy fields take existence. For a more detailed discussion, see Allan Kardec's* The Spirits' Book, *AKES, Philadelphia, PA, 1996, p. 9.*

Principle reacts to impulses of will, and thoughts travel through it as sounds travel through air. The chief difference is that, while sound vibrations are limited in reach, those of thought travel infinite distances in the Cosmic Principle.

When a thought is directed at someone on earth or in the spirit world—from an incarnate to a discarnate being, or vice versa—a current of energy is established between them that transfers the thought from one to the other, just as air transmits sound waves. The power of the current is relative to the strength of the thought and desire. This is how spirits, no matter where they are, hear the prayers directed to them. It's how spirits communicate with each other, and how they send their inspirations to us. Finally, it's how incarnates can potentially establish (telepathic) contact with each other even at a distance.

This explanation is aimed especially at people who can't see any usefulness in prayer because they see it as a mere act of mysticism. It isn't meant to "materialize" prayer but rather, by making its effect understandable, to show that prayer can have direct and powerful results. This doesn't make prayer any less subordinate to God's Will. God is the Supreme Judge of all things, and it's only through God's Will that the action of prayer can take effect.

11. It's also through prayer that we receive the help of the good spirits, who support us in our good resolutions and inspire us with encouraging thoughts. In this way, we acquire the inner strength to go through life's difficulties and to return to the straight and narrow path when we stray from it. With prayer we can also avert the troubles that are the natural product of bad personal decisions. For example: A woman spoils her health because of her self-indulgence and lives in poor health till the end of her days. Does she have the right to complain if she can't be cured? No. If she had prayed early on she would have had the strength to resist the temptations that led to her troubles.

12. If we divided the troubles of life into two groups—the first, the hardships we can't avoid; the second, the ones our carelessness and intemperance lead us into—we'd see that the evils in the second group far outnumber those in the first.[5] We are the authors of most of our own difficulties, which we could avoid if we took care and behaved wisely.

It's obvious that these difficulties come from our disregarding the Law and that, if we observed the Law, our happiness would

[5] *See Chapter 5, item 4.*

be more complete. If we didn't go beyond the limit of the necessary to satisfy our needs, we wouldn't have the ailments or experience the hardships that our excesses bring about. If we put limits on our ambition, we wouldn't have to fear financial disaster; if we didn't try to climb higher than we can go, we wouldn't be afraid of falling; if we were humble, we wouldn't be hurt in our pride; if we lived by the law of love, we wouldn't speak evil of others, we wouldn't be jealous or envious, and wouldn't have to quarrel with anyone. If we wronged no one, we wouldn't fret about their feelings for us.

If we were to admit that we can't do anything about certain unavoidable adversities and that prayer won't save us from them, wouldn't it still mean a great deal if we could spare ourselves the harm that comes from our own behavior? It's easy to see the role that prayer plays here, since its aim is to attract beneficial inspirations from the good spirits and to gather strength to resist bad thoughts, especially those whose realization leads to disastrous consequences for ourselves. In this case, the good spirits won't do away with the hardships, but they will turn us away from the bad thoughts that may cause them. The good spirits won't prevent the fulfillment of God's Laws or suspend the Laws of Nature for us. They will inspire us, in the use of our free will, to honor those laws. They do so in a most subtle and intuitive way, so as never to violate our free will. We're in the position of someone who asks for good advice, but who is still always free to take the advice or not. Providence wants life to be like this, so that we can take responsibility for our actions and take full credit for choosing correctly between good and evil. This much everyone should trust in when they pray with sincerity of heart. This above all is the kind of situation where we can apply the words "Ask and it will be given to you."[6]

Wouldn't the effects of prayer, even in this limited sense, produce enormous benefits? To the Spiritist Doctrine has been left the task of demonstrating prayer's positive action by revealing the relationship between the physical and spirit worlds. But the effects of prayer aren't limited to these results alone.

Prayer is recommended by all advanced spirits. Not to pray is to fail to acknowledge the goodness of God, to reject the assistance that loving spirits can lend to us, and ignore the good we can do for others.

---

[6] *Translator's Note: Matthew 7:7.*

13. In answering a prayer, God wants to reward the intent, the devotion, and the faith of the person who prays. This is why a good person's prayers have greater merit in God's eyes, and are always more effective. The prayers of someone who's ill-meaning and full of vice can never have the devotion and fervor that only come from a heart that feels genuine reverence. A person who has a selfish heart prays only with the lips and so produces only words, never the loving impulse that gives prayer its power. We understand this so clearly that when we ask someone else to pray for us, we instinctively prefer an individual whose behavior we feel is more pleasing to God and who will be more readily heard by God.

14. One might conclude that, because the action of prayer involves a magnetic action of sorts, its effects depend only on the mental power and faith of the one who prays. This is true only in part. For the power of prayer may be increased by the intervention of good spirits willing to second the act of supplication. Or the good spirits may help by sustaining the devotion of the person who prays, with thoughts of encouragement. This only happens when the person is worthy, or when the prayer has a truly useful aim.

   People who don't think well enough of themselves to put forth a supplication abounding in tenderness shouldn't stop praying for someone in the mistaken belief that they aren't worthy to be heard. This awareness of their limitation shows sincere humility—a disposition that is always pleasing to God, Who then takes into account the loving intent behind the prayer. These persons' faith and trust in God are the first steps in the return to the straight path, and the good spirits consider themselves blessed in being able to encourage this return. In fact, prayer is rejected only when it comes from the prideful who believe more in their own power and merits, and who think that their will has precedence over the Eternal One's Will.

15. The power of prayer lies in the thought. It doesn't depend on words or on the place or time in which the prayer is said. A person can pray anywhere, at any time, alone or in a group. The influence of place or time is relevant only to the extent that these induce quiet concentration. In addition, group prayer has a more powerful effect only when all the participants join together in a heartfelt thought and focus on the same objective. The situation is akin to that of a group of people whose voices are amplified when they shout at one time. Communal prayer doesn't do any good, however, when everyone is going their own way with their

thoughts. Hundreds of self-absorbed people can pray together; but if two or three people, joined by the same desire, pray like true brothers and sisters in God, their prayers will be more powerful.[7]

INTELLIGIBLE PRAYERS

16.   *If then I do not grasp the meaning of what someone is saying, I am a foreigner to the speaker, and he is a foreigner to me.*

For if I pray in a (foreign) tongue, my spirit prays, but my mind is unfruitful. If you are praising God with your spirit, how can one who finds himself among those who do not understand say "Amen" to your thanksgiving, since he does not know what you are saying?

(I Corinthians, 14: 11, 14, 16-17)

17. The value of prayer lies in the thought that gives life to it. Therefore, the person who prays cannot be inspired by words he or she doesn't understand. What isn't understood can't touch the heart. For the majority of people, prayers said in an unknown language become just a hodgepodge of words that say nothing to the soul.[8] For a prayer to be deeply felt each word must awaken an idea, which is impossible when the words are unintelligible. A prayer said under these circumstances becomes merely a formula, its value assumed to be dependent on the number of times it's repeated. Consequently, we find that many people pray only out of a sense of obligation, others out of social habit. Once they've said a predetermined prayer a certain number of times and in the correct order, they consider that their duty to pray is done. But God sees what goes on in the depths of our hearts and carefully considers our thoughts and our sincerity. To suppose that God is really more sensitive to the words than the feeling is to discredit the Divine.[9]

PRAYERS FOR THE DEAD AND FOR SUFFERING SPIRITS

18. Suffering spirits need prayers, which can be quite comforting to them. The awareness that someone is thinking of them tenderly

---

[7] *See Chapter 28, items 4-5.*

[8] *Translator's Note: The author makes reference to the use of Latin, which dominated the religious practices of the Roman church for eighteen centuries. It wasn't until 1963, in the decree "Sacrosanctum Concilium" by the Second Vatican Council, that the liturgy (mass) and the rites of the church were allowed to be translated from the Latin language into the modern vernacular.*

[9] *See Chapter 28, item 2.*

makes these spirits feel less neglected and hapless. But prayer can have an even more direct effect: It rebuilds their strength and rekindles in them the resolve to repent and make up for their wrongs, in order to advance. Prayer may also turn them away from thinking bad thoughts. Prayers not only ease their suffering but actually shorten it.[10]

19. As for prayers for the dead, there are people who don't believe in offering them. In their view, only two alternatives exist for the soul: It will either be saved or eternally damned. In either case, prayer would be useless. Now, without discussing the merits of this view, let's admit for a moment the idea that eternal and unpardonable punishment is a reality and that our prayers can do nothing to end their suffering. Even given this hypothesis, we ask if it would be logical, humane, or Christian to refuse prayers for those hopeless souls. Although our prayers might be powerless to free these souls, wouldn't they represent an act of compassion that might help ease their suffering? On earth, when someone is sentenced to life in prison, with no possibility of pardon, nothing prevents a kind person from helping to ease the weight of that sentence! Likewise, when someone catches an incurable disease, and there's no hope of a cure being found in time to save her, should we abandon this person to her luck without providing any comfort? Suppose that among these souls you find a loved one— a friend, a father, a mother, a son, a daughter. Ask yourself if, just because you believe that a reprieve is impossible for them, you would deny them a glass of water to quench their thirst a little or a salve that would heal their wounds. Or if one of them had been condemned to forced labor, wouldn't you show them kindness, or say a good word? Not to do it would be unChristian. And a faith that hardens the heart can't be related to a God Who puts the duty of loving our neighbors before everything else.

Still, the fact that eternal punishment doesn't exist doesn't mean that temporary penalties don't exist either. God, Who is all just, never mistakes wrong for right. In this case, denying the effectiveness of prayer for a suffering soul is akin to denying the uplifting value that words of comfort, encouragement, and guidance possess for us—which is itself equal to denying the strength we gather from the moral support of those who wish us well.

20. Other people base their objections to this kind of prayer on a more specific reason: the unchanging nature of divine decrees. The

[10] *See* Heaven and Hell, *Part II*, *"Examples."*

designs of Providence, they say, can't be changed just because someone asks. If this happened, nothing would be stable in the world. According to this view, we don't really have anything to ask of God; our only recourse is to submit and adore the Divine.

But we find here an incorrect interpretation of the principle of the stability of Divine Laws. More exactly, such an interpretation reveals an unawareness of the Divine Code as it relates to future penalties. The spirits of the Lord are now revealing the meaning of these laws, because we're mature enough at last to understand what, within our faith, conforms and what runs contrary to the attributes of God.

In the dogma of eternal punishment, the contrition and repentance of wrongdoers aren't taken into account. Any desire to do and become better, then, is useless because they've been condemned eternally to evil. But if they were condemned (as some interpret the dogma[11]) for a specified period of time, the punishment ends when that time runs out—and who knows whether or not the wrongdoers' attitudes will have improved by then? Just like criminals on earth, they may be just as bad on leaving prison as they were on entering it. It is evident here that, in the first case (eternal punishment), a regenerated person will be forced to endure unceasing punishment; in the second (punishment for a specified time), pardon could be given to an unrepenting offender. Divine Law is wiser than either of these alternatives. Always fair and merciful, it does not have pre-set times for correction, no matter what the case. This Law can be summed up in the following way:

------

[11] *Translator's Note: The duration of the punishments of hell has been a subject of theological controversy in the traditional church since early Christian times. The third century Christian theologian Origen taught that the purpose of these punishments was purgatorial, and that they were proportionate to the guilt of the individual. This doctrine was condemned by the Second Council of Constantinople in 553 A.D., and belief in the eternity of the punishments in hell became characteristic of both the Orthodox and the Roman Catholic church. It also passed into the creeds of the churches of the Reformation. In modern times the belief in physical punishment after death and the endless duration of this punishment has been rejected by many, but the controversy still exists. Opinions range from holding the pains of hell to be no more than the remorse of conscience to the traditional belief that the "pain of loss"'(the conciousness of having forfeited the vision of God and the happiness of heaven) is combined with the "pain of sense" (actual physical torment).*

21. "Human beings always suffer the consequences of their errors. There is no violation of God's Laws that doesn't bring about a fitting penalty.

"How severe the penalty is depends on the seriousness of the violation.

"The length of a penalty is not definite; rather, it is subordinate to the wrongdoer's contrition and subsequent desire to right his life. The punishment lasts only as long as the person remains on the wrong path. Only if the individual persisted on the wrong path forever would the punishment be eternal; likewise, an early show of remorse makes for a short correction.

"From the moment the wrongdoer cries for mercy, God listens and encourages hope. But repentance by itself isn't enough. The wrongdoer must also make amends. This is why he or she will be granted new opportunities in which, out of their free will, they will be able to do good to make up for the wrong that was done.

"In this way we are the sole arbiters of our destiny. We can shorten our suffering, or prolong it indefinitely. Our happiness or unhappiness depends on our will to do good."

This is the Law—the unchanging law that affirms the Goodness and Justice of God.

Stray and suffering spirits can always redeem themselves, because the Law prescribes the conditions under which redemption becomes possible. In many cases, what these spirits lack is will power, the strength, and the courage to do what needs to be done. Consequently, if our prayers inspire the will to change, if they encourage and sustain, if they help enlighten these souls who are still in the dark, these prayers, far from constituting mere pleas for God to revoke this or that law, turn us into accessories to the law of love and compassion. In allowing this to happen, God permits us to express the kindness of our hearts.[12]

SPIRIT TEACHINGS

THE WAY TO PRAY

22. ■ The first duty of every human being, the first act that should mark the return to the business of the day, is prayer. Most people pray—

---

[12] *See* Heaven and Hell, *Part II, Chapters 4, 7-8.*

but only a very few really know how to pray! The majority recite sentences mechanically. By force of habit, they perform a duty, and it weighs as heavily on them as any other duty. But ask yourselves, What importance can God actually attach to such prayers?

The prayers of a Christian—whether a Spiritist or a member of some other denomination—should be made as soon as the spirit returns to its earthly bonds. Your prayer should raise your soul up to the feet of the Divine Majesty in an attitude of humility and deep awareness. You should be thankful for all the benefits you have received until that day, and for the night you've just had. Even though you might have no conscious knowledge of what happened while you slept, chances are you were allowed to enjoy the presence of friends and guides from which you took new strength and renewed fortitude. Your prayer should ascend humbly to God, acknowledging your frailties and pleading for God's help, tolerance, and mercy. Your prayer should come from deep within and raise your soul to the Creator transfigured, as Jesus was on Mount Tabor, in the full splendor of love and trust.

Your prayer should be an entreaty for God's blessing on all the things you need. Here we speak of real needs. It serves no purpose to simply ask God to shorten your tests and trials or give you happiness and money. It's more sensible to ask for more precious things: patience, fortitude, faith. Don't say, as many people do, "Praying isn't worth it because God doesn't answer my prayers." In most cases, what do you ask God for? Do you ever remember asking for help as you strive for self-improvement? No, you seldom do this. Instead you ask for success in your earthly affairs and then complain that God doesn't bother about you, otherwise there wouldn't be so many injustices in life. How foolish and ungrateful! If you looked deep inside your own conscience, you would realize that most of your life problems have their cause in your own choices. Foremost, then, ask God to help you to become a better person and you'll see yourself showered with graces and solace.[13]

You should pray always, and by that we don't mean that you should confine yourself to a temple or even fall on your knees in a public place. The daily praying we refer to takes place whenever you attend to your higher duties, whatever they may be. After all, isn't it an act of devotion to God to help your brothers and sisters at a time of need, either material or spiritual? Isn't it an act of

---

[13] *See Chapter 5, item 4.*

thanksgiving to lift up your thoughts to God when something wonderful happens, or when you manage to avoid an accident or even when the common nuisances of life only lightly brush you? Don't forget to say, in those moments, "Blessed be God in heaven!" And isn't it also an act of contrition to humble yourself before the Supreme Judge when you realize that you've committed a wrong and say, even if only in a brief thought: "Forgive me, O God, for I have erred (from arrogance, selfishness, or lack of love). Give me the strength not to fail again and the courage to make up for my faults!"

This kind of prayer is quite apart from regular morning and evening prayers and those said on sacred days. As you see, your prayers can take place at any time, without interrupting your activities. Rather than harming your endeavors, it makes them whole. And you can be sure that God will listen to any one of your prayerful thoughts, when heartfelt, far more closely than to the long prayers said out of habit and without any stronger motive than the arrival of the hour of prayer. ■ —V. Monod (Bordeaux, 1862).

THE JOY OF PRAYER

23. ■ All of you who want to believe, come! The celestial spirits are here to announce great things! Children, the divine treasury is open and God is giving out precious gifts. O unbelieving humanity! If only you knew how much good faith can bring to your hearts and how much it can inspire the soul to mend its ways and to pray! Prayer! How moving words are when they are uttered by the lips of someone in prayer! Prayer is the divine dew that puts out the fire of desires. It is the darling child of faith, shepherding you along the path to God. In those moments of silent meditation and solitude, you are with God; the mysteries of life are unveiled to you. Apostles of the mind, life is meant for you. Your soul is free to sail to infinite and ethereal realms of which most humanity is as yet unaware .

March forward! March along the path of prayer and you'll hear the voices of the angels! What harmony they make! The confused noises and harsh sounds of earth disappear, and you will hear only the lyres of archangels and the soft, sweet voices of the Seraphim—more delicate than the morning breeze as it plays among the leaves of the forest. What delights you will walk among, then! Your earthly language can't express such bliss, it envelopes you so completely. When you pray you drink from a live and refreshing spring. Sweet voices and thrilling scents are what the soul experiences when it enters through prayer into the unknown realms. All aspirations are sublime once free from the desires of the flesh. You too can pray, as Jesus did while taking His cross to Calvary. So take up your cross. You too will experience the soothing comfort He felt, though His was the cross of infamy. He was going to die, but only in order to live the celestial life in the abode of God. ■ —Saint Augustine (Paris, 1861).

Chapter 28

A Collection of Spiritist Prayers

PREAMBLE

1. The spirits have always said, "The form means nothing, the thought is everything. Say your prayers in a way that is in harmony with your convictions and in the way most inspiring to you, because a good thought is worth more than countless unfeeling and unfelt words."

   The spirits don't impose a rigid formula for prayers. When they do give us a prayer, it's to help us get a better sense of our ideas and, above all, to call our attention to certain principles of the Spiritist Doctrine. At times, these prayers are also intended to give guidance to people who find it hard to express their ideas. Some persons believe they haven't prayed the right way if they haven't been able to frame their thoughts well.

   The prayers collected in this chapter are a selection from a body of prayers dictated by the spirits on various occasions. Without doubt, the spirits could have dictated other prayers in different words and related to differing ideas and special cases. But if the thought is basically the same, the style doesn't matter. The object of prayer is to raise up our souls to God. Thus, the many forms of prayer available to us shouldn't make any difference to those who believe in God, and even less to the followers of the Spiritist Doctrine, because God accepts all prayers when they're sincere.

   You shouldn't think of this collection, then, as establishing absolute formulas, but as a varied selection received from the spirits. The prayers herein simply apply the moral principles of the Gospel, which have been developed in this book. They are a complement to the spirits' teachings about our duties before God and our neighbors, and remind us anew of all the doctrine's principles.

   The Spiritist Doctrine respects the prayers of all religions as good, i.e., as long as they come from the heart and not just from the lips. The doctrine doesn't impose prayers or condemn them.

God is far too noble to consider rejecting a voice that pleads or sings praises just because these aren't done in this or that manner. So people who reproach ways of praying that fall outside their own concepts prove they don't comprehend God's magnanimity. To believe that God has some kind of special fondness for a certain formula is to credit God with narrow-mindedness and human sentiments.

According to the apostle Paul, one of the essential conditions of a prayer is that it be understandable, so that it will move our spirit.[1] For this to happen, it is enough for us to say a prayer in ordinary language. There are prayers that, even though couched in modern terms, say little more to the intelligence than does a prayer recited in an unknown foreign language—and for this reason they fail to touch our hearts. The few ideas these prayers contain are usually smothered in an overabundance of words and mystical expressions.

The principal quality of a prayer is its clarity. It should be simple and concise, uncluttered by useless phrases or multiple adjectives (these are simply decoration). Each word should be valuable in helping express an idea, in touching a fiber of the soul. In short, a prayer should cause us to reflect. This is the only way it can reach its goal; otherwise, it's nothing but noise.

In most cases, we realize how distractedly and inconsistently people pray. We see their lips move, but by the expression on their faces and in the sound of their voices, we have proof that their prayer is mechanical, a solely exterior act that the soul cares nothing about.

The prayers in this collection are divided into five categories, as follows: (I) General Prayers; (II) Prayers for Oneself; (III) Prayers for Others; (IV) Prayers for Those No Longer on earth, (V) Special Prayers for the Sick and the Spiritually Disturbed.

With the aim of calling special attention to the purpose behind the various prayers, and making their meaning more accessible, they are preceded by opening comments that give an explanation of each. These comments we have subsumed under the title "Preface."

---

[1] *Translator's Note: 1 Corinthians 14: 11, 14-17.*

GENERAL PRAYERS

THE LORD'S PRAYER

2. *Preface:* The Spirits recommended that we begin this anthology with the Lord's Prayer, not simply as a prayer but also as a symbol. This prayer, among all others, is considered the most important—first, because it came from Jesus Himself[2] and second, because it can substitute for all the others, depending on the thought and intention that go with it. It is the most concise and perfect model of a prayer, and in its simplicity a sublime work of art. In its very concise form, it effectively manages to summarize all our duties before God, ourselves, and our neighbors. In it we find an affirmation of faith, an act of adoration and reverence, an entreaty for the things we need in life, and a celebration of love. Anyone who says this prayer for another person, asks for them what they would ask for themselves.

Still, because it's so short, the profound meaning of some of its words escapes many people. This is usually because they say it without thinking about the meaning of each of its phrases. They say it like a mechanical formula, some thinking that its effectiveness depends on the number of times it's repeated. This number is almost always cabalistic—three, seven, or nine[3]—with its origins in ancient belief in the power of numbers and other magic rituals.

In order to fill the void often felt due to the conciseness of the Lord's Prayer, the illuminated spirits have suggested a commentary to each of the phrases. This commentary reinforces the prayer's meaning and tells us how to embrace it in our daily lives. Depending on individual circumstances and the time you have at any given moment, you can say the Lord's Prayer in its simple form or in the more developed one here.

3. Prayer:

(i) Our Father in heaven, hallowed be your name,

O God, we believe in You, because everything around us reveals Your goodness and Your power. The harmony of the Universe gives proof of a wisdom, a sense of judgment, and a foresight that surpasses human comprehension. From the tiny

---

[2] *Translator's Note: Matthew 6: 9-13.*

[3] *Translator's Note: refers to the Roman Catholic practice of prescribing a set number of prayer repetitions, e.g., novena, a devotion consisting of prayers on nine consecutive days.*

blade of grass and smallest insect up to the stars and planets in space, we see the imprint of a sovereignly noble and wise Being. Everywhere we see proof of Your love. Thus, the person who doesn't praise You is too proud; the one who doesn't thank You is ungrateful.

(ii) Your kingdom come,

God, You gave us Laws that are full of wisdom and that would make us happy if only we observed them. With these Laws, we could establish justice and peace. Each of us could help the other instead of doing harm to one another, as we often do. Under these Laws, the strong would support the weak instead of crushing them. We could avoid the evils that give rise to all sorts of abuses and excesses. All the hardships of this world stem from the violation of Your laws, because there isn't one infraction that doesn't bring its inevitable consequences.

You gave the animals instinct, thus setting the range of their needs and behavior. To us, You gave intelligence and reason as well as instinct. Still more, You gave us the freedom to observe or disobey Your Laws regarding our personal lives. That is, You gave us the power of choosing between good and evil, so that we have both the merit and the responsibility for our acts.

No one can claim to be ignorant of Your Laws because, in Your foresight, You caused them to be engraved in the consciousness of each person, regardless of their religious orientation or nationality. In this way the people who violate them do so because they despise You.

The day will come when, according to Your promise, everyone will practice these Laws. Then unbelief will have disappeared. Everyone will recognize You as Supreme over all things and the reign of Your Laws will proclaim Your reign here on earth.

God, privilege us and bring the day of Your glory closer by illuminating our journey on the path of truth!

(iii) Your will be done on earth as it is in heaven.

If the duty of the child is to respect the parents, the worker to respect the boss, how much greater is our duty to respect God, our Creator! By the words "Your will be done" we acknowledge that it is up to us to observe Your Laws and accept with respect Your designs. One day all of us will come to respect your designs. We will come to understand that You are the source of all wisdom and that without You we can do nothing. Then each person will do Your bidding on earth as Your elected ones do it in heaven.

(iv) Give us today our daily bread.

Give us the food we need to maintain our physical strength. And give us also spiritual nourishment for our inner growth.

The animals find their pastures, but we must rely on our own effort and intellectual activity to produce our food because You gave us freedom.

You said, "By the sweat of your brow you will eat your food."[4] With these words You made work a duty and a means for us to employ our intelligence as we search for the means to provide for our needs and attend to our well-being. Without work, whether of an intellectual or physical nature, we would remain stationary and couldn't aspire to the happiness of the more advanced spirits.

We know You give to the people of goodwill who trust in You for their needs, but not to those who are lazy and want everything without effort, or to those who only seek the superfluous.[5]

So many there are who flounder because of their own faults, their negligence, their thoughtlessness, their ambition, or because they aren't content with what You gave them! Yet they're the authors of their own misfortune and can't really complain, because their plight is of their own doing. But in Your infinite mercy, You won't abandon even these. You will extend help to them if they return to You sincerely, as the prodigal son came back to his father.[6]

Help us not to complain about our destiny, and to seek within ourselves whether or not our suffering isn't our own doing. With each misfortune that happens, help us to see how we could have avoided it. Help us to realize that we have been given intelligence in order to deliver ourselves from any predicament, and that it is only up to us to find the means.

Since work is the Law of Life on earth, give us, God, the courage and strength to honor this Law. Also give us discernment, foresight, and moderation so that we don't waste its fruits.

Give us our daily bread—or rather the means of providing for our needs through work, because none of us has the right to ask for more than we need. If we can't work, help us have confidence in Your Divine Providence.

---

[4] *Translator's Note: Genesis 3:19.*

[5] *See Chapter 25.*

[6] *See Chapter 5, item 4. Translator's Note: Luke 15:11-31.*

If it is part of Your plan to test us with scarce means, despite our best work efforts to improve our lot, we accept this as a just correction for wrongs we've committed, either in this life or in a previous one. We know that every hardship serves a just purpose and that we are never corrected without a reason.

Save us, God, from envying people who have what we don't, or people who live in abundance while we ourselves lack life's necessities. Forgive those people, God, if they've forgotten the law of charity and love toward one's neighbor, which You have taught.[7]

Also, God, save us from ever harboring in our souls doubts about Your justice when we see bad people prospering while godly ones are burdened with suffering. We now know, thanks to the new light that You shed upon us, that Your justice always follows its course. The prosperity of bad people is as fragile as their bodily existence, and reversals of fortune do happen. As for those who go through it all with fortitude, their bliss will be endless. [8]

(v) Forgive us our debts, as we also have forgiven our debtors.

God, with each infraction of Your Law, we commit an offense against You. Each new infraction is a debt that we have to redeem. So, trusting Your mercy, we supplicate Your forgiveness and promise You our utmost not to incur new debts.

You made charity (love) a law. But charity doesn't only mean helping our fellow beings in their time of need. It also consists in our forgetting and forgiving offenses against us. What right would we have to expect Your mercy if we ourselves aren't forgiving toward people who've wronged us?

Dear God, give us the strength to erase all the resentment, hate, and bitterness inside us. Don't let death surprise us with a desire for revenge in our hearts. Whenever You call us back from this world, help us present ourselves to You free of animosity, as Christ was when, with His last words, He blessed His tormentors.[9]

The torment we endure at the hands of ill-natured people is part of our earthly trials and we should handle it without complaint, as we should accept all other trials. We should not curse those who, through their wrongdoing, afford us an opportunity to advance on the pathway to eternal happiness—for Jesus, by

[7] *See Chapter 16, item 8.*

[8] *See Chapter 5, items 7, 9, 12, and 18.*

[9] *See Chapter 10.*

Your inspiration, said, "Blessed are those who hunger and thirst for righteousness." In this sense, we should learn to bless the hand that injures and humiliates us. The suffering of the flesh strengthens the soul, and a humiliating offense received today may well raise us to new levels in the future. [10]

Praised be Your name, O God, for giving us the understanding that our destiny isn't unalterably determined after death; and that in other lives we'll have the means for making amends and learning from our mistakes. Praised be Your name for the understanding that each life is a new opportunity to do all the things necessary to our progress and that we weren't able to do in the current life.[11]

In this way, all of life's apparent oddities are finally explained. This understanding is a light trained on our past and our future, a brilliant sign of Your supreme justice and goodness.

(vi) And let us not fall into temptation, but deliver us from evil. [12]

God, give us the strength we need to resist the suggestions of misguided spirits who, by their wicked thoughts, try to turn us away from the path of goodness.

We're imperfect spirits ourselves, incarnated on earth in order to expiate the harm we've brought about and to better ourselves. The root of our wrongdoing still lies in our souls, and the unevolved spirits only take advantage of our lower tendencies to tempt us. Each of our imperfections represents an open door to their influence, and by the same token, we know they are powerless before an upright person. All our efforts to shake them off are in vain if we don't confront them with a will firmly committed to good and a genuine hatred for all evil. For this reason, we must focus our energies on changing ourselves. Thenceforward, the lower spirits will naturally leave us alone since it's the evil in us that attracts them and our uprightness that repels them.[13]

Dear God, support us in our weakness. Let the angels and good spirits inspire us with the desire to correct our imperfections so that no ill-meaning spirit will have access to our souls.

---

[10] See Chapter 12, item 4.

[11] See Chapter 4; and Chapter 5, item 5.

[12] Translator's Note: The NIV text, "And lead us not into temptation, but deliverer us from evil," departs from the original understanding. The original French sense was maintained here.

[13] See "Prayers for the Spiritually Disturbed" later in this chapter.

Evil isn't Your work, God, because the Source of All Goodness can't bring about evil. We ourselves create evil when we violate Your Laws and make bad use of the freedom of choice You give us. When we have learned to observe Your Laws, evil will disappear from earth, just as it has already disappeared from the more advanced realms.

Wrongdoing is not an inescapable condition for anybody. It only appears to be so to those who are complacent about it. Indeed, if we can exercise our will to do wrong, we can just as well use it to do good. So if we will evil, we can equally will good. For this reason, beloved God, we supplicate Your help and that of the good spirits in resisting temptation.

(vii) Amen!

O God, we pray for the realization of our desires, but willingly accept the dictate of Your infinite wisdom. In all the things we can't understand, may Your Will be done and not ours, since You only want our improvement and know better than we do what is best for us.

We say this prayer, God, not only for ourselves, but also for every suffering human being, both incarnate and discarnate. For our friends and enemies, for all those who need our help, and especially for [insert name]. We ask Your mercy and blessing for all.

(Note: Here you can offer thanks to God for everything you have received and express any request you may have, either for yourself or others [see Prayers 26-27 below].)

PURPOSE: SPIRITIST MEETINGS

4.   *"For where two or three come together in my name, there am I with them."*

(Matthew, 18: 20)

5.   *Preface:* In order to gather together in the name of Jesus, our physical presence isn't enough. We need to gather in the spiritual sense as well, through a mutual consideration of our common purpose and by directing our thoughts toward goodness. In this way we will find Jesus among us—that is, either He will come to us or the pure spirits who represent Him will come. The Spiritist Doctrine helps us understand the way in which spirits can be with us. A spirit can be physically present, so to speak, with its spiritual form having an appearance that we would be able to recognize if we could see it. Alternatively, the higher in the spiritual hierarchy spirits are, the greater their power of radiation is.

This is what gives the more evolved spirits an apparent ability to be in more than one place at the same time—a feat they perform by the power of thought.

With these words Jesus wanted to show the effect of union of purpose and good fellowship. It isn't the greater or fewer number of people which attracts Jesus' presence, but the feeling of love that unites and inspires those who have gathered together. If numbers were important He would have said ten or twenty instead of two or three people. But for this purpose two persons are enough. And if these two people pray separately, even if they direct themselves to Jesus, there won't be a communion of thought between them if they aren't motivated by genuine goodwill. If they carry within themselves feelings of hatred, jealousy, or envy, the energy currents of their thoughts will repel each other; empathy, the impulse toward harmony, won't unite them. Consequently, they won't be united in the name of Jesus, Who will only be the pretext for that meeting and not the true reason for it.[14]

This doesn't mean that Jesus will never listen only to one person. However, if He didn't say, "I'll help anyone who calls Me," it was because He expects first, that, we are able to love our neighbor. It is easier to show this when we are around other people than when isolated, more so because self-centeredness distances us from Him. As a result, if in a large meeting two or three people join their love-filled hearts together while everyone else stays by himself or herself and concentrates on selfish and worldly things, Jesus will be with the first group and not the second. It isn't the simultaneous saying of words, singing of songs, or performance of exterior acts that brings the gathering together in Jesus' name. Rather, it's the communion of thought inspired by the true spirit of love, of which Jesus is the personification.[15]

This should be the character of all serious Spiritist meetings in which the participants sincerely desire the assistance of the good spirits.

6. *Prayer (for the beginning of a meeting):* We implore You, O God, the All Powerful, to send us the good spirits to help us and keep away any spirits that may lead us into error. Give us the necessary light to distinguish truth from falsehood.

---

[14] *See Chapter 27, item 9.*

[15] *See Chapter 10, items 7-8; and Chapter 27, items 2 through 4.*

Keep away wicked spirits, whether incarnate or discarnate, that might try to cause dissension among us and turn us away from charity and the love of our neighbors. If any such spirits try to disturb our meeting, don't let them have access to our hearts.

Good spirits, who see fit to come and teach us, make us yielding to your direction. Turn us away from all selfish, proud, jealous, and envious thoughts. Inspire in us tolerance and goodwill toward our fellow human beings, present or absent, friend or enemy. Finally, help us to acknowledge your uplifting presence in the feelings that hearten our souls.

God, give the mediums who have been charged with the responsibility of transmitting higher teachings an awareness of their high commission. Give them a sense of the seriousness of their task so that they can undertake it with the necessary fervor and introspection.

If, at our meeting, there are individuals motivated by feelings other than goodwill, open their eyes to the light and forgive them—as we forgive them—for any bad disposition they may display.

We ask especially that the Spirit *[insert name]*, our spiritual guide, help us and watch over us.

7.   *Prayer (for the close of a meeting):* We give thanks to the good spirits who have come to communicate with us, and ask them to help us put the advice they've given us into practice. We also ask that, when we leave this gathering, they help us to feel strengthened in the practice of goodness and love toward our fellow human beings.

We hope that today's teachings are healing to all the suffering, unaware, or misguided spirits who've been present at this meeting. For them we implore God's mercy.

PURPOSE: FOR THE MEDIUMS

8.   *"'In the last days, God says, I will pour out my Spirit on all people. Your sons and daughters will prophesy, your young men will see visions, your old men will dream dreams. Even on my servants, both men and women, I will pour out my Spirit in those days, and they will prophesy.'"*

(Acts, 2: 17-18)

9.   *Preface:* God wanted everyone of us to see the light and for the voices of the spirits to be heard everywhere so that every individual could obtain his or her own proofs of immortality. It is for this reason that the spirits make their presence felt in all parts of the

globe, and that the gift of prophecy (mediumship) is given to people of all ages and all conditions—men and women, young and old. This is one of the signs that the predicted times have arrived.

So that we can understand the physical world and discover the secrets of nature, God has given us bodily vision, the senses, and the ability to invent instruments such as the telescope with which we can reach into the vastness of space, and the microscope with which we have explored the world of the infinitely small. Likewise, in order to allow us to penetrate the invisible world, God has given us mediumship.

Mediums are interpreters (channels) capable of transmitting to us the teachings of the spirits. To see it from a somewhat different perspective, one could imagine mediums as the physical apparatus the spirits use to express themselves intelligibly to human beings. Thus, mediums fulfill a sacred mission, that of opening up the horizons of eternal life.

Through mediums, the spirits come to instruct us concerning our destiny. The high spirits have as their purpose the task of leading us toward the good path. They do not come to save us from the toil of this world, or to stimulate ambition and greed (by attending to our material requests). This is something mediums must clearly understand or risk making bad use of their gift. Those who fully realize the seriousness of their commission, carry it out in a truly religious spirit. Their conscience would judge them harshly if, in what amounts to a sacrilegious act, they turned their gift into mere showmanship or a pastime for themselves or others. Their gift was given to them for a serious purpose—to put them in communication with those living in the spirit world.

As interpreters of the spirits' teachings, mediums should play an important part in the moral transformation now in progress. But the value of their services is related entirely to the direction their gift takes. Mediums who follow an incorrect path do more harm than good to the Spiritist cause, and more than one person will experience a delay in their progress as the result of the unfortunate impressions some medium has produced. That is why those endowed with this gift will have to account for the use to which they have put it, since they only received it in order to do good to their fellow human beings.

The mediums who want to be assisted by good spirits must work toward self-improvement. The ones who want their gift to

unfold further and become richer must enrich themselves morally and refuse to do anything that will turn mediumship away
from its providential purpose.

If good spirits sometimes use morally imperfect mediums, it is
in order to give them good advice and so lead them toward the
road to goodness. If, however, the spirits meet with hardened
hearts and their advice is ignored, they'll leave and the field will
be open for the entrance of any ill-meaning spirits.[16]

Experience has shown that, in the case of mediums who don't
take advantage of the good spirits' advice, communications that
at first showed some brilliance will deteriorate little by little, and
become confusing, verbose, and riddled with errors. These are
undeniable signs that the assistance of good spirits has stopped.

All truth-serving mediums should have one goal in common: to
honor the trust of good spirits and close the doors to mischievous
and deceptive ones. Without this commitment, mediumship
becomes a hollow gift and can even become harmful to the person
who has it, since it may degenerate into a spiritual disturbance.

The mediums who understand the nature of their responsibilities aren't proud of a faculty that isn't theirs and recognize that
it can be taken away from them. They will always credit God for
the results of their work. If their communications are praised,
they don't become conceited because they know that these messages are independent of their personal merit. Instead, they
thank God for allowing the good spirits to share their wisdom
through their mediation. On the other hand, if the communications bring on criticism, they're never offended because the communications aren't their own work. They are willing to accept
that they are imperfect instruments and that they don't yet have
all the required qualities that would prevent interference from
inferior spirits. Consequently, they aim to acquire these qualities
and ask in their prayers for the strength that they are lacking.

10. *Prayer:* Almighty God, let the good spirits come and help me with
the requested communication. Keep me from presuming that I
am immune to the influence of wrongdoing spirits; to pride,
which can lead me to misinterpret the value of what I receive;
and to any feelings of uncharitableness toward other mediums. If
I make mistakes, inspire someone to alert me to this fact, and give
me the humility to accept the deserved criticism. May I also real-

---

[16] *See Chapter 24, items 11-12.*

ize that the advice the good spirits give through me is not only directed to others but also to me.

If I am tempted to abuse, in any form, the gift bestowed on me by Your grace, or if I become proud of it, I ask that You take it back rather than let it stray from its providential objective, which is the good of all and my own moral improvement.

PRAYERS FOR ONESELF

PURPOSE: TO GUARDIAN ANGELS AND PROTECTING SPIRITS

11. *Preface:* From the moment each of us is born we have a good spirit assigned to us that constantly protects us. At our side this spirit carries out a mission similar to that of a parent to a child—that is, it guides us along the path to goodness and progress throughout our various tests in life. When we respond to its care and advice, that spirit rejoices; when we surrender to wrong, it agonizes over us.

The spirit's name isn't important; it's quite possible that no one on earth knows that name. This is why we refer to it as "Guardian Angel" or "Good Spirit." We could even call it using the name of some higher spirit who has inspired in us special ties of affection.

Apart from our guardian angels, which always come from the ranks of higher spirits, we have other spirit protectors. These are less elevated than our guardian angels but are also good and generous. They are the spirits of friends and relatives, or even people we didn't know in the present life. They give us helpful advice and often intervene in the events of our lives.

Empathetic spirits are those connected to us by similarities in taste and inclination. They may be either good or bad, depending on the tendencies in us that have attracted them to us.

Impure and frivolous spirits try to lead us away from the path of goodness by suggesting bad thoughts to us and by taking advantage of our imperfections, which they see as so many open doorways into our souls. Some of them hold on to us as if we were their prey. But the moment they realize that they're powerless to fight against a will set on good, they make a quick retreat.

In the form of the guardian angel, God gives us a primary and superior guide; in the form of protecting spirits, God gives us secondary guides. It's incorrect, however, to believe that we have an evil spirit assigned to be at our side to counterbalance the influence of the good spirits. Wrongdoing spirits willingly seek us out as long as they see they can associate themselves with us through our moral frailties and our indifference to putting into action the advice of the good spirits. Thus, we're the ones who attract them. We can conclude, then, that the assistance of the good spirits is always available, while the withdrawal of ill-intending spirits is entirely in our own power. In most cases, it's our imperfections that form the principle cause of our suffering, and so often we are, so to speak, our own evil influence.[17]

The purpose of a prayer to guardian angels and protecting spirits should be to ask them to intercede with God on our behalf, to ask for strength in resisting bad suggestions, and to ask for help in meeting life's demands.

12. *Prayer:* Wise and well meaning spirits, messengers of God, whose mission is to help us and lead us toward the straight path, support me in life's trials. Give me the strength to suffer without complaining. Turn away from me any negative thoughts, and don't let me open myself up to wrong-doing spirits, knowing that they'll try to persuade me to embrace their intentions. Make my conscience clear so that I can see my imperfections, and take away the veil of pride that prevents my seeing and admitting them to myself.

    Particularly to *[insert name]*, my Guardian Angel, who watches over me especially, and all the other protecting spirits who take an interest in me, I beg you to help me become worthy of your protection. You know my needs. May you attend to them as God wills.

13. *Prayer:* Dear God, let the good spirits who assist me help me in my times of trouble and hold me up when I stumble. Let them inspire me with faith, hope, and charity; let them be a source of support, an inspiration, and a testimony of Your mercy. May I always find in them the strength I lack to overcome the hardships of life and the power to resist lower suggestions, and to find the faith that saves me and the love that nourishes me.

14. *Prayer:* Beloved spirits and guardian angels, sent by an infinitely merciful God to assist all humanity, be our protectors during all life's trials! Give us the strength, the courage, the fortitude we need. Inspire us to follow after everything good, and keep us from going down the incline that leads to evil. May your sweet

[17] *See Chapter 5, item 4.*

influence fill our souls. Make us feel that we have by our side devoted friends who care about our suffering and take part in our joys.

And you, my Good Angel, never leave me alone. I need all of your protection to be able to support the trials appointed by Providence with faith and love.

PURPOSE: TO TURN AWAY WRONG-DOING SPIRITS

15.   *"Woe to you, teachers of the law and Pharisees, you hypocrites! You clean the outside of the cup and dish, but inside they are full of greed and self-indulgence. Blind Pharisees! First clean the inside of the cup and dish, and then the outside also will be clean.*

"Woe to you, teachers of the law and Pharisees, you hypocrites! You are like whitewashed tombs, which look beautiful on the outside but on the inside are full of dead men's bones and everything unclean. In the same way, on the outside you appear to people as righteous but on the inside you are full of hypocrisy and wickedness."

(Matthew, 23: 25-28)

16. *Preface:* Wrong-doing spirits can only be found where they have a chance to satisfy their desires. To keep them at bay, it isn't enough simply to ask them to go away or even to order them to go. It's essential first that we eliminate from ourselves whatever in us is attracting them. Bad spirits discover the ulcers of the soul in the same way flies discover wounds on the body. So, just as you wash your wounds in order to avoid maggots, clean your soul of its impurities in order to avoid bad spirits. We live in a world that teems with these spirits, and the good qualities of our hearts aren't always enough to stop their attempts on us. Nevertheless, these qualities will give us strength in resisting them.

17. *Prayer:* In the name of the Almighty God, may the evil spirits stay away from me and the good spirits protect me from their influence.

Wicked spirits that inspire bad thoughts, deceiving and lying spirits that delude the unwary, mocking spirits that abuse the naive, I repel you with all the strength in my soul and close my ears to your suggestions. And I pray also that God have mercy on you.

Good spirits that undertook to guide me, give me the strength I need to resist the influence of lower spirits and the discernment not to become a victim of their designs. Keep me safe from pride and presumption. Turn my heart away from all thoughts of jealousy, hate, badness, and any feelings opposed to charity [love], since these are all open doors to wrong-doing spirits.

PURPOSE: TO ASK FOR SELF-IMPROVEMENT

18. *Preface:* Our bad inclinations result from imperfections in our spirits, not our physical bodies. If this weren't true, we wouldn't be responsible for any of our acts. Our progress depends on each of us individually, since every person whose faculties are whole is free to act or not to act in every situation. In order to do good the only thing we need is will power.[18]

19. *Prayer:* Dear God, You gave me the necessary intelligence to tell right from wrong. The moment I recognize that something is wrong, I am guilty to the extent that I don't struggle to resist the temptation to give in to it.

    Save me from pride, which can keep me from becoming aware of my faults, and also from the bad spirits, who can influence me to continue taking the wrong path.

    Among my imperfections I realize that I'm especially inclined to [name the fault] and if I can't resist, it's because I've allowed it to become a habit.

    Being just, You didn't create us guilty, but with an equal potential for good and bad. If I've preferred the bad road it was because of my own free will. But for the same reason I am free to do wrong, I am also free to do good and so can change my path.

    My current defects are the remains of imperfections I brought with me from my past existences. This is my original sin, from which I can free myself through the action of my will and with help from the good spirits.

    Kindly spirits who look after me, and above all, my Guardian Angel, protect me. Give me the strength to resist evil suggestions and to be victorious in this battle.

    Our flaws are barriers that separate us from God, and each time we overcome one of them we take a step further along the pathway of progress that will draw us closer to God.

    O God, in Your infinite mercy You saw fit to grant me this present life so that it could help me advance. Good spirits, help me to take advantage of this opportunity and don't let me squander it. When God decides to remove me from this world, help me to leave it in better condition than I found on entering.[19]

---

[18] *See Chapter 15, item 10; and Chapter 19, item 12.*

[19] *See Chapter 5, item 5; and Chapter 17, item 3.*

PURPOSE: TO ASK FOR STRENGTH TO RESIST TEMPTATION

20. *Preface:* Bad thoughts can have two origins: our own spiritual flaws and the action of a harmful influence. The latter is also indicative of our inner flaws and reveals a preexisting imperfection in our souls. Consequently, someone who does wrong can't use the influence of a bad spirit as an excuse, since this spirit couldn't have led the person to wrongdoing if he or she wasn't already susceptible to that spirit's influence.

    When we have a bad thought, we should picture it as the suggestion of an evil spirit, leaving us completely free to give in or resist, just as if we were being invited by a living person. At the same time, we could picture our guardian angel or spirit guide fighting the bad influence, and anxiously awaiting our decision. Our hesitation in acting on the evil intimation is like the voice of the good spirit resonating in our conscience.

    We recognize that a thought is bad when it detracts from love, which is the basis of every moral principle; when that thought appeals to our pride, vanity, and selfishness; or when acting on it would cause harm to another person. In short, a thought is bad when it leads us to do to others what we would not like someone to do to us. [20]

21. *Prayer:* Almighty God, don't let me give in to temptation. Well-wishing spirits who protect me, turn this bad thought away from me and give me the strength to resist it. If I give in, I'll deserve the consequences of my decision—be they in this or a future life—because I have free will to make my choice.

PURPOSE: TO GIVE THANKS FOR VICTORY OVER A TEMPTATION

22. *Preface:* People who overcome temptation by the help of good spirits, or by acting on their advice, should thank God and their guardian angel for their help.

23. *Prayer:* My God, I thank You for giving me victory in the battle I fought against evil. May this victory give me strength to resist new temptations. And you, my Guardian Angel, thanks for the help you gave me. Let my acceptance of your advice make me worthy to receive your protection again.

---

[20] *See Chapter 28, item 15; and Chapter 15, item 10.*

PURPOSE: TO ASK FOR ADVICE

24. *Preface:* When we're unsure about something we have to do, we should ask ourselves, before anything else, the following questions:

    1. Will what I am hesitating about cause anyone harm?

    2. Will it be useful to anyone?

    3. If someone did this to me, would I be pleased?

    If what we think of doing concerns only ourselves, it's acceptable to consider the personal advantages or disadvantages that might come about. If it concerns others, and if in doing good for one person we may hurt someone else, it's necessary to consider the advantages and disadvantages before deciding whether or not to act. Finally, even when dealing with the best of things, it's necessary to consider the opportunity and the circumstances at hand, since a thing good in itself can result in something bad when it's in the wrong hands or isn't wisely and cautiously undertaken. Before acting on it, it's better to assess our abilities and resources to carry it out.

    In any case, we can always ask for the help of our spirit guides, remembering this wise precept, "When in doubt, do nothing."[21]

25. *Prayer:* In the name of God, the Almighty, I ask the good spirits who protect me to inspire me to make the best decision in this moment of uncertainty. I ask them to always lead my thoughts toward goodness and protect me from the influence of those who would lead me into error.

PURPOSE: HELP TO FACE THE DIFFICULTIES OF LIFE

26. *Preface:* We may ask God for earthly favors, and God may grant them when they serve a useful purpose. But we must remember that the perspective from which we see the usefulness of a favor is limited to the here and now. As a result, we don't always realize the negative side of favors—prompting God, Who has a better view of these things than we do and only wants the best for us, not to grant our requests, just as a parent would refuse to give a child something that would harm it. When a request is not answered, we shouldn't be disappointed; on the contrary, we should take it as a test or an expiation and remember that we'll be rewarded in proportion to the acceptance we show toward the situation.[22]

---

[21] *See Chapter 28, item 38.*

[22] *See Chapter 27, item 6; and Chapter 2, items 5-7.*

27. *Prayer:* God Almighty, Who knows all our struggles, please hear my plea at this moment. If my request is inconsiderate, forgive me. If, in your view, it's just and appropriate, let the good spirits—the executors of Your wishes—come to my aid and help me to realize it.

Whatever happens, God, let Your Will be done! If my request isn't answered, it will be because Your wish is to test my strength, and I willingly accept it. Help me to be strong and let neither my faith nor my acceptance of Your designs be shaken. (Then formulate your request.)

PURPOSE: TO GIVE THANKS FOR RECEIVING A FAVOR

28. *Preface:* Successes in important endeavors aren't the only blessings we should consider. Our destiny is often influenced to a much greater extent by small events. We easily forget the good things we've received and prefer to dwell on our pains. But if we kept count of all the blessings that have come our way day after day, even without our asking, we'd be surprised to find how many of them were dismissed from our memory and we'd feel ashamed of our ungratefulness.

When we lift up our souls to God each night, we should remember in our innermost self the many favors God has granted us during the day and give thanks for them. Most especially, at the very moment when we enjoy a favor, our natural reaction should be to bear witness to our thankfulness. To do so, it's enough to direct a thought attributing the favor to God—we needn't even interrupt our work.

Nor are God's favors limited to material things. We should also offer thanks for our good ideas and fortunate inspirations. A self-centered person will credit all of these things to his or her personal merits, and the unbeliever to mere chance. But the person with faith gives thanks to God and the good spirits. Nor do we need long sentences to do this. "Thank you, dear God, for the inspiration of that good thought," says more than a long prayer. A spontaneous attitude of crediting God for what's happened to us, demonstrates humbleness of heart and assures us the sympathy of the good spirits.[23]

29. *Prayer:* Beloved God of Infinite Goodness, may Your name be blessed for all the many gifts I've received from you! I would be unworthy if I were to attribute these favors to mere chance or to my own merit.

---

[23] *See Chapter 27, items 7-8.*

Good spirits, who carry out God's Designs, I thank you—and most especially my Guardian Angel. Purge from me any thoughts of pride and help me to use what I have received exclusively for doing good. Most of all, I thank You for... *[insert the name of the granted favor]*.

PURPOSE: TO SHOW SURRENDER AND ACCEPTANCE

30. *Preface:* When we are confronted with a distressing occurrence, we may nearly always trace the cause of it—that is, if we look hard enough—to our own carelessness, lack of foresight, or to some past action. In these cases, it's obvious that we only have ourselves to blame for our situation. But if the cause of our suffering can't be found to stem from our own actions, then we're either dealing with a test in this life or a correction for a wrong we committed in a past one. In this instance, the nature of the expiation reveals the nature of the wrong, since the correction always corresponds to the fault that gave rise to it.[24]

    In general, we only see the bad in our suffering and don't think of the good that will come from it later on. Good things often follow a difficult event, just as the cure for a disease follows a painful treatment. In any case, we must surrender to God's Will and endure life's trials with courage if we want them to count in our favor. May Christ's words then apply to us: "Blessed are those who mourn."[25]

31. *Prayer:* Dear God, You are sovereignly just and thus the suffering we experience in this world must have a just cause and purpose. I accept this suffering as a correction for my past wrongs and as a test for the future. Good spirits that protect me, give me the strength I need to bear my suffering without complaining. Help me look at it as a providential warning. Let it enrich my experience, subdue my pride, and lessen my ambition, foolish vanity, and selfishness. Let it contribute to my progress.

32. *Prayer:* Dear God, I feel the need to ask You for the necessary strength to support the test You have sent me. Enlighten my spirit with the necessary understanding that will let me appreciate the full extent of Your love, a love that yearns for my salvation. I surrender myself, dear God, but in my frailty I fear to fail without Your support. Don't abandon me, God, because without You, I am nothing.

---

[24] *See Chapter 5, items 4-10.*

[25] *Translator's Note: Matthew 5:4. See Chapter 5, item 18.*

33. *Prayer:* I lift my eyes up to You, Eternal One, and feel renewed. You are my strength, dear God, don't abandon me. I'm crushed under the weight of my frailties—help me! You know my weaknesses! Please, don't take Your eyes from me!

A terrible thirst consumes me. Make a spring of living water leap up to quench my thirst. May my lips open only to sing Your praises and not complain about my sufferings. I am weak, Lord, but Your love will sustain me.

Eternal One, You alone are the reason and purpose of my life! Blessed be Your name even when You put me through trials. Lord, I am still a flawed servant. I bow down before You in acceptance because You are all-knowing and the final aim of all our lives.

PURPOSE: TO AVOID IMMINENT DANGER

34. *Preface:* Through the dangers we face, God, reminds us of how frail our existence really is. We are shown that our lives are in God's hands, that we are held only by a thread that may break when we least expect it. From this vantage point, privilege doesn't exist for anyone: The same options exist for great and small alike.

If we look at the nature and consequences of danger, we'll see that in most cases the consequences, if the dangerous situation does materialize, will have been a correction for a wrong done or a duty neglected.

35. *Prayer:* Almighty God—and you, my Guardian Angel—help me! If I must die, may God's Will be done. If I'm to be saved, let the rest of my life be used to repay the wrongs I've done, for which I'm truly sorry.

PURPOSE: TO GIVE THANKS FOR HAVING ESCAPED A DANGER

36. *Preface:* By the dangers we pass through, God shows us that from one moment to another we may be called on to account for the way we've lived our lives. A danger alerts us to the fact that we should examine ourselves and change our ways.

37. *Prayer:* Dear God! Dear Guardian Angel! Thank you for the help I received during the danger that threatened me. Let this danger be a warning to me; let it make me aware of the wrongs that brought it to pass. I understand, God, that my life is in Your hands and that You can take it away whenever You see fit. Inspire me, through the good spirits that protect me, with ideas on how to make the best use of the time You've given me in this world. Guardian

Angel! Support me in my decision to correct my ways and to do all the good in my power, so that I can arrive in the spirit world with fewer imperfections when God chooses to call me.

PURPOSE: TO BE SAID AT BEDTIME

38. *Preface:* The purpose of sleep is to rest the body. The spirit, however, doesn't need rest, so while the physical senses are in a passive state, it partly frees itself from the body and in this state enjoys all its faculties. Sleep allows us to renew ourselves both at the organic and the psychic level. While the body recovers the energy it expended during its waking hours, the spirit renews itself through contact with other spirits. From what it is given to see, listen, and learn in this state, the soul derives resolutions that afterwards will occur during the day as intuitions. Sleep, then, represents the temporary return of the exile to the true world; it is analogous to a moment of freedom granted to a prisoner.

But sometimes—just as in the case of an unrepenting prisoner—the spirit doesn't always use its moments of freedom for its own progress. If it is inclined to wrongdoing, it will spend its time in the company of like-minded spirits instead of in the company of good spirits and will go to places where it can give free rein to its desires.

Consequently, people who are convinced of the truth of spirit life will lift up their thoughts to God before they go to sleep. They'll ask for guidance from the good spirits and from those whose memory is dear to them, and to join them in the brief time of freedom they will have. When they awake, they'll feel themselves renewed, allowing them to overcome all that is negative and to be more courageous when facing difficulties.

39. *Prayer:* God, for a few short instants, my soul will be together with other spirits. I beg the good spirits to come and advise me. Guardian Angel, please help me keep a lasting and beneficial impression of this encounter when I wake!

PURPOSE: TO BE SAID ON SENSING THE APPROACH OF DEATH

40. *Preface:* If during our lives we have shown ourselves to have faith in the future by often raising our thoughts to contemplate the soul's future destiny, the process of freeing the spirit from its physical ties will be briefer. Such an attitude helps to weaken the bonds that hold the spirit to the body—often to such an extent that, even before the physical body expires, the soul, eager to be

free, launches itself into the great immensity. On the contrary, the person who has focused the mind solely on the material aspect of life finds these bonds harder to break and the separation from the body more painful and difficult. Such a person will likely awake into the afterlife full of confusion and anxiety.

41. *Prayer:* Dear God, I believe in You and Your infinite kindness. Therefore, I can't fathom the idea that You would endow us with the intelligence that makes us become aware of You and aspire to Eternity, only to plunge us into nothingness at death. I believe that my body is only a perishable covering for my soul and that when I die I'll awaken in the spirit world.

Almighty God, I sense the bonds that hold my soul to my body are loosening, and in a short while, I'll be ready to give an account for the use I've made of the life that's now slipping away from me.

I know that I'll experience the consequences of the good and bad that I've practiced. There will be no possibility of illusions, no way of hiding what I've done. My past will unfold before me and I'll be judged according to my works.

I'll take no earthly possession with me—not honors, wealth, the satisfactions of vanity or pride. Everything that belongs to the body will stay in this world. Not even the most minute particle of these things will go with me, since they would be of no use to me in the spirit world. I'll take with me only what belongs to my soul—that is, the good and bad qualities I possess, which will be weighed in the scale of an exact justice. I know the judgment will be even more severe according to the number of times I neglected the opportunities to practice good that my position on earth gave me.[26]

Merciful God, may the sincere contrition of my soul reach out to You! May You see fit to cast over me Your forgiveness!

If You see fit to prolong my present life, may I use my remaining time to correct, as far as I can, all the wrongs I've done. But if my hour has really come, I take with me the comforting thought that I'll be allowed to redeem myself by means of new tests, so that one day I may deserve the happiness of the elected ones.

If it happens that I am not deserving of such perfect happiness immediately—a state reserved only for the preeminently just, I trust wholeheartdly that this goal is not beyond my reach. I know that, sooner or later and according to my own efforts, I'll reach that goal.

---

[26] *See Chapter 16, item 9.*

I know that the good spirits and my Guardian Angel are nearby to receive me and that I'll see them soon, just as they see me now. I know, too, that if I deserve it, I'll meet again with all those I loved here on earth, and that the ones I leave behind will later come to join me. One day we'll be united forever, and until that time arrives, I'll be able to come and visit them.

I know, too, that I'll meet once again with everyone I've offended. May they forgive me for whatever it is they blame me for—my pride, my hardness, my injustice—so that their presence won't overwhelm me with shame!

I forgive everyone who has either done or tried to do me harm. I hold no bitterness against them and beg You, dear God, to forgive them.

God, give me the strength to leave the material pleasures of this world without regrets, especially since they're nothing compared to the pure delights of the world I'm about to enter. There, for the just, no more torments or sorrows exist and only the guilty suffer. But even they always have the comfort of hope before them.

Good spirits—and you, my Guardian Angel, do not to let me fail at this crucial moment. If my faith should waver, cause the divine light to shine in my eyes, so that I will be strengthened. [27]

PRAYERS FOR OTHERS

PURPOSE: FOR SOMEONE WHO IS SUFFERING

42. *Preface:* If it's in the suffering person's interest to endure a challenging circumstance, no request we make on that person's behalf will shorten it. But to get discouraged ourselves, just because our requests aren't being met, denotes a lack of faith on our part. Even when our prayers can't bring the hardship to an end, they can console the person to some degree and thus lessen the suffering. Further, what someone undergoing a test will really find useful is courage and resignation—qualities without which everything he is experiencing will have no positive result, forcing him to live through the test again. With the aim of nourishing these qualities, we should ask the good spirits to help the person. We should also try to lift his or her morale with our

---

[27] *See "Prayers for the Sick and Spiritually Disturbed" item 5, in this section.*

advice and encouragement and, where necessary, offer material help if we can. In such cases, prayer can have a decisive effect by directing spiritual energy toward the person that will renew his or her disposition.[28]

43. *Prayer:* Dear God of Infinite Goodness, if it pleases You and is according to Your Will, soften the painful situation of *[insert name]*.

Good spirits, in the name of God Almighty, I implore you to help [name] through this suffering. If it isn't in [name]'s interest to be spared it, help him/her realize that this suffering is beneficial for his progress. Instill in [name] confidence in You and the future, which will make him/her less bitter. Also give [name] the strength to resist surrendering to despair, which would mean wasting the fruits of this experience and undergoing future days of even greater distress. Lead my thoughts to [name] so that they might help sustain his/her courage.

PURPOSE: TO GIVE THANKS FOR A FAVOR RECEIVED BY SOMEONE ELSE

44. *Preface:* Unselfish people celebrate the good things that come to their neighbor, even if they didn't pray for the neighbor's success.

45. *Prayer:* Lord, thank You for the happiness granted to [name]. Good spirits, help [name] see that this gift is the result of God's goodness. If the resulting good is a test, please inspire [name] with thoughts of how to make the best use of it, sparing her/him from becoming conceited, which would turn the gift into a future harm. You, good spirit who looks after me and desires my happiness, keep me safe from feelings of jealousy or envy.

PURPOSE: TO BE SAID FOR OUR ENEMIES AND ILL-WISHERS

46. *Preface:* Jesus said, "Love your enemies."[29] This precept reveals everything that is high and sublime in Christian love. Jesus didn't mean that we should feel the same affection for an enemy that we do for a friend. Rather He teaches us to pardon offenses, to forgive the wrongs done to us, and to repay evil with good. Besides the merit this behavior has in God's eyes, it also shows everyone the essence of true lofty living.[30]

---

[28] *See Chapter 5, items 5 and 27; and Chapter 27, items 6 and 10.*

[29] *Translator's Note: Luke 6:27.*

[30] *See Chapter 12, items 3-4.*

47. *Prayer:* Dear God, I forgive [name] for the evil he/she's done and may still want to do to me, just as I ask You to forgive me. I also pray that he may forgive any offenses I may have committed against him. If he has come into my life as a test, may Your Will be done. But keep me safe, dear God, from the temptation of slandering him and from any other negative feeling I might have against him. Don't let me feel a tinge of satisfaction for any misfortune that might happen to him/her, or pain for the good that may happen to him/her. Such feelings would only blemish my soul with thoughts that aren't worthy of a Christian.

Lord, may Your goodness be bestowed upon [name] and lead him/her to better sentiments toward me!

Good spirits, inspire my heart to forget all evil and remember only the good. Don't let hate or bitterness or the desire to repay evil with evil enter my heart, because these feelings can only find harbor in a mean individual, whether incarnate or discarnate. On the contrary, let me be prepared to extend a friendly hand to him/her, to repay evil with good, and to help him/her if that is possible.

To test the sincerity of my words, I beg You to give me a chance to be useful to [name]. But above all, God, don't let me act out of a sense of superiority and for mere show, embarassing [name] with a humiliating generosity that would only cause me to lose the fruits of my action. In that case, I would indeed have earned Christ's judgment, "You have already received your comfort."[31]

PURPOSE: TO GIVE THANKS FOR BLESSINGS RECEIVED BY OUR ENEMIES

48. *Preface:* Not wishing ill on your enemies is only half of true charitableness. True charity consists in also wishing them well and in feeling happy about the good that comes to them.[32]

49. *Prayer:* Dear God, in Your justice You saw fit to shower [name] with joy, and I, too, praise your mercy, despite wrongs [name] has done to me and still tries to do. If [name] uses this gift to humiliate me, I accept this as a test of my capacity to love unconditionally.

Good spirits that look after me, don't let me regret *[name]*'s happiness. Safeguard me from jealousy and envy, which only degrade. Inspire in me a generosity that will lift me up. Shame comes from evil and not from goodness, and we know that sooner or later we will all receive justice according to our works.

---

[31] *Translator's Note: Luke 6:24. See Chapter 13, items 1 and following.*

[32] *See Chapter 12, items 7-8.*

PURPOSE: TO BE SAID FOR THE ENEMIES OF THE SPIRITIST DOCTRINE

50. *"Blessed are the meek, for they will inherit the earth."*

(Matthew, 5: 5)

"Blessed are those who are persecuted because of righteousness, for theirs is the kingdom of heaven. Blessed are you when people insult you, persecute you and falsely say all kinds of evil against you because of me. Rejoice and be glad, because great is your reward in heaven, for in the same way they persecuted the prophets who were before you."

(Matthew, 5: 10-12)

"Do not be afraid of those who kill the body but cannot kill the soul. Rather, be afraid of the One who can destroy both soul and body in hell."

(Matthew, 10: 28)

51. *Preface:* The most sacred of all liberties is that of thought, which includes the liberty of conscience. To condemn anyone simply because they don't think as we do, is to demand that liberty for ourselves but refuse it to others—a violation of Jesus' first commandment, which is to show charity and love toward our neighbor. To persecute other people for their beliefs, is to attack the most sacred human right, the right to believe in whatever we wish and to worship God as we see fit. To require others to worship in a manner similar to our own, is to show that we're more attached to the form than the essence and to appearances than to conviction. To force someone to renounce a belief or practice we don't share, will never produce faith. It can only create hypocrites. It's also an abuse of power, which in no way creates conviction. Truth is sure of itself; it convinces without the need to impose itself on anyone.

The Spiritist Doctrine represents a concept of life, a faith. But even if it were a religion, why shouldn't its followers be free to call themselves Spiritists, just as Catholics, Jews and Protestants, or the adherents of this or that philosophy, this or that economic system, call themselves by those names? A belief is either true or false. If it's false, it will fall by itself, since falsehood can't stand up against an awakened human reason. And if it's true, no amount of opposition will make it false.

Persecution is the baptism that awaits all new ideas that are great and just. The greater and more important an idea is, the more it will be attacked. The rage and antipathy expressed by the enemies of an idea is in direct proportion to the fear it inspires in them. This is why Christianity was persecuted in the past; it is why the Spiritist Doctrine is the object of attacks today. The only difference is that the first was persecuted by pagans, and the second by so-called Christians. Nowadays, of course, there are no more bloody persecutions. But if modern persecutors no longer kill the body, they torture the soul. They assault one's innermost feelings and all for which one cares deeply.

They divide families; they stir up mothers against daughters and wives against husbands. They even threaten one's livelihood by taking aim at one's bread-winning occupation as if, through hunger, they could win one's soul.[33]

Spiritists, don't be angry because of the blows you receive, for they show that you have the truth. If you didn't, your attackers would leave you alone and not bother with you. This is a test for your faith; through your courage, strength, and determination in these times, God will recognize you as a faithful servant—and count you among those who will receive according to their works.

Follow the example of the first Christians and carry your cross with dignity. Trust the promise of Christ when He said, "Blessed are those who are persecuted because of righteousness, for theirs is the kingdom of heaven."[34] "Do not be afraid of those who kill the body but cannot kill the soul."[35] He also said, "Love your enemies, do good to those who hate you, bless those who curse you, pray for those who mistreat you."[36] Show yourselves to be His true disciples and show the goodness of your doctrine by following what He said and did.

The persecution won't last long. Be patient. The dawn is coming and the morning star is already appearing on the horizon. [37]

52. *Prayer:* God, through the lips of Jesus, Your Messiah, You have told us, "Blessed are those who suffer persecution for love of justice; forgive your enemies; pray for those who persecute you." He Himself gave us an example by praying for His tormentors.

Following this example, O God, we ask that You show mercy to those who despise Your most sacred precepts—the only precepts that can bring peace in this world and the next. Like Christ, we also say, "Father, forgive them, for they do not know what they are doing."[38]

[33] *See Chapter 23, items 9-18*

[34] *Translator's Note: Mathew, 5:10.*

[35] *Translator's Note: Mathew, 10:28.*

[36] *Translator's Note: Luke, 6:27-28.*

[37] *See Chapter 24, items 13-19.*

[38] *Translator's Note: Luke, 23:34.*

Give us strength to bear their mockery, insults, slander, and persecutions patiently and with courage since these are tests of our faith and humility. Free us from the idea of reprisal, because the hour of justice comes to everyone, and we wait for it submitting ourselves to Your holy Will.

PURPOSE: PRAYER FOR A NEWBORN CHILD

53. *Preface:* Only after they've passed through the tests offered by incarnate life can spirits reach perfection. Those who still freely dwell in the spirit realm wait for God's permission to return to an earthly existence. In that existence, they will have a chance to progress, either by expiating their faults through the trials they endure or by undertaking missions that will benefit humanity. Their progress and future happiness will be in proportion to the way they use the time given them on earth. The responsibility of guiding their first steps and leading them toward goodness belongs to their parents, who will have to account to God for the extent to which they fulfilled this duty. To help them, God made parental and filial love a Law of Nature, a Law that can never be broken without incurring a penalty.

54. *Prayer (to be said by the parents):* Dear spirit that has incarnated in the body of our child, we welcome you. We thank You, Almighty God, for the blessing of this child.

We know this is a trust You have given us and that one day we'll have to account for it. If the child belongs to the new generation of spirits that are to live on earth, we thank you, God, for · the blessing! If it's an imperfect spirit, we know that our duty is to help our child progress toward goodness through our teaching and good example. If, through our fault, he or she turns to wrongdoing, we alone will be responsible for it, since we will have failed in our mission.

Support us in this task, God, and give us the strength and will power we need to perform it. If this child has come as a test for us, may Your Will be done!

Good spirits that have watched over this birth and will accompany this child throughout life, don't abandon him [or her]. Keep our child safe from all the bad influences that will try to tempt him [or her] to take the wrong path. Give him [or her] the strength to resist their suggestions and the courage to suffer, with patience and fortitude, the tests that wait here on earth. [39]

---

[39] *See Chapter 14, item 9.*

55. *Prayer:* Dear God, You've entrusted me with the destiny of one of Your spirits. Make me worthy of this task. Give me Your protection. Enlighten me so that I can see right from the start the tendencies of the one I must prepare to ascend to Your peace.

56. *Prayer:* God of Infinite Goodness, You've seen fit to let the spirit of this child come once more to undergo the earthly trials that will allow it to progress. Give it, then, enough enlightenment to come to know You, love You, and worship You. Through Your all-embracing power may this soul renew itself from the source of Your Divine Teachings. Under the protection of its guardian angel, may it grow and advance in intelligence, aspiring to move ever closer to You. Let the knowledge of the Spiritist Doctrine be a brilliant light that will illuminate it in the many choices it will make in life. Finally, let it learn to appreciate the full extent of Your love, which gives us challenging endeavors so that we can purify ourselves.

    God, watch over our family—to which You have entrusted this spirit—with a parent's eye. May we come to understand the importance of our mission. Let the seeds of goodness in this child grow until, through its own aspirations, it rises upward to You.

    O God, answer, if it pleases You, this humble prayer—in the name of and by the worthiness of Jesus, Who said, "Let the little children come to me, and do not hinder them, for the kingdom of heaven belongs to such as these."[40]

PURPOSE: TO BE SAID FOR ONE WHO IS DYING

57. *Preface:* Agony is the prelude to the separation of the soul from the body. At this moment, we can say, the person has one foot on earth and the other in the next world. This phase can be quite painful for people who are deeply attached to worldly things—for those who live more for the possessions of this world than the next one—and whose consciences are troubled by regret and guilt. By contrast, the seekers after the Infinite disengage themselves from matter more easily, breaking the links that tie them to the earth without pain in their last moments. Only a thin thread links the physical body to their souls, whereas in the first case, thick roots hold the departing soul. In every case, prayer produces a powerful action in the work of separation.[41]

---

[40] *Translator's Note: Matthew 19:14.*

[41] *See below "Prayers for the Sick" and A. Kardec's* Heaven and Hell, *Part II, Chapter 1, "The Passing."*

58. *Prayer:* Merciful and all powerful God, here is a soul that is about to leave its earthly covering and return to its real home in the spirit world. Let it have peace in this passing and extend Your mercy to it.

Good spirits that have accompanied this person on earth, don't desert him in this ultimate moment. Give him the strength to endure the last sufferings he must undergo, the sufferings that will allow him to pass out of this world for the sake of his future progress. Inspire him to use the last glimmerings of physical awareness to repent any wrongs he has done. Let my thoughts act to help him achieve this separation with greater ease, and may hope bring comfort to his soul at the moment it leaves earth.

PRAYERS FOR THOSE NO LONGER ON EARTH

PURPOSE: TO BE SAID FOR SOMEONE WHO HAS JUST DIED

59. *Preface:* We don't pray for souls that have just left earth only to show our sympathy. Our prayers also help release these souls from their earthly ties, shortening the period of agitation that always follows the separation and allowing for a more peaceful awakening on the other side. In this, as in all other circumstances, the effectiveness of a prayer depends on how sincere our thoughts are, not on the number of grandiose words we say— very often such words don't come from the heart.

Prayers that truly are of the heart resonate with the spirits they're directed to. The ideas of the departing soul at this point are still in a state of confusion. Our prayers are like sweet voices that come to awaken them from sleep.[42]

60. *Prayer:* Almighty God, show mercy to the soul of [name] whom You have just called back. We beg and implore that the trials he/she suffered here on earth be counted in his/her favor and that our prayers will soften and shorten the anguish he/she may still have to experience.

Good spirits that have come to welcome this soul, and especially his/her Guardian Angel, help him/her to free herself from matter. Give light and self-awareness and help her to overcome the temporary confusion that accompanies the return to spirit life. Inspire this soul to repent for any wrongs and encourage to

---

[42] *See Chapter 27, item 10.*

seek ways of improving, thus quickening his/her growth toward a blissful eternal life.

And you, *[name]*, you've just entered into the world of the spirits, and yet you may still feel that you are one of us. You still hear and see us: The difference between you and us is the perishable physical body that you have just left, which will quickly turn to dust.

You've now let go the gross envelope that served you on earth, which was subject to constant hardships and death. Now you have your spiritual body, which is imperishable and free from the aches of the flesh. You no longer live in a physical body but live instead as spirit, and the spirit life is free from the tribulations that torment human kind.

Now your eyes are no longer covered by the veil that hides the glory of the future existence from us. Now you will contemplate new wonders, while we go on immersed in the fog.

Now you will travel through space and freely visit other worlds, while here on earth we struggle through life—under the burdensome weight of a physical body.

Infinite horizons open before you. Seeing such grandeur, you'll understand the uselessness of earthly desires and aspirations, and how futile are the so-called joys that human beings surrender themselves to.

For us, death is nothing more than that quick moment when the soul is separated from matter. From this place of exile where we continue living by the Will of God, and where we remain in order to carry out our duties, we'll continue to follow you in thought until the time comes when we can join you again, just as you've now rejoined those who went before you.

Even though we can't go where you are, you can come here. Come, then, to the ones who love you and whom you love. Help them in their life trials. Watch over your dear ones and protect them as much as you can. Lessen the pain of your absence by suggesting to them the thought that you're happier now and that one day, for a certainty, you'll be reunited in a better world.

In the new realm where you are now, there should be no room for old earthly grudges. Don't let them tinge your feelings again, for the sake of your future happiness. Forgive anyone who's committed an offense against you, just as those you offended now forgive you.

Comment: If appropriate, add to this generic prayer your own special words according to the circumstances of the family, your relationship with the deceased, or the deceased's accomplishments. In the passing of an infant, the Spiritist Doctrine explains that the spirit is not a recently created being but one that has already lived other lives and may be well advanced on its path. In cases in which the newly concluded life has been short, we can deduce that it was needed only to complete a test or trial, or to serve as a needed test for the parents.[43]

61. *Prayer:* All-Powerful God, let Your mercy extend over those who have just left earth! Let Your light shine on them! Don't leave them in darkness. Open their eyes and ears. Let the good spirits come for them and help them discern Your words of hope and peace.

God, although we may not be worthy ourselves, we dare ask you to show mercy toward those who have recently been recalled from earthly exile. Receive them as the father received the prodigal son. O God, forgive the wrongs they may have committed and consider the good they've done. Your justice is firm, as we know, but Your love is immense. We ask You, then, to supplement Your justice with the fountain of kindness that springs forth from You.

You who've just left the earth, may the light shine brightly before your eyes! May the good spirits be near you, surround you, and help you shake off your earthly bonds. Now you understand and see the grandeur of God—so accept God's Justice without complaining, and never fail to trust God's Mercy. Dear brother [or sister], may a sincere review of your past open the doors to a new future. Let it help you understand the wrongs you left behind, and the work that needs to be done to straigthen them out! May God pardon your faults and may the good spirits sustain and encourage you! We, your loved ones on earth, will pray to God for you, and ask that you equally pray for us.[44]

PURPOSE: TO BE SAID FOR A BELOVED ONE

62. *Preface:* Horrible is the idea of nothingness! We pity those who think that the words of a person who mourns a loved one are lost in a void, resonating nowhere and receiving no response. Those who embrace the thought that everything dies with the body

---

[43] *See Chapter 5, item 21.*

[44] *This prayer was dictated to a medium from Bordeaux just as the funeral procession of an unknown person was passing by the medium's residence.*

have never known a pure and devout affection. For them, the genius who amazes the world is simply the result of a combination of atoms and, like a flame, will be put out forever at death. For them, all that will remain of a dearly loved person—a father, a mother, an adored child—is a handful of dust, which time will inevitably scatter!

How can anyone with a heart remain unmoved by this idea? Why doesn't the idea of absolute nothingness freeze them with terror? And yet they don't wish even that the opposite might be true. But if reason hasn't, until now, been enough to dispel their doubts, the Spiritist Doctrine has come to eliminate all uncertainty about the future by providing concrete evidences of the survival of the soul and the existence of beings in the beyond. Such evidence is coming at such a rate it is being received with joy everywhere. Confidence is reborn, because from now on, humanity will know that the earthly life is only a brief passage leading to a better existence, that work done in this world isn't lost, and that the truly pure affections aren't shattered beyond hope.[45]

63. *Prayer:* O God, receive this prayer favorably in the name of *[name]*. Help him/her see the divine lights that will make his/her pathway to eternal happiness easier. Let the good spirits take my words and thoughts to him/her.

You, who were so loved by me in this world, listen to my voice: It calls to renew my vows of affection. God gave you your freedom before me and to complain about this would be selfish, since it would be the same as wishing that you were still subject to life's sufferings. I wait with resignation, then, for the moment when we'll reunite in that happier world to which you've gone before me.

I know that our separation is only temporary and that, however endless it might seem, its length is nothing compared to the blessed Eternity God has promised the chosen ones. So may God's goodness prevent me from doing anything that might delay this longed-for moment, so that I won't have to experience the pain of not meeting you when I finish my earthly sojourn.

The certainty that there's nothing between us but a material veil that hides you from me is a sweet and comforting thought! So, too, is the knowledge that you can even be here with me and hear me speak as you used to do, or perhaps even better; that you

[45] *See Chapter 4, item 18; and Chapter 5, item 21.*

haven't forgotten me as I haven't forgotten you; that we are constantly exchanging thoughts and that your thoughts accompany and support me.

May the peace of God be with you.

PURPOSE: TO BE SAID FOR SUFFERING SPIRITS WHO ASK FOR PRAYERS

64. *Preface:* To appreciate the soothing relief that prayer gives to suffering spirits, we have to remember how such relief can come about; this has been explained previously.[46] Persons convinced of this fact will be able to pray more enthusiastically, since they're certain that their prayers won't be in vain.

65. *Prayer:* God of Compassion and Mercy, may Your goodness extend to all the spirits who seek our prayers, especially the spirit of *[name]*.

Good spirits, whose only charge is to do good, intervene along with me for their relief. Shine a ray of hope before their eyes and show them the imperfections that keep them distant from the homes of the blessed. Open their hearts to repentance and to the desire to correct themselves so that they can advance more quickly. Help them understand it's their own efforts that will shorten the length of their trials.

May God, Who is all goodness, give them the necessary strength to follow through on their good resolutions!

May these well-meaning words ease their trials, and so show them that there are people on earth who sympathize with them and wish them happiness.

66. *Prayer:* We ask, God, that You pour out the blessings of Your love and mercy on everyone who suffers, whether they're incarnate or not. Have compassion on our frailty. You gave us the freedom to make choices and the ability to resist temptation and overcome evil. Let Your mercy reach all spirits who couldn't resist their base tendencies and who continue to drag themselves along dark pathways. May the good spirits assist them; may Your light shine before their eyes; may they be so attracted by the life-giving warmth of this light that they return to You in humbleness, with a sense of contrition, and reverence.

Merciful God, we also pray for our brothers and sisters who haven't had the strength to resist their earthly trials. God, You gave us a burden to carry, which we must lay only at Your feet.

---

[46] *See Chapter 27, items 9-15.*

But our weaknesses are great and sometimes, in the course of our journey, our courage fails us. Have pity on the weak servants who left their work before quitting time. In Your Justice, spare them and let the good spirits take them some relief, comfort, and hope for the future. The expectation of a pardon strengthens the soul. God, give this pardon to all the guilty ones who've surrendered to despair so that, upheld by new hope, they can, amid the enormity of their failings and sufferings, gather enough motivation to leave behind the past and prepare themselves to conquer the future.

PURPOSE: TO BE SAID FOR AN ENEMY WHO HAS DIED

67. *Preface:* Charity toward our enemies should accompany them into the spirit world. We have to understand that the wrongs they committed against us were a test for us—a test that we can use in our spiritual progress if we know how to take advantage of it. It can be even more beneficial to us than purely material difficulties, since it allows us to join together courage, resignation, charity, and the forgetfulness of offenses.[47]

68. *Prayer:* Lord, it pleased You to call the soul of [name] before You called me.

   I forgive him/her all the wrongs he/she did against me and the bad intentions he/she developed toward me. As he/she releases himself/herself from the illusions of this world, may he/she now find the path of repentance.

   Dear God, let Your mercy descend on him/her and keep me from any thought of rejoicing at his/her death. If I am indebted to him/her for any reason, may he/she forgive me, as I forgive all his/her wrongs against me.

PURPOSE: TO BE SAID FOR A CRIMINAL

69. *Preface:* If the effectiveness of prayers depended on their length, the longest ones would be reserved for the guiltiest, since they need prayer more than people who've lived upright lives. To refuse to pray for criminals is to lack charity toward them and to be unaware of the mercy of God. To believe your prayers would be useless because someone has committed this or that serious crime is to prejudge the Almighty's justice.[48]

[47] *See Chapter 10, item 6; and Chapter 12, items 5-6.*
[48] *See Chapter 11, item 14.*

70. *Prayer:* Lord God of Mercy, don't disown this criminal who has just left earth! Human justice has condemned him, but this doesn't excuse him from Your justice if his heart hasn't been touched by remorse.

Take away the blindfold that hides the seriousness of his wrongs from him. May his repentance earn Your kindly treatment and ease the sufferings of his soul. May our prayers and the intercession of good spirits offer him hope and comfort, inspire in him the desire to make up for his actions in another lifetime, and give him the strength not to give up in the new battles he will undertake.

Lord, have pity on him!

PURPOSE: TO BE SAID FOR A SUICIDE

71. *Preface:* We have no right to dispose of our lives; only God can decide when to set us free from the bonds that keep us on earth. Though Divine Justice does take into account mitigating circumstances, it is very severe with those who deliberately seek to escape the trials of life.

In a sense, the suicide is like a prisoner who breaks out of prison before serving his full sentence and who's kept under stricter conditions once he's been recaptured. Like the prisoner, the suicide might imagine that he's escaping the miseries of the moment, but he will only find that he's plunged himself into greater difficulties than before.[49]

72. *Prayer:* We know, God, the destiny awaiting people who violate Your Law by deliberately shortening their lives. But we know, too, that Your mercy is infinite. Please, extend this mercy to the soul of [name]. May our prayers and Your pity lessen the harshness of the sufferings being experienced for not having been courageous enough to wait until all trials were over.

Good spirits whose mission is to help the unfortunate, take this soul under your protection; encourage him/her to regret the error committed. Let your assistance strengthen him/her so that she can bear with greater fortitude the new trials he/she has to go through to make up for this act. Keep [name] from troubling influences that can drive him/her once more toward the wrong path and so extend suffering and put at risk the fruits of trials yet to come.

We also direct ourselves to you whose plight is the reason for our prayers. May our expression of sympathy help soothe your pain and encourage you toward a better future. That future lies in

---

[49] *See Chapter 5, item 14-17.*

your hands. Trust the merciful ways of God, Whose bosom opens to accept all repentance and is closed only to hardened hearts.

PURPOSE: TO BE SAID FOR REPENTANT SPIRITS

73. *Preface:* We would be unfair if we included in the category of wicked spirits all the suffering and repentant ones who thirst for prayers. They may have been bad once; but they stopped being so from the moment they recognized the errors of their ways and rejected them. They're only unhappy now. Some of them have even begun to enjoy a small measure of happiness.

74. *Prayer:* God of Mercy, Who welcomes the sincere repentance of wrong-doers, be they incarnate or disincarnate, here are souls who used to take pleasure in evil, but now recognize their errors and seek the right path. Receive them, God, like the prodigal son and forgive them.

    Good spirits that they wouldn't listen to but now seek eagerly, let them glimpse the happiness of the evolved ones, so that they'll persist in the desire to cleanse themselves in order to join them. Support them in all good resolutions and give them the strength they need to resist baser tendencies.

    To the repentant spirit of [name], we rejoice for your new attitude and thank the good spirits who've helped you in this undertaking.

    If you previously enjoyed doing wrong, it was because you didn't understand the sweet pleasures that go hand in hand with doing good and because you didn't feel good enough to enjoy those pleasures. But, from the moment you first stepped onto the path of goodness, a new light shone in you. Then you began to enjoy moments of joy you had never known, and hope entered your heart. This is because God always hears the prayers of an individual who repents sincerely. God never rejects anyone who is seeking after the Divine.

    To be completely in God's grace again, you have to apply yourself from now on—not only to avoid committing evil again but to do good and, above everything, to correct the wrongs you've done. Then you'll satisfy God's Justice; each good action you practice will wash away the errors of your past.

    You've taken the first step. Now, as you continue to advance on this path, it will become easier and more pleasant. Stay on it, and one day you'll have the glory of being counted among the good spirits and the blessed.

PURPOSE: TO BE SAID FOR HARDENED SPIRITS

75. *Preface:* Bad spirits are those that haven't been moved to repent, that delight in wrongdoing without feeling guilty about it. These spirits are insensitive to criticism, reject prayer, and frequently take God's name in vain. They are the hardened spirits. After death they seek revenge on others for the suffering they underwent, and they pursue with hatred anyone who wronged them during their lifetime, either by causing those persons to become spiritually disturbed or by directing their disastrous influence toward them. [50]

These spirits fall into two distinct categories: the plainly evil and the hypocritical. Reclaiming the first for good is infinitely easier than reclaiming the second. More often than not, the spirits in the first group have coarse, uncultivated natures, just as we observe in people amongst ourselves; they practice evil more from instinct than calculation and don't try to appear better than they are. Yet inside them there's a latent seed waiting to bloom; and it will bloom as long as others do not give up on them and are willing to guide them with a steady hand, goodwill, good advice, encouragement, and prayer. Incidentally, it's been noticed in automatic writing that these spirits have a hard time writing the name of God. This is a sign of an instinctive respect for the inner voice of conscience that tells them they're still unworthy. It's at this point that they're ready to change and we can have high hopes for them. We only need to find the point of access to their hearts.

Hypocritical spirits are almost always very intelligent. But in their hearts they lack the grain of sensitivity; nothing touches them. They pretend to have all the right attitudes as a way of gaining others' confidence and are happy when they meet with people who are gullible enough to accept them as saintly spirits—for these people they can control as they like. Far from inspiring fear and trembling in them, the name of God serves them as a mask behind which they hide their foulness. In both invisible and visible worlds, the hypocrites are the most dangerous beings because they operate in the shadows, often without raising suspicion. They often profess a faith, but it is never sincere.

76. *Prayer:* God, look kindly on the imperfect spirits who find themselves in the darkness of ignorance and who still don't know You, especially the spirit of [name].

---

[50] *See Chapter 10, item 6; and Chapter 12, items 5-6.*

Good spirits, help us make these imperfect spirits come to the realization that by leading human beings into evil, by disturbing their lives and tormenting them, they only perpetuate their own sufferings. Help them to see you as examples of happiness in which they can find encouragement.

You, spirit who still enjoys doing evil, you have just heard the prayer we made on your behalf. This should convince you that we only mean you well, regardless of the harm you create.

You're unhappy because happiness is impossible while we persist in wrongdoing. Why choose to suffer when the ability to avoid it depends on you yourself? Look at the good spirits around you at this moment and see how blessed they are! Wouldn't it be much more pleasant if you enjoyed the same happiness?

You think this is impossible. But nothing's impossible to someone who wants something badly enough—especially since God gave you, along with every intelligent being, the freedom to choose between good and evil, that is, between happiness and misfortune. No one is created to do evil. As you now use your will to spread harm, you may equally use it to do good and, therefore, to be happy.

Raise your sight toward God. Elevate your thoughts toward God for an instant and a ray of divine light will illuminate you. Say these simple words together with us, "Dear God, I repent, forgive me!" Then honestly try to repent and do good instead of bad works, and you'll soon feel the mercy of God descend on you. An indescribable sense of well-being will replace the anguish you're experiencing now.

Once you've taken the first step on the path to goodness, the rest of the way is easy to follow. You'll understand that you've lost a long period of happiness as the result of your imperfections. Nevertheless, a radiant, hopefilled future will open before you. You'll forget your miserable past, so full of upsets and mental distresses—a true hell for you if they were to last through Eternity. Indeed, the day will come when these sufferings will be so great that you'll want them to stop at any price. Yet the longer you put off repenting, the more difficult repenting will be.

Don't believe that your present state is permanent; this is an impossibility. You have two prospects ahead of you: You can suffer far more than you have until now, or you can be blessed like the good spirits around you. The first is bound to happen if you insist on being stubborn, although a little effort on your part would be enough to remove you from the bad situation in which you find yourself. So hurry to the path of good, because each day that you delay is a lost day of happiness!

Good spirits, let these words echo in the mind of this struggling soul and help it to return to God. We ask this in the name of Jesus Christ, Who has such great power over stray spirits.

PRAYERS FOR THE SICK AND SPIRITUALLY DISTURBED

PURPOSE: TO BE SAID FOR THE SICK

77. *Preface:* Physical illnesses are part of the hardships and challenges of earthly life. They are an inherent element of our coarse physical bodies and of the harsh natural environment where we live. Here our uncontrolled appetites and physical excesses produce the conditions for some illnesses; others have a hereditary basis. By contrast, on more physically and morally advanced realms, the physical body is much more purified and less material. It doesn't suffer from the same ailments that attack it on earth, and it isn't subject to the abuses of our uncontrollable appetites.[51] Accordingly, we have to resign ourselves to the consequences of the environment in which our unadvanced state has placed us until we earn the right to pass on to a better one. Yet, while we're waiting, there's nothing to prevent us from doing whatever we can to improve our present lot. And if we can't manage to do so, despite our best efforts, the Spiritist Doctrine is the support that encourages us to bear our temporary pains with fortitude.

If God hadn't wanted the body's sufferings to be relieved and eased, the possibility of cure wouldn't have been placed within our reach. Providence's care and our instinct of self-preservation suggest that it's our duty to find these means of cure and apply them.

Besides ordinary medications used in medical science, medical research makes us aware of the power of spiritual healing. The Spiritist Doctrine, in addition, reveals the immense healing power of prayer.[52]

78. *Prayer (to be said by the sick person):* God, You are all Justice. The illness You saw fit to send me I must deserve, since You never allow suffering without a just cause. So I entrust my cure to Your

---

[51] *See Chapter 3, item 9.*

[52] *See below the note concerning the mediumship of healing.*

infinite mercy. If You decide to restore my health, blessed be Your Name! And if it's necessary for me to suffer more, blessed be Your Name just the same. I submit to Your wise purpose without complaining, knowing that what You do can only be for the good of Your creatures.

Dear God, let this sickness be a timely warning to me—one that will cause me to meditate on myself. I accept it as correction for my past and a test of my faith, and out of respect for Your Will [see Prayer 40].

79. *Prayer (to be said for the sick person):* Dear God, Your plans are inaccessible to us and in Your wisdom You have allowed this illness to afflict [name]. I implore You, God, to look on this suffering with pity and, if You see fit, to bring it to an end.

    Good spirits, ministers of the Almighty, I ask you to second this request to ease [name]'s sufferings. Direct my thoughts so that a balm is poured over his/her body and comfort poured into his/her soul.

    Inspire *[name]* with patience and the acceptance of God's Will. Give [name] the strength to support the pain with Christian resignation so that the fruits of this test won't be lost *[see Prayer number 57].*

80. *Prayer (to be said by the healer):* Dear God, if it pleases You, use me as an instrument, even if I'm not yet worthy of such opportunity. Let me cure this sickness if You so desire it, because I have faith in You. I know that I can't do anything alone. Let the good spirits concentrate their beneficial energy in me so that I can send it to the sick person. Free me, too, from all thoughts of pride and selfishness that might alter its purity.

PURPOSE: TO BE SAID FOR THE SPIRITUALLY DISTURBED

81. *Preface:* A spiritual disturbance[53] is the persistent action that an unevolved— bad— spirit exercises over an individual. This action may take many forms, from a simple psychological influence lacking any perceptible outward sign, to a complete physical and mental breakdown. It may even interfere with the gifts of a medium. We see this in cases of automatic writing where only one spirit insists on communicating to the exclusion of all other spirits.

    Ill-meaning spirits are all around because people on earth are lacking in moral development. Their malevolent behavior is part of the

[53]*Translator's Note: See Chapter 10, footnote 1.*

harsh landscape that faces humanity here. Spiritual disturbances, as much as illnesses and all tribulations of life, should be considered as growth challenges and purifications, and accepted as such.

In the same way that sicknesses occur when there are bodily deficiencies, which open the defenses to harmful exterior agents, spiritual disturbances occur when there are moral deficiencies, which weaken the defenses and give access to ill-meaning spirits. Ailments of an organic nature must be treated with a physical antidote; likewise, ailments with a spiritual cause must be treated with a moral-spiritual antidote. In order to prevent illnesses, we strengthen our bodies. To keep ourselves free from a negative spiritual influence, we have to strengthen our souls. This means that the person must work for his or her own betterment—work that's frequent enough to end the spiritual disturbance without the person bringing in outside help. When a disturbance deteriorates into spiritual subjugation and spiritual possession, however, the help of other people becomes essential because often the patient loses all will power and the clarity that allows him to use his free will.

Spiritual disturbances may have their cause in a spirit's desire for revenge. In many cases this feeling is rooted in the relationship the spirit had with its victim in a previous life.[54]

In a case of severe spiritual disturbance, the person is enveloped by a sheath of harmful energies that neutralize and thus deflect the action of healthy energy. The person must be freed from these negative energies, but it's important to remember that a negative energy can't be cleared away by another lower energy. The method is similar to the one used in psychic healing, i.e., bad energies are replaced by healthy ones, which act like a reactive agent. Indeed, this is a mechanistic view of the process, and by itself, it isn't enough. It's also necessary and extremely important to address the spiritual entity with moral authority. Such authority stems from moral superiority: the greater this is, the greater will be the authority.

But even this isn't all. In order to put an end to the condition, the disturbing spirit must also be persuaded to give up its designs, recognize its error, and desire to change. This can be done through skillful counseling in special (mediumistic) meetings set up for the purpose of raising the spirit's moral awareness. It's possible, then,

---

[54] *See Chapter 10, item 6; and Chapter 12, items 5-6.*

to have the double satisfaction in these cases of healing a human being and redeeming a misguided spirit at the same time.

The task is made easier when the disturbed person understands the situation and cooperates with goodwill and prayers. This doesn't happen, however, when the person, seduced by the spirit, remains in delusion and even enjoys the wrongs the spirit urges him or her to commit. In this case, the sufferer, instead of helping, rejects all assistance offered. This is the situation in cases of spiritual fascination,[55] which are infinitely more resistant to treatment than even the most violent cases of spiritual subjugation.[56] In all cases of spiritual disturbances, prayer is the most powerful means of countering the negative interference and helping the person recover her balance.

82. *Prayer (to be said by the person suffering a spiritual disturbance):* Dear God, let the good spirits free me from the troubling spirit that has attached itself to me. If this spirit is looking for revenge as the result of wrongs I may have committed against it in other lifetimes, then You have allowed this to happen, God, and I'm suffering the consequences of my own faults. Let my repentance of those faults make me worthy of Your pardon and my freedom. But whatever the motive, I implore Your mercy for the spirit that oppresses me. God, help it to find the path to progress, which will turn it away from wrongdoing. For my part, let me repay its mean actions with goodness and so encourage it to better feelings and attitudes.

But, dear God, I also know that it is my own imperfections that have opened me up to the influence of imperfect spirits. Give me the light I need to recognize these imperfections; and above all, help me fight off the pride that makes me blind to my own flaws.

How unworthy I must have been to deserve the constant company of an ill-meaning being!

Dear God, let this blow to my vanity be a lesson in the future. Let it strengthen my resolve to purify myself by practicing goodness, love, and meekness of heart so that, from now on, I can keep away all negative influences.

God, give me the strength to endure this test with patience and resignation. I understand that, as with all other tests, it will help

---

[55] *Translator's Note: Spiritual fascination is a hypnotic-like state in which an ill-disposed spirit influences greatly the will and actions of an individual.*

[56] *See* The Mediums' Book, *Chapter 23.*

my progress if I don't spoil its fruits by complaining. I know, too, that it offers me an opportunity to demonstrate my respect for You and to practice charity toward an unhappy fellow spirit through the forgiveness of the harm it has done me.[57]

83. *Prayer (to be said for the person suffering the spiritual disturbance):* Almighty God, may it please You to give me the power to free [name] from the influence of the spirit that is now causing disturbance. If it is in Your plans to put an end to this test, give me the grace to address this spirit with the necessary moral authority.

I ask all good spirits that help me, and you, Guardian Angel, to give me your assistance in freeing this sufferer from the deleterious energies that surround [name].

In the name of Almighty God, I urge the evil spirit that torments this person to withdraw!

84. *Prayer (to be said for the disturbing spirit):* God of Infinite Goodness, I implore Your mercy for the spirit who is disturbing [name]. Help it see the divine light and recognize how false the path it follows is. Good spirits, help me make it understand that it has everything to lose by practicing evil and everything to gain by practicing good. To the spirit who is tormenting [name], please listen to me since I'm speaking to you in the name of God!

If you would think about it for a moment, you would realize that evil can never outdo goodness and that it isn't possible to be stronger than God and the good spirits. It is possible for them to protect [name] from your attacks. If this hasn't been done already, it's because [name] had to go through this test. But when the test comes to an end, all further action against [name] will be blocked. The turmoil that you've created will not, finally, cause any harm. Rather, you will have contributed toward progress and happiness. Consequently, your misguided behavior will backfire and only harm yourself.

God, Who is all powerful, and God's delegates, the superior spirits, are more powerful than you and can end this persecution whenever they want. Before their supreme authority, your persistence will fall. But, being good, God wants you to have the merit of ending this pursuit of your own will. Thus, God offers you a respite; and if you don't take advantage of it, you'll have to live with very unfortunate consequences. In this case, you should

---

[57] *See Chapter 12, items 5-6; and Chapter 28, item 15 and following, and also items 46-47.*

expect a great deal of anguish and painful suffering. When this happens you'll have no alternative but to plead for mercy and for the prayers of your victim. Indeed [name] has already forgiven you and even prays for you. This has great merit in the eyes of God, helping expedite freedom from your influence.

So reflect while there's still time, because God's Justice will fall on you as it does on all unruly spirits. Consider that the evil you do now has a limit; but if you continue to be stubborn in this matter, you'll only increase the extent of your own sufferings.

When you were upon earth, didn't you consider it stupid to sacrifice a great good for a small and temporary satisfaction? It's the same now that you're a spirit. What will you gain by what you're doing? You take a misguided enjoyment in tormenting someone; but that doesn't prevent you from being miserable within yourself—even if you won't admit it—and only leaves you even more unhappy.

On the other hand, look at what you're missing! Look at the good spirits around you and tell me if their lot isn't preferable to yours. Yet their happiness can be yours whenever you like. What do you have to do to receive it? Pray to God, and instead of doing evil, do good. I know that you can't change yourself immediately, but God doesn't demand the impossible. God asks only for good will. Try, and we'll help you. Make an effort and very soon we may be able to offer up, in your name, the prayer for the repentant [Prayer number 73]. We'll no longer include you in the ranks of bad spirits, and will wait for the moment when we can count you among the good [see also Prayer number 75, for hardened spirits].

Comment: Curing serious spiritual disturbances requires much patience, persistence, and devotion. To turn often vicious, hardened, and deceptive spirits toward goodness requires also a great deal of sensitivity and skill. Some are rebellious to the ultimate degree. In most cases, we must flow with the circumstances. Whatever the character of a spirit, nothing is gained by threats or force. Ability to convince a spirit depends on moral superiority. Further, both logic and experience have shown the complete ineffectiveness of exorcism, formulas, sacramental words, amulets, talismans, ritualistic practices, or any kind of material symbols.

Prolonged spiritual disturbances may cause pathological disorders that demand simultaneous or consecutive treatments. These treatments must consider conventional medical therapies and be complemented by spiritual healing. When the cause has been neutralized, we must then look for ways to remedy the effects.[58]

---

[58] *See* The Mediums' Book, *Part II, Chapter 23, "Obsession"; and* Revue Spirite, *February and March 1864, and April, 1865, for examples of cures for spiritual disturbances.*

GLOSSARY

Action and Reaction – see Cause and Effect.

Afterlife – the life after the physical life; the state to which the spirit returns after existence in the physical realm.

Angel – a being that has attained the state of pure spirit. Angels have passed up through all the degrees on the scale of progress and freed themselves from all the impurities of the material world.

Animism -- situation in which the medium's subconscious mind, rather than another spiritual individuality, is the source of a mediumistic message. The term is also used to identify religious practices based in the belief that all living things have a soul. However, only the former notion is recognized in the Spiritist literature.

Astral Body – see Perispirit.

Attachment (spirit) – a temporary situation in which spirits of limited awareness seek connection and enjoy living in close relationship with an incarnate person.

Aura – A field of energy that surrounds human beings. The aura is a form of radiation emitted by the spirit. It should not be confused with the bio-energy that radiates from the human and animal body.

Automatic Writing (Psychography) – the process of receiving written communications without the control of the conscious self. Writing of truly automatic kind, when the arm and hand are under spirit control, is rare. More often the writing is the product of mind-to-mind communication between the medium and the communicating spirit. By its very nature, the process may be more or less affected by the medium's mind.

Bio-Energy – the vital life force that sustains physical life (see also Vitalism).

Cause and Effect (Action and Reaction) – a law of nature according to which every effect must have a generating cause. In the moral realm, every conscious human action produces an effect. Logically, good actions are likely to generate good reactions, and vice-versa. In the ultimate sense, however, the effect is more than just an equivalent outcome. For instance, a person who seriously harms another doesn't need necessarily to experience the same form of harm, because the person may neutralize the negative effect by doing good to others. This interpretation of the principle of Cause and Effect is more attuned with Jesus' instruction "For she loved much, her sins are forgiven"(Luke 7:47), and the concept of Divine Justice.

Cord (Spiritual) – see Silver Cord.

Catalepsy – A condition in which consciousness and feeling are suddenly, temporarily lost, and muscles become rigid; it may occur in epilepsy and schizophrenia.

Clairaudience – A paranormal perception in which the person 'hears' spirit communications and perceives events taking place in the spirit realm.

Clairvoyance – A paranormal kind of perception in which the human mind perceives images, more or less well defined, of events, scenes, or objects in the spirit realm.

Christianity – Christian beliefs or practices; Christian qualities or character. In the Spiritist tradition, Christianity defines a mental attitude and a relationship with life in all its expressions, rather than a religion in the conventional sense of the word.

Christian Spiritist – the person who sympathizes with or embraces the spirit philosophy and is committed to the work of personal transformation following the ideal defined by Jesus Christ.

Cosmic Principle – the subtle, fundamental, unifying substance that gives rise to phenomena such as heat, magnetism, and electricity, and to matter itself.

Cult – A religion or religious sect regarded as unorthodox, with its followers often living in an unconventional manner under the guidance of an authoritarian, charismatic leader.

Death – The exhaustion of the bodily organs and with that the complete liberation of the spirit from the physical body.

Demon – spirits of scanty moral progress who nurture hatred and harbor base sentiments and inclinations.

Destiny – predetermined course of events in human life. The Spiritist Doctrine does not endorse the view that the circumstances of a person's life were scripted beforehand. They are usually the result of a person's own actions, or choices made before incarnation. Human beings are the creators of their own destiny.

Determinism – the notion that every event, including human choices and decisions, have sufficient causes. The Spiritist philosophy does not support this view in all that regards the moral and spiritual aspects of human life.

Devil – same as Demon.

Divine Justice – The system of laws and norms that flow from God. They are eternal and unchanging. The Divine Justice assures that every person receives according to his or her merit. It is not a strict system of punishments and rewards. God always considers the causes of our actions and does not punish any one. Love is the fundamental essence of the Divine Justice.

Dream – Dreams are often the recollection of what the spirit experiences and happen during sleep of the body. The spirit is never inactive during the bodily rest. The dreams referred to in the original works of the Spiritist Doctrine are known, in modern dream literature, as psychic dreams.

Ectoplasm (From the Greek: ektos, external and plasma: substance) – Visible substance that exhales from the body of certain mediums in the production of materializations.

Ecstatic Trance – A state of profound inner concentration in which the person shows little awareness of the immediate environment. In this state the person may have visions and manifest special mediumistic powers. It is distinguished by an intense feeling of joy.

Euthanasia – the act of interrupting human life in a painless manner to, supposedly, relieve the pain and suffering of a terminal illness. From a continuous life perspective, euthanasia generates a complex stream of consequences that may bring more suffering than what the person still had to endure.

Evil Spirits – same as Demons.

Evolution (Spiritual) – the process of development of the spirit. Spirits were created simple and in a state of unawareness. They develop and grow through experiences in this and various other spheres of life. The spirit's evolution is a continuous and progressive movement. Evolution is a forward movement, it never regresses. Every spirit has to tread the path of evolution; none is left behind or condemned to unawareness.

Exorcism – ritual ceremonies or formulas used by certain religions to remove a harmful or disturbing spirit from a place or a person's life.

Expiation – the means and circumstances by which a person atones, provides reparation, for wrongs done to self or others. Used in the Spiritist literature to refer to experiences in which there is a great deal of suffering or difficulty unconnected to a person's past actions or choices.

Family (Spiritual) – any group of spirit beings that share mutual affection, and have affinity of ideas and values. They may choose to be born in the same family of kin. Their connections have roots in past life experiences. This affinity may draw these spirits together in the physical life. Their ties strengthen with their progress.

Fatalism – same as Determinism.

Fate – same as Destiny.

Free Spirits – The temporary state of spirits between incarnations.

Free Will – the notion that human action expresses personal choice, rather than the intervention of divine forces. Free will is a fundamental right of the human consciousness. Without free will, human life would be either a series of predetermined movements or a sequence of random events. As a spirit progresses, the exercise, so to speak, of its free will expands, i.e., the spirit takes responsibility for a wider range of choices.

Gender (in spirits) – spirits have no gender.

Gift (Spiritual) – a special sensorial ability, usually identified as paranormal, that allows a person to interact with subtler dimensions of life, i.e., spirit reality.

God – The Supreme intelligence of the Universe, the First Cause of All things.

Ghost – in the popular culture, word used in reference to the soul of a dead person that wanders among or haunts living persons. Such occurrences are indeed the sighting of the spiritual body, or perispirit, of those persons who after their physical death are temporarily unable to adjust themselves to the spirit realm.

Golden Rule – 'do to others as you would have them do to you' (Luke 6:31).

Guardian Angel – same as Guide.

Guide (Spiritual) – A spirit who has achieved a high stage, relatively speaking, of moral and intellectual development. They may be identified as teachers, guides, or counselors. They take interest in the growth of an individual or group. Other schools of thought call them angels, and spiritual masters.

Healing (Spiritual) – treatment of physical or spiritual illnesses by means of bio-energy transfer and prayer. Through cleansing or replenishing the energies of the spiritual body, the physical body is able to restore itself to health. The healer works in close association with spiritual beings. The therapy is based on the power of prayer, faith, and love.

Healing Energy – the energy that enables spiritual healing to take place. It is the energy produced through prayer and faith during the spiritual healing therapy. See also Healing.

Hell – in traditional Christian theology, the place in which the evil-doers are condemned to live for all eternity. The Spiritist philosophy rejects the notion of Hell as a place of perpetual punishment because all God's creatures are destined to progress and attain happiness. In the Spiritist literature the word Hell is employed only as metaphor to describe a place where distraught, rebellious, and anger souls gather temporarily.

Hypnotism – the science of dealing with the induction of hypnosis, an artificially induced state resembling sleep in which the subject is highly susceptible to suggestion.

Hypnotic Power – the power held by certain individuals, as well as spiritual beings, to induce another into a hypnotic state.

Incarnate Spirit – A spirit that is temporarily wearing the garment of a physical body; the soul of a living person.

Induced Trance – usually a self-induced trance in preparation for mediumistic, psychic practice.

Inner Transformation – the renovation of moral values, views, and behavior that constitutes the essential purpose of incarnate life. It is the striving to acquire the perfections inspired by becoming conscious of God. The enlightened spirits who dictated the Spiritist Doctrine considered inner transformation as the fundamental task of the spirit in the course of time, and have presented Jesus as our divine point of reference.

Inner Voice – the voice of conscience in its purest expression. St. Francis of Assisi used this expression to identify the Christ voice that guided him in critical decisions.

Intelligent Principle – one of the essential principles of the universe; the core constituent of the spirit.

Intuition – The ability to understand a situation or draw conclusions about complex events without the use of rational process. Also, a form of presentiment about future events. For some spiritually sensitive persons, the ability to sense the ideations of enlightened spirits who take interest in a particular area of human development.

Invocation – the act of invoking a spiritual being, Jesus, or God, for aid, protection, inspiration, or guidance.

Jesus – in the words of the enlightened spirits who laid the basis of Christian Spiritism as a philosophy of life, 'the most perfect example that God has offered to us as a guide and model.'

Last Judgment – according to the traditional dogma, 'the final trial of all mankind.' This notion is not supported in the Christian Spiritist philosophy because the doctrine views the process of life and evolution as continuous and infinite.

Laying On Of Hands – a form of spiritual healing in which the healer, in a state of profound meditation or prayer, places hands over the patient's head without physical touch. In this state the healer gives off the bio-energy that replenishes or helps rebalance the patient's energy field. This is the purest form of spiritual healing as it was practiced by Jesus.

Karma – Hindu and Buddhist ethical doctrine of "as one sows, so shall one reap" in this or in a future reincarnation. According to the law of karma, every conscious human action—in thought, word, or deed—leads to consequences, good or bad, depending on the quality of the action. Karma implies strict causality. A positive act will lead to a positive result. Accordingly, the result will directly correspond to the nature of the cause. In the Christian Spiritist application the notion of direct causality between the action and the result of the action is amended with Jesus' precept '"For she loved much, her sins are forgiven" (Luke 7:47). See Cause and Effect.

Kirlian -- A photographic method that captures bio-fields of persons or objects through a high voltage discharge process. The process of Kirlian photography is named after Seymon Kirlian, a Russian inventor. The interpretation of the coronas that surround the animate objects photographed is open to controversy. Some researchers argue that they are a paranormal phenomenon, the aura. Others counter that they show nothing more than electricity being discharged which can be produced under certain conditions. Although we are far from a conclusive interpretation, there is growing evidence that energy flows in the body are influenced by mental states, medical conditions, healing treatment, prayer, etc.

Levitation – the raising of a person or object through psychic or paranormal methods.

Magnetic Healing – similar to Spiritual Healing but reliant only on the energy and mental power of the healer (as opposed to healing with the assistance of spiritual guides, and prayer).

Materialism -- the philosophical principle that matter is the only reality and all phenomena, including thought and feeling, can be explained in terms of matter and physical processes. Alternatively used to signify the attitude that possessions are the greatest good and highest value of life, and that spiritual values are not relevant.

Materialization – It is one of the several types of mediumistic phenomena produced by conscious or unconscious mediums who possess such a gift. During materialization, a spirit takes a visible form to make itself materially visible.

Medium (From the Latin: medium, intermediate) – a person endowed with a superior sensitivity who serves as an intermediary for communication between the physical and spirit world.

Mediumship – The faculty of mediums. There are many types of mediumship. The more common are: Trance, Automatic Writing, and Clairvoyance.

Mentor – same as Guide.

Mesmerism -- A healing method developed by F. A. Mesmer (1733-1815) involving the induction of hypnotic trances and the transfer of physical energy, originally named animal magnetism, from the therapist to the patient. People in trance often showed paranormal abilities.

Metempsychosis – the ancient doctrine by which a soul (spirit) may enter another human body or that of an animal according to its deeds in a previous life.

Miracle – A physical event that appears inexplicable by the known laws of nature and is considered of Divine or supernatural cause. Christian Spiritism proposes that the so-called miracles, even the more amazing healing and paranormal phenomena, appear so as the result of our still limited understanding of the laws of nature.

Mission (spiritual) – the kind of assignment trusted to more advanced spirits, as opposed to the trials and expiations experienced by the majority of the souls on Earth. Missions are attributions that impact a large circle of people, rather than just the individual or the individual's immediate family.

Moral Conscience – A well developed ability to understand right from wrong coupled with a resilient willingness to act accordingly. To act in such a manner requires cultivation of emotions and integration of spiritual values in the management of physical needs and desires.

Obsession – in Spiritist studies, the temporary influence exercised by an ill-meaning spirit over a person. The causes range from a person's own behavior all the way to mutual hatred between the besetting spirit and its victim, and may have origin in this as well as in a previous lifetime. It is a condition that requires spiritual treatment, behavior change, and inner transformation. In severe cases it may cause physical and mental ailments.

OBE – Out-of-Body Experience - the temporary freedom obtained by an incarnate spirit during deep trance or sleep to travel outside the human body. The spirit may visit places or friends on Earth, travel to places in the spirit realm, or take part in benevolent endeavors under the guidance of a spiritual mentor.

Occult – related to magic, astrology, and other disciplines that rely on secret, mysterious, or supernatural forces

Original Sin – in traditional Christian theology, the sin committed by Adam, the first man. As a consequence of this first sin, we are all born with a tendency to be evil. This notion is not endorsed by the Spiritist Doctrine, which postulates that all spirits are created equal, with the same propensity for good and evil.

Paranormality -- deals with events beyond the range of normal sensorial experience or scientific explanation; for instance, a medium's intuition of a future event.

Perispirit – From the Greek, Perí means surrounding. It is the subtle body of the spirit. It serves as interface between the spirit and the physical body. Also known as spiritual body, astral body or double.

Poltergeist – a paranormal phenomena involving the movement of objects, rapping, and sounds produced by spiritual entities. Usually the presence of a person with the proper type of sensitivity is necessary for the phenomena to occur.

Possession (spiritual) – an aggravated spiritual obsession (see Obsession) in which the ill-meaning spirit is able to have a controlling influence over a person's actions. Spiritual possession tends to have a longer course. Deep-seated hatred or vengeance usually are the motivating forces behind these relationships. Cure requires spiritual assistance and specialized medical treatment.

Premonition -- An intuitive anticipation of a future event.

Pure Spirits – beings that have reached the higher states of moral and intellectual perfection.

Purgatory – according to the theology of some traditional Christian denominations, the place of temporary punishment reserved for the penitent souls that had their sins forgiven on Earth. The Spiritist Doctrine does not subscribe to this view.

Psychometry – a psychic gift with which the medium is able to sense the history of an object by holding it, or the past of a person by simply touching or shaking hands with the person.

Regresssion (Past Lives) – psychological therapy by which persons under hypnotic trance access memories of events that have supposedly taken place in past lives. It has been successfully used in the treatment of phobias and a variety of traumatic experiences. Although not without controversy, this therapy is receiving increasing attention from the medical community.

Reincarnation -- The notion that a spirit (soul) can be reborn in a new body, as part of the continuous progress toward higher levels of spiritual existence. The purpose of reincarnation is to offer the spirit opportunities to grow in awareness, love, and intellectual ability. In addition, reincarnation provides the time and circumstances for the spirit to provide reparation for wrongs committed in prior existences.

Remote View – a type of psychic technique in which the medium, or subject, is able to acquire information about a person, place, or event which is distant in time or space.

Resurrection – in traditional Christian theology, the belief that at a point in time there will be a final judgment and that God will then raise into heaven all the saved who have been dead. When this occurs, their physical bodies will rise from being dead and will be reunited with their souls. The Spiritist Doctrine does not subscribe to this view.

Revelation – The act of revealing divine truth, or that which is revealed by God to man. Revelation is the supernatural communication of truth to the mind of a teacher or writer, who, in traditional Biblical lexicon, is called a prophet. The Spiritist Doctrine was given to humanity by the ennobled intelligences who fulfilled a design of God. According to this notion, the Spiritist Doctrine is a revelation of our true spiritual nature, purpose, and destiny as eternal spirits. However, the Spiritist philosophy endorses the notion that revelation is a continuous process, and that the progress of humanity is accomplished by the incarnation of exceptional individuals with responsibilities in every major field of human endeavor to reveal or expand continuously the frontiers of our knowledge (see question 622). The Doctrine in no way claims to have access to the absolute truth. This enlightened stance is cemented in the motto: "The Only Unshakeable Faith Is That Which Can Withstand Reason, Face to Face, In Every Stage Of Humankind's Development." Besides, Allan Kardec made it a cornerstone of the Spiritist thought that the Doctrine is dynamic and that its evolution should occur always in agreement with the development of scientific knowledge.

Ritual -- The repeated performance of ceremonial acts prescribed by tradition or religion. Religious rituals are dependent upon some common belief system. Rituals are part of the fabric of every human society.

Second-sight – same as Clairvoyance. It gives the medium the ability to see spirits and perceive events and circumstances of the spirit world. It is a complex and difficult gift in which the medium is responsible for interpreting and communicating what is seen. Because of this element of intellectual interpretation, which opens the doors to personal biases and beliefs, the issue of reliability is always a concern.

Seer – a person endowed with the gift of Clairvoyance or Second-sight.

Silver Cord – the metaphorical link between the spiritual and the physical body. When the cord is broken, the physical body dies, and the spirit is free to continue life in the spirit world.

Sin – in religious theology, willful and deliberate transgression of Divine law, the violation of some religious or moral principle.

Sin (Original) – see Original Sin.

Soul -- An incarnate spirit (question 134 in this book). Before uniting to the body, the soul is one of the many distinct beings inhabiting the invisible world.

Spirit -- The intelligent beings of Creation. They populate the entire universe and can be found beyond the boundaries of the material world.

Spirit World – the essential world that pre-exists and survives everything else. Spirits are everywhere in the universe. The spirit world has beauty, life, and harmony beyond anything that incarnate beings can conceive.

Spirit of truth (The) – in the Christian Spiritist perspective, a collective of enlightened spirits who represent the purest aspect of the Christian thought and ideal. The ideas proposed in messages signed by 'the Spirit of truth', in this book and other works, are Divine in a logical sense, if one considers that these ideas were produced by beings who live in oneness with Jesus, and are inspired purely by their love of God. In the Spiritist Doctrine "the Spirit of truth" reaffirms the morality of the Gospel as the highest creation of human conscience, and encourages the quest for knowledge through science and reason.

Spiritual Body – see Perispirit.

Spiritist Doctrine or Christian Spiritism -- The philosophy that deals with the nature, the origin and the destiny of Spirits, as well as their relationship with the corporeal world.

Spiritist (or Christian Spiritist) – A follower of the Spiritist Doctrine.

Spiritual Family – see Family.

Spiritualism -- in philosophy, the notion that human beings are more than just matter. As a doctrine, Spiritualism denies that the contents of the universe are limited to matter and the properties and operations of matter. It maintains that the real being (spirit) is radically distinct in nature from matter. Plato is practically considered as the father of Spiritualism, as he articulated the distinction between the irrational, or sensuous, and the rational functions of the soul. For him the rational soul was related to the body merely as the pilot to the ship or the rider to his horse. In this sense, all religions which accept the existence in the human being of a principle independent from matter, are Spiritualist.

Spiritualism, in daily American and British usage, however, is commonly defined as a belief that the dead communicate with the living through mediums. In this case, the usage is more closely associated with the religion of Modern Spiritualism. While there are many parallels between Modern Spiritualism and the Spiritist Doctrine, the differences are very significant, and they should not be confused, or used as equivalents.

Spontaneous Trance – the individual is temporarily without control of his will or awareness; commonly observed in the religious ecstasy that accompanies the phenomenon of speaking in tongues.

Suicide – the deliberate taking of one's own life. Suicide is an act that carries profound and long lasting consequences for the spirit as it is a transgression of natural laws.

Table Turning – the phenomenon where tables and other objects move without human contact. Table turning was very popular in the mid 1850's. The phenomenon was characterized by a table moving in irregular ways, in various directions, rising, and remaining suspended in the air. The invisible agents that produced the table movements later identified themselves as spirits. In the context of Modern Spiritualism and the Spiritist Doctrine, the tables provided the first and crudest form of communication with the spirit world. The methods of communication have since changed. Tables are no longer employed as means of communication, as other more reliable and accurate methods have become available; for instance, automatic writing, and clairvoyance.

Telepathy – communication between minds without the use of ordinary sensory channels.

Tiptology – A language of beats, raps or tilts. A name given to a kind of spirit communication system using beats or other noises. Alphabetical typology is the designation of letters (or ciphers) by raps or tilts.

Trance – This is an expanded state of consciousness characterized externally by apparent sleep or unconsciousness. During a trance the medium may willingly serve as an instrument for a spirit communication.

Transitional Worlds – Way stations that serve as resting places for free spirits.

Trial – a life or state of pain or anguish that tests patience, endurance, courage, or belief. In the Spiritist literature, two other conditions are discussed: life of expiation in which the spirit repairs the wrong or harm done in a previous life, and life of mission, in which the spirit is assigned a task that impacts the social, cultural, spiritual, scientific, or artistics of a group or society.

Vital principle – The principle that gives organic life to all beings; it has its source in the cosmic principle.

Vitalism – The doctrine that life processes arise from or contain a nonmaterial vital principle and cannot be explained entirely as physical and chemical phenomena. The vitalist concept is at the heart of the Spiritist view of the origin of life. Christian Spiritism maintains that this vital force has its origin in God, the Divine source, the First Cause of all things, and that life is not solely the result of biochemical processes and organic evolution.

Biographical Appendix

Erastus, one of the early Christians who assisted Paul the apostle. Just before the revolt in Ephesus, Paul sent Erastus and Timothy from Ephesus to Macedonia (Acts, 19:22). This Erastus is probably the same one mentioned in 2 Timothy, 4:20 as an inhabitant of Corinth. It is also possible that he was the same Christian who occupied the high post of town treasurer in Corinth. This senior civil servant, together with Paul, greeted the Christians in Rome as recorded in Romans, 16:23.[1]

Fénelon, François de Salignac de la Mothe (1651-1715), French writer, prelate, and liberal theologian, whose theories and publications, despite the opposition of Church and state, eventually became the basis for profound political and cultural changes in France.

Fénelon was born August 6, 1651, into a noble family in Dordogne and educated at the University of Cahors and the seminary of Saint Sulpice. In 1695 Fénelon was made archbishop of Cambrai but soon afterwards became involved in a controversy with Bossuet over the quietist doctrines of Madame Guyon. Fénelon had been influenced by quietism, which stressed the contemplative life, and his *Explication des Maximes des Saints* (*Maxims of the Saints*, 1697) was attacked by Bossuet as inconsistent with traditional Christian teachings. The two prelates appealed to Rome, and parts of the book were condemned by Pope Innocent XII in 1699. Louis XIV, who had sided with Bossuet, exiled Fénelon to his diocese. In addition, Louis had been offended by Fénelon's *Télémaque* (*Telemachus*, 1699), the book for which he is best known. A political novel, it states that kings exist for their subjects; it also expresses an ardent denunciation of war and a belief in the fraternity of nations. He died January 7, 1715, in Cambrai.[2]

Girardin, Delphine Gay (1804 – 1855), French writer. The daughter of Sophie Gay, she was raised in a very literary environment. She published, beginning in 1824, the *Essais Poétiques* (*Poetical Essays*) and other poems that earned her the unofficial title, *"Muse de la Patrie"* (Nation's Muse). These writings show her to have been a very noble soul. After a long trip to Italy (1826-1827), where she won acclaim, and her marriage to Émile de Girardin, she wrote many other romances (*Le Lorgnon, Le Marquis de Pontanges*) and a charming story

---

[1] Nouveau Dictionnaire Biblique. *Edition Emmaüs, Switzerland.*

[2] *"Fénelon, François de Salignac de la Mothe," Microsoft® Encarta® 98 Encyclopedia.* © *1993-1997 Microsoft Corporation. All rights reserved.*

("La Canne de M. Balzac"). Using the nom de plume Vicomte de
Launay, she wrote from 1836 to 1848 the *Lettres Parisienne* (published
in her husband's newspaper *La Presse*), a witty collection that had a
total success. For the theater, she composed a number of both
tragedies and comedies.[3]

Hahnemann, Samuel-Chrétien-Frédric (1753-1843), German
physician and chemist. He initiated the study of homeopathy in 1796,
after becoming disillusioned with conventional medical practices.
Hahnemann based his innovative medical treatment on the healing
power of a good diet, exercise, fresh air, and minimum doses of natural medications. He created homeopathy after observing the effects of
Peruvian Bark and other products on the human organism. This
approach to medicine was a radical concept at the time.[4] Hahnemann
moved to Paris in 1835 due to the great hostility toward homeopathic
doctrine in Germany. He died there in 1843 at the age of 90.

Heine, Heinrich (1797-1856), German poet, who gained lasting
fame for his lyrical poems and ballads, which are noted for the variety of moods and emotions they express. In his own time, he was also
well known for his liberal political opinions and for his satirical
attacks on German nationalism. His writings and controversial activities brought him into disfavor in Germany but made him famous
throughout Europe.

John the Evangelist (died about AD 101), in the New Testament,
one of the twelve apostles, son of Zebedee and younger brother of
Saint James the Great. He is also known as St. John the Divine. He
became a disciple first of John the Baptist and then of Jesus, who made
him an apostle and called him and James "Boanerges" (Greek, "sons
of thunder") for their zeal (see Mark 3:17). John, together with James
and Peter, made up the group of disciples who witnessed Jesus' trans-
figuration and were present during the agony in Gethsemane. Next to
Peter, John was the most active of the apostles in organizing the early
church in Palestine and, later, throughout Asia Minor.

According to tradition, during a period of Roman persecution of
Christians, John was banished to Pátmos, where he is believed to
have written the Apocalypse, or Book of Revelation. Later he is
believed to have gone to Ephesus, where the same tradition relates
that he wrote three Epistles and the fourth Gospel. He is venerated as
the patron saint of Asia Minor. In art, he is represented by several

[3] Le Petit Robert de Noms Propes - *Grand Format. Dictionnaires Le Robert.*

[4] "Homeopathy," *Microsoft® Encarta® 98 Encyclopedia.* © 1993-1997 *Microsoft
Corporation. All rights reserved.*

emblems, among them an eagle, relating to his position as evangelist, and a kettle, referring to the tradition that he survived an attempted execution by immersion in burning oil. His feast day is December 27.[5]

Lacordaire, Jean Baptiste Henri (1802-61), French ecclesiastic and leader of the Roman Catholic revival in France following the Revolution of 1789. He was born in Recey-sur-Ource. After practicing law in Paris, he became a priest in 1827. He joined the small group of intellectuals under the influence of French philosopher and political writer Félicité Robert de Lamennais, and was one of the founders of the controversial journal *L'Avenir*. The journal was discontinued, however, after the papacy condemned Lamennais's ideas in 1832. Lacordaire submitted to the papal decree and turned his energies to preaching. He became known as the greatest Roman Catholic preacher of the day; his sermons at Notre Dame in Paris were considered to be literary and social events. Lacordaire entered the Dominican order in Rome in 1839. His major contribution was the reestablishment of the order in France. He was elected to the French Academy in 1860. His major writings were religious and devotional.[6]

Lamennais, Félicité Robert de (1782-1854), French philosopher and political writer, who attempted to combine political and theological liberalism.

Lamennais was born on June 19, 1782, in Saint-Malo. During his early years, he steeped himself in the works of the French philosopher Jean Jacques Rousseau and other Enlightenment authors. His first important work, cowritten with his brother Jean in 1808, was a reflection on the state of the Church in France. The book, advocating a revival of the Roman Catholic Church in France, came into conflict with Napoleon's antichurch policy and was suppressed by the government.

In 1816, Lamennais was ordained a priest. He soon became the most celebrated clergyman of his day, gaining an enthusiastic following of intellectuals. Together with the French ecclesiastic Jean Baptiste Henri Lacordaire and the French political leader and writer Comte de Montalembert, Lamennais founded (1830) the controversial journal *L'Avenir*, which advocated democratic principles and the separation of church and state. The journal was discontinued, however, after Lamennais's ideas were condemned by the papacy in 1832. With the publication of *Paroles d'un croyant* (*Thoughts of a Believer*,

[5]*"John the Evangelist," Microsoft® Encarta® 98 Encyclopedia. © 1993-1997 Microsoft Corporation. All rights reserved.*

[6]*"Lacordaire, Jean Baptiste Henri," Microsoft® Encarta® 98 Encyclopedia. © 1993-1997 Microsoft Corporation. All rights reserved.*

1834), Lamennais left the Church. He devoted himself to literary and philosophical work until his death, February 27, 1854.[7]

Paul the Apostle (circa A.D. 3-62), the greatest missionary of Christianity and its first theologian, called Apostle to the Gentiles. Born to Jewish parents in a thoroughly observant home in Tarsus (now in Turkey), Paul was originally named for the ancient Hebrew king Saul. As a young Jew of the Diaspora (the dispersion of Jews into the Greco-Roman world), Saul took, as his everyday name, the Latin Paul, a name with a sound similar to that of his Hebrew birth name.

Paul's letters reflect a keen knowledge of Greek rhetoric, something he doubtless learned as a youth in Tarsus. But his patterns of thought also reflect formal training in the Jewish Law as preparation for becoming a rabbi, perhaps received in Jerusalem from the famous teacher Gamaliel the Elder (flourished A.D. 20-50). By his own account, Paul excelled in the study of the Law (see Galatians 1:14; Philippians 3:6); and his zeal for it led him to persecute the nascent Christian church, holding it to be a Jewish sect that was untrue to the Law and that should therefore be destroyed (see Galatians 1:13). Paul became a Christian after experiencing a vision of Christ during a journey from Jerusalem to Damascus (see Acts 9:1-19, 22:5-16, 26:12-18). Paul viewed his call to be a Christian and his call to be an evangelist to the Gentiles as a single and indivisible event. He recognized the legitimacy of a mission to the Jews, as carried out by Peter, but he was convinced that Christianity was God's call to the entire world, and that God was making this call apart from the requirements of the Jewish Law.

From Acts it is known that Paul was arrested in Jerusalem after riots incited by his Jewish opponents, and that he was finally taken to Rome. In Acts, Paul also speaks of the possibility of his own death (see Acts 20:24; see also Acts 20:38). He was executed in Rome, probably in A.D. 62; Christian tradition from the fourth century fixes the day as February 22.[8]

Pascal, Blaise (1623-1662), French mathematician, physicist, religious philosopher, and writer who, in association with Fermat, laid the foundation of modern probability theory. His ideas on inner religion influenced Jean-Jacques Rousseau, Henri Bergson, and the Existentialists. He invented the first digital calculator (1642-1644) to assist his mathematician father in local administration. Further stud-

---

[7]*"Lamennais, Félicité Robert de," Microsoft® Encarta® 98 Encyclopedia. © 1993-1997 Microsoft Corporation. All rights reserved.*

[8]*"Paul, Saint," Microsoft® Encarta® 98 Encyclopedia. © 1993-1997 Microsoft Corporation. All rights reserved.*

ies in geometry, hydrodynamics, and hydrostatic and atmospheric pressure led him to invent the syringe and to discover Pascal's Law of Pressure (1647-1654) and the principle of the hydraulic press (1650).

By 1653 Pascal had begun to feel religious scruples, and, though he never became one of the solitaries at the Janseist convent of Port-Royal, it was henceforth only at their request that he was ever to take up his pen. In 1655 he entered Port-Royal, where he wrote *Les Provinciales* (*Provincial Letters*), a defense of Janseism against the Jesuits, and the *Pensées* (*Thoughts*). *Les Provinciales* was an immediate success: For the first time, the bombastic, and tedious rhetoric of traditional French prose are replaced by variety, brevity, tautness, and precision of style. These literary innovations mark the beginning of modern French prose. Pascal spent his last years in scientific research and good works.[9]

Augustine, Saint (354-430), greatest of the Latin Fathers and one of the most eminent Western Doctors of the Church.

Augustine was born on November 13, 354, in Tagaste, Numidia (now Souk-Ahras, Algeria). Between the ages of 15 and 30, he lived with a Carthaginian woman whose name is unknown; in 372 she bore him a son, whom he named Adeodatus, which is Latin for "the gift of God." Inspired by the philosophical treatise *Hortensius* (by the Roman orator and statesman Marcus Tullius Cicero), Augustine became an earnest seeker after truth. For nine years, from 373 until 382, he adhered to Manichaeism, a dualistic Persian philosophy then widely current in the Western Roman Empire. Disillusioned by the impossibility of reconciling certain contradictory Manichaeist doctrines, Augustine abandoned this philosophy and turned to skepticism.

About 383 Augustine left Carthage for Rome, but a year later he went on to Milan as a teacher of rhetoric. There he came under the influence of Neoplatonist philosophy and also met the bishop of Milan, St. Ambrose, then the most distinguished ecclesiastic in Italy. Augustine presently was attracted again to Christianity. One day, according to his own account, he seemed to hear a voice, like that of a child, repeating, "Take up and read." He interpreted this as a divine exhortation to open the Scriptures and read the first passage he happened to see. Accordingly, he opened to Romans 13:13-14, where he read: "...not in revelry and drunkenness, not in debauchery and licentiousness, not in quarreling and jealousy. But put on the Lord Jesus Christ, and make no provision for the flesh, to gratify its desires." He

[9] The New Encyclopedia Britannica, *15th edition. Encyclopedia Britannica Inc., Chicago.*

immediately resolved to embrace Christianity. Along with his natural son, he was baptized by Ambrose on Easter Eve in 387.

He returned to North Africa and was ordained in 391. He became bishop of Hippo (now Annaba, Algeria) in 395, an office he held until his death. Augustine's doctrine stood between the extremes of Pelagianism and Manichaeism. Against Pelagian doctrine, he held that human spiritual disobedience had resulted in a state of sin that human nature was powerless to change. In his theology, men and women are saved by the gift of divine grace; against Manichaeism he vigorously defended the place of free will in cooperation with grace. Augustine died at Hippo, August 28, 430. His feast day is August 28.

Among his many works are *Confessions* (circa 400), *The City of God* (413-26), *Retractions* (428), *Epistles* (386-429), *On Free Will* (388-95), *On Christian Doctrine* (397), *On Baptism: Against the Donatists* (400), *On the Trinity* (400-16), *On Nature and Grace* (415); and Homilies upon several books of the Bible.[10]

Saint Louis (1214- 1270), King of France (1226-1270). After attaining his majority, he fought and won a revolt led by the Comte de Lamarche, signing the Treaty of Paris in 1259. In order to free Palestine from Egypt, in 1248 he decided that his obligations as a son of the Church outweighed those of his throne, and he left his kingdom for a six-year adventure. Since the base of Muslim power had shifted to Egypt, Louis did not even march on the Holy Land. Any war against Islam now fit the definition of a Crusade. Louis and his followers landed in Egypt on June 5, 1249, and the following day captured Damietta. The next phase of their campaign, an attack on Cairo in the spring of 1250, proved to be a catastrophe. The Crusaders failed to guard their flanks, and as a result, the Egyptians retained control over the water reservoirs along the Nile. By opening the sluice gates, they created floods that trapped the whole Crusading army, and Louis was forced to surrender in April 1250. After paying an enormous ransom and surrendering Damietta, he sailed to Palestine, where he spent four years building fortifications and strengthening the defenses of the Latin kingdom. In the spring of 1254 he and his army returned to France.

King Louis also organized the last major Crusade, in 1270. This time the response of the French nobility was unenthusiastic, and the expe-

[10]*"Augustine, Saint," Microsoft® Encarta® 98 Encyclopedia. © 1993-1997 Microsoft Corporation. All rights reserved.*

dition was directed against the city of Tunis rather than Egypt. It ended abruptly when Louis died in Tunisia during the summer of 1270.[11]

Vincent de Paul, Saint (1581-1660), French priest, founder of the Congregation of the Mission, called the Vincentians or the Order of the Lazarists.

Vincent was born near Pouy (now Saint-Vincent de Paul), in Gascony, on April 24, 1581. He attended the universities of Dax and of Toulouse. It is said Vincent was seized by pirates while going from Marseille to Narbonne in 1606. Sold into slavery in Tunisia, he escaped and returned to France some months later. He spent some 20 years as a parish priest and chaplain to an aristocratic family. He was also chaplain general of the galleys of France and as such, tried to aid the galley slaves. In 1617 he founded the first Confraternity of Charity, made up of wealthy women working among the sick and poor in Châtillon-les-Dombes, near Lyon. In 1622 the French prelate St. Francis of Sales appointed him superior of the Parisian convents of the Order of the Visitation of Holy Mary.

With the support of the family he served as chaplain, Vincent founded the Congregation of the Mission to preach to the peasants on the family's estates. A community of the congregation was formally established at the College des Bons-Enfants in Paris in 1626, where Vincent served as principal. The alternate name, Lazarist Fathers, was given to the group when it established headquarters at the former priory of Saint Lazare, in Paris in 1632. Vincent not only headed the order but also founded several other charitable organizations, notably the Daughters of Charity, formed under his direction in 1633. The foundling hospital of Paris owes its origin to this group. The Congregation of the Mission organized several seminaries for the training of priests as a result of work done by Vincent de Paul with young men about to be ordained. He was also concerned with relief work during the religious wars in France. His opposition to Jansenism is believed to have been responsible for its suppression. He died in Paris on September 27, 1660. He was canonized in 1737 and was named patron of works of charity in 1855. Vincent's feast day is September 27.[12]

---

[11]"Crusades," *Microsoft® Encarta® 98 Encyclopedia.* © 1993-1997 *Microsoft Corporation. All rights reserved.*

[12]"Vincent de Paul, Saint," *Microsoft® Encarta® 98 Encyclopedia.* © 1993-1997 *Microsoft Corporation. All rights reserved.*

Jean-Marie-Baptiste Vianney, Saint (1786 -1859), French priest, confessor, and patron saint of parish priests. He was born and grew up during the Napoleonic era. Because of religious persecutions at that time, he had to make his First Communion secretly. He was drafted into Napoleon's army but, because of ill health, he found himself absent without leave and branded a deserter. In 1815, he was ordained even though he had been dismissed from the seminary for failing the examinations and for his inability to learn Latin. After serving as an associate for three years in the parish of Ars, he became pastor (Fr., curé) in 1818. He soon became famous as a spiritual counselor and confessor. It is said that he spent eighteen hours a day hearing confessions, being a model of the parish priest totally devoted to his congregation, without regard for personal recognition or reward. He was canonized in 1925.[13]

---

[13] The Harper Collins Encyclopedia of Catholicism, *Harper Collins, 1995.*

SUBJECT INDEX

Gospel At Home

The Gospel comes alive when its message is explored in an environment of trust. As new interpretations evolve from the sharing of personal ideas, they will gently nourish your soul and guide your actions. The Gospel At Home is a practice that you and your loved ones will enjoy and come to look forward to every week. It will bring spiritual peace to your home life. For information and literature on how to start a Gospel At Home study, please contact the Allan Kardec Educational Society.

For information on other works by Allan Kardec
or to start or join a study group write to:

Allan Kardec Educational Society
P.O. Box 26336
Philadelphia, PA 19141-6336
Phone: (215) 329-4010

AKES – Book Distribution Center
P.O. Box 30692
Phoenix, AZ 85046
Phone: (602) 996-3123
Fax: (602) 996-1937

or visit our website:
www.allan-kardec.org

Notes

Notes

_____

_____

_____

_____

_____

_____

_____

_____

_____

_____

_____

_____

_____

Notes

Notes

_____

_____

_____

_____

_____

_____

_____

_____

_____

_____

_____

_____

_____

_____